BEST

OLD-GROWTH FOREST HIKES

Washington & Oregon Cascades

John & Diane Cissel

THE MOUNTAINEERS BOOKS

Published by
The Mountaineers Books
1001 SW Klickitat Way, Suite 201
Seattle, WA 98134

First edition, 2003

Published simultaneously in Great Britain by Cordee, 3a DeMontfort Street, Leicester, England, LE1 7HD

Manufactured in Canada

Acquiring Editor: Cassandra Conyers
Project Editor: Betsy Wilcox
Copyeditor: Erin Moore
Cover and book design: The Mountaineers Books
Layout: Mayumi Thompson
Cartographer: Diane Cissel, Richard Cissel, Katie Cissel
Photographer: John Cissel
Illustrations: Diane Cissel

Cover photograph: *Western redcedar and Douglas-fir, Clackamas River, Mount Hood National Forest.* John Cissel

A cataloging in publication record for this book is on file at the Library of Congress.

Printed on recycled paper

TABLE OF CONTENTS

CENTRAL OREGON CASCADES

SOUTHERN OREGON CASCADES

ACKNOWLEDGMENTS

We wish to thank our children Richard and Katie Cissel for their many contributions and inspiration. Without their assistance with map production, and their participation in our many family hiking adventures, this book would not have been possible.

Numerous friends and family provided transportation, a place to stay, editorial advice, or company on the trail. In particular, we would like to thank Dawn Adams, Doug and Patrick Bloem, Lillian Bloem, Al Brown, Rosemary Camozzi, Barbara Canavan, Howard and Lucille Cissel, Ken and Lori Humphreys, Rich Lechleitner, Scott and Carol Rose, and David Wallin.

Many individuals provided information concerning where to find old growth along the trail. We especially thank Al Brown, Rich Lechleitner, Howard Rondthaler, Lewis Sullivan, and the many individuals working in Forest Service, Park Service, Bureau of Land Management, Washington State Parks, and Bellingham County Parks Department offices who contributed useful information and reviewed all hike descriptions and maps for accuracy. We thank you for your attention to detail, and assistance in creating an accurate product for public use and enjoyment.

A special thanks to fellow cartographer Peter Eberhardt who helped create our first old-growth map in 1991.

FOREWORD

Visions of gigantic old trees extending to the base of spectacular, snow-clad peaks pulled us to the Pacific Northwest thirty years ago. We knew little about old-growth forests at the time and found almost no help in bookstores and outdoor stores. General-purpose hiking guides often used a variety of vague terms to describe forests, such as virgin forest, deep forest, primary forest, and native forest. But we wanted to know where to find the big, old trees and lush forests that are so symbolic of the Northwest, and we wanted to learn more about the ecological forces that shape these forests.

Over the decade of the 1990s we collected information about old-growth hikes throughout the Cascade Range and self-published three guide maps describing old-growth hikes in a substantial portion of the Cascades. Now we extend this information throughout the Cascades and bring it forward in a book format. These hikes describe the very best old growth left near trails in the Cascade Range of Washington and Oregon. The book represents more than 2,000 miles of observation on the trails of the Cascades, and is intended for novice hikers and serious old-growth buffs alike. We hope that this book can bring you pleasure and enrich your understanding of the majestic forests of the Pacific Northwest. It is certainly our pleasure to share this volume with you.

John and Diane Cissel

INTRODUCTION

USING THIS GUIDE

This book is intended as a comprehensive and authoritative guide to hiking in old-growth forests in the Cascade Range of Washington and Oregon. Old-growth forests are one of the defining features of the Pacific Northwest, and the Cascade mountains still harbor a broad assortment of impressive old forests. The classic image of awe-inspiring giants towering over richly carpeted forest floors is inviting and accurate. But that is only part of the story. Old forests also occur in near-desert and near-arctic settings, on sites exposed to frequent forest fires, and even on top of lava flows! This book describes the full suite of old-growth forest types found in the Cascades as seen from the trails of one hundred day hikes. In addition, more than fifty sidebars highlight short nature trails through old growth or noteworthy big trees. Readers looking for very easy or wheelchair-accessible trails should consult the sidebars.

We use the tools of narrative, cartography, illustration, and photography in a complementary fashion so the reader can better understand old forests as they are encountered along the trail. Text descriptions lead hikers through the trail connections that need to be made, highlight key features of the trailside forest, and identify ecological factors influencing the forest. Detailed hike maps depict the location of old-growth forests along the trail, while regional locator maps show major roads, towns, and other features useful for navigating to the trailhead. An illustration is included with each hike that highlights a plant or animal species present near the trail. Together these images provide the reader with enough orientation to navigate the trail, and enough ecology to understand the general features of old-growth forests in the Cascades.

Selecting a hike

Hikes are grouped by geographic region for easy reference. The Cascades of Washington and Oregon are subdivided into five regions: northern Washington Cascades, southern Washington Cascades, northern Oregon Cascades, central Oregon Cascades, and southern Oregon Cascades. Choose the region that interests you and find hike locations on the corresponding regional map. Hike descriptions for that region follow the regional map. Each hike is introduced by an information summary block, which provides a quick snapshot of basic considerations for each hike. Scan these summaries to find hikes suitable for your time, interests, energy level, and likely hiking season. Each block contains the following information:

Hike length in miles is given to either a logical turnaround point for two-way day hikes, or for the total length of a loop. Although hike lengths are generally displayed to the nearest tenth of a mile, distances should be regarded as approximations since considerable variation occurs in measurement methods and devices, and measurement error is inevitable. Some hikes include one-way hike options using a vehicle or bus shuttle.

Each hike is rated for *Difficulty*. Generally, easy means that the total hike distance is less than 5 miles and the elevation gain is less than 1,000 feet. Moderate means that the total hike distance is between 5 and 10 miles and there are no extended periods of very steep trail grade. Difficult means that the total hike distance is greater than 10 miles, or there are extended periods of very steep trail grade.

The *Season* when the trail is generally open for use is given in broad terms. Snowpack accumulation and snowmelt are the key factors controlling trail access. Trail access may vary from one year to the next by four to six weeks or more due to high year-to-year variation in snowpack depth.

The *Lowest point* and *Highest point* for each hike refer to the lowest and highest elevations along the hike. The difference between the two may or may not equal the total elevation gain of the hike. Many hikes start at the lowest point and head up, but most have ups and downs. Refer to the topographic map for each hike to identify extended grade changes.

The *Human imprint* rating is a totally subjective way to convey the degree to which human presence is perceivable. Minimal means that little obvious evidence of human presence is detectable, and the trail receives light use. Moderate means that one or more various forms of human presence is noticeable, but these do not generally intrude on the nature of the hike. High means that a significant presence is noticeable, and the character of the hike is strongly influenced by this presence. Very high means that human activity dominates a portion of the hike. The sources of human imprint are listed in parentheses (e.g., roads, clearcuts, hikers, and developed recreation sites).

Primary *Information* sources are also listed for each hike. Most hikes are on national forests, and both the national forest and local ranger district office are listed. The visitor map for the listed national forest is a helpful resource and guide to local campgrounds and access roads and can be obtained from the local office. Contact information for each office is provided in Appendix E.

Another heading, given for each hike below the information summary is the *Primary Old-Growth Feature*, a brief phrase describing the key old-growth characteristics of the hike. Unusual aspects of the forest, such as extreme size or age, are listed here.

Following the hike description, the last paragraph for each hike, *How to Get There*, gives concise directions to the trailhead. Read this section to better understand the length of time needed to get to the hike's start. Although road mileages are generally given to the nearest tenth of a mile, distances should be regarded as approximations since vehicle odometers can vary significantly. Directions for potential shuttle options for one-way hikes are given where those options are described in the text.

Maps

The maps in this book are intended to help hikers find the location of old-growth trails in the region, and then guide hikers to specific old-growth forests along trails. The introductory section for each geographic region contains a map showing the major features and roads in that region, as well as the general location of each of the described hikes. These maps contain sufficient detail to get you from towns and cities in or near the region onto the state, county, and major forest roads leading to the hikes in that geographic region. National Forest visitor maps, available at national forest and ranger district offices, and at other information centers and outdoor stores, will prove helpful when navigating forest roads to the trailhead, and are highly recommended.

A detailed, to-scale map is included with each hike depicting the topography, roads, streams, trails, and other features of interest. The location and type of old growth along the trail, particularly impressive old-growth groves, scenic viewpoints, and hike mileage marks are also shown on these maps. Old growth was mapped in two categories: old growth and partial old growth. Stands mapped as old growth contain all of the characteristics of old-growth forests (see Introduction, Old-growth forests); partial old growth means some, but not all, old-growth characteristics are present. Most stands mapped as partial old growth are either mature forest on the verge of becoming old growth, or forest that has experienced a disturbance, usually fire, which regenerated a new stand around large trees that survived the disturbance. Only old growth located near the route described for the hike was mapped. Fluctuations in the width of mapped old-growth corridors occur due to topography, roads, past cutting units, streams, and other features. No attempt was made to map all old growth within the borders of the map.

Accurate maps are indispensable to hikers, and great effort was made to ensure that the maps in this book are as accurate as possible. Public domain USGS topographic maps were used as background layers to create basic map features. These features were all ground-checked; and additional features unique to this book, such as the mapping of old-growth corridors, were based entirely on field reconnaissance. Draft maps were reviewed by the officials responsible for the trails in their areas, and all known errors were corrected. Still, there are 105 maps in this book and each map contains dozens of details. Additional errors are guaranteed. Please let us know if you find one (John Cissel c/o The Mountaineers Books). Appendix D lists USGS 7.5-minute topographical map(s) and Green Trails map(s) for each hike.

Identifying trees

Several components of the book can be used in a complementary fashion to help readers identify key tree species found along the trail. Appendix B lists basic identifying characteristics, habitat preferences, and the geographic range of major conifer species in the Cascades. The needles and cones of these trees are depicted in some of the illustrations that accompany each hike, and the color photograph section shows the general appearance and bark of many tree species. The largest known living specimens of most of the conifers discussed in the book are catalogued in Appendix C.

FOREST AGE

The age of conifers can be reasonably estimated by counting tree rings. Tree cells are larger and have thin cell walls early in the growth season when moisture is abundant, and are smaller with thick cell walls later in the season. The result is a recognizable pattern of annual growth rings. Forest ages given in the book are from published sources and agency data where available, or from tree ring counts conducted in the field by the author. Several factors affect the accuracy of field counts, including the condition of the cut surface and the width between annual rings. The degree of accuracy of forest ages given in this book is reflected in the precision used in the referring language: e.g., "720 years" versus "over 700."

THINGS YOU SHOULD KNOW

Forest roads

Hiking in the forest generally requires traveling in a vehicle on forest roads to the trailhead. Although most forest roads are gravel surfaced, and many are steep, negotiating forest roads is not overly difficult. Trailheads needed for the hikes described in this book can usually be reached by a careful driver in a full-sized sedan.

Road conditions are subject to change due to weather, and to infrequent road maintenance. Annual snowpack varies from year to year, and extreme events such as major windstorms or floods can block access for extended periods of time even on principal roads. Road maintenance funding has declined rapidly on national forest lands, and many roads are more likely to have heavy brush, potholes, washboards, and big rocks on the road surface today than in past years. Most national forests and parks have websites where relatively current information on road status can be obtained (see Appendix E), and numerous websites provide current weather conditions and forecasts. If in doubt, contact a local Forest Service or Park Service office for the latest information.

Most hikes in the book require travel on U.S. Forest Service roads. Fortunately, the national forests in the Northwest use a standardized road numbering system. Three types of roads reflect the level of use and maintenance roads receive. Primary roads are designated with a two-digit number (e.g., Forest Road 23) and are marked on the ground with a trapezoid-shaped sign. These are the best roads through the forest. They are frequently paved and connect forest roads with state and county roads. A horizontal, rectangular sign is used to mark secondary roads. These roads are labeled with four digits, the first two of which are the same as an adjoining primary road (e.g., Forest Road 2320 is connected to FR 23). These roads are also generally well maintained and could be either gravel surfaced or paved. Shorter, local roads that branch off at the ends of the road network are more likely to be rough or infrequently maintained. Local roads are designated with a three-digit number (e.g., Forest Road 100) and are marked on the ground with a vertical, rectangular sign. The four-digit secondary road it joins with is usually numbered on the top of the sign.

Safety

With reasonable precautions and advance planning, hiking is a safe activity. However, hiking does require physical exertion in a wild and constantly changing environment, and hikers assume the inherent risks. Inclusion of a hike in this book does not guarantee a hiker's safety, or even that hikers will find conditions on the ground to be identical to those described in this book. Fires, windstorms, floods, and gravity all subject the forest, trails, and roads to periodic change. Hikers need to be knowledgeable and alert, follow basic safety guidelines, and take personal responsibility for safety decisions.

Ten Essentials: Basic safety preparation means carrying a few things with you that you most likely will never use. The point is to be prepared for the "what if": what if you do get lost or somehow break an ankle and have to spend the night in the woods. A good start for basic safety is to carry what are widely known as the Ten Essentials:

1. Extra clothing—include long pants, insulating layers, and raingear
2. Extra food and water—high-energy food to replace lost calories, and a lot of water
3. Sunglasses—protects eyes, especially if traveling over snow
4. Knife—helpful for emergency fire building or first aid
5. Firestarter—a candle or other firestarter, some flammable material
6. First-aid kit—include any special medications
7. Matches—essential for emergency fire building, in waterproof container
8. Flashlight—carry an extra, or extra batteries and bulbs
9. Map—maps in this book show sufficient detail for the hikes described; see Appendix D for other maps
10. Compass—essential if lost or confused, otherwise fun to use

Driving there: The most dangerous part of a hiking trip is driving to and from the trailhead, and the high-speed roads closer to civilization generally pose more risks than forest roads. Nevertheless, caution is warranted when driving in the forest. Defensive driving is the rule, and recommendation number one is to take every corner as if there is a truck on the other side coming toward you. Just because you have not seen another vehicle for the last fifteen miles does not necessarily mean you are the only one in the vicinity. Cutting corners is the best way to have a serious vehicle accident in the forest. Watch out for black ice, particularly during fall and winter mornings on paved roads along valley bottoms. Remember to use lower gears, especially on steep grades, and note that four-wheel drive just means you can go farther before you get stuck.

Hypothermia: The most serious risk to hikers on the trail is hypothermia. Weather conditions change rapidly in the Cascades, and cold rain is common at higher elevations. Know the weather forecast, take and use protective raingear, and keep the body supplied with calories in wet, cold weather.

Contacts: Make sure somebody knows where you are going and when you will be back. Have a positive contact system set up in advance, which means that somebody will check on you and your party if you do not show up on time. The Forest Service and Park Service do not perform this service, and cell phones do not generally work in the mountains.

Car clouting: Clouting (breaking and entering, or vandalism) does happen at trailheads, but very infrequently. Some trailheads have more problems with car clouting, generally those closer to urban areas. One school of thought is to leave your vehicle unlocked at the trailhead so it is not trashed by someone trying to get in. The other point of view is to always lock up so casual clouters do not rip the interior apart. The clear answer is to not leave anything of value in the vehicle

Water: Don't drink the water. At least be aware that anytime you drink untreated water from a stream or lake there is a risk of infection with *Giardia,* an intestinal parasite capable of seriously disrupting your lifestyle. Bring a couple quarts of drinking water per person with you. Iodine tablets or lightweight water filters are suitable methods for treating water.

Animals: The wild animals most likely to harass hikers are mosquitoes and various flies. July and early August can be ugly in the high Cascades. Be prepared; carry either repellent or protective netting. Black bears are shy of humans. Count it as good fortune if you get a good look at a bear. Cougars are even more difficult to spot in the woods. Injury to hikers from these large predators is almost unheard of. In the highly unlikely event you encounter a bear or cougar, do not run, back away slowly. Most charges by black bears are bluff charges, but if the bear keeps coming, fall to the ground and protect your neck. If charged by a cougar, fight back vigorously and stay on your feet. Rattlesnakes are very uncommon and less potent than those in the Southwest, but do occasionally occur at low elevations in the southern Cascades. Check for ticks after hiking, especially in spring and early summer, and off-trail wandering can stir up yellow jackets, especially in the late summer and early autumn. Individuals allergic to bee or wasp stings should carry prescription bee-sting kits.

Poison oak: Poison oak is a three-leaved shrub common at low elevations on dry sites in Oregon. Learn to identify and avoid it. If you come into contact with poison oak, wash yourself and your clothes as soon as possible. Tecnu® is a product that does a particularly good job of removing poison oak oils.

Good manners

Good manners are mostly a matter of respect, for fellow travelers and for the forest. The goal is simple: leave no trace of your passing, and do not disturb animals, plants, or other people. The following guidelines make life better for everyone:

- Do not shortcut switchbacks; shortcutting is unsightly and leads to erosion.
- Do not pick flowers or disturb other natural features.
- Do not leave any litter, not even orange peels.
- Yield the right-of-way to horses by stepping off the trail, to the downhill side if feasible.
- Leave pets at home; if you must bring your dog, keep it on a leash and bury dog feces. (Note: pets are not allowed on trails in national parks and are discouraged in designated wilderness.)
- Respect private property.
- Be courteous to rangers and other officials in the field. They do not set policy or fees.
- Human waste should be buried 200 feet or more from a stream. Pack out toilet paper.

Additional considerations apply if you plan to camp overnight:

- Cook food using backpacking stoves.
- Minimize use of fires. Use existing fire rings where possible, and use only dead and down wood gathered away from the campsite.
- Hang food out of the reach of animals, at least 4 feet from the tree trunk and 8 feet off the ground. Ground squirrels and mice are the most likely intruders.
- Camp on hardened or previously used sites. Avoid fragile areas such as meadows.
- Wash at least 100 feet from a water source, even if you use "biodegradable" soap.
- Camp out of sight from trails and lakes, and at least 100 feet from lakeshores.

Other trail users

Trails on public lands are managed for multiple uses. In practical terms that means that mountain bikes, horses and other stock, and even motorbikes could be encountered on the trail. Nonmotorized bikes are generally allowed on trails unless signed otherwise, except in wilderness where bikes are prohibited. Horses and other stock are also generally allowed on most trails, unless posted otherwise. Motorized bikes are prohibited on most trails frequented by hikers. Only a handful of trails in this book are heavily used by bike or horse riders, and they are so noted in the hike descriptions. Hikers wishing to avoid these trail users should visit these areas during the week and avoid weekends. In any case, do not confront other trail users in the forest. If their use bothers you, inform local officials and work through your local hiking club for better protection.

Wilderness rules

Most wilderness areas require each party of hikers to carry a self-issued wilderness permit. These permits are usually available at the trailhead. Certain heavily used locations require special permits issued from the local information office. None of the hikes in this book currently require special permits.

General rules governing wilderness use are as follows:

- Group size must be no larger than 12, including both stock and humans.
- Entry is banned from areas marked as rehabilitation sites.
- All motorized and mechanical devices are prohibited, including mountain bikes.
- Live vegetation should not be damaged.
- Fires are generally prohibited within 100 feet of streams, lakes, and trails.

Some wilderness areas have additional restrictions, such as lower limits on group size. If in doubt, contact the local information office (see Appendix E).

Fees

Fees are a controversial topic for some folks. We treat them here as a fact of life. Fees are now charged to park at most trailheads on national forests in the Northwest and in the North Cascades National Park. It costs $5 per day to park at a designated trailhead, or $30 per year for an annual pass known as the Northwest Forest Pass. We just pay our annual fee, always put the permit on the rearview mirror, and do not worry about it anymore. Not all trailheads are in the program, but most are and more are being added. The program is still evolving and more changes are likely. If in doubt, contact the local information office (see Appendix E).

The other main fees hikers will likely encounter are national park entrance fees. Mount Rainier and Crater Lake National Parks do not participate in the Northwest Forest Pass program and charge a $10 entrance fee. The fee is good for seven consecutive days after entry.

OLD-GROWTH FORESTS

Grandeur, mass, and antiquity

Old-growth enthusiasts are motivated by something far deeper than the arguments that lawyers conjure out of scientific papers, the mumble-jumble of environmental assessments, and legal precedent. Political arguments rage around the ecology and economics of Northwest old-growth forests, but it is the sheer beauty, the richness of life, the awe-inspiring dimensions, and the sense of a living connection to a primeval past that ignites such passions in the first place. African, Asian, European, and Indian cultures all have great works of art and architecture connecting them to centuries and millennia past. In the Pacific Northwest it is the great works of living nature that link us back to an ancient time.

Old forests occupy an important place in the soul and psyche of forest lovers throughout the world, and the forests of the Northwest are truly world-class wonders. Douglas-fir are known to stretch thirty stories or more in height, or more than fifty times the height of adult humans. Western redcedar reach 15 or more feet in girth, requiring ten or so adults to extend arms around the larger specimens. Old trees are commonly 500 years of age and some exceed 1,000 years old, almost fifteen times the average life span of humans. This great age enriches our sense of time, and lends perspective to the travails of the day.

Regardless of season and weather, old-growth forests of the Cascades reflect an unrivaled splendor of color and form. Stout, cinnamon-brown trees arise from rich, organic soils carpeted with thigh-high ferns. Centuries in the making, life springs out of every crack and crevice in these fertile forests. Broad, irregular branches high up in the old trees support communities of mosses, lichens, and ferns whose life and death cycles produce pockets of soil perched on branch surfaces. Ancient decomposing snags still standing decades past death now sprout hemlock seedlings and red huckleberry bushes from their broken tops.

What are old-growth forests?

Forty years ago the term "old-growth forest" referred simply to a forest older than the preferred timber harvest age. Now we see such a forest as a complex ecological community with unique characteristics. Defining the term is made difficult by great variability in ecological conditions across the Pacific Northwest, and by differing perspectives. Old-growth forests could be defined based on some arbitrary minimum age, say, older than 200 years. Another approach is based on the presence of species known to use older forests, such as spotted owls. But both of these methods prove overly simplistic and difficult to apply in real, highly variable forests. A third approach, based on the structural attributes of a forest, has proven more practical to apply, as these attributes are more readily measured and include many of the unique features of old growth.

The structure of a forest refers to the size, number, and condition of both live and dead trees present in a given area of forest. Ecologists differ on the specifics, but generally agree that four characteristics of forest structure can be used to describe old-growth forests. First and foremost are large live trees that dominate the forest canopy. These craggy monarchs often have distinctive shapes with broken tops and stout lateral branches. Big standing dead trees (snags), formed when these giants die, are the second major component. Snags can remain standing for many decades, gradually breaking down and succumbing to the forces of gravity and decay. Standing trees, both live and dead, eventually crash to the forest floor, creating a third component—large, down logs. Down logs may persist for centuries (e.g., western redcedar), or may turn to mush in a few decades (e.g., Pacific silver fir). The final general characteristic included in most old-growth definitions is a multi-layered or continuous forest canopy stretching from the forest floor to the tops of the tallest trees. Older forests typically contain gaps in the uppermost layer of trees where light can penetrate into the understory and stimulate growth of smaller trees, shrubs, and understory herbs.

Each of these components contributes to the overall diversity and functioning of a forest. Big live trees support massive crowns of branches and needles, which power the food web and support arboreal lichens, mosses, spiders, insects, and small mammals. Many of these species are much more abundant in old forests, and some contribute significantly to forest nutrient cycles. Numerous birds, bugs, and mammals use big snags as foraging and nesting habitat. Certain bats have been observed roosting on large snags underneath slabs of bark starting to separate from tree trunks. Down logs shelter amphibians and small mammals, act as nurse logs to seedlings, and store vast amounts of carbon and water. Together these habitats, species, and ecological processes form a unique ecosystem worthy of recognition, study, protection, and enjoyment.

Ecology

Images of old-growth forests conveyed through various popular media typically portray enormous Douglas-fir in lush, verdant forest. Such forests certainly exist, and, in fact, are icons of the Northwest. Yet the old forests that hikers actually see on the landscape are quite varied, reflecting a wide range of environmental conditions. An understanding of basic ecological processes, and experience interpreting their expression across the landscape, enhances appreciation of Northwest forests.

The amount of sunlight, heat, and moisture available to a tree varies greatly, as does a tree's ability to tolerate high or low levels of each. Trees and other plants need sunlight to create food through photosynthesis; species differ in their tolerance of low light conditions. The degree of shade cast by an upper canopy of trees is the most significant factor affecting the availability of sunlight to other plants. Differing shade tolerance among tree species has a strong affect on which species are present and the relative abundance of each species in very old forests. Theoretically, over the long term, tree species that can regenerate and grow in shade, such as western hemlock and Pacific silver fir, will eventually move into the upper canopy and dominate the forest.

Species also differ in their ability to withstand temperature extremes, particularly in the early stages of forest establishment when tree seedlings struggle to root themselves and out-compete surrounding plants. Cold-

and snowpack-tolerance directly affect which tree species can colonize a site at higher elevations in the Cascades where heavy and persistent snow is the rule. Changes in the tree species present due to changes in elevation and latitude follow predictable patterns. For example, Douglas-fir seedlings can not tolerate deep snowpacks; consequently Douglas-fir is rare at high elevations.

The amount of water available to tree roots through the soil strongly influences the growth of trees. Too little moisture, and trees turn down basic life-maintenance functions; too much moisture reduces the availability of oxygen in the soil for vital physiological processes. Soils vary widely in their moisture-holding capacity based on exposure to the sun, soil depth, rock content, geologic history, and many other factors. Some tree species are better able to tolerate either high (e.g., western redcedar) or low (e.g., ponderosa pine) levels of moisture in the soil, giving them a competitive advantage over other species on these soils.

These environmental factors set the stage for the cast of conifers likely to occupy a site. The tree species present often change over time though, as a forest grows and develops in a process called "forest succession." Commonly, the tree species most capable of establishing a new forest when there is ample sunlight do not regenerate or compete as well in a shady environment—Douglas-fir for example. Consequently, shade-tolerant species tend to become more abundant as succession progresses. Succession can also refer to changes in forest structure over time as big trees and snags develop, and the forest canopy becomes more diverse and irregular.

Over the very long term, 800 to 1,000 years or more, forest succession can lead to a condition known as a "climax" forest. Theoretically, if enough time passes without major disruption, such as fire, only shade-tolerant trees survive and regenerate, creating a forest with trees of all ages from the same species. In reality such theoretical conditions rarely exist. Fires have historically occurred often enough throughout most of the Cascade Range to reset the forest prior to development of a climax forest. Also, shifts in climate, such as those experienced over the last thousand years or so, are sufficient to alter the competitive balance between tree species and interrupt progression toward a climax forest.

Variability in environmental conditions and changes over time through succession create a broad template of forest patterns over the landscape. But it takes understanding of still another ecological process, known as "disturbance," to grasp the range of forest conditions encountered in the Cascades. Disturbance occurs when some kind of event, such as fire or flood, brings rapid change to a forest. Disturbances may occur relatively frequently (e.g., tree blowdown), or infrequently (e.g., volcanic eruptions).

Historically, fire was a pervasive disturbance in the Cascade Range, varying widely in frequency and severity. In general, fires occurred less frequently but burned more severely in the northern Cascades, and burned more frequently but with lower severity in the southern Cascades. More severe fires killed most of the trees on a site, essentially resetting the successional clock and initiating a new stand. Less severe fires left substantial amounts of live trees and other organisms on the site, while simultaneously creating space and conditions for a new generation of trees to become established. Surviving trees, sometimes known as "legacy" trees, facilitated re-establishment of biological communities following disturbance. Modern fire suppression has significantly reduced the role of fire in the Cascades, allowing dense stands of young trees to develop on sites where frequent fire formerly maintained a more open forest.

In the last century or so a new form of disturbance—timber cutting and removal—has greatly affected vast portions of the Cascade Range. As with fires and other disturbances, timber harvest can occur with varying frequency and severity. Unfortunately though, timber cutting has generally been both very severe (clearcutting) and very frequent (short rotations), especially on private industrial lands where old growth has essentially been liquidated. Millions of acres of old growth have also been felled or fragmented by clearcutting on federal forest lands in the Cascades, although substantial old growth remains.

Conservation

Great strides have been made in recognizing the ecological and aesthetic values of old-growth forests and the need to protect these values now and into the future. Historically, timber harvest of old-growth forests was the assumed objective, and clearcutting proceeded at a rapid pace. Harvest was concentrated first on privately owned land, and then spread to federal lands after World War II. When old-growth values were considered, the goal was to preserve a few small, extraordinary stands while minimizing the effect on timber available for future harvest. Old growth was included in some formally designated wilderness areas starting in 1964, but these were generally high-elevation forests or small stands on the margins of the wilderness. Starting in the late 1970s and continuing through the 1980s, large blocks of low-elevation mature and old forest were featured in a few newly legislated wilderness areas.

New scientific information concerning the unique characteristics of old-growth forests, and forest protection campaigns organized by environmental interest groups, increasingly brought old-growth forests onto the front pages and television screens of the Northwest throughout the 1980s. Ultimately, a series of lawsuits in the late 1980s culminated in the listing of the northern spotted owl as a threatened species in 1990, and a federal injunction halting all cutting in northern spotted owl habitat on federal lands was issued in 1991. As a result, timber harvests on federal lands in the Northwest plummeted and controversy escalated.

Former President Bill Clinton campaigned on a promise to develop a balanced solution to the forest controversy in the Northwest and quickly embarked on a path leading to the Northwest Forest Plan. Formally adopted in 1994, this new plan created large "late-successional reserves" and extensive "riparian reserves" throughout the range of the northern spotted owl. Projections showed that timber harvest volume on federal lands managed under the new plan would drop approximately 80 percent as compared to the harvest levels in the 1980s. Still, timber harvest volume in the plan would come primarily from old and mature forests.

Attempts by the federal agencies to implement this new timber harvest level have largely been unsuccessful. High costs, complex interagency procedures, and lack of public support for continued harvest of old and mature forest on federal lands at any level have prevented the Forest Service and the Bureau of Land Management from selling many timber sales in older forests under Northwest Forest Plan guidelines. Meanwhile, the timber industry has transformed itself to process smaller logs. Very few mills capable of processing large logs still exist. Federal agencies are generally focusing on thinning young stands, which are abundant due to past clearcutting.

Isolated cases of old-growth logging still occur, and major changes in social values or political control could potentially usher in a new era of old-growth logging. On the whole though, it is hard to believe that widespread cutting of old forests in the Northwest will ever again be politically sustainable. An ever-changing array of forest advocacy groups closely monitor federal agencies and are quick to protest, appeal, and litigate violations of environmental guidelines. The bigger threats could come if serious attempts are made to repeal environmental protections afforded through the Endangered Species Act, National Forest Management Act, and other environmental protection laws. Continued vigilance is prudent.

Old growth along the trails in this book falls into a variety of categories with respect to protection from timber cutting. Trails in designated wilderness are legislatively protected from timber harvest. Other trails are mostly in administrative reserves of various form (e.g., late-successional reserves, riparian reserves, unroaded recreation areas) where logging of older forests is generally prohibited. Portions of a few trails are in general forest where some type of timber harvest could still occur. In practice though, the odds of the trails in this book being affected by harvest of old growth appear to be slim. We monitor approximately two hundred trails that pass through old growth in the Cascades and only a couple have been affected by timber harvest in the last decade. If you have questions or concerns about the future of forests along a specific hike, contact the local agency office (see Appendix E).

Timber harvest is not the only human activity that can negatively affect our grand old forests. Air pollution, climate change, and the introduction of exotic pathogens all pose significant threats to our forests. Even fire suppression, which at first glance would appear to protect forests, can result in a build-up of fuels and more damaging fires. These agents of change are more pervasive, more difficult to observe and mitigate, and potentially more significant over the long term than likely levels of timber harvest on federal lands.

Efforts to conserve old growth are also challenged by our mental models and the tools we employ. Most people view old-growth forests as static entities that can be preserved. Yet, old forests are dynamic and will continue to change regardless of our intentions. It is quite natural for forests to be disturbed, and throughout much of the Cascades disturbance is ultimately essential to renew old forests characteristic of the native landscape. Middle-aged forests, often referred to as mature forests, are the old forests of tomorrow and an essential component of landscapes intended to sustain old forests. Even young forests are integral to the concept of healthy landscapes. Diverse young forests provide unique habitats, and may very well support species essential for the food web of species associated with old forests.

Preservation of existing old growth has been a critical first step. The challenge for future generations will be to employ a broader mix of approaches that can sustain old-growth characteristics on a wide variety of land ownership types, and within a wide range of political and environmental contexts. We will have to open our minds to tools and approaches that involve forest management activities on some lands to ultimately be successful. Preservation should remain a central tool. But in the long term, if take-it-all or leave-it-all approaches are the only options on the table, the result may be lose-it-all.

The goal of a healthy landscape that maintains options for the continual maintenance and renewal of old-growth forests can be a cornerstone of our regional identity. Using our collective understanding of forest ecosystems and political systems, and remaining humble in the face of our ignorance, may improve our odds of meeting this goal for future generations.

A NOTE ABOUT SAFETY

Safety is an important concern in all outdoor activities. No guidebook can alert you to every hazard or anticipate the limitations of every reader. The descriptions of roads, trails, routes, and natural features in this book are not representations that a particular place or excursion will be safe for your party. When you follow any of the routes described in this book, you assume responsibility for your own safety. Under normal conditions, such excursions require the usual attention to traffic, road and trail conditions, weather, terrain, the capabilities of your party, and other factors. Keeping informed on current conditions and exercising common sense are the keys to a safe, enjoyable outing.

The Mountaineers Books

Opposite: *Douglas-fir, Huckleberry Creek*

LEGEND

- old-growth area
- partial old-growth area
- extraordinary grove or tree
- TH trailhead for featured hike
- TH alternative trailhead for featured hike
- featured hike trail
- unofficial trail
- other trail
- 3557 trail number
- 3 trail mileage
- view
- unbridged crossing
- wheelchair-accessible trail
- mountaintop
- lookout tower
- wet meadow or swamp
- lake, stream
- waterfall
- glacier
- lava flow
- national forest boundary
- administrative boundary (national park, state park, etc.)
- wilderness area
- private land
- RS ranger station
- guard station
- point of interest
- campground
- picnic area
- gated road
- paved road
- gravel road
- rough gravel or dirt road
- railroad
- powerline
- 90 interstate freeway
- 12 U.S. highway
- 123 state route
- 54 primary forest foad
- 5407 secondary forest road
- 100 local forest road
- 30 county road

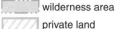

NORTHERN WASHINGTON CASCADES

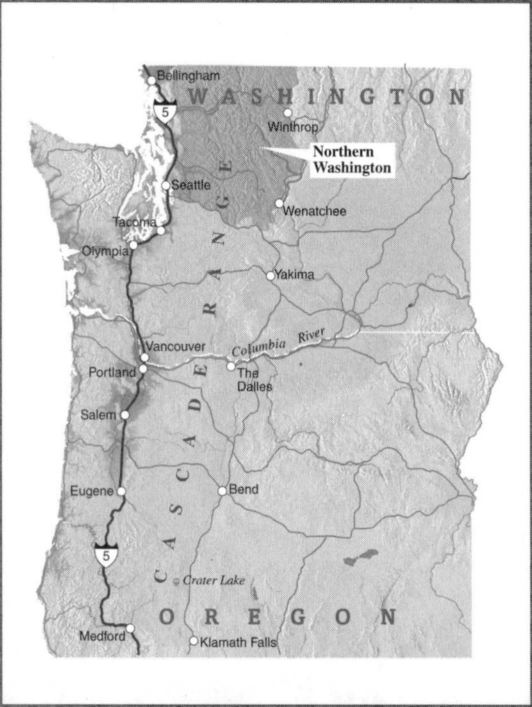

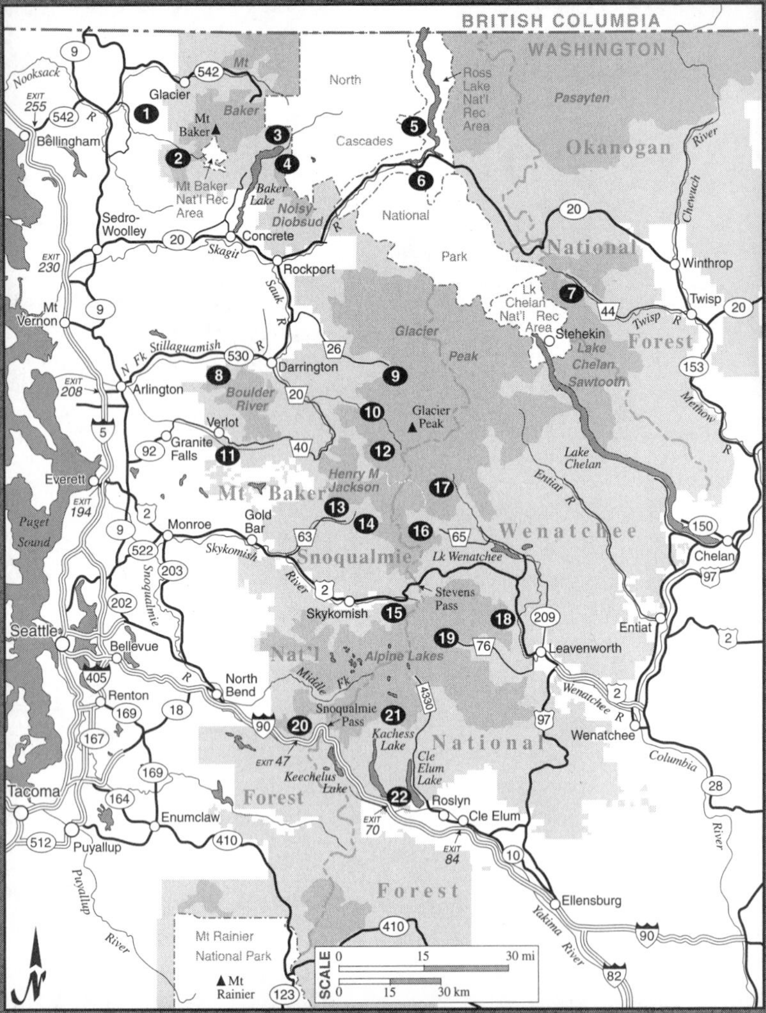

Hike locations

1 CANYON LAKE CREEK COMMUNITY FOREST

Length	**4 miles one way**
Difficulty	Moderate
Season	Summer
Lowest point	2,320 feet
Highest point	4,460 feet
Human imprint	Very high (clearcuts and roads)
Information	Whatcom County Parks and Recreation Department

Primary Old-Growth Feature
Very old mountain hemlock, Alaska-cedar forest

A unique parcel of ancient, high-elevation forest covers the upper slopes at the head of Canyon Lake Creek. Once privately owned and slated for the same fate as the surrounding clearcut lands, an unusual public-private partnership formed to procure this tract. Now known as the Canyon Lake Creek Community Forest, the property is jointly owned by the Whatcom County Land Trust, Western Washington University, and Whatcom County, and is open for public use.

The great age of the forest was the catalyst that sparked efforts to move

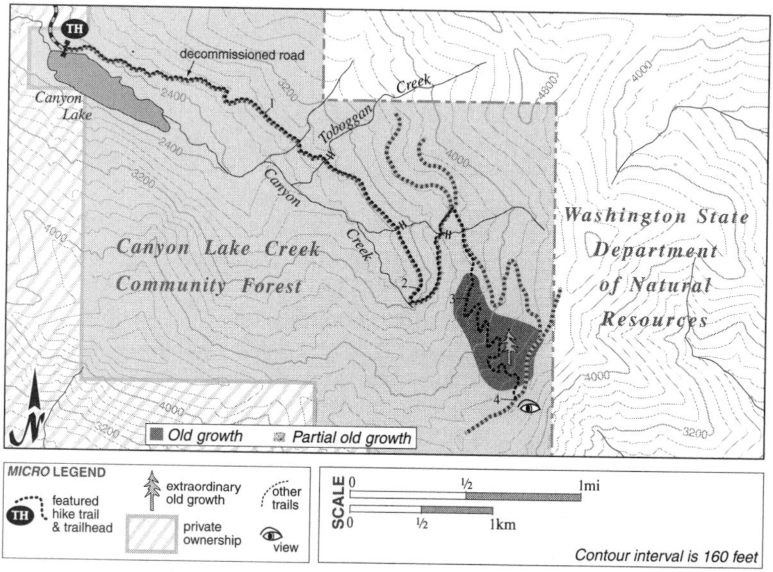

Douglas' squirrel

this land into public stewardship. A study of the forest identified a wave of Alaska-cedar and mountain hemlock that regenerated following a fire in approximately 1170, and another pulse of mountain hemlock established following a fire that occurred around 1410. Survivors from these age-classes are still standing today. There are likely other high-elevation forests of similar vintage in the North Cascades, but few such tracts have been identified to date.

Visiting the forest requires hiking 2.5 miles along a decommissioned logging road through what is essentially one huge recovering clearcut. The road is blocked to vehicular traffic near the mouth of Canyon Lake, an interesting feature formed by a massive landslide off the south valley wall. Extensive rehabilitation work has been done to the road itself—fifty-seven culverts were pulled, stream crossings were excavated, waterbars were constructed, and the road surface was strewn with large boulders. Mountain bikes and horses are not allowed on the old road surface.

The old growth is in sight nearly the whole way up the road, and provides a welcome relief when the trail is finally reached. The trail itself switchbacks repeatedly up through the forest past very old mountain hemlock and Alaska-cedar, and somewhat younger Pacific silver fir. The trees are short at this elevation and generally 2 to 4 feet in diameter, although a few reach 5 feet in girth. The trail emerges from the forest after a mile and enters a 1990s clearcut at the top of the ridge. Continue a hundred yards or so to the crest for a fabulous view of Mount Baker and the Twin Sisters.

How to get there: Head east on the Mount Baker Highway (State Route 542) from Interstate 5 in Bellingham (exit 255). Turn right on Mosquito Lake Road 16.8 miles from the freeway (3.5 miles past Deming). Turn left onto gravel-surfaced Canyon Lake Road in 1.7 miles. Follow the little green signs with white arrows 6.6 miles to the trailhead parking area. The road travels through private land, and a gate 1 mile up the road may be closed during periods of high fire danger. Call the Whatcom County Parks and Recreation Department if in doubt (see Appendix E).

SKYLINE DIVIDE

To see a nearby high-elevation forest of similar stature, check out the Skyline Divide Trail (678). Although the forest is not of such great antiquity as the Canyon Lake Creek Community Forest, big mountain hemlock and Pacific silver fir abut the trail for the first 1.25 miles or so. The trail continues up to Skyline Divide reaching a large, flower-filled meadow 2 miles from the trailhead. Head south, up and down the ridgeline, for increasingly stunning views of glacier-packed Mount Baker.

How to get there: Continue east on the Mount Baker Highway past Glacier and turn right onto Forest Road 39 about two-thirds of a mile past the Glacier Public Service Center. Take an immediate left onto FR 37 and follow it 12.8 miles to the trailhead.

2 ELBOW LAKE

Length ■ **3.5 miles one way**
Difficulty ■ Moderate
Season ■ Summer to early autumn
Lowest point ■ 2,060 feet
Highest point ■ 3,520 feet
Human imprint ■ Minimal
Information ■ Mount Baker–Snoqualmie National Forest (Mount Baker Ranger District)

Primary Old-Growth Feature
Very old western redcedar, western hemlock, Pacific silver fir forest

Elbow Lake and Lake Doreen sit in a saddle atop Sisters Divide: the dividing line between the Middle Fork Nooksack River and the South Fork Nooksack River watersheds, and the landform that connects the Twin Sisters to Mount Baker. Most people access the lakes via a shorter route from the south, but the northern approach features a peaceful path through excellent old forest and is well worth the extra distance. A couple of openings along the way allow close-up views of the Twin Sisters.

Head downhill on the Elbow Lake Trail (697) through younger forest, and cross the raging Middle Fork Nooksack River on a big, cedar plank bridge. Veer right and swing around to the Green Creek valley, soon entering old growth. Big western hemlock and Pacific silver fir dominate the forest for the next 3 miles, although scattered western redcedar on the lower slopes are larger. Two single Douglas-fir stand near the trail, each reaching 8 feet in diameter. These solitary veterans appear to be the last survivors of a generation established long ago following a forest fire.

Banana slug

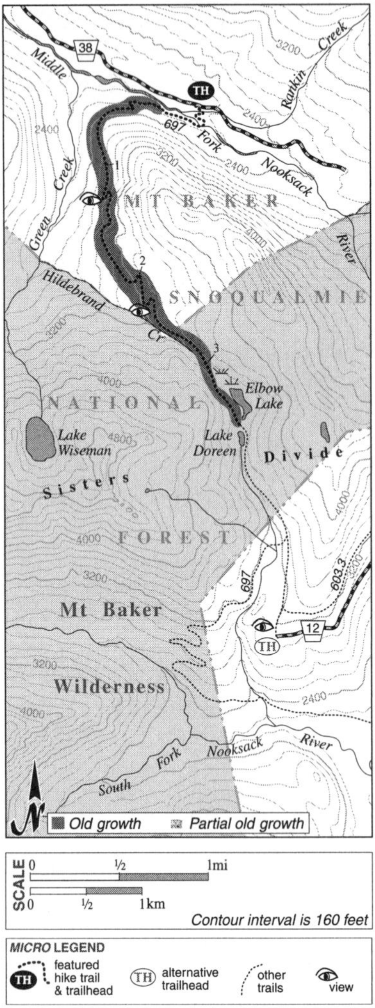

The trail climbs moderately, switchbacking in places, and gradually swerves around to parallel Hildebrand Creek and enter the Mount Baker Wilderness. The valley tightens as the path nears the pass, finally flattening out where the trail crosses the stream near a small pond in the saddle. From here the trail traverses a slope above emerald-green Elbow Lake through shapely Pacific silver fir. A few Alaska-cedar are sprinkled through the forest on the upper slopes.

The southern approach starts in a plantation where Twin Sisters rise prominently to the west. The trail soon enters an old Pacific silver fir forest, joined by western hemlock, mountain hemlock, and Alaska-cedar. Stay left at the first junction, and right at the second, reaching Lake Doreen about 1 mile from the trailhead. A 6-foot-wide western hemlock signals close proximity to the lake. Another couple hundred yards or so past Lake Doreen brings you to the southern end of Elbow Lake.

How to get there: To reach the northern trailhead, head east on the Mount Baker Highway (State Route 542) from Interstate 5 in Bellingham (exit 255). Turn right on Mosquito Lake Road 16.8 miles from the freeway (3.5 miles past Deming). Turn left on an acute angle onto gravel-surfaced Forest Road 38 in 4.8 miles. Take the left fork, angling uphill, 4.9 miles later. Follow this road 6.2 miles to the parking area on the left.

To reach the southern trailhead from the North Cascades Highway (State Route 20), turn north onto Baker Lake Road, heading toward the Mount Baker National Recreation Area. After 12.1 miles turn left onto Forest Road 12 and continue to its end, approximately 17 miles from Baker Lake Road. Stay left at a junction 1.8 miles from Baker Lake Road, go straight at a junction in 3.5 miles, and stay left again at a gate in 8.3 miles. Note that the gate is closed from November 1 to June 30 each year for wildlife protection.

3 Baker River

Length	**2.6 miles one way**
Difficulty	Easy
Season	Early spring to late fall
Lowest point	810 feet
Highest point	880 feet
Human imprint	Moderate (hikers)
Information	Mount Baker–Snoqualmie National Forest (Mount Baker Ranger District); North Cascades National Park

Primary Old-Growth Feature
Immense western redcedar along river corridor

Gargantuan redcedar along a rollicking river attract a steady stream of visitors to Baker River. Low elevations mean the trail is open much of the year, and a nearly level trail grade accommodates hikers of most abilities. The wild river roams over a wide, unconstrained channel littered with large logs on broad gravel bars. Graceful hardwoods add beauty to riparian terraces and floodplains.

The Baker River Trail (606) heads out of the parking lot on an old road through a young forest for the first quarter mile. Occasional large trees a little ways off the trail foreshadow the groves of giant western redcedar dead ahead. The trail soon emerges on an old river terrace stocked with redcedar, western hemlock, Pacific silver fir, grand fir, black cottonwood, and red alder. A few dominant redcedar approach 10 feet in diameter.

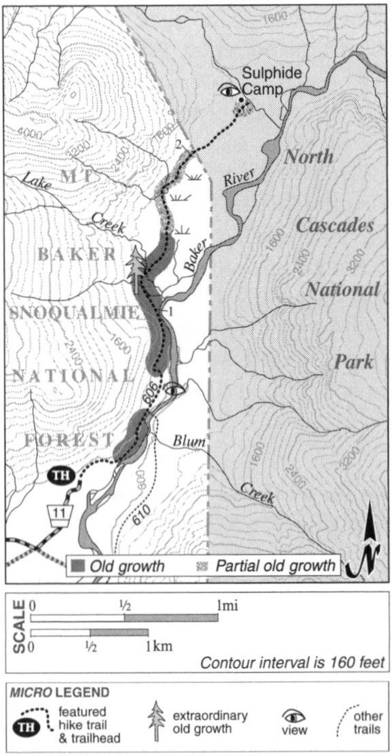

A junction with the Baker Lake Trail (610) is soon encountered on the west side of the bridge over Baker River. Pause a moment and stroll out to the middle of one of the most impressive trail bridges in the Cascades. Views to the east of Mount Blum and its resident glaciers open up from the trail just beyond the bridge.

After a short interlude passing through a vine maple arbor and patches of red alder, the trail reenters old forest. Two amazing western redcedars, each approaching 15 feet in diameter, stand by the trail about two-thirds of a mile above the bridge. The trail then crosses several small streams before entering a delightful bigleaf maple glade dotted with large western redcedar. Beyond the maples the trail skirts a network of marshes, beaver ponds, and a couple more mega-trees, including a lonesome Douglas-fir close to 10 feet thick.

Finally the trail enters North Cascades National Park, traversing a mature forest of conifers for about a half mile before terminating beside unbridged Sulphide Creek and Sul-

Pileated woodpecker

phide Camp. A few large trees shade campsites by the creek. A short stroll up the streambank reveals Jagged Ridge and Crystal Glacier on the east shoulder of Mount Shuksan.

How to get there: Turn north onto Baker Lake Road off the North Cascades Highway (State Route 20) approximately 16 miles east of Sedro-Woolley. The road becomes Forest Road 11 approximately 16 miles later, and becomes gravel surfaced just past the Baker Lake Resort in another 4 miles. Stay left on the main road at a junction 5.4 miles past the resort, and park in the large lot in another half mile.

SHADOW OF THE SENTINELS

A wheelchair-accessible, interpretive trail off of Baker Lake Road provides easy, year-round access to a splendid stand of lowland old growth. The half-mile-long trail alternates among asphalt and boardwalk, winding past well-crafted exhibits explaining ecological features of an old-growth forest. Western hemlock and Pacific silver fir dominate portions of the stand, while impressive Douglas-fir 5 to 7 feet in diameter cluster along the far edge of the loop. **How to get there:** Turn right into the parking lot off of Baker Lake Road, approximately 14.5 miles from the North Cascades Highway.

4 Baker Lake

Length ■ **4.5 miles one way**
Difficulty ■ Moderate
Season ■ Early spring to late fall
Lowest point ■ 810 feet
Highest point ■ 1,160 feet
Human imprint ■ Moderate (motorboaters)
Information ■ Mount Baker–Snoqualmie National Forest (Mount Baker Ranger District)

Primary Old-Growth Features
Lakeshore groves of large western redcedar; an immense Douglas-fir

Beautiful groves of western redcedar and bigleaf maple ornament portions of the Baker Lake Trail along the southeast shore of upper Baker Lake. The low-elevation trail is open during all seasons except midwinter, providing an excellent early season opportunity to enjoy the splendors of our native forest. A noteworthy stand

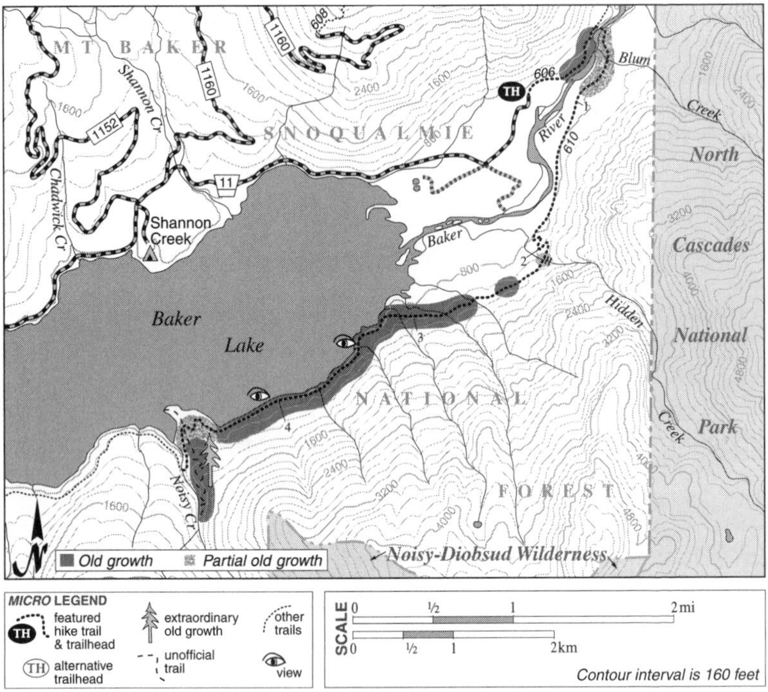

of old-growth Douglas-fir on the lower slopes east of Noisy Creek provides a suitable destination for a day hike.

Start out on the Baker River Trail (606), first through young forest, then past ancient western redcedar. Turn right onto the Baker Lake Trail (610) at the trail junction a little over a half mile from the trailhead, and cross an awesome trail bridge over Baker River. Turn back south and head toward Baker Lake on the east bank of the river. Several big redcedar and a lovely glade of bigleaf maple and cottonwood are the chief attractions over the next 1.5 miles.

The trail then switchbacks up to a bridge over Hidden Creek where a few chunky conifers are sheltered. The trail alternates between old growth and mature forest for the next half mile before settling into an extended stand of superb western redcedar and Douglas-fir. A few of the western redcedar approach 10 feet in diameter. Another gorgeous grove of bigleaf maple and western redcedar adorns the trail about 3 miles from the trailhead. The trail then heads back down to the lakeshore where the forest canopy opens for a couple of dead-on views of resplendent Mount Baker.

A trail junction is reached on a small peninsula just before crossing Noisy Creek, 4.5 miles from the trailhead. Continuing straight, the trail tracks the lakeshore for almost 9 miles to the lower Baker Lake trailhead; heading right on an unofficial trail leads down to a couple of campsites on the lakeshore. Turn left here instead to climb through a spectacular stand of Douglas-fir old growth, including the Noisy Creek Fir about a quarter mile up the trail. This renowned titan measures 12.7 feet in diameter and 210 feet tall, and is currently the sixth largest known Douglas-fir by volume at 9,810 cubic feet (personal communication from Robert Van Pelt). The trail is steep and unmaintained but distinct for three-quarter mile or so and well worth the effort.

Bigleaf maple

How to get there: Turn north onto Baker Lake Road off the North Cascades Highway (State Route 20), approximately 16 miles east of Sedro-Woolley. The road becomes Forest Road 11 another 16 miles later, and changes from paved to a gravel-surface just past the Baker Lake Resort at 20 miles. Stay left on the main road 5.4 miles later, and park in the large lot in another half mile.

ROCKPORT STATE PARK

Surprisingly, Rockport State Park, located in the lower Skagit River valley adjacent to the North Cascades Highway, still holds remnant old-growth patches in a heavily cut-over area. Although approximately 5 miles of trail in the park wander through mixed-age, Douglas-fir forest, the best examples of old growth lie along two short loops across the highway to the south. These loops highlight large Douglas-fir and western redcedar intermingled with attractive bigleaf maple. The Sauk Springs Loop (a third of a mile long) passes several big Douglas-fir up to 7 feet thick and a trio of impressive redcedar, the largest of which approaches 10 feet in diameter. The two-thirds-mile-long South Loop (alternatively signed as "Skagit View Loop") also features an old-growth Douglas-fir forest.

How to get there: Turn north into the Rockport State Park entrance from the North Cascades Highway (State Route 20), approximately 30 miles east of Sedro-Woolley (1 mile west of Rockport). Turn right and park in the day-use area.

5 BIG BEAVER CREEK

Length ■ **7.5 miles one way**
Difficulty ■ Difficult
Season ■ Summer to early autumn
Lowest point ■ 1,610 feet
Highest point ■ 1,840 feet
Human imprint ■ Minimal
Information ■ North Cascades National Park

Primary Old-Growth Feature
Groves of enormous, ancient western redcedar

A hike along well-known Big Beaver Creek reveals some of the finest groves of western redcedar found anywhere. While the trail is more often hiked as a backpack trip connecting with the Little Beaver Trail, a day hike with a lake approach is feasible with a little advance planning. The main trick is to schedule a water taxi operated by Ross Lake Resort (call ahead at 206.386.4437; or contact *www.rosslakeresort.com*). The twenty-minute ride costs $25 each way for up to six riders. The resort operates the taxi on request from Memorial Day to the end of October from 8 A.M. to 6 P.M., leaving sufficient time for a memorable day hike through grove after grove of gigantic redcedar.

To reach the water taxi dock from the Ross Dam trailhead, head downhill toward Ross Lake through a young, post-fire stand, passing a few older Douglas-fir near Happy Creek. Take a right onto a road after about three-quarters mile and follow it for a quarter mile toward the

Common loon

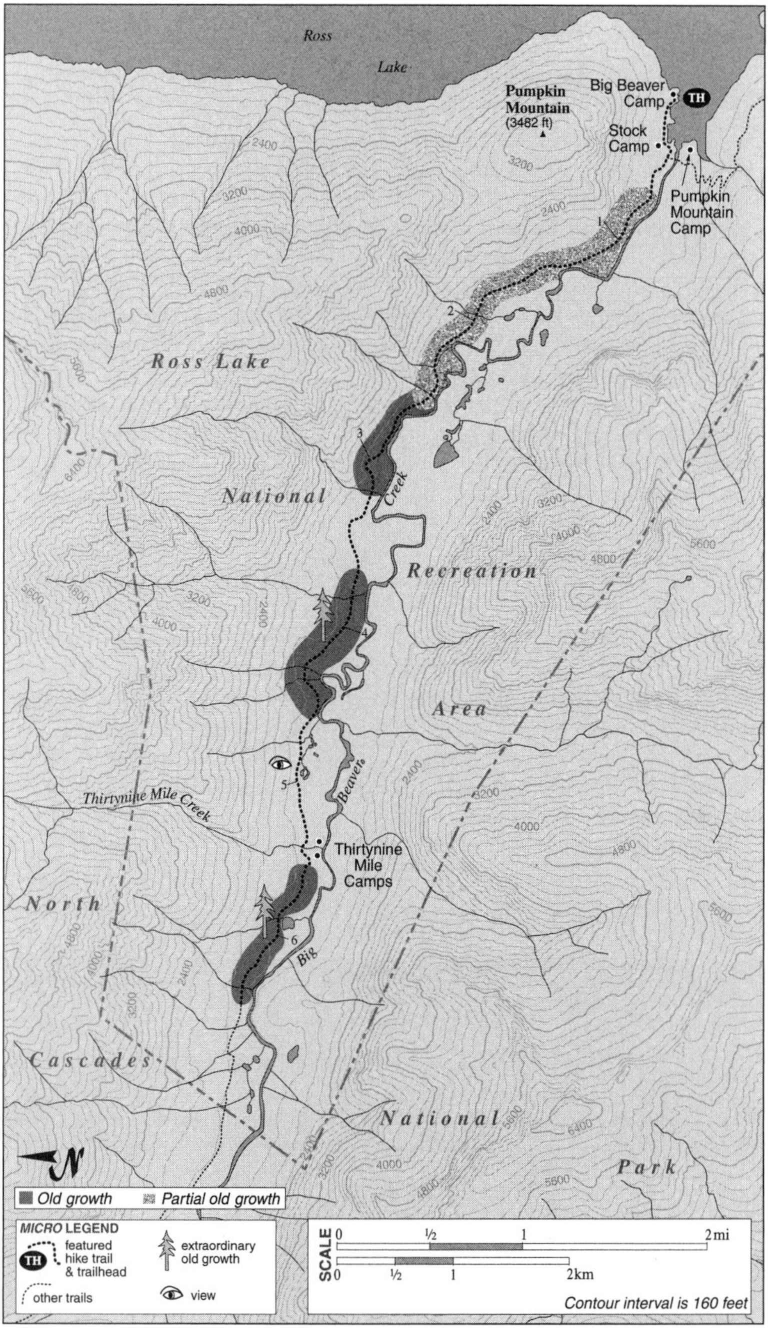
Ross Lake
Pumpkin Mountain (3482 ft)
Big Beaver Camp
TH
Stock Camp
Pumpkin Mountain Camp
Ross Lake National Recreation Area
Creek
Beaver
Big
Thirtynine Mile Creek
Thirtynine Mile Camps
North Cascades National Park
1
2
3
4
5
6
2400
3200
4000
4800
5600
6400
Old growth
Partial old growth
MICRO LEGEND
featured hike trail & trailhead
other trails
extraordinary old growth
view
SCALE
0 ½ 1 2mi
0 ½ 1 2km
Contour interval is 160 feet

dock. Call the resort using the telephone by the lakeshore just before reaching the dock.

After a short ride up the lower end of Ross Lake disembark at Big Beaver Camp. The taxi service is reliable, but it never hurts to double-check your pickup time with the taxi captain. Wind your way behind the campground over to the north shore of the bay, and turn right on the Big Beaver Trail a few hundred yards later.

Head northwest up the valley on an almost level grade, passing for 2 miles or so through a young, post-fire Douglas-fir forest with a few scattered older survivors. The first western redcedar grove is reached about 2.5 miles from the landing. Magnificent redcedar up to 8 feet in diameter and Douglas-fir 4 to 6 feet thick stand gracefully by the river and on the adjoining lower slopes.

A more impressive western redcedar grove stands less than a half mile farther up the trail. A narrow band of old growth arrayed along the river contains enormous redcedars rooted in the riparian area. A few of these spectacular specimens stretch more than 10 feet across at breast height. Huge Douglas-fir reaching 6 feet in diameter are surpassed by these colossal cedars.

All too soon the ancient redcedars are left behind and the trail enters younger forest. The trail crosses Thirtynine Mile Creek about 5.5 miles from the landing where Thirtynine Mile Camps (one camp is for stock campers, one for hikers only) occupy mirror-image sites adjacent to the stream. Shortly after passing the camps the trail enters a third grove of sensational cedar. Most day hikers will have had enough by the end of this patch about 6.5 miles from the landing. Those with more energy can continue a half mile farther up the trail and find still another giant redcedar grove.

How to get there: Park on the north side of the North Cascades Highway (State Route 20), in the Ross Dam trailhead parking lot approximately 13.5 miles east of Newhalem.

HAPPY CREEK FOREST WALK

Pull off the North Cascades Highway and take the Happy Creek Forest Walk for a pleasant and educational break. Interpretive signs explain basic forest ecology on this short (one-third mile) loop through an attractive old forest. The elevated boardwalk is wheelchair accessible, although there is a slight grade. Fire-scorched Douglas-fir and western hemlock 3 to 4 feet thick shade the chuckling creek.

How to get there: The parking area is located on the south side of the North Cascades Highway 13.8 miles east of Newhalem (approximately a quarter mile past the Ross Dam trailhead).

6 THUNDER CREEK

Length ■ **6.7 miles one way**
Difficulty ■ Moderate
Season ■ Spring to autumn
Lowest point ■ 1,220 feet
Highest point ■ 1,900 feet
Human imprint ■ Moderate (hikers)
Information ■ North Cascades National Park

Primary Old-Growth Feature
Western redcedar grove

Multiple generations of Douglas-fir and an exceptional grove of western redcedar cloak the slopes of Thunder Creek in the Ross Lake National Recreation Area. Ironically, while the basin holds the largest concentration of glaciers in the Lower 48, evidence of several forest fires is abundant along the trail. Trail use is high for the first mile or two, but rapidly tapers off as the campground recedes.

The Thunder Creek Trail quickly enters an old-growth Douglas-fir forest. A couple hundred yards later the Thunder Woods Nature Trail takes off uphill to the right (see sidebar). The trail crosses over the tip of Thunder Arm (an appendage of Diablo Lake) on a substantial steel suspension bridge and starts upstream on the silt-capped floodplain. The next half mile passes through an exceptional stand dominated by gnarly western redcedar up to 9 feet thick. Large Douglas-fir (some reaching 6 feet in girth) in the stand likely regenerated following a fire 400 or more years ago.

Shortly after passing the turnoff to Thunder Camp old forests are replaced by a mature stand of Douglas-fir that originated following a fire in the 1800s. Scattered individuals and small patches of older trees overtop the main canopy where the fire burned less intensely. About 2 miles later the trail enters a much younger Douglas-fir stand that arose from the ashes of a 1970 fire. Again, scattered survivors of the fire cast their shadow over the younger forest. Openings in the vicinity provide great views of Colonial Peak, Snowfield Peak, and other glacier-clad peaks to the southwest.

Osprey

For the next mile the trail passes through mixed mature and old forest before entering another young postfire stand of primarily Douglas-fir, this one in a patch burned by the McAllister Fire in 1990. Here, too,

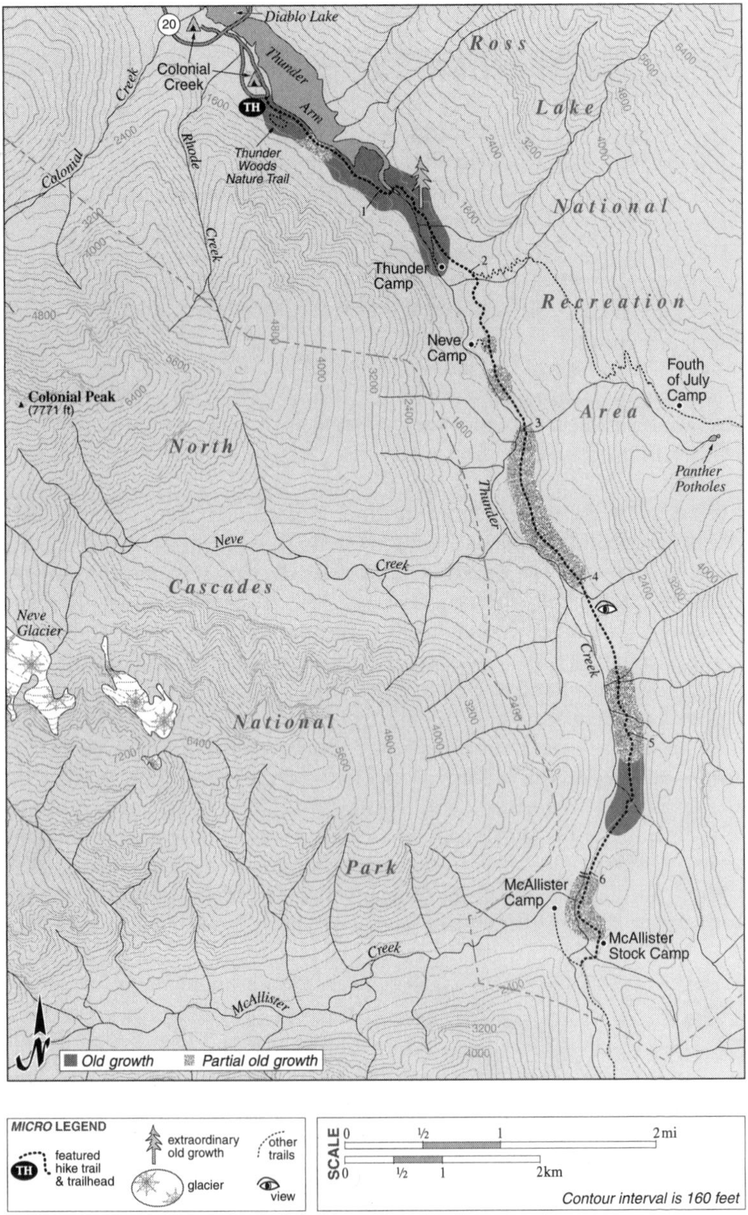

older fire survivors provide a legacy from the pre-burn forest to help maintain forest species and ecological processes. For example, canopy-dwelling lichens and insects are available to help repopulate the younger forest by dispersing from the older trees to the new stand.

The trail quickly descends to Thunder Creek near a hidden gorge where the stream rockets through a narrow slot. From here the trail winds past McAllister Stock Camp down to a junction with the spur trail to McAllister Camp approximately 6.7 miles from the trailhead. A relatively open and attractive mature Douglas-fir forest on the other side of the stream makes a logical turnaround point for day hikers. Mixed mature and old forest continues for another mile up Thunder Creek to Triconni Camp.

How to get there: Turn south off of the North Cascades Highway (State Route 20) into Colonial Creek Campground 9.6 miles east of Newhalem. Stay to the left and park at the trailhead by the amphitheater at the far end of the campground.

THUNDER WOODS NATURE TRAIL

The Thunder Woods Nature Trail offers an easy way to sample an old-growth forest close to the North Cascades Highway. Take a right onto the nine-tenths-mile-long loop just a couple hundred yards from the Thunder Creek trailhead. The trail circles across the slope through an open stand of classic lowland old growth. Although the trail tread is steep and uneven in places, most will find it an easy hike. An interpretive brochure explains the wonders of this elderly Douglas-fir and western hemlock community.

7 South Creek

Length ■ **7.2 miles one way**
Difficulty ■ Difficult
Season ■ Summer
Lowest point ■ 3,180 feet
Highest point ■ 6,320 feet
Human imprint ■ Minimal
Information ■ Okanogan National Forest (Methow Valley Ranger District)

Primary Old-Growth Features
Patches of large ponderosa pine, Douglas-fir, and Engelmann spruce; scattered alpine larch

The South Creek drainage provides a diverse and scenic option for exploring the dry-side forests of the Twisp River watershed. The South Creek Trail (401) passes through several environmental zones ending at South Pass where a handful of large alpine larch are scattered across the upper slopes. Alpine larch is a distinctive and hardy species inhabiting high, rocky slopes within a narrow range on the east side of the Cascades from Wenatchee north to southern British Columbia.

Most of the South Creek basin lies within the Lake Chelan–Sawtooth Wilderness, part of a complex of national parks, national recreation areas, and national forest wilderness that comprise the core of a region known collectively as the North Cascades Ecosystem (NCE). The NCE may be the only remaining chunk of wild landscape in the Cascades of sufficient size to support rare carnivores such as gray wolf, grizzly bear, Canada lynx, and wolverine.

Start out heading west from the trailhead. The trail soon crosses the Twisp River and enters the South Creek basin. For the first mile or so the trail travels through a generally forested environment dominated by old ponderosa pine and Douglas-fir, becoming more open where snag patches occur. An outbreak of western spruce budworm in the 1970s defoliated portions of the South Creek basin, contributing to extensive tree mortality.

Forest cover is regularly interrupted by shrub fields propagated and maintained by avalanches over the next several miles. Flattened, quaking aspen join a host of shrub species to form semi-permanent early-successional habitat in the avalanche paths. Strips of forest between the avalanche paths are dominated by Douglas-fir and Engelmann spruce, including some impressive spruce as much as 4 to 5 feet in diameter along the forest

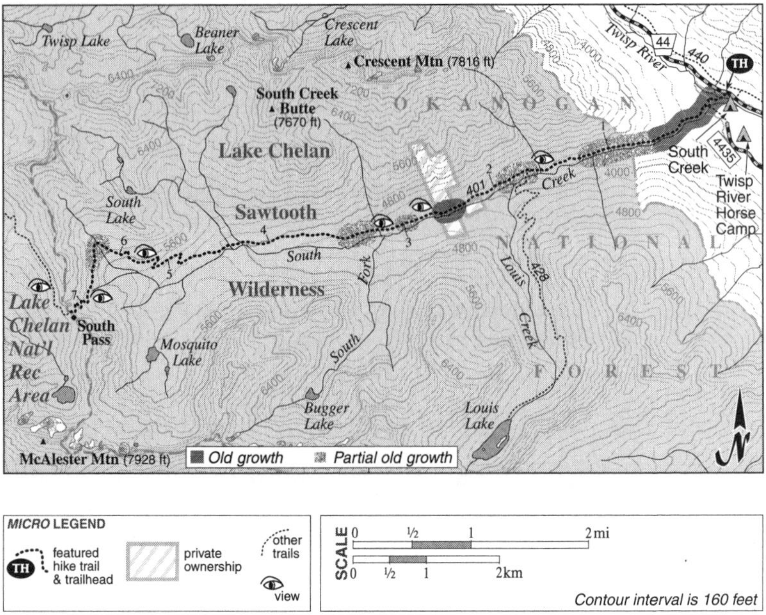

edges. Vistas in the openings reveal the peaks rimming the upper basin.

Continue up the north side of South Creek past the junction with the Louis Lake Trail (428), leaving the large trees behind 1.5 miles later. Dense patches of young forest continue for another mile so until the trail enters a large opening created by a forest fire in 1970. Stumps in the fire area predate wilderness designation (1984). The trail switchbacks up through the opening, finally reentering a small patch of forest in a draw about 6 miles from the trailhead.

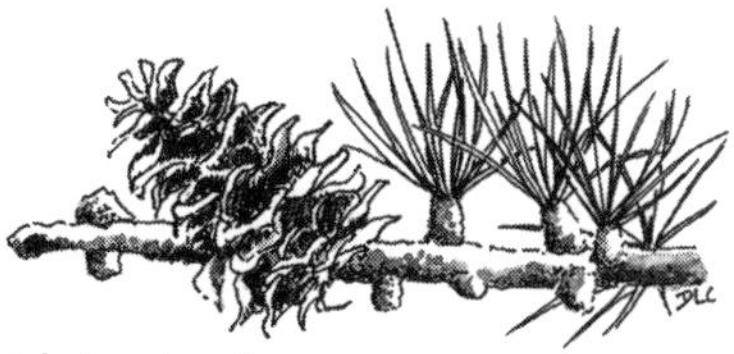

Alpine larch

The last mile of trail above this stand is in a subalpine zone of rocky slopes with scattered alpine larch, whitebark pine, and subalpine fir. Sturdy alpine larch seem to prosper in these high-elevation boulder fields and are best seen in late September when their needles turn yellow before dropping. Continue up past a few old alpine larch to South Pass, for sensational views of McAlester Mountain and the upper Rainbow Creek valley to the west.

How to get there: Head west on Twisp River Road out of Twisp. The road turns into Forest Road 44, becomes gravel surfaced, and reaches the trailhead on the left 24 miles from Twisp just past the South Creek Campground.

8 BOULDER RIVER

Length ■ **4.3 miles one way**
Difficulty ■ Moderate
Season ■ Early spring to late autumn
Lowest point ■ 880 feet
Highest point ■ 1,540 feet
Human imprint ■ High (hikers)
Information ■ Mount Baker–Snoqualmie National Forest (Darrington Ranger District)

Primary Old-Growth Features
Very old forest; huge western redcedar and Douglas-fir

A relatively easy and accessible lowland trail through fine old forest attracts legions of hikers to the Boulder River Wilderness. Immense western redcedar and Douglas-fir impress most visitors, and several delightful waterfalls tumble over the sheer rock wall bordering Boulder River.

The Boulder River Trail (734) is usually open when most Cascade trails are snowbound, leading to a steady stream of hikers and family backpackers during the wet season. High trail use on wet, clay soils have created numerous mucky holes in the trail, some not drying out until late in the season.

Skunk cabbage

The trail begins on an old railroad logging road through younger forest. Boulder Falls can soon be heard roaring below the trail, but can only be partially glimpsed through leafless hardwoods in the winter and early spring. Shortly thereafter the trail enters ancient forest in the wilderness.

The trail generally contours along the sideslopes above the river through old western hemlock and Pacific silver fir. Scattered western redcedar dominate the forest in places. Twice in the first 2.5 miles the trail dips toward the river for striking views of tributary waterfalls dancing down a sheer cliff face across the river. Douglas-fir are scarce, but three impressive veterans, 7 to 8 feet thick, cluster upslope about 2 miles from the trailhead between the waterfall viewpoints.

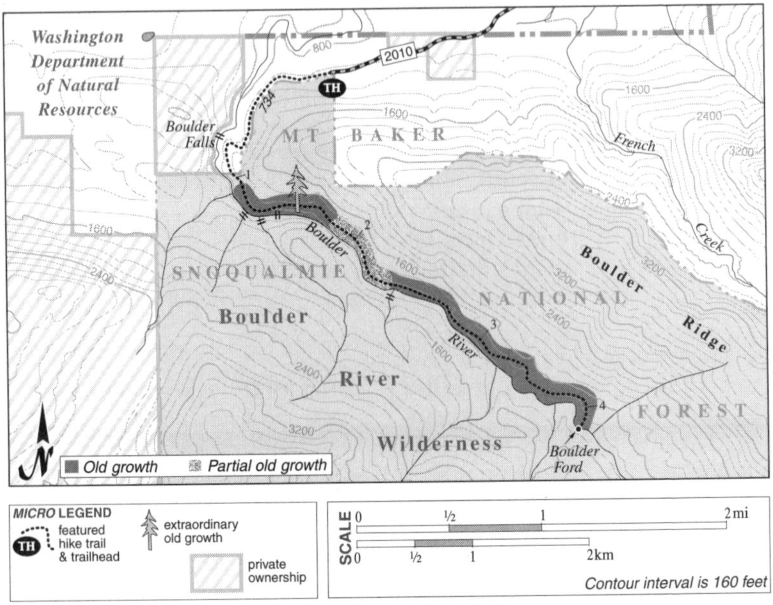

Past the waterfalls, the trail continues through a relatively intact canopy of old Pacific silver fir and western hemlock. A few colossal western redcedar up to 10 feet in diameter dwarf neighboring trees and forest visitors alike. The trail winds away from the river for the last mile or so, returning to the river and ending abruptly at Boulder Ford. A few campsites at the ford receive heavy use on most weekends.

How to get there: Take State Route 530 east from Arlington for 19.6 miles, then turn right (south) onto Forest Road 2010 immediately east of milepost 41. The trailhead is at the end of the road, 3.8 miles from SR 530.

9 ¦ MILK CREEK

Length ■	**6 miles one way**
Difficulty ■	Moderate
Season ■	Spring to autumn
Lowest point ■	1,680 feet
Highest point ■	2,900 feet
Human imprint ■	Minimal
Information ■	Mount Baker–Snoqualmie National Forest (Darrington Ranger District)

The route to upper Milk Creek unfolds for mile after mile in an old-growth paradise. Giant Douglas-fir and western redcedar along the first couple miles slowly yield to massive Pacific silver fir and western hemlock along the valley bottom and lower slopes of Milk Creek. Amazingly enough, this feature-packed, moderately graded trail is relatively lightly used.

> **Primary Old-Growth Features**
> Classic Douglas-fir–western hemlock old growth; immense western redcedar grove; beautiful Pacific silver fir–western hemlock forest

Start out on the Suiattle River Trail (784) and head upriver on an old roadbed through a lush lowland forest of ancient Douglas-fir, western hemlock, and western redcedar. One prodigious Douglas-fir along the way is more than 8 feet in diameter. Veer downhill to the right onto the Milk Creek Trail (790) about three-quarters of a mile from the trailhead. The trail soon enters a red alder gallery and crosses the river on an imposing steel bridge.

Shortly after crossing the river the trail comes to a stream crossing where you are likely to wet your feet up to mid-July. Switchback up the north-facing flank of Lime Ridge through a magnificent stand of 700-year-old Douglas-fir, western hemlock, western redcedar, and Pacific silver fir. The trail then levels out in a grove of enormous redcedar, some reaching 10 feet

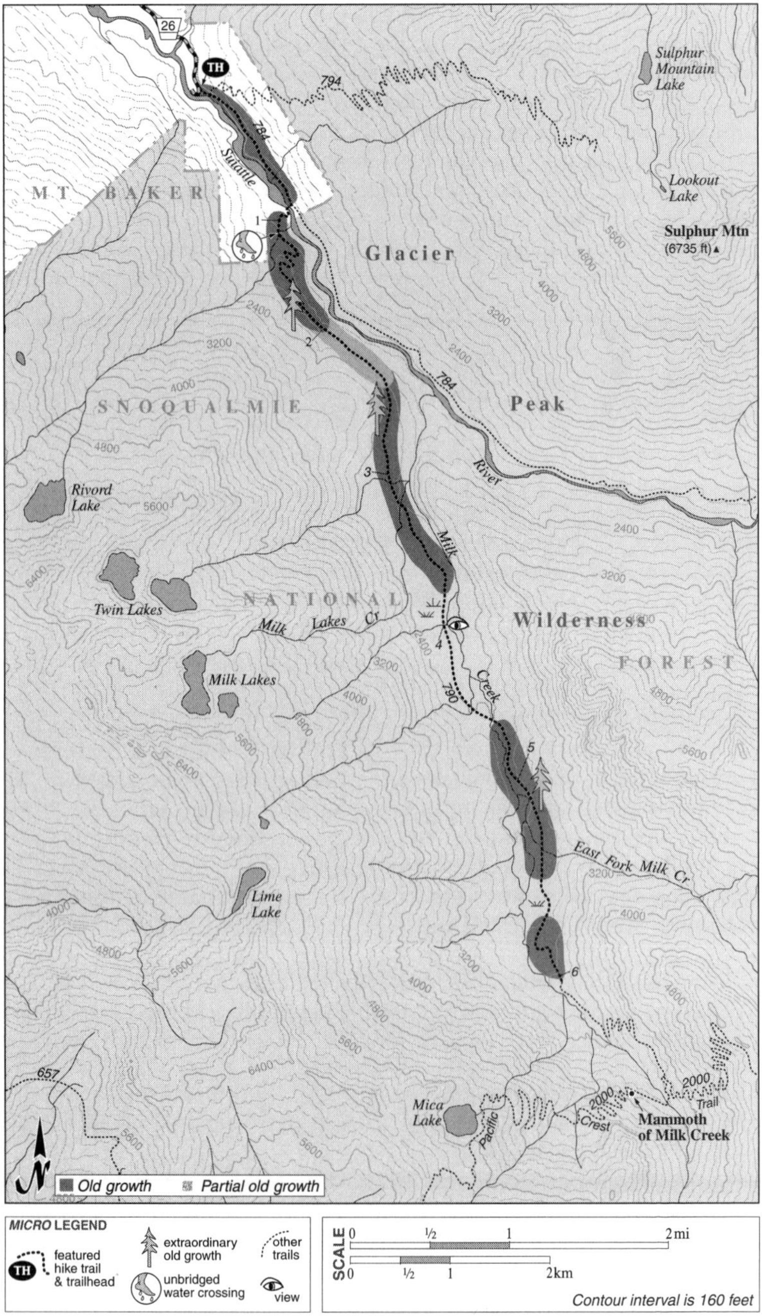

26
TH
794
784
Suiattle
MT BAKER
Glacier
Peak
SNOQUALMIE
NATIONAL
FOREST
Wilderness
Sulphur Mountain Lake
Lookout Lake
Sulphur Mtn
(6735 ft)
River
Milk
Creek
Rivord Lake
Twin Lakes
Milk Lakes Cr
Milk Lakes
790
East Fork Milk Cr
Lime Lake
Mica Lake
Pacific
Crest
Trail
2000
657
Mammoth of Milk Creek
Old growth
Partial old growth
MICRO LEGEND
featured hike trail & trailhead
extraordinary old growth
unbridged water crossing
other trails
view
SCALE
0 ½ 1 2mi
0 ½ 1 2km
Contour interval is 160 feet

in girth. A small stream marks the end of this patch about 2 miles from the trailhead where the trail enters a younger stand.

Awesome old growth featuring immense Douglas-fir resumes in another third of a mile where the trail curves to the south and enters the Milk Creek valley. Just beyond the bridge over Milk Lakes Creek the trail reaches an ancient Pacific silver fir, western hemlock, and western redcedar forest on an extensive flat where fire has long been absent. Abundant devil's club and salmonberry indicate moist, productive soils. The trail then slides over to the west bank of Milk Creek and passes through a riparian alder forest ornamented with scattered black cottonwood, bigleaf maple, and old conifers.

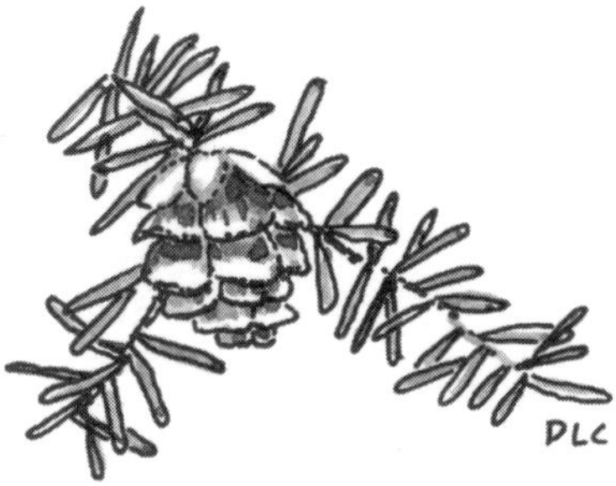

Western hemlock

The trail emerges from the forest into a shrubby, ferny meadow where Glacier Peak dominates the skyline directly ahead. The meadow tends to flood early in the season and may be wet through July. Continue across a bridge over Milk Creek about 4.5 miles from the trailhead and enter a deluxe Pacific silver fir and western hemlock forest. Some titans reach 5 to 6 feet in diameter. The trail then crosses the East Fork of Milk Creek, enters a small meadow, and bisects another patch of old growth. The end of this patch, about 6 miles from the trailhead, makes a fine stopping point for most day hikers. From here the trail steepens amid avalanche chutes and small stands of old growth for about another 1.5 miles before joining the Pacific Crest Trail (see sidebar).

How to get there: From State Route 530, turn east onto Suiattle River Road (Forest Road 26) approximately 11.2 miles south of Rockport (about 7 miles north of Darrington). Follow Suiattle River Road to the trailhead at its end 22.6 miles later. Although the first 10 miles are paved, believe the sign warning of "surface irregularities."

BIG TREE TIP—MAMMOTH OF MILK CREEK

Those with extra energy should continue on the Milk Creek Trail up to the junction with the Pacific Crest Trail (2000), and turn right. The second largest (by volume) recorded western hemlock stands just below the trail at the eastern end of the first complete switchback, approximately one-half mile from the junction. Known as the Mammoth of Milk Creek, this double-topped giant measures 8.9 feet in diameter and 167 feet tall. Several other impressive hemlock and silver fir stand near the Mammoth.

10 WHITE CHUCK RIVER

Length ■ **4.5 miles one way**
Difficulty ■ Moderate
Season ■ Summer to autumn
Lowest point ■ 2,340 feet
Highest point ■ 3,280 feet
Human imprint ■ Moderate (hikers, hot springs)
Information ■ Mount Baker–Snoqualmie National Forest (Darrington Ranger District)

Primary Old-Growth Feature
Mid-elevation riverside old growth

Hefty Douglas-fir and western redcedar join ubiquitous western hemlock and Pacific silver fir along the shores and banks of the White Chuck River. Although the trail is heavily used by bathers seeking the warm waters of Kennedy Hot Spring, the trail is kept in good condition and passes through interesting old forest. Expect a full parking lot and a steady stream of hot-spring hikers if visiting on a weekend.

Coolwort foam flower

The White Chuck River Trail (643) starts out in a predominantly younger forest with scattered old timers stretching above the general canopy layer. The trail enters Glacier Peak Wilderness a third of a mile from the trailhead, and the old forest begins in earnest shortly thereafter. Western hemlock and Pacific silver fir 3 to 4 feet thick are the dominant trees, occasionally leavened with stout western redcedar 4 to 6 feet in girth. Small patches of stocky Douglas-fir also reach 5 to 6 feet through the middle.

Continue southeast, always in earshot and frequently in sight of the churning river. The trail intermittently swings to the shore, and then switchbacks up and over several landslides triggered by extreme precipitation on porous volcanic deposits. Old Alaska-cedar make a welcome appearance about 3 miles from the trailhead and become more common with increasing elevation.

The trail reaches milky Kennedy Creek about 4.5 miles from the trailhead, providing the best view of Glacier Peak from the river. This is a good place to take a break before heading back.

If you're interested in the hot spring, cross a rickety bridge over the creek and find your way through the paths connecting various campsites and outhouses to the main bridge over White Chuck River. Cross the bridge and take a left to the spring where a small pool sufficient to hold about four people was excavated below ground. Bathers' heads bob above the surface of the warm, muddy water.

How to get there: Turn left onto Forest Road 23 from the Mountain Loop Highway about 9 miles south of Darrington. Trailhead parking is at the end of the road 10.2 miles later.

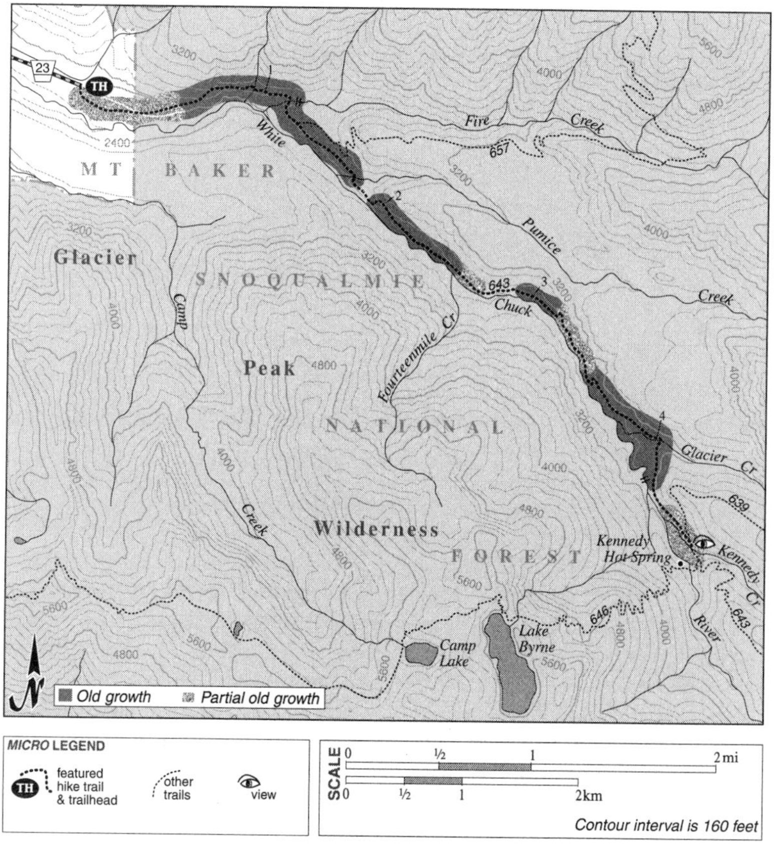

WHITE CHUCK BENCH

The White Chuck Bench Trail (731) offers another scenic old-growth hiking option in the White Chuck drainage. Although the hand of man has more obviously laid on the land near this trail, other benefits will sufficiently compensate many hikers. The White Chuck Bench Trail is snow-free at times when the White Chuck Trail is still snow-covered, receives much lower visitation, and giant western redcedar are common along the eastern half of the 6.5-mile trail. Occasional river and mountain views provide additional attractions. **How to get there:** The eastern trailhead is on the left of Forest Road 23, just after crossing the White Chuck River 5.5 miles from the Mountain Loop Highway.

11 LAKE TWENTYTWO

Length ■ **2.7 miles one way**
Difficulty ■ Moderate
Season ■ Spring to autumn
Lowest point ■ 1,110 feet
Highest point ■ 2,420 feet
Human imprint ■ Very high (hikers)
Information ■ Mount Baker–Snoqualmie National Forest (Darrington Ranger District)

Primary Old-Growth Features
Very old western hemlock, Pacific silver fir forest; grove of huge western redcedar

The well-trodden trail to Lake Twentytwo packs abundant attractions into a relatively short and steepish path. Extremely old forest, colossal western redcedar, numerous waterfalls, views of snow-clad peaks, and a cliff-rimmed lake are sufficient to satisfy all hikers—except maybe those in search of solitude. Save this one for a weekday as weekends are downright crowded on this easily accessible and well-known trail. Fortunately, the trail has been reconstructed and hardened, somewhat mitigating the heavy impact of hikers.

This area is known for extremely heavy precipitation, most likely due to the lack of moisture-catching mountains in the direction of the prevailing winds. Lack of fire over the past 1,000 years or more has allowed shade-tolerant western hemlock and Pacific silver fir to dominate the forest on these wet, north-facing slopes, a true climax forest. Douglas-fir, a tree species that

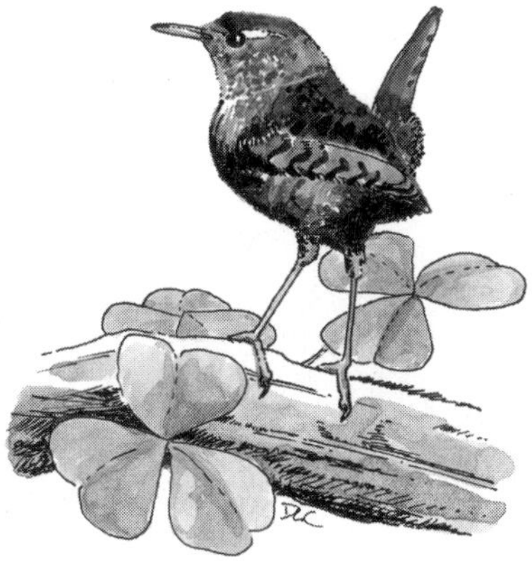

Winter wren

regenerates and often persists for many centuries following a fire, is absent from this stand altogether. Lands around Lake Twentytwo were designated as a Research Natural Area by the Forest Service in 1947 as a sample of an undisturbed western hemlock–western redcedar–Pacific silver fir forest.

The Lake Twentytwo Trail (702) immediately enters this ancient forest. The hemlock and silver fir, although far more numerous, are overshadowed in places by gigantic western redcedar, some reaching almost 12 feet in diameter. Redcedars along the lower slope were cut long ago, but once the trail gets up and away from the river bottom, gnarly old redcedars steal the show. The trail crosses Twentytwo Creek on a distinctive cedar bridge about three-quarters of a mile from the trailhead and proceeds to switchback uphill past several notable unnamed waterfalls.

The trail breaks out into the open about 1.5 miles from the trailhead, entering a steep talus slope. A long switchback leads to a grove of bigleaf maple and vine maple where views to the northeast reveal the dominant peaks of the Boulder River Wilderness and surrounding ridges, including Liberty Mountain and Three Fingers. The trail returns to old forest on the other side of the talus, including mountain hemlock and Alaska-cedar, and arrives at the lake a half mile later. At least a dozen small waterfalls drain the deep snowfields in the basin during snowmelt season. A new 1.25-mile trail around the lake is planned for future construction.

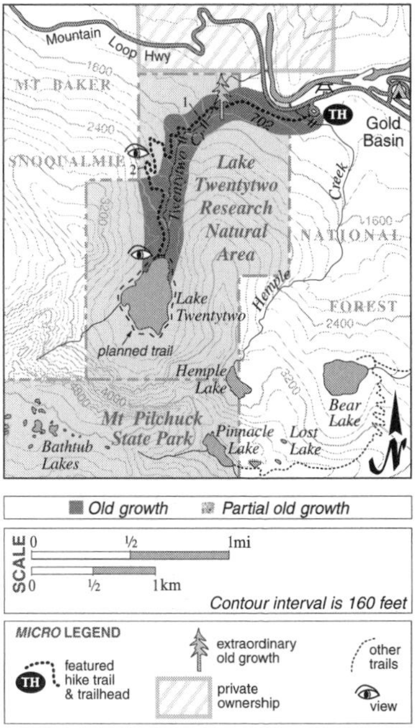

How to get there: Approximately 14 miles east of Everett, head east out of Granite Falls on the Mountain Loop Highway. Stop at the Verlot Public Service Center 11 miles from Granite Falls to see the chronology of a 700-year-old Douglas-fir displayed in a cross-sectional slice. The trailhead parking lot is on the right just over 2 miles past the public service center.

YOUTH-ON-AGE NATURE TRAIL

Impressive examples of 500-year-old Douglas-fir, western hemlock, and Sitka spruce flank this self-guided nature trail on the banks of the South Fork of the Stillaguamish River. Extremely high rainfall in the area supports one of the furthermost inland occurrences of Sitka spruce, a coastal rainforest species. The grove is named for the locally abundant youth-on-age plant, also known as the piggyback plant, a species that is able to reproduce by growing "daughter" plants in buds found along the base of mature leaves. When the leaves fall to the ground the daughter plants are able to send down roots establishing a new plant. This short (one-third mile) paved trail is accessible to wheelchairs.

How to get there: Follow the directions above, and continue past the Lake Twentytwo trailhead another 6.5 miles to park on the right.

12 North Fork Sauk River

Length ■ **4.1 miles one way**
Difficulty ■ Moderate
Season ■ Late spring to autumn
Lowest point ■ 2,070 feet
Highest point ■ 2,840 feet
Human imprint ■ Minimal
Information ■ Mount Baker–Snoqualmie National Forest (Darrington Ranger District)

Primary Old-Growth Features
Spectacular western redcedar groves; classic Douglas-fir old growth

Amazing groves of enormous western redcedar and majestic Douglas-fir line the first few miles of the North Fork Sauk River Trail (649), a primary route into the Glacier Peak Wilderness. Although the forest is superb and the trail gentle, the valley receives less use than other more well-known areas nearby. An unbridged crossing of Red Creek a little more than 4 miles from the trailhead marks a logical turnaround point for day hikers.

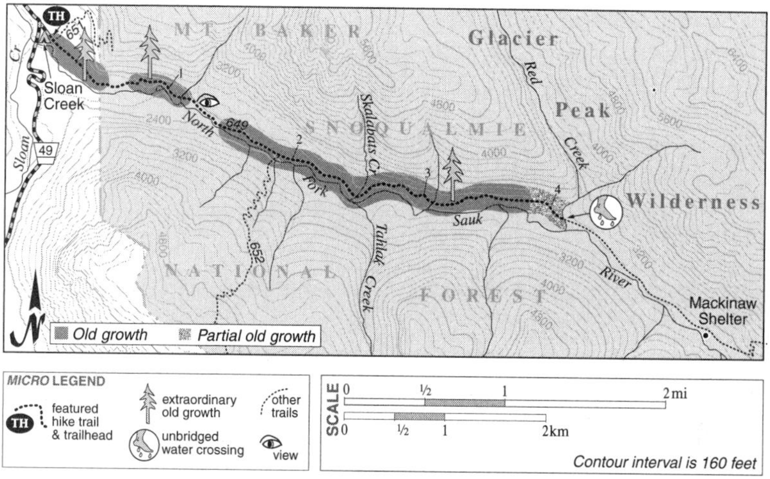

The gently inclined path immediately enters a great grove of cedars and immense Douglas-fir that continues for most of the first 1.25 miles. Some of the larger redcedars reach 9 feet in diameter. A brief break in the forest shortly thereafter allows views across the old growth to glacier-clad Sloan Peak.

The trail comes to a junction with the Pilot Ridge Trail (652) about 2 miles from the trailhead, then enters a beautiful lowland forest that stretches almost all the way to Red Creek. Huge Douglas-firs 4 to 8 feet thick mingle with ancient western hemlock, western redcedar, and Pacific silver fir along the river's north bank. While the river is near and usually within earshot, views of the river are rare.

Most safety-conscious hikers will see Red Creek as a reasonable stopping point. The unbridged creek carries a substantial flow, especially early in the season, and the best old forest has already been traversed. For those who venture across the creek, there are patches of older trees interspersed with avalanche paths for about another 1.5 miles above the stream before the trail veers sharply uphill just past the Mackinaw Shelter. For those with energy to spare, continuing uphill provides increasingly expansive views of the surrounding peaks.

How to get there: Turn left (east) from the Mountain Loop Highway (Forest Road 20) approximately 16 miles south of Darrington onto FR 49. Turn left into the trailhead parking lot 6.7 miles later.

Western redcedar

HAROLD ENGLES MEMORIAL CEDARS TRAIL

This small grove was set aside to honor a long-serving Forest Service District Ranger who worked to protect the western redcedar groves along the North Fork Sauk River more than 50 years ago. An infrequently maintained path through a grove of red alder and large western redcedar stumps leads to a still-standing redcedar 14 feet in diameter, a giant by any standard. Overgrown meandering paths direct visitors to other huge western redcedar nearby. Long pants are recommended along this brushy trail.

How to get there: The trailhead is on the right side of Forest Road 49 approximately 3.2 miles from the Mountain Loop Highway.

13 Blanca Lake

Length ■ **4 miles one way**
Difficulty ■ Difficult
Season ■ Summer to early autumn
Lowest point ■ 1,900 feet
Highest point ■ 4,640 feet
Human imprint ■ Moderate (hikers)
Information ■ Mount Baker–Snoqualmie National Forest (Skykomish Ranger District)

Primary Old-Growth Features
Very old Douglas-fir–western hemlock forest; old mountain hemlock grove

The Blanca Lake Trail (1052) rises rapidly from an impressive Douglas-fir and western hemlock forest on the lower slopes of Troublesome Mountain to stellar mountain hemlock along the ridgeline. Although the steepness of the ascent and descent deter some, hikers crowd this readily accessible trail on summer weekends. Picturesque Blanca Lake cradled below prominent snow-clad peaks provides ample reward at the end of the trail.

The trail starts out relatively level, but soon steepens abruptly. Thirty-seven switchbacks, 2,700 feet of elevation gain, and 3 miles later the trail reaches a saddle along the ridge marking the southern boundary of the Henry M. Jackson Wilderness. Douglas-fir 6 to 7 feet thick crowd the trail along the lower slopes, becoming less abundant as the trail gains elevation. Weathered western hemlock are replaced by mountain hemlock after the first 2 miles. Omnipresent Pacific silver fir is the only tree species that

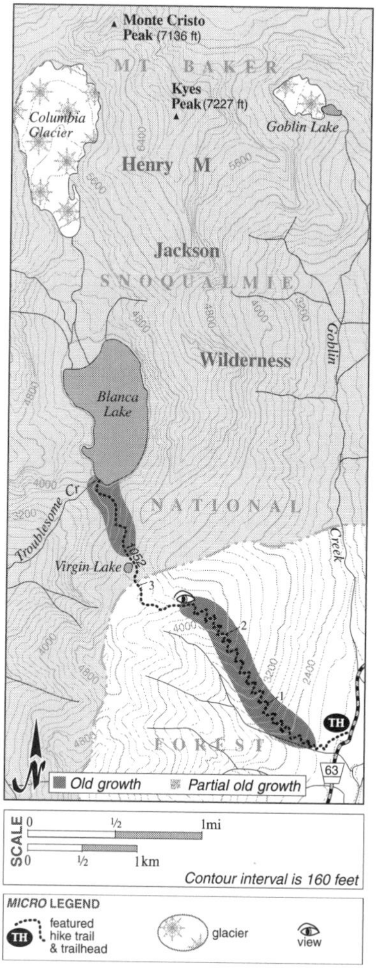

occurs throughout the elevational gradient.

Continuous forest cover ends near the saddle where subalpine meadows are interspersed with patches of mountain hemlock. The trail crests the ridge and immediately starts the descent toward Blanca Lake. Once across the ridge the trail skirts the east shore of

Common raven

tiny Virgin Lake and deteriorates into a well-used but rough path. The trail continues north across the sideslopes of Troublesome Creek basin through an excellent stand of 500-year-old mountain hemlock, near the upper age limit for the species.

The trail finally reaches Blanca Lake pooled in the floor of a glacial cirque approximately 600 feet below the saddle. To sustain lake surface levels, Blanca Lake depends on meltwater from the Columbia Glacier and snowfields draped on the shoulders of Columbia, Monte Cristo, and Kyes Peaks. The greenish hues of the lake contrast memorably with the white snowbanks on the surrounding peaks. After wandering about and recovering some energy, reverse your engine and return the way you came.

How to get there: From Stevens Pass Highway (U.S. Highway 2), turn north toward the town of Index onto North Fork Skykomish River Road (Forest Road 63). Follow paved FR 63 for 15 miles, then turn left (north) onto gravel FR 63 at an unsigned road junction (4 miles past the Troublesome Creek Campground). Two miles later turn left into the trailhead parking area.

TROUBLESOME CREEK NATURE TRAIL

A half-mile-long nature trail showcases some of the larger Douglas-fir and western redcedar standing along Troublesome Creek, the outlet for Blanca Lake. This beautiful cascading stream achieved its moniker because of difficulties in putting a road across the creek in the early days of exploration and mining. Now a double-loop trail highlights 500-year-old conifers scattered among a younger forest. The creek shoots through a cool slot gorge just below the upper bridge, taking on a unique "electric blue" coloration.

How to get there: Turn right into Troublesome Creek Campground off North Fork Skykomish River Road, approximately 11 miles from Stevens Pass Highway. Turn left immediately upon entering the campground and park by the trail bridge 100 yards later.

14 West Cady Ridge

Length ■ **4 miles one way**
Difficulty ■ Moderate
Season ■ Summer to autumn
Lowest point ■ 2,470 feet
Highest point ■ 4,760 feet
Human impact ■ Minimal
Information ■ Mount Baker–Snoqualmie National Forest (Skykomish Ranger District)

Primary Old-Growth Feature
Classic Douglas-fir–western hemlock old growth

The north-facing slopes of West Cady Ridge shelter a magnificent stand of classic lowland old growth. A steady climb through this fine forest leads hikers to ridgetop views of Glacier Peak, Kyes Peak, Columbia Peak, and nearby spires. To top it off, berry-pickin' enthusiasts will love the huckleberry heaven along the ridgeline.

The West Cady Ridge Trail (1054) heads upstream parallel to the North Fork of the Skykomish River before crossing the frothy river on a dependable trail bridge. Then the trail heads upslope through consummate old forest headed by Douglas-fir up to 6 feet in diameter and 700 years old. Craggy old western hemlock, western redcedar, and Pacific silver fir fill out the cast of conifers.

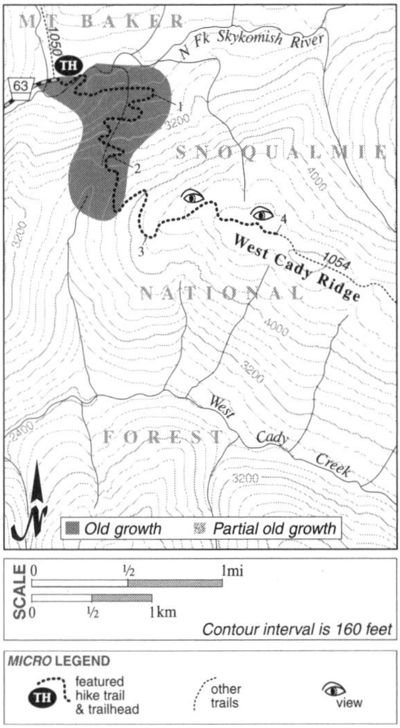

The trail continues switchbacking uphill on a moderate grade angling upwards on long arcs at first, then climbing more steeply in tighter turns. The path repeatedly winds into moist, productive draws armored by patches of spiny devil's club, then out and around drier knolls. After about 2 miles Douglas-fir drops out of the forest and a few Alaska-cedar and mountain hemlock join the ensemble. Shortly thereafter the trail enters a relatively young forest, where an early twentieth-century fire set the stage for a new forest generation.

After 3 miles the trail leaves the forest altogether and enters shrub fields with scattered small trees. Glimpses of snow-clad peaks entice hikers onward. The trail climbs steadily until "the flats" are reached on the top of West Cady Ridge about 4 miles from the trailhead. Here shrub and heath lands provide a picture-perfect setting for wide-ranging views of Benchmark Mountain to the east, Glacier Peak to the north, Kyes and Columbia Peaks to the northwest, and Spire Mountain and other peaks to the southwest.

Ambitious hikers can continue eastward out the ridge another 4 miles to Benchmark Mountain for a still loftier view of Cascade peaks, but most day hikers will be content to meander along the ridgeline for awhile and then head back to the trailhead. Hikers that time their arrival with the seasonal ripening of the huckleberries (roughly late August to September) will find this ridgeline to their liking.

How to get there: From Stevens Pass Highway (U.S. Highway 2), turn north toward the town of Index onto North Fork Skykomish River Road (Forest Road 63). Follow paved FR 63 for 15 miles, then turn left onto gravel FR 63 at an unsigned road junction (4 miles past the Troublesome Creek Campground). The road ends 4.4 miles later at the trailhead parking area.

Devil's club

15 DECEPTION CREEK

Length ■ **5 miles one way**
Difficulty ■ Moderate
Season ■ Late spring to autumn
Lowest point ■ 1,990 feet
Highest point ■ 3,190 feet
Human impact ■ Minimal
Information ■ Mount Baker–Snoqualmie National Forest (Skykomish Ranger District)

Primary Old-Growth Feature
Very old western hemlock and Pacific silver fir forest

The Deception Creek Trail (1059) bisects a long valley holding one of the oldest forests in the Cascades. Mile after mile of gnarly old Pacific silver fir and western hemlock form an excellent example of a "climax forest." A portion of the trail was recently rerouted to stay on the west side of Deception Creek for most of the first 5 miles, a distinct improvement that avoids a couple of log bridges prone to flood damage.

The trail begins in a mature forest (approximately 250 years old) where Douglas-fir still prospers. A solitary blue-hued noble fir stands by the trail about a quarter mile from the trailhead, near the northern limits of noble fir distribution. The trail then enters the Alpine Lakes Wilderness, crosses a solid bridge over Deception Creek, and begins angling across the slope away from the creek.

Soon Douglas-fir disappears and the really old forest begins. Relatively shade-intolerant Douglas-fir is a long-lived species that regenerates and competes well at this elevation following fires. It may take 1,000 years or more with-

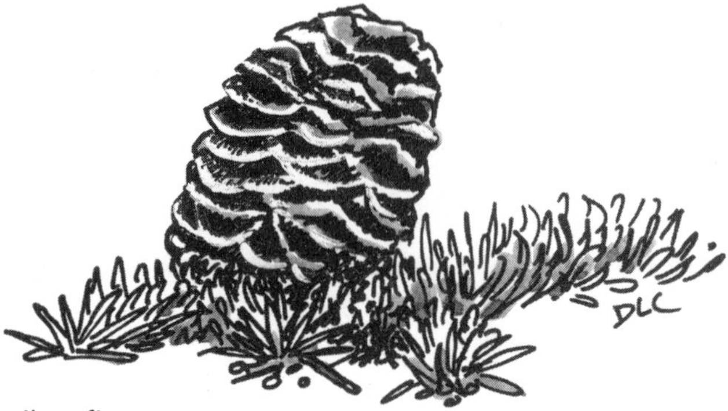

Pacific silver fir

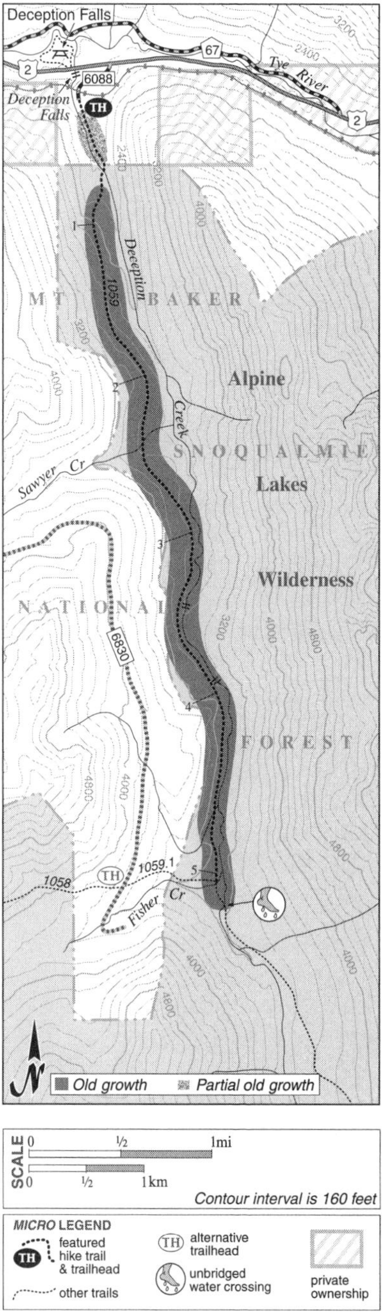

out fire for Douglas-fir to die out, allowing more shade-tolerant conifers to take over. Western hemlock, the Washington state tree, is conspicuous throughout the hike, sometimes reaching 5 feet or more in diameter. Monster western redcedar, some scorched by forest fire, are sprinkled throughout the forest for about the first 2.5 miles. Stately Pacific silver fir increase in prominence as the trail gains elevation, stretching to impressive heights on the better sites.

The trail climbs a bit in the second mile, passing a single Douglas-fir on a knoll, noteworthy as a loner among cousins. The trail levels out near the top of an extended cliff formation approximately 2 miles from the trailhead, and then descends toward Deception Creek. The trail rejoins the creek about 3 miles from the trailhead where a particularly beautiful stand shades a campsite by the old stream crossing.

The trail stays streamside for the next 2 miles, passing an impressive two-step waterfall about 3.5 miles from the trailhead and a smaller falls a half mile later. Above the falls Deception Creek rushes through a rocky gorge and Alaska-cedar make an appearance. The trees again gain girth and height on an old floodplain prior to crossing Fisher Creek, a logical turnaround spot for day hikers. The trail continues upvalley from Fisher Creek, crossing Deception Creek, and heading sharply upslope toward Deception Lakes, Deception Pass, and the Pacific Crest Trail.

How to get there: Turn south on Forest Road 6088 from Stevens

Pass Highway (U.S. Highway 2) a quarter mile east of the Deception Falls parking area (8.25 miles east of Skykomish). Road 6088 passes under a railroad trestle and ends in four-tenths of a mile in the trailhead parking area.

DECEPTION FALLS NATURE TRAIL

Travelers wending their way over Stevens Pass often stop at Deception Falls for a quick break and a peek at the falls. The Deception Falls Nature Trail offers an agreeable way to extend the respite and enjoy the old forest along the confluence of Deception Creek and the Tye River. Pick up the half-mile loop behind the rest rooms and head downhill through large Douglas-fir and western hemlock, with occasional 600-year-old western redcedar. Interpretive signs explain the cultural and ecological history of the area, and point out a noteworthy western white pine by the trail. A short, barrier-free trail leads to a viewpoint where Deception Falls is visible under the highway.

How to get there: Pull into the Deception Falls parking lot on the north side of Stevens Pass Highway (U.S. Highway 2) about 8 miles east of Skykomish.

16 HEATHER LAKE

Length ■	**3.4 miles one way**
Difficulty ■	Moderate
Season ■	Late spring to autumn
Lowest point ■	2,660 feet
Highest point ■	3,960 feet
Human imprint ■	Moderate (hikers)
Information ■	Wenatchee National Forest (Lake Wenatchee Ranger District)

Primary Old-Growth Feature
Very old and impressive stand of western hemlock and Pacific silver fir

The popular path to Heather Lake passes through two splendid stands of old growth, one relatively young and the other truly ancient. The Heather Lake Trail (1526) begins on the level, climbs steeply in the middle, and flattens out again for the final approach to the lake. Glittering Heather Lake sits in a half-mile-long depression beneath Grizzly Peak, just a mile east of the Cascade crest.

An outstanding example of a very old forest clinging to the last vestiges of a post-fire generation of Douglas-fir stands along the trail for about the first 1.5 miles. Shade-tolerant western hemlock and Pacific silver fir dominate the forest, some reaching 4 to 5 feet thick and 500 years of age. A widely scattered handful of battered Douglas-fir are even larger (6 to 7 feet thick) and substantially older. Veteran Heather Lake hikers need to be alert for a temporary trail reroute about a mile from the trailhead. The old bridge over the gorge has collapsed and until the bridge is replaced the trail crosses Lake Creek a third of a mile prior to the old crossing.

The path steepens gradually as it approaches the head of the valley, then abruptly starts switchbacking in earnest just after entering the Henry M. Jackson Wilderness. A much younger, old-growth forest dominated by 2 to 4-foot-thick Douglas-fir and western hemlock drapes across the valley headwall. A rock outcrop about 2.25 miles from the trailhead provides vistas to the east of Labyrinth Mountain and adjacent peaks.

The trail soon levels out, now in higher-elevation forest featuring mountain hemlock and Alaska-cedar. The trail comes to the northeast corner of Heather Lake 3.4 miles from the trailhead. Glacially striated bedrock

Starry false Solomon's seal

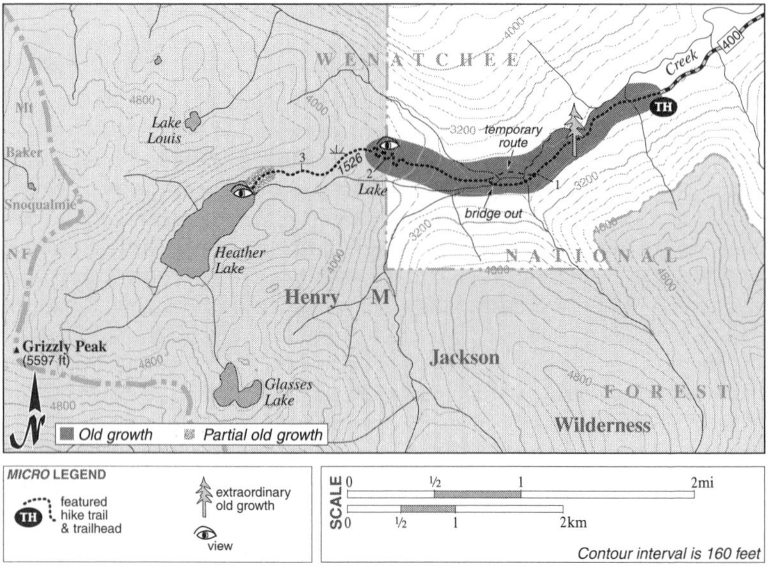

studded with garnet crystals and fringed by heather beckons new arrivals to come sit a spell and marvel at the wonders of the Cascades.

How to get there: Turn north onto State Route 207 off Stevens Pass Highway (U.S. Highway 2) at Coles Corner (14.4 miles north of Leavenworth). Follow SR 207 around the north side of Lake Wenatchee staying left (veering southeast) onto Forest Road 65 at the head of the lake. Turn left onto gravel-surfaced FR 6700 about 4.7 miles later, then turn right onto FR 6701 in another half mile. Turn left onto FR 400 after 4.7 miles. Trailhead parking is at the end of the road in 2.3 miles.

BIG TREE LOOP

This pleasant path provides an excellent way to end a day in the Little Wenatchee River area. The trail drops down to a productive, herb-rich terrace where stout Douglas-fir, western redcedar, and grand fir dignify the flat. A few western white pine and understory hemlock and silver fir round out the roster. Two short paths lead to the river's edge for rock tossing and reflection, then the trail turns back to complete the half-mile loop.

How to get there: Continue to the right on Forest Road 65 at the junction with FR 6700, and follow it 1.5 miles to Soda Springs Campground. Turn left toward the campground and slowly wind downhill one-third of a mile and park wherever you can. The loop starts at the far end of the campground.

17 INDIAN CREEK

Length ■ **4 miles one way**
Difficulty ■ Moderate
Season ■ Summer to autumn
Lowest point ■ 2,310 feet
Highest point ■ 3,120 feet
Human imprint ■ Minimal
Information ■ Wenatchee National Forest (Lake Wenatchee Ranger District)

Primary Old-Growth Features
Riparian old growth; bizarre, mega–western redcedar

Beautiful lowland forest flanks both sides of the middle stretch of the White River, and both sides boast easy riverside trails. The Indian Creek Trail (1502) parallels the west bank of the White River through riparian old growth for 2 miles, before turning west up Indian Creek into younger forest. The White River Trail (1507), along the river's east bank, also bisects groves of old forest for several miles. Both trails

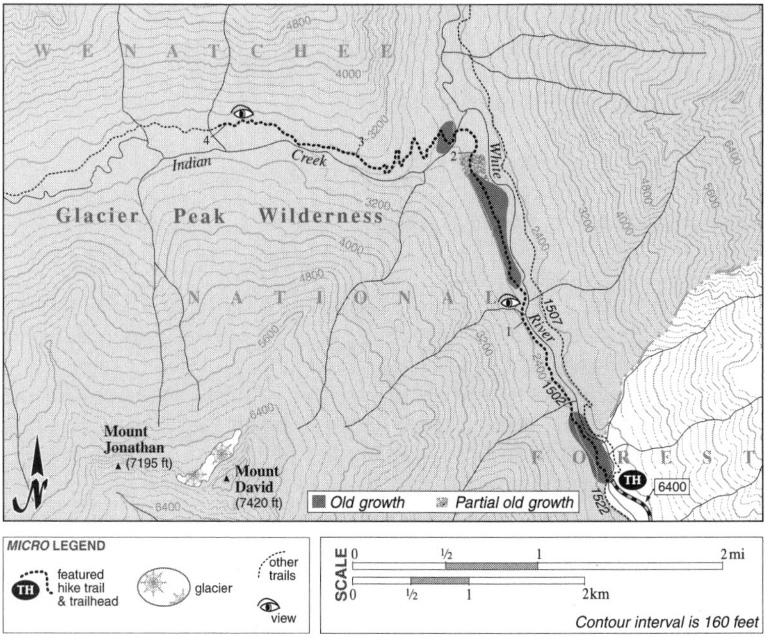

become very difficult farther up where incessant brush fields overrun the trails.

Try the Indian Creek Trail for starters. Cross the bridge over the White River into the Glacier Peak Wilderness and immediately enter a lovely grove of western hemlock and western redcedar. A massive redcedar of truly bizarre form stands to the right of the trail just a couple hundred yards from the trailhead. The surreal specimen reaches a maximum diameter well over 10 feet across at 10 to 15 feet above the ground, and then rapidly tapers off and splits into several thin, short stems.

The trail leaves this grove too quickly and enters a younger stand with occasional large grand fir. The trail comes to the river's edge in places, where glaciated Clark Mountain can be seen rising behind the river. Rock flour derived from glacial grinding gives the river a white, milky appearance.

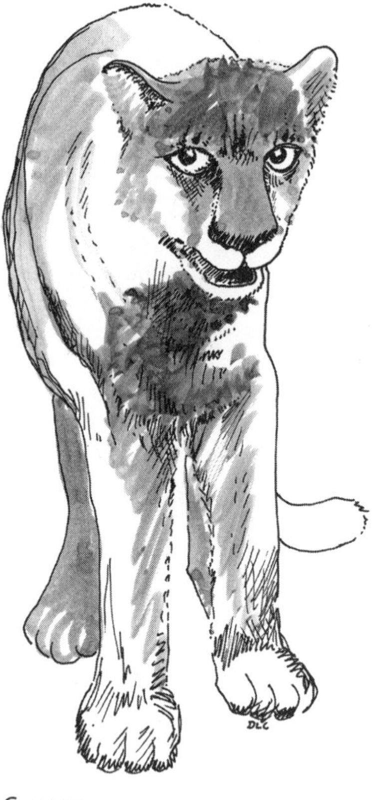

Cougar

The trail soon reenters riparian old growth perched on an old river terrace. Western hemlock, Douglas-fir, and western redcedar star in the show, with able support from occasional western white pine and Engelmann spruce. A few giant redcedar flourish by the river and tributary streams where their roots tap moisture reservoirs.

The old forest is left behind just before crossing Indian Creek about 2 miles from the trailhead. Switchback up the slope through one last little patch of old forest, taking a westerly course into the Indian Creek valley. The trail levels out above a series of small switchbacks where avalanche-induced brush fields begin. A nice view of Mount Jonathan and Mount David to the south marks a practical turnaround point for day hikers.

How to get there: At Coles Corner on Stevens Pass Highway (14.4 miles north of Leavenworth), turn north onto State Route 207 heading toward Lake Wenatchee. Follow SR 207 around the north side of the lake and turn right onto White River Road 10.5 miles from the highway. The road becomes gravel-surfaced Forest Road 6400 in 6.3 miles, and terminates at the trailhead 3.9 miles later.

18 CHIWAUKUM CREEK

Length	**5.5 miles one way**
Difficulty	Moderate
Season	Late spring to autumn
Lowest point	2,180 feet
Highest point	3,320 feet
Human imprint	Moderate (road, clearcut)
Information	Wenatchee National Forest (Leavenworth Ranger District)

Primary Old-Growth Feature
Scattered large ponderosa pine, Douglas-fir, and grand fir

Scattered old conifers characteristic of dry, eastside forests line the pleasant path along Chiwaukum Creek. A mighty stand of majestic ponderosa pine once stood across the trail 4 to 5 miles in, but was largely destroyed by logging prior to coming into public ownership. Fragments of the old forest remain though, and still provide a worthwhile destination.

Start out by the gate across a private road, open to the public only for foot traffic and only for through passage. The road curves up the valley

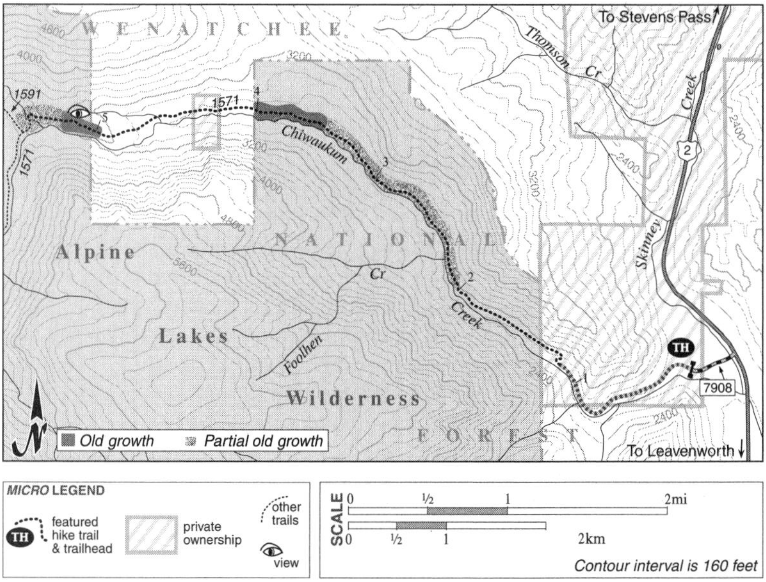

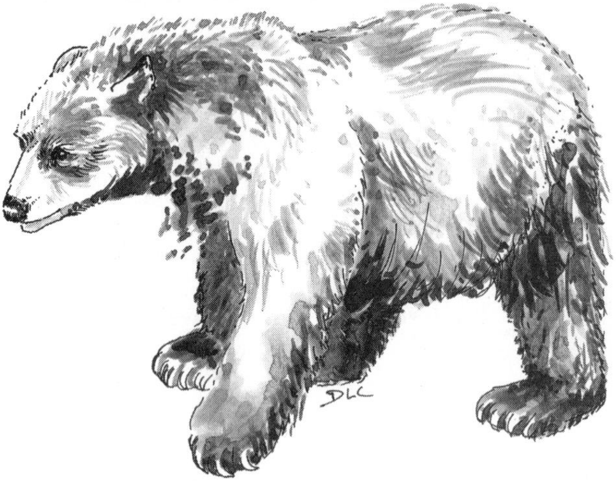

Black bear

floor near the cascading Chiwaukum Creek for a little over 1 mile, then comes to the start of the Chiwaukum Creek Trail (1571). Take the trail and soon enter the Alpine Lakes Wilderness.

The forest along the trail's first 2 miles is highly variable in character. Scattered large ponderosa pine, Douglas-fir, and grand fir stand among dense young forest, snag patches, and small shrubby openings. A handful of old western white pine and western redcedar shade a campsite and streamside break spot about 3 miles from the gate.

Another half mile up the trail brings you to the start of an outstanding and rare example of ponderosa pine old growth. Open and park-like in places, orange-plated pines are shown to best advantage where surrounded by a grass-covered forest floor. The fine stand ends too soon though due to chainsaw liquidation dating to the 1980s. The next mile of trail passes through a dense and fragrant snowbrush thicket. Pine stumps 4 to 5 feet across reveal a 500 to 600-year history, including multiple fire scars.

Continue past the young forest and brush field, finally emerging back in the old pine stand. A cluster of elderly pine crowns a small knoll about 5 miles from the gate, perfect for a picnic and a potential day-hike endpoint. A grove of young quaking aspen in the foreground softens the rocky canyon walls visible in the background.

For the next half mile the trail drops down to the stream, quickly entering a cooler, moister environment favoring western redcedar, grand fir, and Engelmann spruce. The stream crossing and the trail junction that follows mark other logical stopping points.

How to get there: Turn left (west) onto Chiwaukum Creek Road (Forest Road 7908) off Stevens Pass Highway (U.S. Highway 2) approximately 9.5 miles north of Leavenworth. Park at the trailhead one-third of a mile later.

HIDDEN LAKE

For those seeking more old ponderosa pine in the vicinity, try the short path to Hidden Lake. The trail switchbacks up the hill four-tenths of a mile through a few groups of older, fire-scorched pine amid a generally younger forest. A picturesque patch of fiery ponderosa pine graces the northern lakeshore.

How to get there: From the Stevens Pass Highway (U.S. Highway 2), turn north at Coles Corner (14.4 miles north of Leavenworth) onto State Route 207, heading toward Lake Wenatchee. Turn left 3.6 miles later onto Cedar Brae Road toward Nason Creek Campground. Keep to the left and park at the end of Glacier View Campground in another 5.1 miles.

19 ICICLE CREEK

Length	**6 miles one way**
Difficulty	Moderate
Season	Spring to autumn
Lowest point	2,860 feet
Highest point	3,240 feet
Human imprint	Moderate (hikers)
Information	Wenatchee National Forest (Leavenworth Ranger District)

Primary Old-Growth Features
Long stretch of old western hemlock forest; grove of large western redcedar

The long, broad valley of Icicle Creek, long ago a conduit for alpine glaciers, now serves as a conduit for alpine backpackers and day hikers. While the Icicle Creek Trail (1551) provides the backbone for many multiday loop options, the lower portion of the trail makes a fine day hike through diverse old forest. The forest attains westside dimensions on some of the better sites where western redcedars reach 5 to 6 feet in diameter. The well-known trail is readily accessible and practically level, so expect company on summer weekends.

The trail starts out passing two large black cottonwood trees, then enters the Alpine Lakes Wilderness less than a quarter mile from the trailhead. The forest along the first 1.25 miles is quite variable, featuring an assortment of both old and young conifers typical of eastside forests close to the Cascade crest (western redcedar, Douglas-fir, western hemlock,

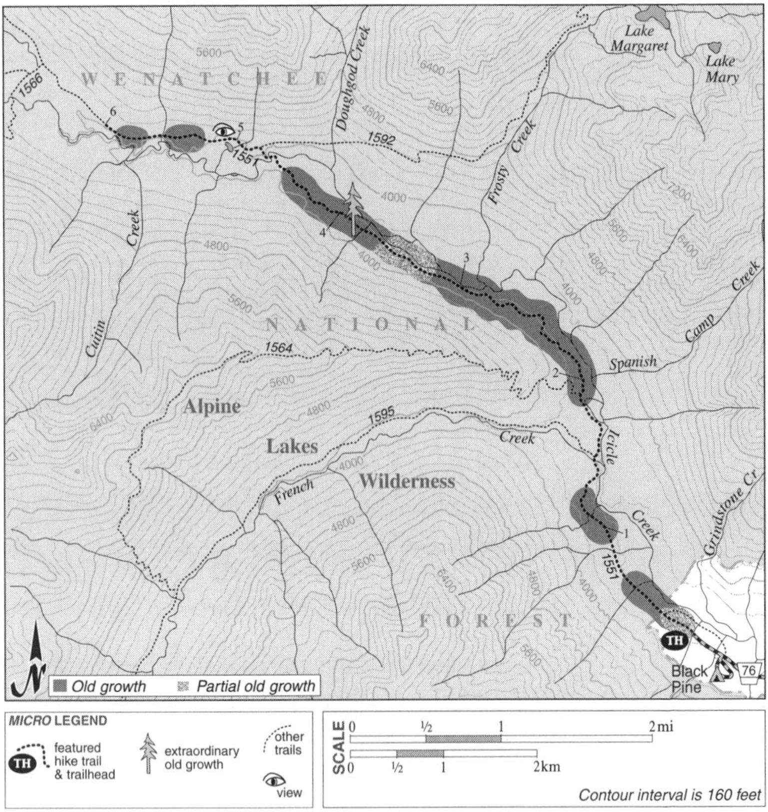

grand fir, Engelmann spruce, western white pine, and Pacific silver fir). A younger forest prevails in the vicinity of French Creek, a common stopping point for families with young children.

Shortly after crossing French Creek, the trail reenters older forest. For the next 1.5 miles or so the trail bisects a forest dominated by moderate-sized (2 to 3 feet thick), 300-year-old western hemlock. The trail continues up the valley parallel to Icicle Creek, coming to an exemplary stand on a fertile flat about 4 miles from the trailhead. Here, western redcedar, western hemlock, and Pacific silver fir are both taller and stockier than elsewhere along the trail. The larger redcedar reach 6 feet or more across. Well-armored devil's club indicates moist, productive soils.

The trail continues in patchy forest until crossing Icicle Creek a little less than 5 miles from the trailhead. Now on the north side of the creek, the path regularly passes through avalanche chutes overrun by a tangle of shrubs. The good news is that the openings allow occasional views across the valley to French Ridge, and the strips of forest between the avalanche paths contain big western redcedar, Pacific silver fir, and Engelmann spruce. Another mile of hiking past the stream crossing traverses most of the big trees.

Mosquito

How to get there: From Stevens Pass Highway (U.S. Highway 2) at the west end of Leavenworth, turn south onto Icicle Road (becomes Forest Road 76). Follow the road westward for approximately 16.5 miles, then stay left at a junction by the Rock Island Campground and cross the bridge over to the south side of Icicle Creek. Continue another 1.8 miles to the trailhead.

20 DENNY CREEK

Length	**4.4 miles one way**
Difficulty	Moderate
Season	Summer to early autumn
Lowest point	2,280 feet
Highest point	4,640 feet
Human imprint	Very high (hikers)
Information	Mount Baker–Snoqualmie National Forest (Snoqualmie Ranger District)

Primary Old-Growth Features
Excellent mid-elevation old growth; mountain hemlock old growth at upper elevations

An abundance of attractions along the path up Denny Creek valley brings crowds of visitors on summer weekends. Stellar old-growth forest, gorgeous alpine scenery, and sparkling waterfalls amply reward visitors, although weekdays are decidedly more enjoyable. The first 1.25 miles of the trail is especially well used by families heading toward or returning from the Denny Creek Waterslide, a spot well-known for water-play.

The first half mile of the Denny Creek Trail (1014) wanders through an outstanding ancient forest of shade-tolerant conifers (western hemlock, Pacific silver fir forest, western redcedar) sandwiched between the two halves of Interstate 90. The trail crosses to the east bank of Denny Creek, then passes under the viaduct supporting west bound Interstate 90 just over a half mile from the trailhead. Another half mile or so later the trail recrosses Denny Creek by a series of short waterfalls popular with families. Smooth rocks and small pools are well suited for sunning and sliding.

The crowd thins out above these falls though the trail remains in superb old growth for another half mile, then abruptly enters an expansive talus slope and shrub field. A small island of stout Pacific silver fir marks a great viewpoint of Keekwulee Falls thundering in the gorge below. Shortly thereafter the trail climbs a series of seven full switchbacks to gain admittance into the upper valley.

The route now levels out in patchy old forest, and Snowshoe Falls can be glimpsed below the trail. Denny Creek is crossed again, and the path bisects another large talus slope and shrub field. The trail starts climbing once more near the north edge of the shrub field, switchbacking in earnest toward Hemlock Pass, 4 miles from the trailhead.

An impressive 500-year-old mountain hemlock and Pacific silver fir forest is draped across the pass and continues on to Melakwa Lake. The trail condition deteriorates a bit over the last third of a mile or so to Melakwa Lake, but the trailside forest is fine and the alpine

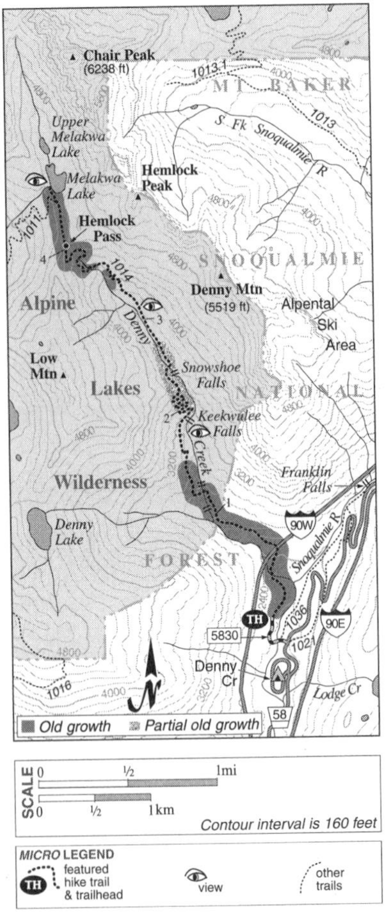

peaks rising around the lake are stunning. Due to the well-deserved popularity of the lake, camping is limited to designated sites, to protect the fragile landscape around the lakes from overuse.

How to get there: Take exit 47 off Interstate 90, approximately 47 miles east of downtown Seattle, and turn left (turn right if westbound). Turn right onto Denny Creek Road (Forest Road 58) at the stop sign. Turn left in one-third of a mile, re-

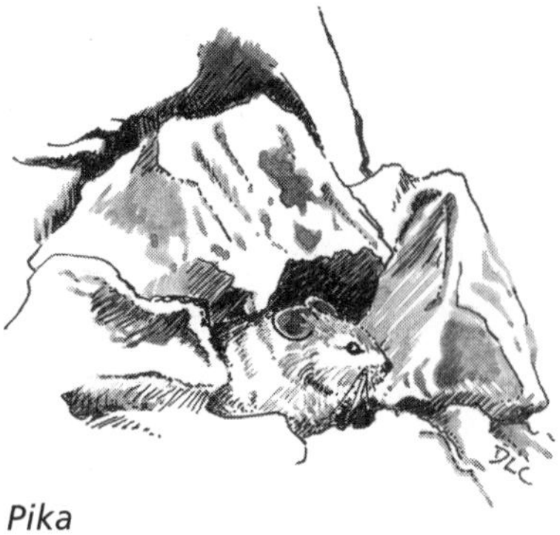

Pika

maining on Denny Creek Road for 2.3 miles. Then turn left onto FR 5830 just past the Denny Creek Campground and park where you can. The trail begins at the end of the road.

ASAHEL CURTIS NATURE TRAIL

The Asahel Curtis Nature Trail—showcasing chunky Douglas-fir, western redcedar, western hemlock, and Pacific silver fir—loops through classic old growth on a hillslope above noisy Interstate 90. The slow pace of change in the old-growth grove contrasts vividly with the freeway traffic whizzing by just downslope. The nature trail works equally well as a short (1 mile) hike in the old growth, or as a rest break from the freeway. A short connector trail leads to the nearby Asahel Curtis Picnic Area.

How to get there: Take exit 47 off Interstate 90 and turn right at the end of the ramp if eastbound (and left if westbound). Turn left onto graveled Forest Road 5590 a couple hundred yards later. The trailhead parking area is on your right after a third of a mile.

21 PETE LAKE

Length ■ **4.5 miles one way**
Difficulty ■ Moderate
Season ■ Summer to autumn
Lowest point ■ 2,810 feet
Highest point ■ 3,020 feet
Human imprint ■ Minimal
Information ■ Wenatchee National Forest (Cle Elum Ranger District)

Primary Old-Growth Features
Impressive eastside old growth; solitary gargantuan Douglas-fir

The Pete Lake Trail (1323) follows a nearly level grade to winsome Pete Lake nestled in the southeastern corner of the Alpine Lakes Wilderness. The path travels through diverse forest of varying ages, culminating in an outstanding grove of conifers near Pete Lake, a stand reminiscent of westside old growth. The trail is well used for family backpacking trips, and many continue past Pete Lake to scenic Spectacle Lake.

Start from the trailhead heading northwest on a gentle, rolling path, through a relatively sparse forest of lodgepole pine and assorted conifers. A few scattered old Douglas-fir, western white pine, and western hemlock preside over a younger post-fire stand for the first mile or so. Exposed bedrock exhibits the telltale striations of glacial grinding.

The Tired Creek Trail (1317) intersects the Pete Lake Trail near the beginning of the first extensive stand of old growth about 1.5 miles from the trailhead. Douglas-fir and western hemlock intermix with abundant Pacific silver fir near the beginning of the stand, but diminish in importance farther up the trail. Younger forest resumes after a mile or so, and the Pete

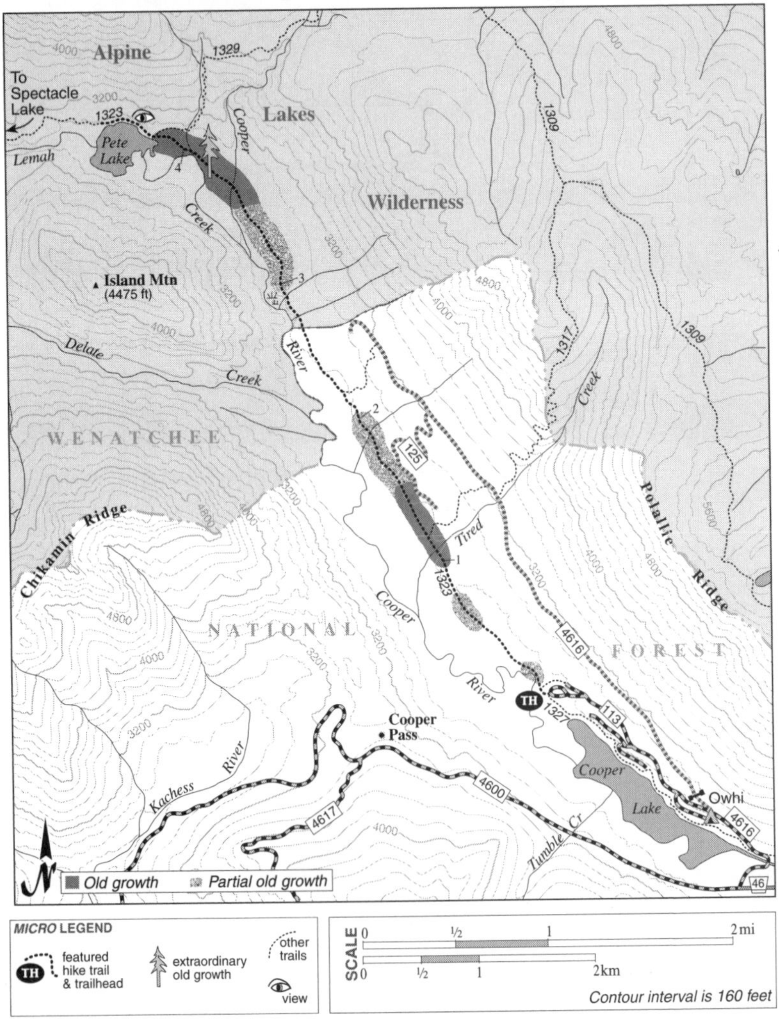

Thimbleberry

Lake Trail intersects a spur trail providing mountain bike access to Forest Road 4616 shortly thereafter. Another third of a mile brings you to the wilderness boundary, about 2.75 miles from the trailhead.

Big trees reappear after the trail passes a small meadow on the left. The destination old growth resides about 4 miles from the trailhead, heralded by a handful of large Alaska-cedar. Majestic Douglas-fir, western hemlock, and Pacific silver fir reach westside dimensions in places. The trail curves left at one point suddenly revealing a 6-foot-diameter Douglas-fir, then continues curving to the right past an even larger Douglas-fir, a full 9 feet in girth—pretty impressive for an eastside forest.

Shortly after the junction with the Waptus Pass Trail (1329), the trail reaches pretty Pete Lake. Numerous side paths head to the lakeshore and to heavily used campsites. Island Mountain stands dead ahead, while loftier peaks along upper Chikamin Ridge and Lemah Mountain dominate the skyline. Though Pete Lake makes an excellent destination, the alpine scenery only gets better farther up the trail, and another fine patch of old growth straddles the trail about three-quarters of a mile past Pete Lake.

How to get there: At Cle Elum, head west on 2nd Street, wind your way through Roslyn on the main road (State Route 903), and head north on the east side of Cle Elum Lake. Route 903 becomes Salmon la Sac Road a few miles past Roslyn. Turn left onto Forest Road 46 toward Cooper Lake 15 miles from Roslyn, then turn right onto Cooper Lake Road (FR 4616) in 4.6 miles. Veer left onto FR 113 by the gate on FR 4616 about three-quarters of a mile later, and park at the trailhead in another mile.

22 Silver Creek

Length ■ **5 miles one way**
Difficulty ■ Difficult
Season ■ Summer to early autumn
Lowest point ■ 2,400 feet
Highest point ■ 4,700 feet
Human imprint ■ Minimal
Information ■ Wenatchee National Forest (Cle Elum Ranger District)

Primary Old-Growth Feature
Beautiful eastside conifer forest in a perched valley

Perched high above Kachess Lake to the west and Cle Elum Lake to the east, the Silver Creek valley shelters a series of diverse habitats, including outstanding, eastside old growth. For years the future of this valley and surrounding lands was threatened by a checkerboard pattern of federal and private land ownership, but a large land exchange completed in 2001 resulted in consolidated federal ownership of the entire valley. Now the area is managed primarily for nonmotorized recreation.

The price of admission to this glorious valley is a very steep ascent on a rocky, south-facing slope. Take the Silver Creek Trail (1315) and begin climbing immediately. After a mile or so of good exercise both the trail grade and the environment begin to moderate.

A notable, partially obscured waterfall in Silver Creek marks a transition to the second phase of the hike. The next mile or so closely follows frothy Silver Creek past stout Douglas-fir, western hemlock, and grand fir 3 to 4 feet thick. The trail crosses over to the east side of Silver Creek 2 miles from the trailhead on an old log just past the junction with lightly used and infrequently maintained Beacon Ridge Trail (1315.3).

Soon thereafter the hike begins a third phase where the trail enters a broad, nearly level valley formed by glacial erosion. Pacific silver fir and western hemlock 3 to 4 feet in diameter dominate the valley bottom where cold air and moisture collect. Numerous moist and wet meadows lie interspersed among the old forest. Several large cottonwoods demonstrate their ability to compete well on wet soils.

The trail resumes climbing at the head of the flat, continuing through attractive Pacific silver fir. Douglas-fir reappears on these well-drained soils, and mountain hemlock becomes common as the trail gains elevation. The trail reaches a junction with Trail 1308.1 approximately 4.5 miles from the trailhead, marking the beginning of still another phase. Beautiful large meadows at the head of the valley provide a perfect picnic spot and ending point for a day hike. Hardy hikers can form a challenging 13-mile loop by returning on Trails 1308.1, 1308, 1308.2, and 1212.

How to get there: From Interstate 90, take exit 70 near Easton (18 miles east of Snoqualmie Pass) and head north toward Sparks Road. Turn left

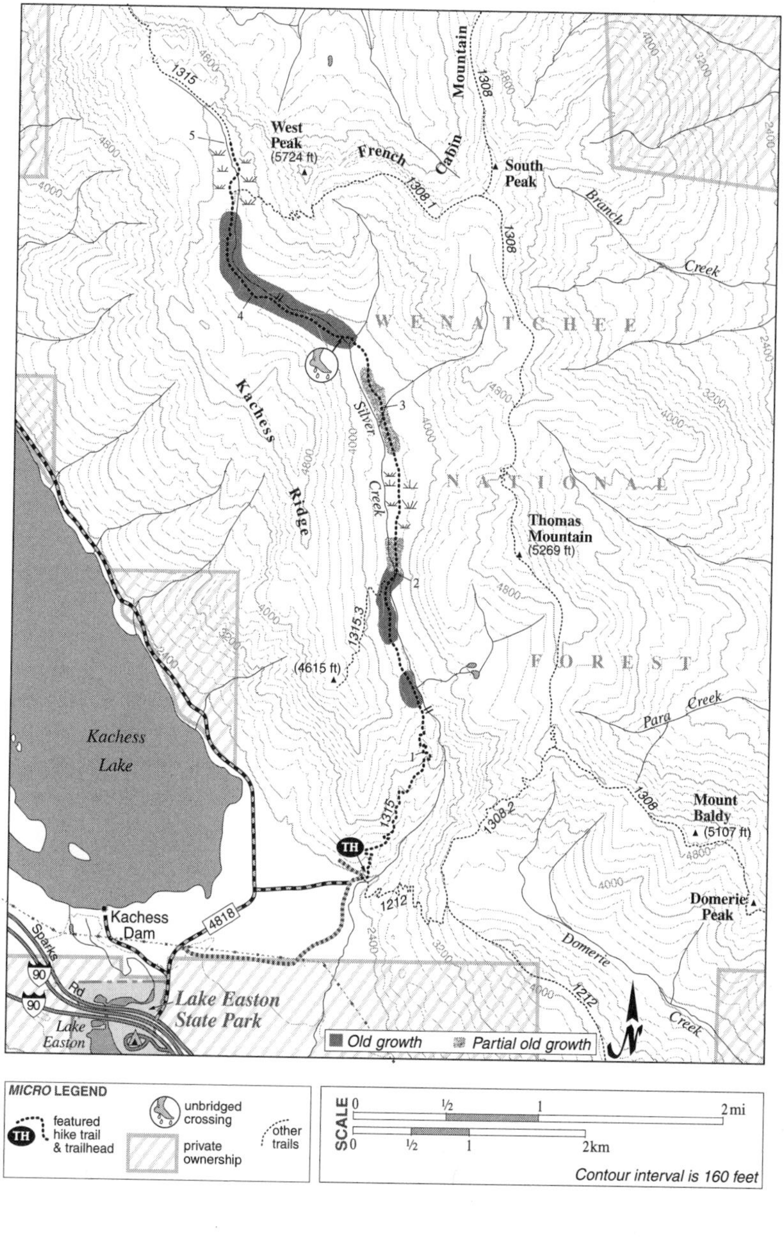

onto West Sparks Road, then turn right onto Forest Road 4818 a half mile later. Turn right toward Trails 1315 and 1212 in about a mile. The trailhead is to the right a half mile later.

KACHESS NATURE TRAIL

A surprising example of sterling old growth stands on the east side of the Cascades by the west shore of Kachess Lake. Take an easy half-mile loop through picturesque Douglas-fir, western hemlock, western redcedar, and grand fir. Cinnamon-barked Douglas-fir of westside character and dimensions highlight the relatively open stand and contrast strikingly with the lime-green vine maple. Veer to the left at the start of the trail and follow the loop clockwise.

How to get there: From Interstate 90, take exit 62 (10 miles east of Snoqualmie Pass) and head toward Kachess Lake on Kachess Lake Road. Turn right into Kachess Campground in 5.2 miles and continue straight past the entrance station. The Northwest Forest Pass covers the entrance fee for day use. Turn right at the first intersection and park on the right. The trail starts on the opposite side of the road by the intersection.

Black cottonwood

SOUTHERN WASHINGTON CASCADES

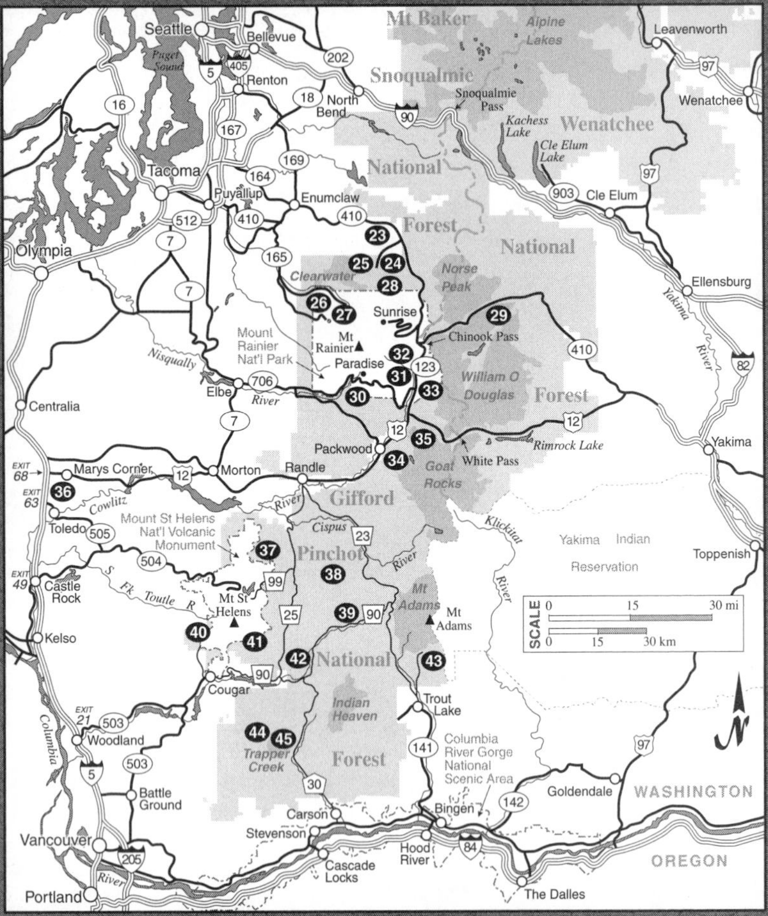

Hike locations

23 Federation Forest

Length ■ **2.6-mile loop**
Difficulty ■ Easy
Season ■ Year-round
Lowest point ■ 1,540 feet
Highest point ■ 1,720 feet
Human imprint ■ High (state highway, hikers)
Information ■ Federation Forest State Park

Primary Old-Growth Feature
Lush lowland old growth, including Sitka spruce

Federation Forest State Park harbors a rare resource —an impressive old-growth forest near a major metropolitan area. Thanks to the efforts of the Washington State Federation of Women's Clubs, 612 acres of prime forest within an hour's drive of Seattle were dedicated as a state park in 1949. A network of trails now lace the park, offering several loop hike options. An autumn, winter, or spring visit will avoid the summertime crowds and take advantage of generally snow-free conditions along the lower reaches of the White River. The parking area off of State Route 410 is recommended for a starting point, although there is parking during summer months through the main entrance by the interpretive center. Three nature trails in the park support the educational mission of the center.

A display shelter a few yards south of the SR 410 pullout marks a three-way trail junction. To see the best forest in the park, veer to the far right. A left turn leads to the West Trail, a nine-tenths-mile-long interpretive loop, and a shorter (one-third mile) interpretive loop lies straight ahead.

Once headed west the trail wanders through lovely lowland forest for more than a mile. Skunk cabbage, devil's club, and other herbaceous species typical of moist sites grow in profusion. Douglas-fir, Sitka spruce, western

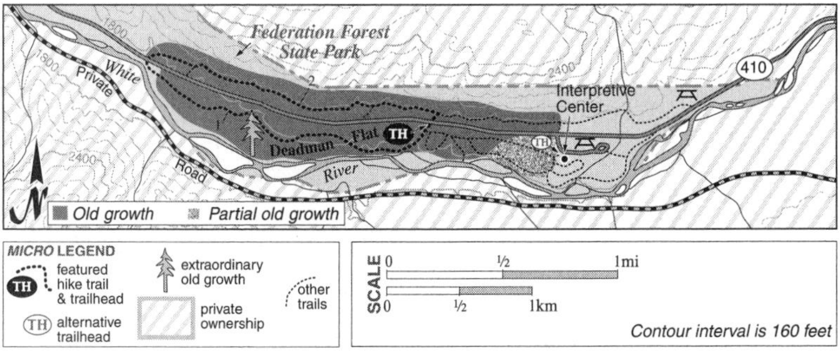

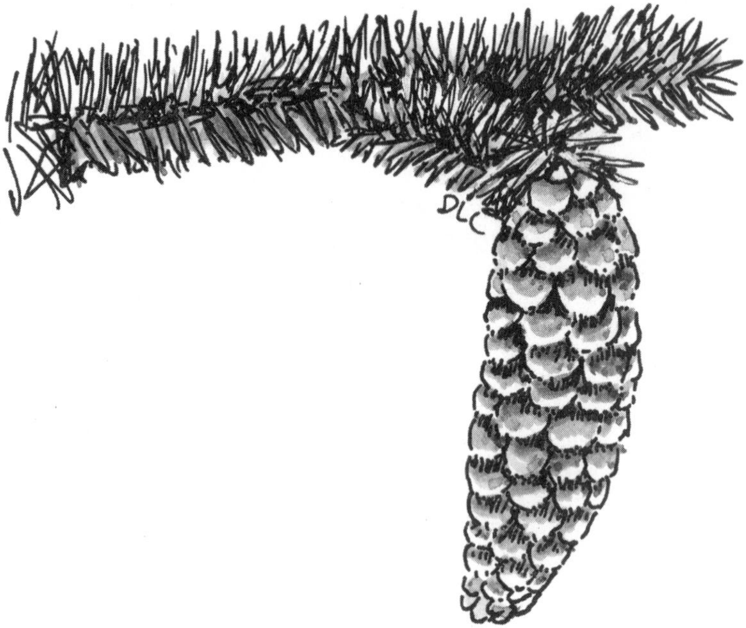

Sitka spruce

hemlock, and western redcedar 3 to 5 feet in diameter grace the trailside, with occasional titans reaching 6 to 7 feet in girth. Sitka spruce, one of the giant trees of the Northwest, is generally confined to a narrow coastal fog belt, and is only found in the Cascades along the lower reaches of a few major rivers in northwestern Washington. A unique trailside feature, the Hobbit House, has been fashioned out of an old stump and decorated in the hobbit custom by young trail walkers.

Cross SR 410 a half mile or so past the Hobbit House (1.4 miles from the trailhead) and begin the eastbound return leg on the north side of the highway. Impressive old growth continues as the trail treads up and down in a mini–roller coaster pattern. Take the third spur down to the road a little over 1 mile from where the trail crossed SR 410 and return to the parking area. Alternatively, continue east another half mile and cross SR 410 by the Catherine Montgomery Interpretive Center. From here take the West Trail and connecting spur trail back to the parking area. Old growth continues along most of these trail segments as well. Be prepared for muddy areas along both sides of the road.

How to get there: From Enumclaw, head east on SR 410, reaching the parking pullout on the south side of the highway in approximately 16.5 miles. To park at the interpretive center (open during summer months), continue another half mile east on SR 410 and turn right.

24 Skookum Flats

Length	**5.5 miles one way**
Difficulty	Easy
Season	Spring to autumn
Lowest point	2,080 feet
Highest point	2,480 feet
Human imprint	High (hikers, highway, nearby forest plantations)
Information	Mount Baker–Snoqualmie National Forest (Snoqualmie Ranger District)

Primary Old-Growth Feature
Easily accessible, big Douglas-fir

The Skookum Flats Trail (1194) offers an easy way to sample the large Douglas-fir and western redcedar growing along the banks of the White River. Though relatively young (250 to 300 years old) by the standards of Northwest old growth, trees growing on the more productive sites reach 5 to 6 feet in diameter. Designated as a national recreation trail, the route is popular with both hikers and mountain bikers due to easy access and a gentle grade. Relatively low trail elevations and high trail use favor an off-season visit.

The forest is best developed and the trees reach their larger dimensions in small patches along the first 3 miles of the trail. Start off heading south in a strip of big trees between plantations to the west and the White River to the east. Portions of the strip have experienced substantial blowdown of the larger trees, likely exacerbated by the openings on the windward side

Chestnut-backed chickadee

created by past clearcutting. The trail then enters a nice stretch of old growth with stout Douglas-fir and western redcedar scattered across a rich riverside flat.

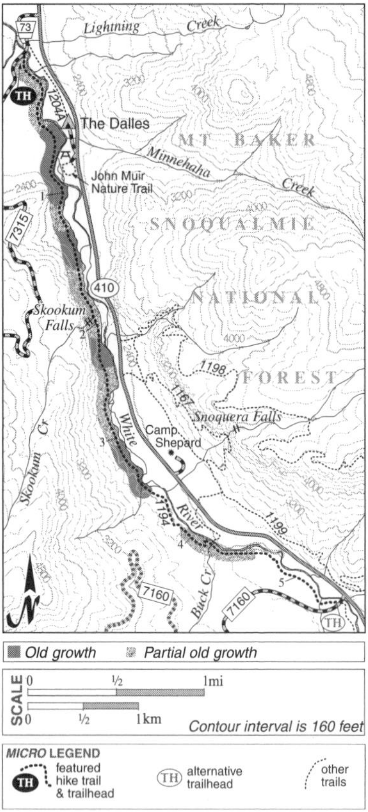

Continue upriver, reaching a small stream spilling over a large cliff in a thin ribbon known as Skookum Falls about 1.8 miles from the trailhead. Enter another nice, riverside glade a quarter mile or so past the falls. The trail continues for about another 1.5 miles in marginal old forest before ascending to a flat above the river occupied by a younger forest. The Buck Creek Trail intersects the path about 4 miles from the trailhead, heading north across White River on a suspension bridge before heading upslope to State Route 410. The trail intersects Forest Road 7160 about 5.5 miles from the lower trailhead, providing a potential pick-up or drop-off point for a one-way hike.

How to get there: From Enumclaw, head east on SR 410 toward Greenwater and Mount Rainier. Turn right onto FR 73 about 6.5 miles past Greenwater (24 miles southeast of Enumclaw). Trailhead parking is on the right a half mile from the highway, just after crossing the bridge over White River.

To reach the upper (southern) trailhead, continue up SR 410 for another 5 miles and turn right on FR 7160. Trailhead parking is on the left after crossing the bridge.

BIG TREE TIP—THE DALLES BIG TREE

While you are in the area take a look at a giant Douglas-fir (9.5 feet thick) that towers over the northeast corner of The Dalles Campground. Stretching upwards to 235 feet in height, this 700-year-old veteran survived a fire in this area approximately 300 years ago. A couple more super-old big guys stand just beyond this tree on The Dalles River Trail.

JOHN MUIR NATURE TRAIL

Another option in the area is to take a short (about one-third of a mile) nature trail originally constructed by a class from the John Muir Grade School out of Seattle. A paved, wheelchair-accessible path winds in and around a few large conifers on a lush flat by the river. Interpretive signs explain a few features of the forest.

How to get there: Turn into The Dalles Campground from State Route 410 1 mile past the junction with Forest Road 73. Stay to the right for the big tree; turn left into the day-use area for the nature trail.

25 UPPER CLEARWATER VALLEY

Length	**5.5 miles one way**
Difficulty	Difficult
Season	Summer to autumn
Lowest point	3,170 feet
Highest point	4,960 feet
Human imprint	Minimal
Information	Mount Baker–Snoqualmie National Forest (Snoqualmie Ranger District)

Primary Old-Growth Feature
Remote stand of old western hemlock and Pacific silver fir

The Carbon Trail traverses an impressive ancient forest tucked away in the remote headwaters of the Clearwater River. The upper slopes of the Clearwater River valley were torched by fires that burned over much of the White River drainage approximately 200 years ago, leading to extensive stands of mid-successional, mature forest across the landscape. A seldom-visited stand of pristine western hemlock and Pacific silver fir in the south end of the Clearwater Wilderness escaped these conflagrations.

Both the Carbon Trail (1179) and the Clearwater Trail (1178) adjoin the trailhead at Martin Gap. Take the Carbon Trail to the left to reach the upper Clearwater valley. The first 1.3 miles or so passes through a mature stand of Douglas-fir and western hemlock casting a dense shade over a sparse understory. A few large noble fir are clustered by stream crossings about three-quarter mile from the trailhead. The trail then enters an older stand of Douglas-fir and western hemlock, switchbacks downhill, and comes to a crossing of the east fork of the Clearwater River.

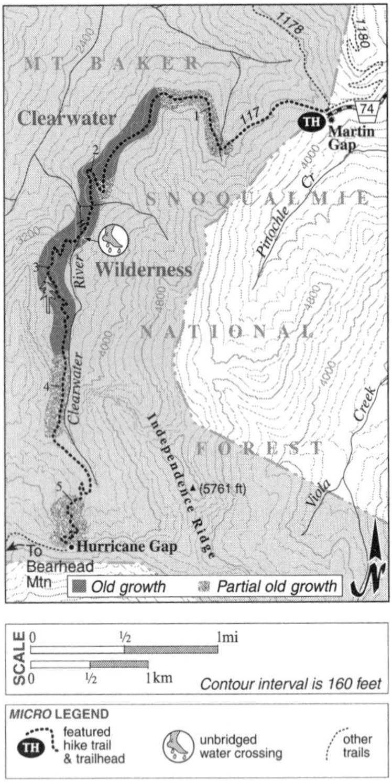

Carefully cross the east fork and start uphill into a delightful stand of large (3 to 5 feet in diameter) western hemlock and Pacific silver fir. This stand may be 800 or more years old as there is no evidence of Douglas-fir observable from the trail. Massive western hemlock reach 5 to 6 feet thick in places. Continue another couple miles up the valley, bisecting a grove of Alaska-cedar and passing an old camp. Finally, switchback up the steep valley headwall to Hurricane Gap passing a few colossal survivors, including a noble fir approximately 8 feet thick.

Unfortunately, the view of nearby Mount Rainier from Hurricane Gap (5.5 miles from the trailhead), is obscured by trees. Energetic hikers can continue along the trail another 2.5 miles to the west to the Bearhead Trail (1179A), coming to an excellent view of the mountain just before the trail junction. Views from the top of Bearhead Mountain are breathtaking.

How to get there: From Enumclaw, head east on State Route 410 toward Greenwater and Mount Rainier. Turn right onto Forest Road 74 about 3.5 miles past Greenwater. Stay right on FR 74 at a junction with FR 75 less than a half mile from the highway, and stay right again in another 7.8 miles. The trailhead is at the end of FR 74, a little over 15 miles from the highway.

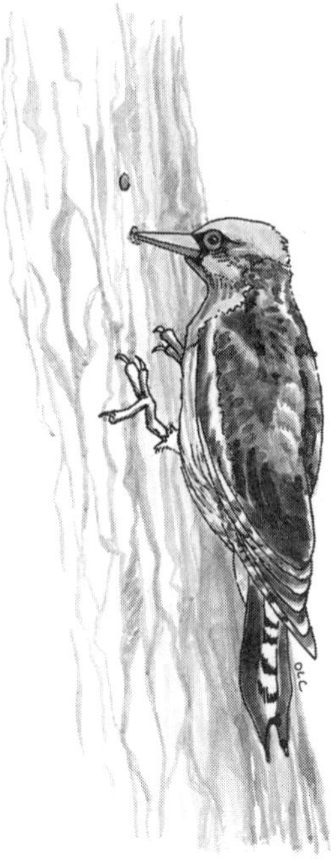

Red-breasted sapsucker

26 GREEN LAKE

Length ■ **1.8 miles one way**
Difficulty ■ Easy
Season ■ Spring to autumn
Lowest point ■ 2,120 feet
Highest point ■ 3,190 feet
Human imprint ■ Moderate (hikers)
Information ■ Mount Rainier National Park

Primary Old-Growth Features
Outstanding grove of enormous Douglas-fir; huge down logs

A short and steady ascent on the well-worn path to Green Lake passes through some of the most impressive old growth found anywhere in the Cascades. This is a must-see forest for all old-growth enthusiasts. Mammoth Douglas-fir are densely stacked across the hillslope in scenes reminiscent of pre-settlement lowland forests. Huge logs lie on the forest floor, adding to the massive amount of carbon stored in this stand.

Green Lake sits in the far northwest corner of Mount Rainier National Park in the Carbon River drainage. Carbon River drains Carbon Glacier, a large ice field on the north slope of Mount Rainier that extends to the lowest elevation (3,520 feet) of any glacier in the Lower 48 states. The low-lying glacier furnishes downslope breezes with chilling moisture resulting in high humidity and cool temperatures similar to coastal conditions. Species generally confined to a narrow coastal band, such as platy-barked Sitka spruce and the speedy, marbled murrelet, are found inland along Carbon River. The cool, moist environment sustains plant growth and inhibits forest fire during summer dry periods, conferring high productivity and great longevity to the forest.

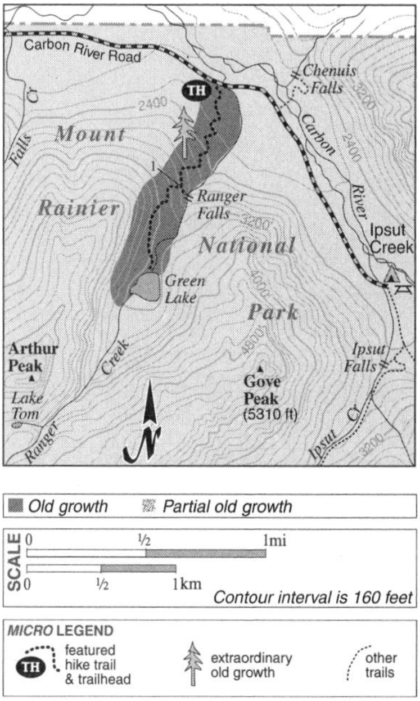

Immense trees along the path to

Green Lake are one result. Douglas-fir 6 to 8 feet thick are numerous, and while huge by any reasonable measure, they appear ordinary next to occasional 8 to 10-foot-diameter giants. Large western redcedar (3 to 6 feet thick) and western hemlock (3 to 4 feet thick) are abundant, but barely merit attention in such a forest.

Switchback upslope for the first mile to Ranger Falls. Heavily armored and appropriately named devil's club, a species indicating moist sites and superior growth potential, is abundant along the lower portion of the trail. An imposing Douglas-fir marks multi-stepped Ranger Falls, visible to the left from a short spur trail about 1 mile from the trailhead.

The forest begins a transition to colder-site species shortly above Ranger Falls and reaches Green Lake 1.8 miles from the trailhead. Although charming in its own right, cliff-rimmed Green Lake is somewhat anti climatic after the splendors of the forest below.

How to get there: From Enumclaw, take State Route 410 south to Buckley, then follow SR 165 through Wilkeson and past Carbonado. Stay left on Carbon River Road at the junction with Mowich Lake Road 10.3 miles from Buckley. The Carbon River entrance to Mount Rainier National Park (fee required) is reached 7.7 miles later. Continue another 3.1 miles to the trailhead and park on the left.

Twistedstalk

27 IPSUT CREEK

Length	**3.2 miles one way**
Difficulty	Moderate
Season	Summer
Lowest point	2,330 feet
Highest point	4,800 feet
Human imprint	Minimal
Information	Mount Rainier National Park

Primary Old-Growth Features
Very old climax forest; near-record noble fir; huge Alaska-cedar

Spectacular Ipsut Creek valley holds one of the oldest forests known in the Cascades and a couple of near record-sized individual trees. According to a study done for Mount Rainier National Park, the last major fire in most of this moist basin was more than 1,000 years ago. Douglas-fir and noble fir, species expected to successfully regenerate following a fire, have long since died out leaving a forest of shade-tolerant western hemlock and Pacific silver fir.

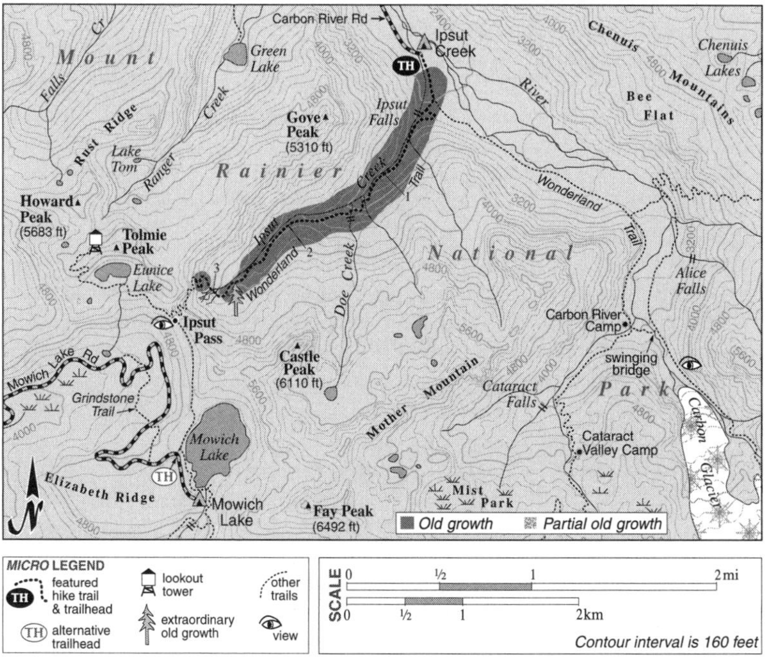

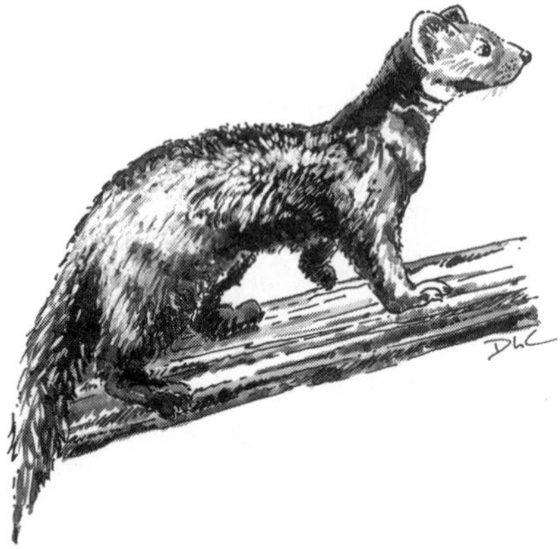

American marten

Head southeast from the Ipsut Creek parking lot, coming to the Wonderland Trail in a half mile. Turn right and start upslope. The forest along this first segment is sprinkled with large Douglas-fir and western redcedar, but the last of the Douglas-fir marks a switchback along the short climb into Ipsut Creek valley. For the next 2 miles the trail heads up Ipsut Creek through a beautiful forest of ancient western hemlock, Pacific silver fir, and western redcedar.

As the trail nears the head of the valley it begins to trace the margin between forest to the left and shrub fields to the right. A few hundred yards later a mammoth noble fir known as the Ipsut Creek Colossus stands right beside the trail. The giant fir is the third largest noble fir known by volume, measuring 8.9 feet in diameter and 217 feet in height. The tree is truly an anomaly, the only noble fir around in a sea of hemlock and silver fir.

Leaving the Colossus behind, the trail emerges into a shrub patch where the trail crosses several small tributaries before entering a forested island containing Pacific silver fir, mountain hemlock, and truly ancient Alaska-cedar. One Alaska-cedar has been aged at over 1,200 years old, and another was once a national champion at almost 12 feet in diameter. This massive Alaska-cedar is somewhat disguised and difficult to spot as the trunk tapers rapidly and the largest part is below the trail.

Beyond the island the trail continues switchbacking steeply up through shrubs and talus to Ipsut Pass. From the pass the Colossus comes into view far below as a solitary blue-hued crown emerging above the surrounding hemlocks. From here it is another mile to Mowich Lake, an alternative trailhead.

How to get there: From Enumclaw, take State Route 410 south to Buckley, then follow SR 165 south from Buckley through Wilkeson and past Carbonado. Stay left on Carbon River Road at the junction with Mowich Lake Road 10.3 miles from Buckley. The Carbon River entrance to Mount Rainier National Park (fee required) is reached 7.7 miles later. Continue for another 4.9 miles until reaching the Ipsut Creek Campground and large parking area at the end of the road.

To reach Mowich Lake, turn right onto Mowich Lake Road at the junction and follow it for 16.7 miles to the lake.

CARBON RIVER

A relatively level path along milky, glacier-fed Carbon River leads through marvelous old forest in a 6.5-mile loop to Carbon Glacier and back. From the Ipsut Creek trailhead head southeast for a half mile, then stay left onto the Wonderland Trail. The terrace below the trail in the first mile is particularly lush, hosting many 4 to 6-foot-diameter Douglas-fir, western hemlock, and western redcedar. Another nice patch of huge Douglas-fir is encountered just before reaching a trail junction about 2 miles from the trailhead. Stay right on the Wonderland Trail; the trail to the left is the return leg of the loop. Continue upstream west of the river for another mile or so until reaching a bouncy suspension bridge, always a thrill to cross for young and old alike. A short side trip heading southeast from the east side of the swinging bridge leads to a flank of the Carbon Glacier and a spectacular view of the glacial snout. Return to the trail junction by the bridge and complete the loop on the east side of the river.

28 HUCKLEBERRY CREEK

Length ■ **7 miles one way**
Difficulty ■ Moderate to difficult
Season ■ Summer
Lowest point ■ 3,000 feet
Highest point ■ 5,660 feet
Human imprint ■ Minimal
Information ■ Mount Rainier National Park; Mount Baker–Snoqualmie National Forest (Snoqualmie Ranger District)

Primary Old-Growth Feature
Long wilderness valley with large patches of old forest

The bottom of Huckleberry Creek valley is lined with splendid old forest, yet this readily accessible trail receives relatively little use. The trail travels up the floor of a deep glacial

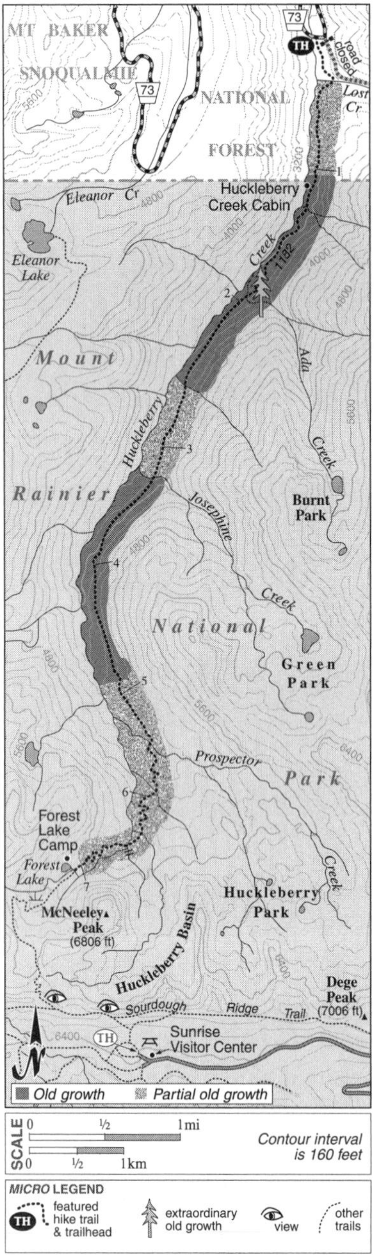

trough for 6 miles, climbs up the head of the basin for another 3 miles, and finally emerges on Sourdough Ridge for jaw-dropping views of Mount Rainier. Forest Lake, 7 miles in, is a suitable destination for a long day hike, although hikers can sample the best of the old forest by hiking in only 3 miles and returning by the same route.

The Huckleberry Creek Trail (1182) starts out in Mount Baker–Snoqualmie National Forest on the east bank of Huckleberry Creek. Follow the path upstream for a third of a mile on an old roadbed to a crossing of Lost Creek. An old forest dominated by Douglas-fir and western hemlock begins south of the creek and continues for the next several miles.

The trail enters Mount Rainier National Park about 1 mile from the trailhead and comes to the historic Huckleberry Creek Cabin shortly thereafter. Over the next 1.5 miles the trail passes through an exceptional stand of stout old-timers standing tall on a streamside flat. Prodigious Douglas-fir 5 to 7 feet thick and 700 to 800 years old dominate the stand, although big western hemlock and western redcedar are also plentiful. Favorable topographic position along the valley bottom has protected these forests from the forest fires responsible for regenerating the younger forests covering the valley walls.

The trail steepens as it continues up the basin moving through patches of 300 to 400-year-old forest and some younger forest. Pacific silver fir, mountain hemlock, and Alaska-cedar phase in and eventually replace their lowland kin. The trail reaches tiny Forest Lake approximately 7 miles from the trailhead, signaling the beginning of a subalpine zone where forests interfinger with meadows. The trail continues to climb above the lake headed south toward Sunrise Visitor Center, a potential drop-off point for a 9.5-mile, one-way, downhill hike.

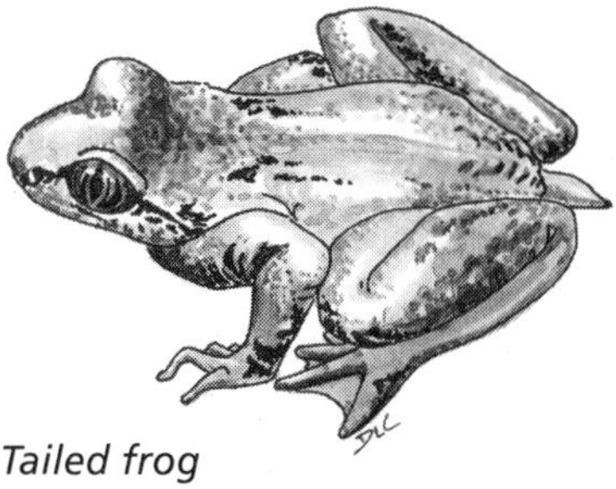

Tailed frog

How to get there: From Enumclaw, head east on State Route 410 toward Greenwater and Mount Rainier. Turn right onto Forest Road 73 about 6.5 miles past Greenwater (24 miles southeast of Enumclaw). Follow FR 73 for 6 miles to the trailhead just before the bridge over Huckleberry Creek.

To reach Sunrise Visitor Center, follow SR 410 another 12.8 miles past the FR 73 junction to the White River entrance of Mount Rainier National Park (fee required), and follow the main road 15.4 miles to the large parking lot by the visitor center.

29 Pleasant Valley

Length ■ **3 miles one way; 14.6-mile loop**
Difficulty ■ Easy; difficult
Season ■ Late spring to early autumn
Lowest point ■ 3,270 feet
Highest point ■ 3,475 feet
Human imprint ■ Moderate to high (highway, campgrounds)
Information ■ Wenatchee National Forest (Naches Ranger District)

Primary Old-Growth Feature
Old-growth western larch

Distinctive western larch populate the valley bottom and hillslopes of the American River canyon, a dramatic piece of scenery east of Mount Rainier and Chinook Pass. Western larch stands out to landscape viewers during the growing season due to its soft, kiwi-green appearance, and in the autumn as it turns golden prior to losing its needles. Its deciduous habit is an uncommon trait for Northwest conifers.

Originally built by the Cascadians, an outdoor club from Yakima, the

14.6-mile Pleasant Valley Loop Trail (999) provides a convenient way to traverse the old forest on the valley floor. For those looking for a shorter venture, the first 3 miles of the loop showcases the best of the forest and beautiful views of the meandering river. Spring chinook salmon are able to spawn in the gravel beds found in this stretch of the American River.

Head southwest from the trailhead parking area, immediately entering the William O. Douglas Wilderness. The trail is on the southeast bank of the river for most of the first 2 miles, but only intermittently thereafter. Continue southwest paralleling the river in and out of old forest until returning to the highway 8 miles from the trailhead. Hefty western larch and Douglas-fir 3 to 4 feet thick are abundant in places. Cross the bridge and highway to pick up the trail on the north side of the road.

The return half of the loop skirts Mather Memorial Parkway and passes through a more-disturbed forest. Large trees are scattered throughout most of the western half of this segment, however, and a particularly nice pocket of 600-year-old Douglas-fir stands on an alluvial fan about a mile east of the Union Creek trailhead. The trail follows old two-track roads in places, and joins a popular cross-country skiing loop for the last 2 miles or so. Cross the bridge and highway to return to the trailhead on the south side of the road. The entire loop is marked with blue diamonds, placed to be visible above the snowpack in winter.

An unusual feature of Pleasant Valley sure to attract hikers' attention are the numerous ant mounds found near the western half of the loop. These

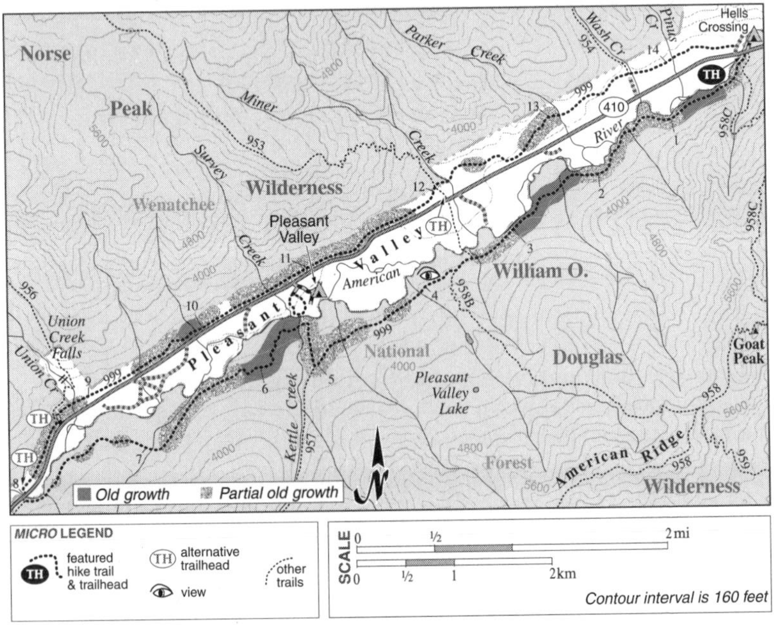

Western larch

mounds are typically 2 to 4 feet high and several feet in diameter, each hosting a queen and a colony of worker ants. Corridors of ants radiate out from each mound during warm weather as ants search for food and housing material. In fact, hikers may first take notice of these ants by observing a black strip of ants 6 to 10 inches wide crossing the trail. One corridor of ants even uses the trail bridge over Kettle Creek. These ants are known as thatch ants, and belong to a group of fifty or so mound-building ant species distributed throughout the northern hemisphere.

Although ant mounds have been present in the valley for decades, one reason the thatch ants may be booming now is an outbreak of western spruce budworm in this area. These ants are known to be voracious predators of spruce budworm caterpillars. The forested hillslopes appear brown where budworm has consumed the current years' needles from grand fir, Douglas-fir, and Engelmann spruce. Western larch are avoided by the budworm and are conspicuous by their healthy crowns.

How to get there: Turn right into the roadside parking area from the Mather Memorial Parkway (State Route 410) across from Hells Crossing Campground, approximately 19 miles east of Cayuse Pass (15.5 miles east of Chinook Pass).

BIG TREE TIP—PLEASANT VALLEY LARCH

The Pleasant Valley Larch stands tall, very tall, on a productive riparian terrace in the Pleasant Valley Campground. This western larch is the sixth largest western larch by volume, and the largest known in Washington state. Such status is earned by the Pleasant Valley Larch owing to its great height (189') and diameter (6.1'). Big Engelmann spruce and black cottonwood stand near the full-crowned larch.

PLEASANT VALLEY NATURE TRAIL

A new, one-mile-long nature trail circles through forest that is typical of Pleasant Valley. Scattered Douglas-fir and western larch up to 500 years old and 2 to 4 feet thick dwarf a dense stand of much younger trees. The path is paved for wheelchair access, and interpretive signs explain a few features of the forest.

How to get there: Turn south into the Pleasant Valley Recreation Site from the Mather Memorial Parkway (SR 410) approximately 14.5 miles east of Cayuse Pass (11 miles east of Chinook Pass). Stay to the left to find the big larch behind campsite #3. Stay to the right and pick up the nature trail behind the signboard.

30 PARADISE RIVER

Length ■ **4.7 miles one way**
Difficulty ■ Easy to moderate
Season ■ Summer to early autumn
Lowest point ■ 2,780 feet
Highest point ■ 4,500 feet
Human imprint ■ Moderate (hikers, sightseers)
Information ■ Mount Rainier National Park

Primary Old-Growth Features
Very old Douglas-fir; riverside old growth

This popular stretch of the Wonderland Trail rambles through noteworthy old forest along the valley bottoms of two glacier-fed rivers in Mount Rainier National Park. Longmire Inn, Cougar Rock Campground, and Narada Falls supply the trail with a steady stream of hikers, although most do not venture far from the trailhead.

From Longmire, the trail starts off on the east side of the main road by the Wilderness Information Center and heads up the west side of the Nisqually River following the Wonderland Trail. After passing through young forest in the first half mile, the trail comes closer to the river and enters an older forest where unimpressive, relatively small Douglas-fir are widely scattered. Surprisingly, the forest age map for the park shows this forest as more than 700 years old. In fact, Douglas-fir in nearby Cougar Rock Campground have been aged at more than 1,000 years old, some of the oldest known Douglas-fir anywhere. Unproductive soils derived from glacial outwash may account for this apparent paradox of great age and

Hairy woodpecker

relatively small size. These thin, rocky soils are likely low in nutrients and microbial life essential for rapid tree growth.

Spur trails from well-used Cougar Rock Campground enter from the left just under 2 miles from Longmire. The trail then crosses the Nisqually River a couple hundred yards above the Paradise River junction, and picks up an old service road on the other side. The trail continues up the west side of Paradise River alongside a wooden conduit used to pipe water down to Longmire several decades ago. Alaska-cedar highlights the riparian forest assemblage along this segment, some reaching 5 to 6 feet in diameter. Tumbling Carter Falls and shorter Madcap Falls are encountered a mile or so above the river crossing.

After crossing Paradise River a half mile above the falls, the trail heads upslope through outstanding western hemlock old growth. At the next trail junction bear left to view fan-like Narada Falls, 4.7 miles from Longmire. Hikers can cross the road from the parking lot above the falls and continue another 1.2 miles up the river to Paradise Visitor Center. Another option is to continue to the southeast on the Wonderland Trail from the junction below Narada Falls, heading through old forest for another mile or so to Reflection Lakes.

How to get there: Drive to Longmire, 21 miles east of Elbe on State Route 706 (6 miles east of the Nisqually entrance to the park). Pull into Longmire and park in the lot behind the Longmire Museum and the National Park Inn. The hike can also be accessed from Cougar Rock Campground and Narada Falls farther up the Nisqually-Paradise Road.

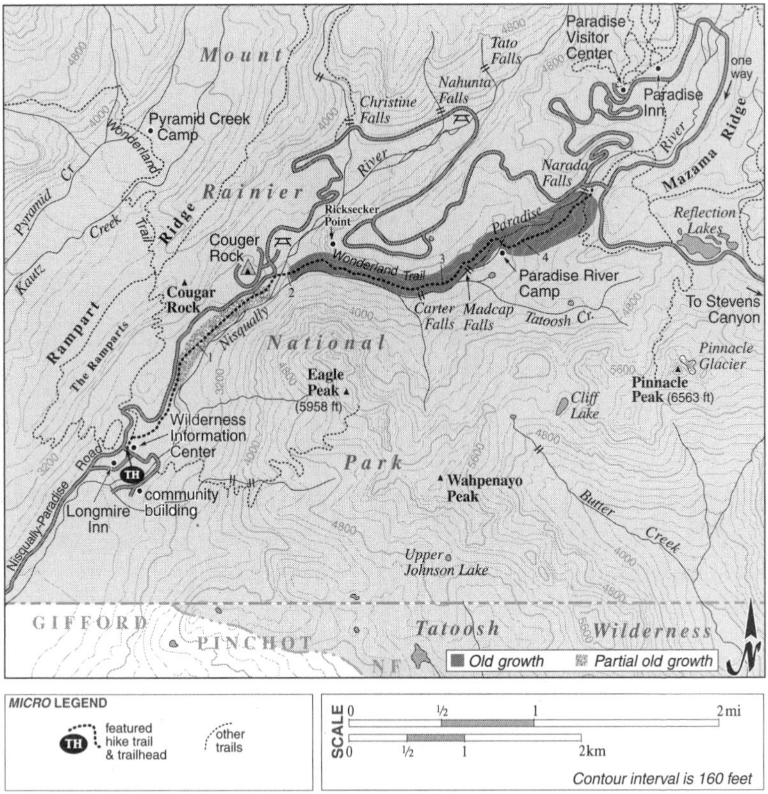

TWIN FIRS

This half-mile loop showcases a superb example of a late-successional forest in transition from shade-intolerant Douglas-fir to shade-tolerant western hemlock. Impressive Douglas-fir 6 to 8 feet thick still stand, although the overstory canopy of Douglas-fir is clearly deteriorating. Large dead wood, both standing and down, is abundant. Gaps in the canopy from tree mortality provide sunlight and growing space for opportunistic understory trees to expand. Barring future disturbance, such as fire, emerging western hemlock will take over this stand.

How to get there: Parking is located on the north side of the Nisqually-Paradise Road approximately 4 miles east of the Nisqually entrance to the park. A display board and a couple of huge Douglas-fir mark the pullout.

31 OLALLIE CREEK

Length ■ **4 miles one way**
Difficulty ■ Moderate
Season ■ Summer
Lowest point ■ 2,380 feet
Highest point ■ 4,720 feet
Human imprint ■ Minimal
Information ■ Mount Rainier National Park

Primary Old-Growth Feature
Large stand of huge Douglas-fir and western hemlock

The Olallie Creek basin harbors an impressive and lightly visited patch of old growth on the east side of Mount Rainier National Park. Overshadowed by better known trails in the park, the Olallie Creek Trail offers a quiet, 4-mile path through superb old growth along a half-mile elevational gradient. With a vehicle shuttle the hike can be extended another 3 miles over to Box Canyon for a one-way trek.

The trail climbs steadily on the east-facing slopes of Cowlitz Divide for 1.5 miles through gargantuan Douglas-fir and western hemlock, many 500 to 700 years old. Large western redcedar and abundant Pacific silver fir fill out the roster on these lower slopes. Where the trail makes a right-angle turn to the left onto a cooler, north-facing slope, Alaska-cedar and mountain hemlock replace Douglas-fir.

The trail drops down to a crossing of Olallie Creek and to Olallie Creek Camp 2.6 miles from the road, continuing the ascent to Cowlitz Divide on the north side of Olallie Creek. Large Douglas-fir briefly reappear on these warmer, south-facing slopes before dropping out of the stand as the trail starts climbing to the ridge in earnest. Pacific silver fir and mountain hemlock dominate the forest on these upper slopes; The trail joins the Wonderland Trail in a gap on Cowlitz Divide 4 miles from the road.

How to get there: Turn right into the Stevens Canyon entrance of the park (fee required) from State Route 123, approximately 11 miles south of Cayuse Pass (13.25 miles northeast of Packwood). Trailhead parking is on the right in about three-quarters of a mile, approximately one-half mile past the Grove of the Patriarchs parking area.

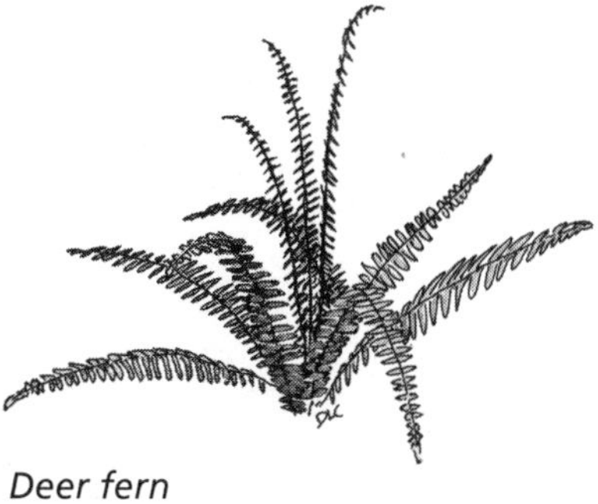

Deer fern

SILVER FALLS

The 250-year-old forest along this pleasant 3-mile loop provides an interesting contrast to the much older forest along Olallie Creek (500 to 700 years old). Here the forest canopy is still intact, large snags have not yet formed, and understory trees are still small. The Douglas-fir are large (2 to 4 feet thick) compared to many forests but relatively small for Pacific Northwest old growth. Occasional fire-scorched, older trees—which survived the mid-eighteenth-century fire that birthed this forest—are scattered among the younger trees. Ground-shaking Silver Falls rockets through a slot in the rocks near the northern apex of the loop.

How to get there: The loop can be accessed from the Olallie Creek trailhead and the Grove of the Patriarchs parking area (described above, fee required), or from the Ohanapecosh Visitor Center (fee not required). To reach the visitor center, turn west into the Ohanapecosh Campground from State Route 123, approximately 13 miles south of Cayuse Pass (11.5 miles northeast of Packwood), and stay to the right for a quarter mile.

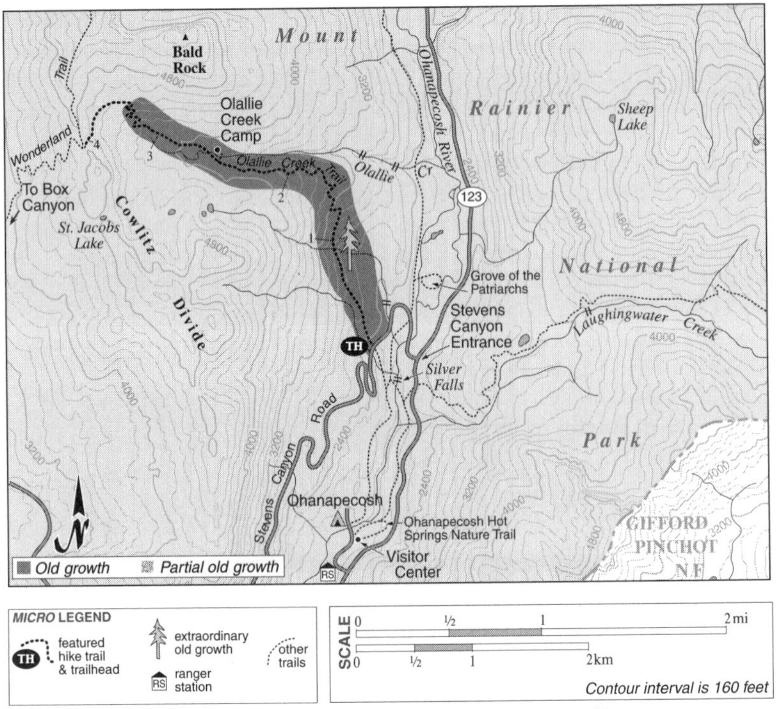

32 OHANAPECOSH RIVER

Length ■ **3.8 miles one way to Ohanapecosh Falls; 9.5 miles to Cayuse Pass**
Difficulty ■ Moderate to difficult
Season ■ Spring to autumn
Lowest point ■ 2,220 feet
Highest point ■ 4,580 feet
Human impact ■ Minimal (except first half mile)
Information ■ Mount Rainier National Park

Primary Old-Growth Features
Very old forest; long valley stuffed with groves of huge Douglas-fir and western redcedar; abundant large dead down and standing wood

The valleys on the east side of Mount Rainier National Park hold extensive stands of some of the finest old forest in the Northwest. Fortunately, the Eastside Trail travels through the best of this forest bisecting some stands aged at more than 700 years old. A convenient day hike stretches 3.8 miles from the trailhead by the Stevens Canyon park entrance to Ohanapecosh Falls. Hikers can continue another 3 miles to the Deer Creek trailhead, or up to the Cayuse Pass trailhead (9.5 miles one way) in dynamite old growth nearly the entire way. Easy shuttles can

Bunchberry

be arranged from these trailheads for one-way hikes.

Throngs of visitors pack the first half mile north from the Stevens Canyon trailhead, almost all of whom are headed for the Grove of the Patriarchs (see sidebar). Tremendous old Douglas-fir and western hemlock tower over trail-bound trekkers along this particularly lush segment. After paying your respects at the Grove of the Patriarchs, continue upriver through 500 to 600-year-old forest for another 3 miles to two-tiered Ohanapecosh Falls.

Cross the falls on a wooden bridge and continue north on the west bank of Chinook Creek where forest fires have been absent nearly a millennium. Great age is obvious above Stafford Falls where widely scattered, massive Douglas-fir 6 to 8 feet or more in diameter are the sole-survivors from an ancient post-fire generation. The ragged forest canopy and abundant large dead wood provide additional evidence of antiquity.

The trail crosses over to the east bank of the river a little over a half mile above Stafford Falls, entering a forest devoid of Douglas-fir or any other early-successional trees. All age-classes of shade-tolerant western hemlock and Pacific silver fir are present in a classic example of a "climax" forest. A short spur trail leading up to the Deer Creek trailhead joins on the right approximately 3 miles above Ohanapecosh Falls.

Recross Chinook Creek for the final trail segment, coming to an intersection with the Owyhigh Lakes Trail just past the bridge. Continue

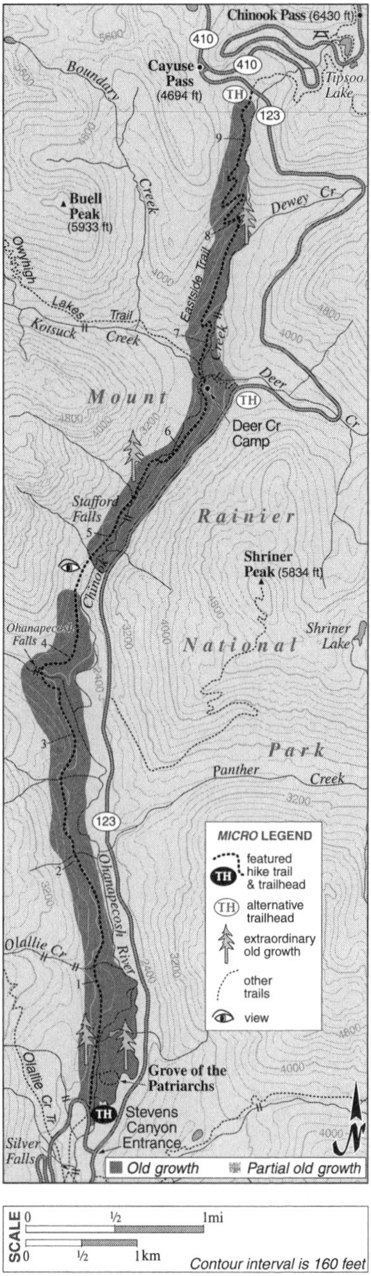

up Chinook Creek arriving at a nice waterfall vista at the elbow of a switch-back. Big Douglas-fir reenters the forest where a fire burned 500 to 600 years ago. Western hemlock and Pacific silver fir become more common with increasing elevation, eventually replacing Douglas-fir altogether. Mountain hemlock enters the forest just before the trail reaches the Cayuse Pass trailhead.

How to get there: Turn right into the Stevens Canyon entrance of the park (fee required) from State Route 123 approximately 11 miles south of Cayuse Pass (13.25 miles northeast of Packwood). The trail begins behind the rest rooms by the parking area on the right a quarter mile later.

The Cayuse Pass trailhead is located approximately a half mile south of the pass. Turn into the large parking lot west of the highway and find the trail down the road 100 feet or so from the parking area.

GROVE OF THE PATRIARCHS

This justly famous grove is an obligatory stop for big-tree enthusi-asts. Head up the Eastside Trail from the Stevens Canyon entrance and turn right over a steel suspension bridge a little under a half mile from the trailhead. A 300-yard loop through immense western redcedar and Douglas-fir 8 to 11 feet in diameter begins on the other side of the bridge. The grove is nourished by rich soil and ample moisture on an island protected from fire. Interpretive signs explain features of the forest.

33 LAUGHINGWATER CREEK

Length ■	6 miles one way
Difficulty ■	Moderate to difficult
Season ■	Summer
Lowest point ■	2,240 feet
Highest point ■	4,880 feet
Human imprint ■	Minimal
Information ■	Mount Rainier National Park

The Laughingwater Creek Trail as-cends steadily through several dis-tinct stands of old forest in the southeastern corner of Mount Rainier National Park. Charming Three Lakes is the destination of

Primary Old-Growth Features
Excellent Douglas-fir and western hemlock old growth; large Alaska-cedar

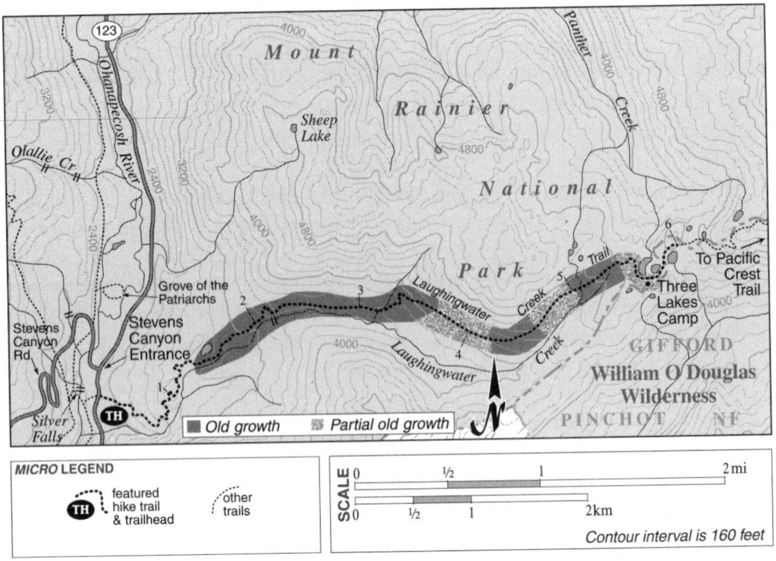

choice for most day hikers, and backpackers frequently use the trail as a portal to the Pacific Crest Trail.

Begin by switchbacking steadily up through a mature Douglas-fir and western hemlock forest on a slightly unstable slope. Tension cracks running down the slope and tipsy trees indicate a slow-moving earthflow on this lower hillside. After about 1.5 miles and seventeen switchbacks, the trail reaches a flat area holding an unnamed pond and a much older forest. Scattered big Douglas-fir and western hemlock preside over a dense stand of younger trees. The upper canopy is rapidly disintegrating allowing shade-tolerant species growing in the understory to move into the dominant canopy layer.

The trail climbs again soon coming to another flat approximately 3 miles from the trailhead, where an intact and much more attractive stand of Douglas-fir and western hemlock tower overhead. Some of the older Douglas-fir exceed 700 years of age. The flat soon ends though and the trail makes a right-angle turn to the left, and then to the right into a younger forest. Old remnant trees that survived a stand-initiating fire lend old-forest character to the stand.

The trail continues climbing and bends northeast into a patch of notable Pacific silver fir and Alaska-cedar. Some of the cedars are quite impressive and picture worthy. A crest holding a small, lupine-filled meadow is reached 5.5 miles from the trailhead.

The trail trends downhill from here reaching Three Lakes a half mile later. Old mountain hemlock and Pacific silver fir surround the picturesque lakes,

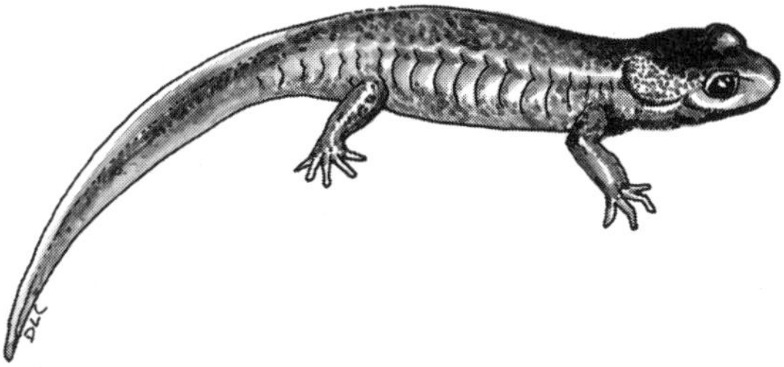

Northwestern salamander

home to bugling elk, campsites, and a historic patrol cabin. For extensive mountain views though, a journey of another couple miles to the Pacific Crest Trail will be needed.

How to get there: Park on the west side of State Route 123 approximately 1.5 miles north of Ohanapecosh Campground (one-third mile south of the Stevens Canyon entrance to the park). This point is about 13 miles south of Cayuse Pass and 11.5 miles northeast of Packwood. The trail is on the east side of the road.

34 PACKWOOD LAKE

Length ■ **4.4 miles one way to Packwood Lake; 8 miles to end of old growth**
Difficulty ■ Moderate to difficult
Season ■ Spring to autumn
Lowest point ■ 2,860 feet
Highest point ■ 3,190 feet
Human imprint ■ High (ATVs, equestrians, hikers)
Information ■ Gifford Pinchot National Forest (Cowlitz Valley Ranger District)

Primary Old-Growth Feature
Groves of large western redcedar and Douglas-fir

Busy Packwood Lake sits in the midst of superlative old forest and dramatic, glacially sculpted scenery. Although the trail to the lake travels through the Goat Rocks Wilderness, and wilderness surrounds the upper portion of the lake, the area around the lake outlet lies outside the wilderness. Motorized all-terrain-vehicle (ATV) access to the lake is provided via a separate, parallel trail (Pipeline Trail, 74) that noisily conveys multitudes of

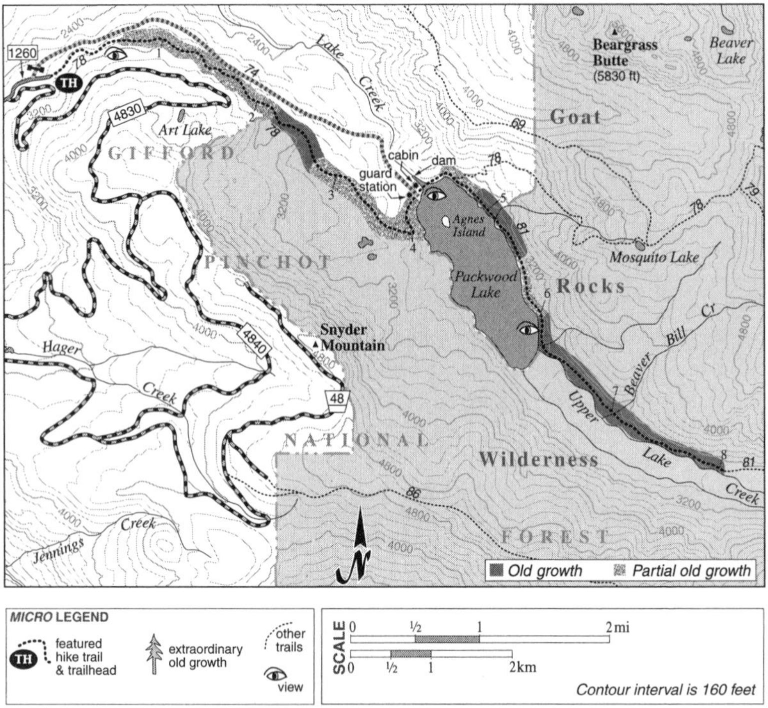

visitors to the lake. Still, it is a gorgeous setting studded with impressive old growth, and a midweek or autumn visit should minimize encounters with motorized contraptions and large parties.

Start out on the Packwood Lake Trail (78) through fire-regenerated young forest laced with varying amounts of older fire survivors. Two small strip clearcuts about three-quarters of a mile from the trailhead provide expansive views of Mount Rainier and the upper Cowlitz River valley. The trail enters the Goat Rocks Wilderness after 2 miles, then leaves the wilderness and descends to the lake after 4 miles. On a clear day, the view over the lake to Johnson Peak is phenomenal.

Packwood Lake initially formed when an immense landslide came off the northeast face of Snyder Mountain about 1,200 years ago damming Lake Creek. More recently the natural dam has been expanded by the Washington Public Power Supply System to supply hydropower. Most hikers will want to speed past the congested area near the lake outlet and move on to quieter spots. A guard station, historical cabin, and ATV parking lot are all clustered near the lake outlet.

Hikers with energy to burn and old growth as a destination should bear right onto the Upper Lake Creek Trail (81) about 4.7 miles from the trailhead, and reenter the wilderness on the northeast side of the lake. Continue south along the lakeshore to reach excellent old growth near the head of the lake, including a productive flat sporting chunky western redcedar 6 to 8 feet thick. Look back to a marvelous view of Mount Rainier.

Rattlesnake-plantain

South of the lake the trail tracks along the edge between lower slopes stuffed with big conifers and the floodplain where Upper Lake Creek roamed during a major flood in February of 1996. The raging stream simultaneously captured existing down trees, killed standing trees with extensive sediment deposits, and created a substrate for establishment of a new generation of trees. The trail runs out of old growth about 8 miles from the trailhead where it veers upslope towards Packwood Saddle.

How to get there: From U.S. Highway 12 in Packwood, turn east onto Forest Road 1260 next to the Packwood Information Center. FS 1260 ends 5.8 miles later at the Packwood Lake Trail parking lot.

35 CLEAR FORK COWLITZ RIVER

Length ■ **6.5 miles one way**
Difficulty ■ Moderate
Season ■ Summer
Lowest point ■ 3,600 feet
Highest point ■ 3,680 feet
Human imprint ■ Minimal
Information ■ Gifford Pinchot National Forest (Cowlitz Valley Ranger District)

Primary Old-Growth Features
Very old Douglas-fir; long expanse of old forest

Head up the Clear Fork Trail (61) into the remote and pristine forest of the Goat Rocks Wilderness to experience truly ancient forest. While most of the trees are not particularly large (3 to 4 feet thick), many are exceptionally old. Elderly forest rolls on for mile after mile as the trail undulates within a

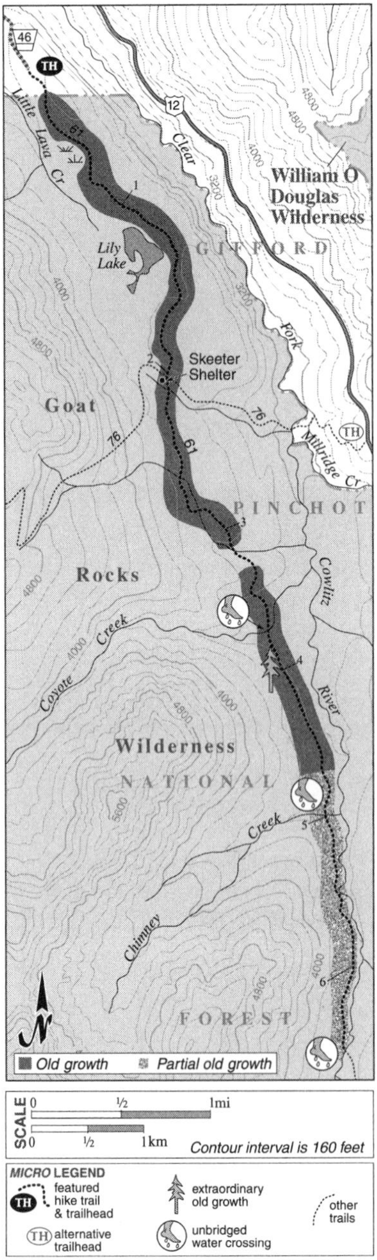

narrow elevation range. Logical stopping points for a day hike include the Skeeter Shelter (2 miles), the Coyote Creek crossing (3.7 miles), and the Clear Fork Cowlitz River crossing (6.5 miles).

Quickly pass through the trailhead plantation and enter a very old stand of widely spaced Douglas-fir. Many of these trees are well over 700 years old, although accurate tree ring counts in the field were next to impossible to attain due to the extremely narrow growth rings. Although very old, the trees are of quite ordinary girth (2 to 5 feet thick) and relatively short. Droughty, infertile soils limit tree growth potential on these sites.

Pathfinder

The trail passes reedy Lily Lake about 1.5 miles from the trailhead, and intersects the Clear Lost Trail (76) at Skeeter Shelter a half mile later. Right on Clear Lost Trail heads up to Coal Creek Mountain; left leads to U.S. Highway 12. Continue straight on the Clear Fork Trail through more ancient forest for another mile, then briefly pass through a younger forest. Switchback down a sideslope and come to a campsite at Coyote Creek.

The forest along the next mile between Coyote Creek and Chimney Creek has aged to the point where very few Douglas-fir remain. Broken-topped Douglas-fir are widely scattered through the forest, while shade-tolerant western hemlock and Pacific silver fir dominate both overstory and understory canopy layers. Alaska-cedar, capable of living over a thousand years, are also prevalent through this part of the forest.

Beyond Chimney Creek the forest is noticeably younger. Douglas-fir and noble fir are abundant as the trail follows the rim of a bench overlooking the Clear Fork. The trail finally drops down to the river for an unbridged crossing.

How to get there: Turn south onto Forest Road 46 from US 12 approximately 4.4 miles northeast of Packwood. Follow FR 46 for almost 9 miles where it ends at the trailhead. The last three-quarters of a mile is rocky and steep, but passable.

36 Lewis and Clark State Park

Length ■ **0.3-mile loop; 1.3-mile loop**
Difficulty ■ Easy
Season ■ Year round
Lowest point ■ 400 feet
Highest point ■ 530 feet
Human imprint ■ High (campers, hikers, highway, edge effects)
Information ■ Lewis and Clark State Park

Primary Old-Growth Feature
Remnant patch of lowland old growth

Lewis and Clark State Park contains one of very few old-growth stands left in the Puget Lowlands of western Washington. The park is ideal for short winter trips due to elevations below 600 feet and ideal also for a road-trip rest stop due to close proximity to Interstate 5. Though park facilities are closed from October through March, the park is open for hiking year round.

The forest itself is still impressive in places, although nearby roads, homes, private lands, and park visitors impart a distinct feeling of a disturbed ecosystem. In addition, severe damage sustained during the Columbus Day windstorm (1962) and subsequent salvage operations is still evident. Over half of the forest volume was blown down in that extreme event. Large snags characteristic of old growth are essentially absent from most of the forest.

The Old-Growth Forest Trail makes a one-third-mile-long loop through the best old forest remaining in the park. Burly Douglas-fir, western redcedar, and western hemlock dwell on the flat above a ravine to the east. Fire scorches on some of the larger trees show that these survivors have endured multiple disturbances. The more obvious entry to the loop is straight ahead of the road where a couple of immense Douglas-fir 6 to 8 feet thick stand next to the trail in the first hundred yards or so. Bear left at an unsigned trail junction just past these two behemoths to travel counterclockwise around the loop.

The Trail of the Deer is actually a set of three short loops linked together to form an easy 1.3-mile hike. Take one side of each loop on the way up, and the other sides on the way down. Although the main trailhead is by the park entrance, the trail can be accessed from several other points by short spur trails, including one from the parking area for the Old-Growth Forest Trail. Douglas-fir, western hemlock, and western redcedar 3 to 5 feet

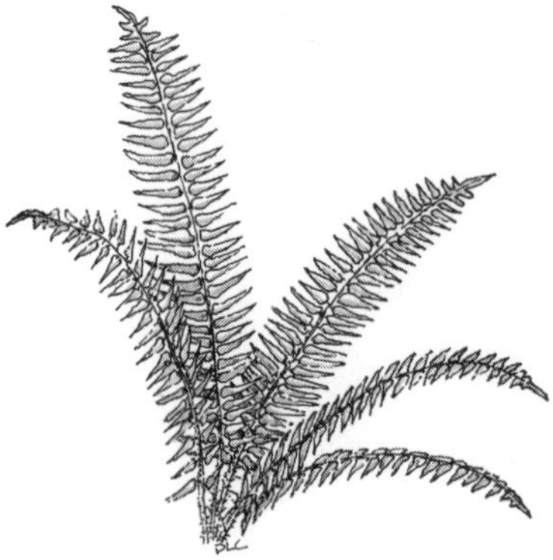

Western swordfern

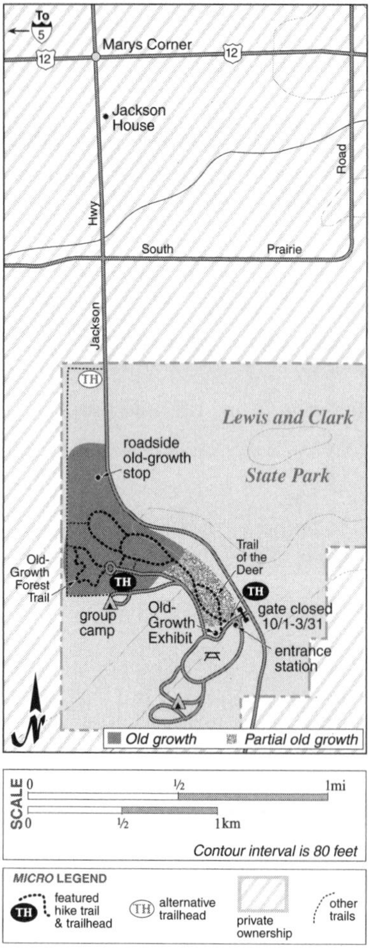

thick are arrayed along the wayside, with occasional giants reaching 6 to 8 feet in diameter.

How to get there: Head east on U.S. Highway 12 from Interstate 5 (exit 68, 10 miles south of Chehalis). Turn right onto Jackson Highway in Marys Corner 2.5 miles east of the freeway, then turn right into the park 1.75 miles later. Follow the road to the right past the entrance station for just under a half mile, then turn right again onto the road to the "Old-Growth Forest." Look for the sign "Big Trees" by the loop at the end of the road in four-tenths of a mile. The primary trailhead for the Trail of the Deer is to the right near the park entrance station. Park by the gate during the off-season (October-March).

37 GREEN RIVER

Length ■	**4 to 6.5 miles one way**
Difficulty ■	Moderate to difficult
Season ■	Late spring to autumn
Lowest point ■	1,880 feet
Highest point ■	2,790 feet
Human imprint ■	Moderate (salvage logging)
Information ■	Gifford Pinchot National Forest (Cowlitz Valley Ranger District); Mount St. Helens National Volcanic Monument

Primary Old-Growth Feature
Classic low-elevation old growth in the midst of a volcanic blast zone

A segment of the Green River watershed in the northern portion of Mount St. Helens National Volcanic Monument is well-known for the classic old-growth forest still standing on its valley floor. Fortunately, the lower slopes of the basin were protected from the eruption of Mount St. Helens in 1980 by a high ridge to the south. The gently graded Green River Trail (213) travels this valley bottom, bisecting several miles of prime old forest.

From Forest Road 2612, the trail first passes through 2 miles of plantations established in the early 1980s after salvage of trees killed by the volcanic blast. The ash-laden slopes above the trail produced numerous landslides and debris torrents during the February 1996 flood, including a couple that sliced through the trail. Beyond the plantations the trail enters a short stretch of unsalvaged blast zone where you can see how the fury of the eruption was felt 10 miles north of Mount St. Helens.

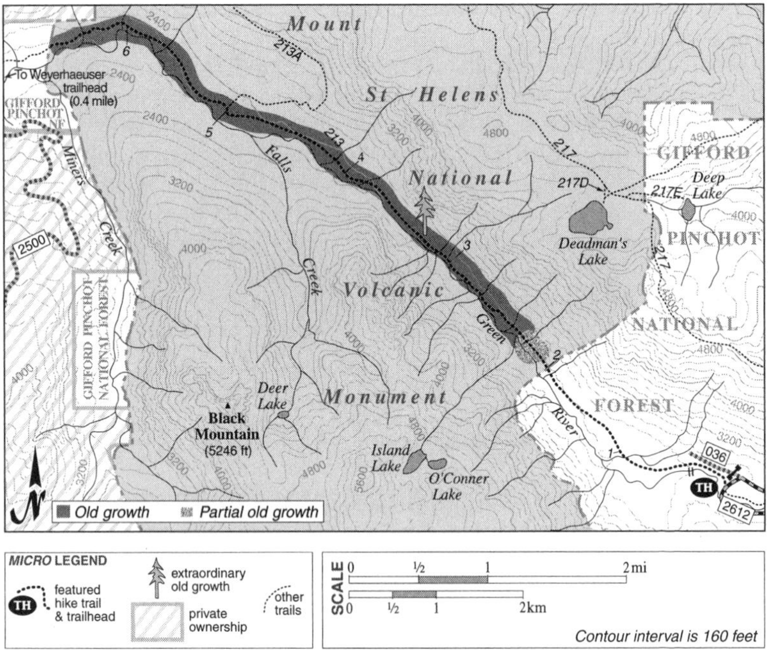

Then the parade of patriarchs begins. Big Douglas-fir, western hemlock, and western redcedar each take their turn leading the pageant on these rich, riparian surfaces. Some of the larger trees reach 6 to 7 feet in girth and are more than 600 years old. The mesmerizing old forest continues for another 5 miles downriver until the trail exits the old growth and reenters the blast zone. Shortly thereafter the trail ends on private land.

How to get there: Turn right onto Cispus Road from U.S. Highway 12 in Randle (just under 50 miles east of Interstate 5) and head south. Veer right onto Forest Road 25 at a junction just under a mile later. Follow FR 25 for 7.7 miles, then turn right onto FR 26 just after crossing the Cispus River. Climb steadily for 12.5 miles until reaching FR 2612 by Ryan Lake. Turn right, follow FR 2612 for 2.5 miles, and park by the junction with FR 036. Walk down FR 2612 a hundred yards or so to pick up the trail on the right.

If FR 26 is still closed by damage from the 1996 flood, continue south on FR 25 and turn right onto FR 99 about 20 miles from Randle. Turn right on FR 26 9 miles later by Meta Lake, then turn left onto FR 2612 in another 4.6 miles by Ryan Lake.

The western trailhead is on the Weyerhaeuser St. Helens Tree Farm and is generally open to public use on weekends. The route to the trailhead sometimes changes due to winter damage and logging operations, and may be closed at times due to fire danger or other reasons. Call 866.636.6531 (toll free) for current information.

QUARTZ CREEK BIG TREES

An easy, half-mile trail circles through a lush valley bottom along Quartz Creek where some of the largest trees anywhere in the Cascades are sheltered. Jaw-dropping Douglas-fir 6 to 10 feet thick are scattered throughout the grove. Western redcedar and western hemlock 4 to 5 feet across pale in comparison to the enormous 550 to 650-year-old Douglas-fir nearby. The compacted-gravel path is suitable for wheelchairs, but is rated as "more challenging" due to short, steep pitches (up to 12 percent grade).

How to get there: On your way to Green River, turn right onto Forest Road 2608 from FR 26 about 7.75 miles from FR 25. Trailhead parking is in 1.25 miles. Contact the Cowlitz Valley Ranger District to make sure the roads are open.

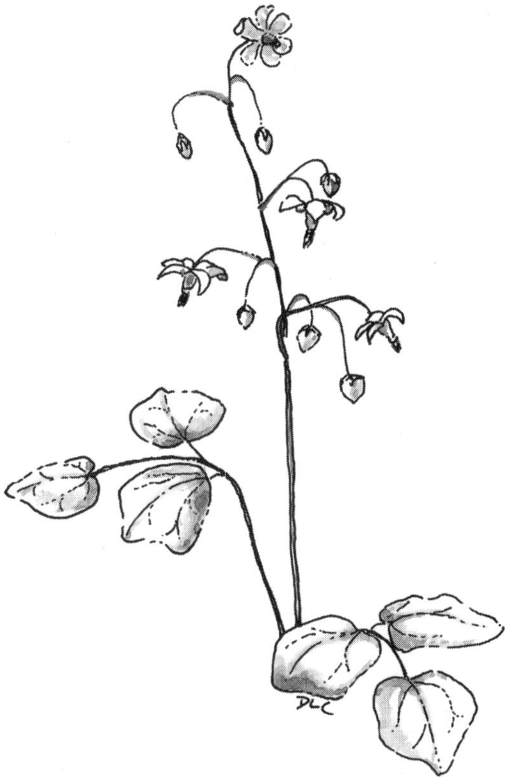

Inside-out flower

38 Craggy Peak

Length ■ **5.5 miles one way**
Difficulty ■ Difficult
Season ■ Summer
Lowest point ■ 3,870 feet
Highest point ■ 5,240 feet
Human imprint ■ Moderate (motorbikes)
Information ■ Gifford Pinchot National Forest (Cowlitz Valley Ranger District)

Primary Old-Growth Feature
Pacific silver fir and mountain hemlock old growth on a scenic ridgeline

Elderly Pacific silver fir and mountain hemlock forests drape the ridgeline separating the Cowlitz River watershed to the north and the Lewis River watershed to the south. The Boundary Trail (1), a historic route along the boundary of the old Rainier and Columbia National Forests, runs east–west along this divide for more than 32 miles. The segment described here approaches Craggy Peak from the east through cloud-catching old growth. Unfortunately, the trail is also open to motorbikes, though a weekday visit should minimize encounters.

Head west through younger forest for the first 2 miles past great views of Mount Adams. The third mile travels in and out of old forest until reaching a cliff-top perch peering into the upper Yellowjacket Creek basin. Here is a fine spot to spend a few moments identifying Hat Rock, Craggy Peak, Shark Rock, Kirk Rock, and Badger Peak.

Carpenter ant carrying cheese

Continue west and enter a striking stand of sturdy mountain hemlock and Pacific silver fir. As you descend toward Yellowjacket Pass on warmer slopes western hemlock, noble fir, and Douglas-fir appear. As you climb out of the pass, aged Pacific silver fir resume prominence.

The trail starts curving to the south about 5 miles from the trailhead where the east shoulder of Craggy Peak meets the ridge. Continue southwest to an open area and potential turnaround point south of

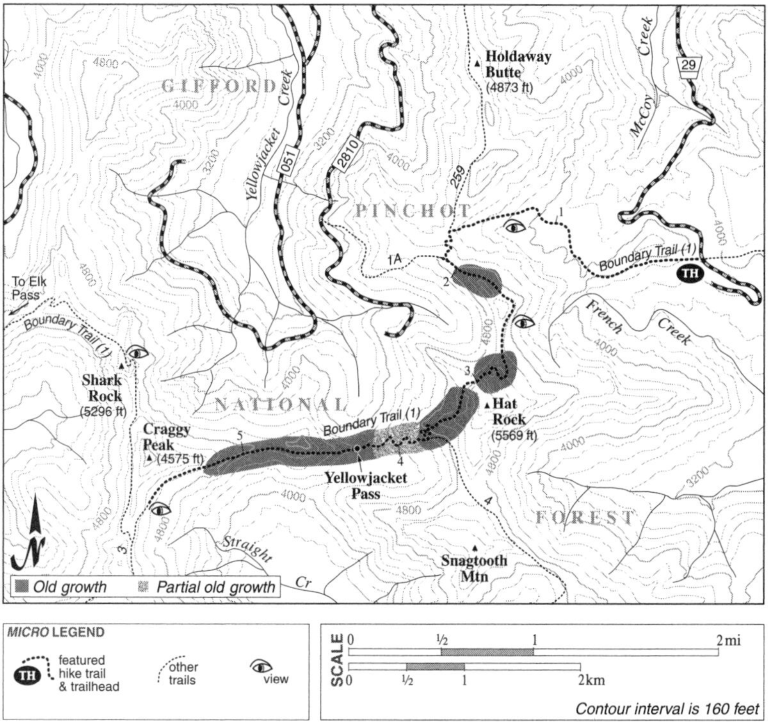

Craggy Peak where Mount Adams commands the skyline to the southeast. Wind around the south shoulder of Craggy Peak to see Shark Rock rising dramatically from the ridge. The viewpoint marks a logical turnaround point for day hikers.

The trail, however, continues westward through more snow-zone old growth, to emerge on Forest Road 25 at Elk Pass about 6 miles from Craggy Peak. Elk Pass is an alternative starting point or pick-up spot for a one-way hike with a shuttle. A long stretch of old forest straddles the ridge from Kirk Rock to Badger Lake, and a short side trip to the top of Badger Peak leads to breathtaking mountaintop views.

How to get there: From U.S. Highway 12 in Randle (just under 50 miles east of Interstate 5), turn right onto Cispus Road and head south. Veer left onto Forest Road 23 just under a mile later. Follow FR 23 for approximately 9 miles, then turn right onto FR 28 and cross the Cispus River. Turn left onto FR 29 in 1 mile, and follow it for almost 15 miles to the ridgetop trailhead.

To reach Elk Pass, continue south on FR 25 at the junction a mile south of Randle, and follow it for approximately 22 miles to the ridgeline.

IRON CREEK

The barrier-free, Iron Creek Campground Loop Trail (187) lies on a fertile floodplain stacked with husky trees. Two particularly immense Douglas-fir (8 feet thick, 265 to 280 feet tall, and 600 years old) stand near the western side of the 1.5 mile loop. Multiple, short spur trails radiate out from the campground providing access to the encircling loop. A one-third-mile interpretive loop is appended to the main loop, and can also be accessed from the adjacent Iron Creek Picnic Area.

How to get there: Follow Forest Road 25 for 9.5 miles south of Randle, then turn left into the Iron Creek Campground. A day-use parking area is on the left a couple hundred yards into the campground. Walk toward the Cispus River to pick up the loop.

39 QUARTZ CREEK

Length	**4.6 miles to Quartz Creek Camp; 7.3 miles to Quartz Creek crossing**
Difficulty	Difficult
Season	Spring to autumn
Lowest point	1,760 feet
Highest point	2,960 feet
Human imprint	Minimal
Information	Gifford Pinchot National Forest; Mount St. Helens National Volcanic Monument

Primary Old-Growth Feature
Large roadless area with Douglas-fir and western hemlock old growth

Long embroiled in the political wrestling match over the Dark Divide Roadless Area, the Quartz Creek basin is justly famous for copious old growth. Old forest extends for several miles along the Quartz Creek Trail (5), attaining noteworthy proportions in places. Although the net elevation change is not large, the trail is more difficult than it appears, ascending and descending short pitches repeatedly.

The first 2.5 miles pass through old-growth leave strips, younger natural stands, and rapidly growing plantations. Then evidence of the industrial chainsaw disappears, and splendid old growth prevails. The old forest reaches its zenith on deep-soiled benches and in well-watered draws about halfway between Straight Creek and Snagtooth Creek, and again near Quartz Creek Camp. Enormous Douglas-fir and western redcedar (4 to 6 feet thick) are tightly packed in these forest oases. Veer right on the Quartz Creek Butte Trail (5B) a half mile above Snagtooth Creek to reach the eminent old forest near the camp. The creek crossing nearby makes a relaxing break spot and sensible turnaround point.

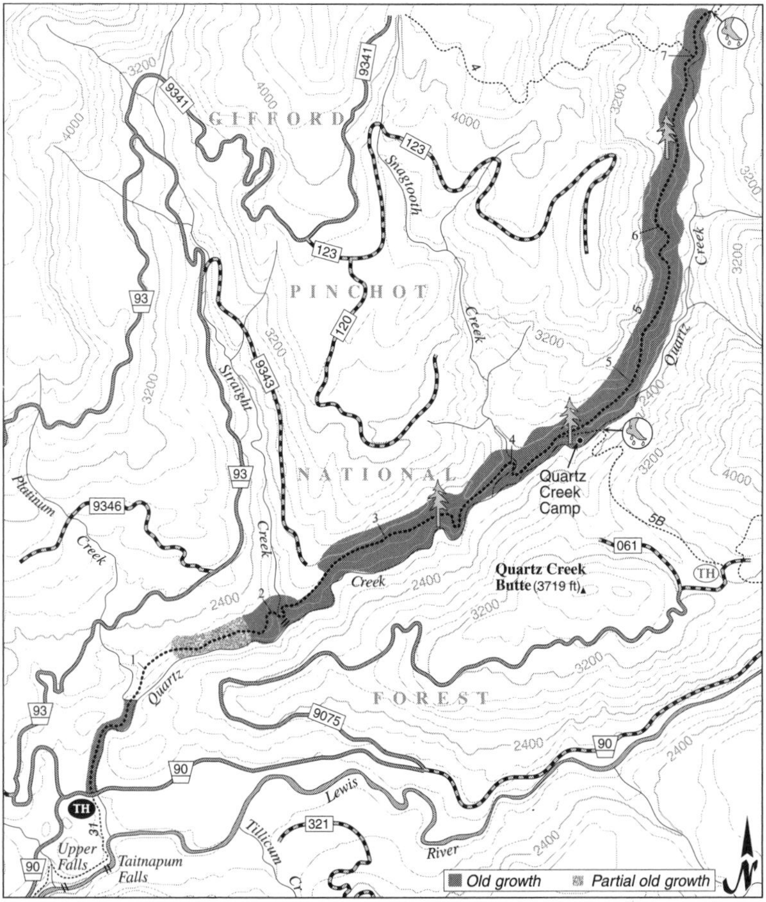

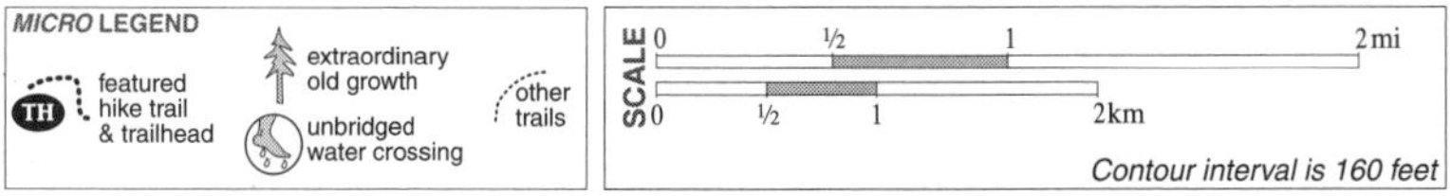

The little-used Quartz Creek Butte Trail also provides an alternative access route to the heart of Quartz Creek valley, or a starting point for a one-way downhill hike to the lower trailhead. The upper half of the trail slopes moderately downhill through an overstory of scattered old fire survivors, while the lower half of the trail pitches steeply down the valley wall through first-class old growth.

Windflower

Above Quartz Creek Camp, the Quartz Creek Trail continues the roller coaster hike through exemplary old growth for another 3 miles to a crossing of upper Quartz Creek. A noteworthy patch of older forest stands astride the trail about 2 miles above the camp. Only a handful of big Douglas-fir remain in this stand of shade-tolerant conifers (western hemlock, Pacific silver fir, and western redcedar).

How to get there: From Interstate 5 at Woodland (exit 21), go east on State Route 503, which becomes 503-Spur at Yale, and then Forest Road 90 about 3 miles east of Cougar. At the junction with FR 25 less than a quarter mile past the Pine Creek Work Center (approximately 48 miles east of Interstate 5), turn right, staying on FR 90. Continue on FR 90 for 16.8 miles to a parking area on the right just before crossing Quartz Creek. The trail is across the road to the left.

To find the Quartz Creek Butte trailhead, continue east on FR 90 for another 1.9 miles and turn left onto FR 9075. Follow the pavement uphill for 4.5 miles, then turn right onto a gravel road. The trailhead is on the left where the road curves right less than a half mile from the junction.

LEWIS RIVER FALLS

The Quartz Creek trailhead also marks the upper terminus of the Lewis River Trail (31). Head downriver for 3.5 miles through a riverine ribbon of old growth past four major waterfalls. The forest reaches maximum development between Upper Falls and Middle Falls. Here fire-scorched Douglas-fir up to 8 feet thick join large western redcedar and Pacific silver fir in a riparian rhapsody. Although the big trees gradually peter out below Middle Falls, exquisite Lower Falls must be seen.

40 SHEEP CANYON

Length ■ **11 miles one way from Blue Lake trailhead; 7-mile loop from Sheep Canyon trailhead**
Difficulty ■ Difficult
Season ■ Summer
Lowest point ■ 3,230 feet
Highest point ■ 4,720 feet
Human imprint ■ Minimal
Information ■ Mount St. Helens National Volcanic Monument

Primary Old-Growth Feature
Outstanding, highly productive noble fir old growth

The luxuriant old-growth forest in the Sheep Canyon area contrasts vividly with the relatively barren slopes and stream channels nearby. The violence of Mount St. Helens's most recent eruption scarred the landscape at an astonishing scale. This fertile forest was sliced into chunks by large-scale mudflows that scoured Sheep Canyon and nearby streams during the volcanic blast in 1980. Disturbed areas have experienced remarkable recovery since the outburst, but will require many centuries, if not millennia, to regain their former opulence.

Segments of three trails can be joined together to form a dramatic 7-mile loop around Sheep Canyon. However, a mudflow triggered by heavy rain in November 2001 came thundering down Coldspring Creek high off of Mount St. Helens, severing the access road to the Sheep Canyon trailhead. Fortunately, the Toutle Trail (238) runs from the Blue Lake trailhead to the Sheep Canyon Trail (240), passing through spectacular old growth most of the way. Hiking this stretch of the Toutle Trail to reach the Sheep Canyon loop adds about 4 miles to the total distance hiked.

Noble fir

Pick up the Toutle Trail on the other side of Coldspring Creek, quickly coming to and skirting aptly named Blue Lake. The trail reaches a superlative noble fir and Pacific silver fir forest about a mile from the trailhead. In places a near-solid layer of clover-like oxalis underlies columns of noble fir 4 to 6 feet in diameter. The presence of oxalis indicates deep, well-watered, and fine-textured soils perfect for growing big trees. The old growth is interrupted by a half-mile-long plantation of rapidly growing, young noble fir before the stunning old forest resumes. The trail reaches the Sheep Canyon Trail about 2.5 miles from the Blue Lake trailhead and a half mile from the Sheep Canyon trailhead.

Continue straight on the Toutle Trail (238) and cross the bridge over Sheep Canyon. The Sheep Canyon mudflow devoured the adjacent forest leaving a scoured trough in its wake. Reenter outstanding old growth on the other side of the canyon where lofty noble fir and associated conifers shade a carpet of herbs. After another half mile or so the trail emerges from the forest into the vast blast zone. Switchback down the slope in and out of the blast zone edge above several beaver ponds. Head toward the South Fork of the Toutle River where adjacent slopes were leveled and incinerated by the blast.

Turn right onto the Loowit Trail (216) by the riverbank and head sharply upslope toward the forest. The trail then climbs steeply on Crescent Ridge near the blast zone edge until emerging above the old forest. Mount St.

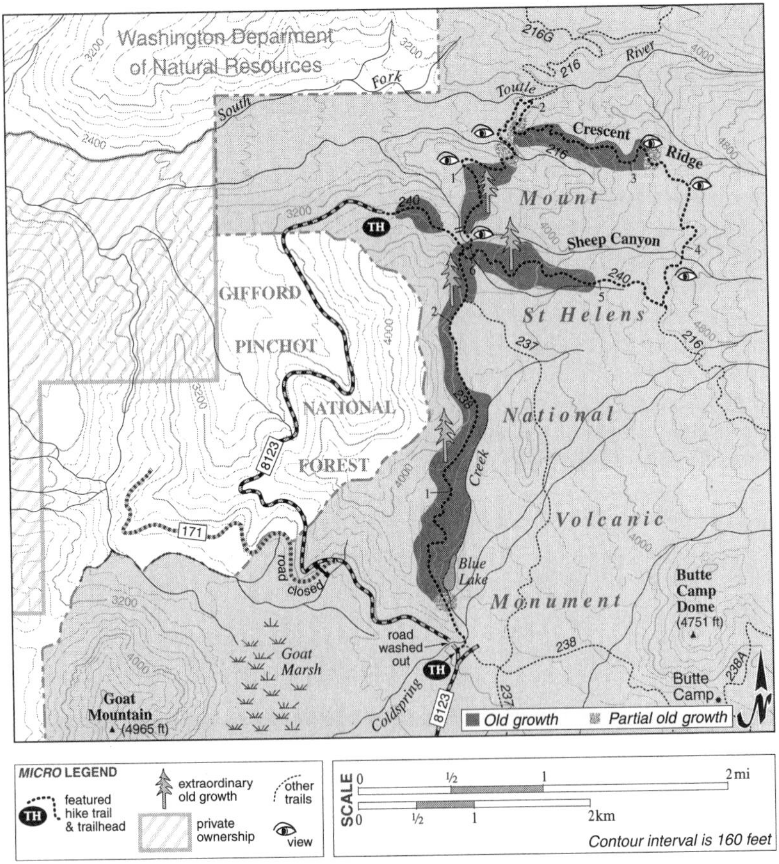

Helens looms dramatically above the skyline as the trail swings around to the south, recrosses the braided stream channels of Sheep Canyon, and arrives at a junction with the upper end of the Sheep Canyon Trail (240). Turn right and head downhill toward the junction with the Toutle Trail through majestic noble fir and Pacific silver fir old growth most of the way.

How to get there: From Interstate 5 at Woodland (exit 21), go east on State Route 503, which becomes 503-Spur at Yale. Turn left onto Forest Road 81, heading toward the Kalama Recreation Area, 4.5 miles east of Yale (27.5 miles east of Interstate 5). Follow FR 81 for 11.5 miles, then turn left (north) onto FR 8123. The Blue Lake trailhead is to the right by Coldspring Creek 1.7 miles later. If the road crossing has been reestablished, continue another 6.5 miles to the Sheep Canyon trailhead for the 7-mile loop.

41 Ape Canyon

Length	**4.5 miles one way**
Difficulty	Moderate
Season	Summer to fall
Lowest point	2,850 feet
Highest point	4,180 feet
Human imprint	Moderate (hikers, mountain bikers)
Information	Mount St. Helens National Volcanic Monument

Primary Old-Growth Features
Classic Douglas-fir and western hemlock old growth; large noble fir and Pacific silver fir

Although apes are not abundant along the Ape Canyon Trail (234), broad conifers and dramatic views are certainly plentiful. The trail ascends a narrow ridge holding an island of old forest along the southeast flank of Mount St. Helens. A massive mud and ash flow (lahar), a plantation, a shrub field, and the seared slopes of Mount St. Helens border this isolated patch.

The trail sets out along the edge of the sparsely vegetated lahar and an older plantation. Although the volcano blew out to the north in 1980, decapitation of the peak and rapid melting of the remaining snowpack initiated this lahar off the south slope. Dead-on views of Mount St. Helens open up where the trail skirts the edge of the lahar.

The trail leaves the plantation 1.3 miles from the trailhead and enters a patch of stately Douglas-fir and western hemlock old growth. The trail stays to the west of the ridgeline for the next mile penetrating the heart of the grove, and then switchbacks up to the ridgeline. The next 1.5 miles passes through a mix of shrub patches and old growth on and near the ridgeline. Forest composition shifts toward the more cold- and snow-tolerant true firs as the trail gains elevation. One particularly chunky noble fir straddling the ridgeline reaches more than 7 feet in girth.

Ruffed grouse

The trail finally emerges above the forest onto the pumice ejected by Mount St. Helens. Ape Canyon appears as a narrow chute sliced down the valley bottom to the east. Watch your footing in this area. Just before the junction with the Loowit Trail (216), a view to the east through a rock slot perfectly frames Mount Adams. If you have a little extra energy, turn right on the Loowit Trail toward the Plains of Abraham where pumice bombs are strewn across the surface and grand views abound in all directions.

How to get there: From Interstate 5 at Woodland (exit 21), go east on State Route 503, which becomes 503-Spur at Yale, and then Forest Road 90 about 3 miles east of Cougar. Turn left onto FR 83 about 6.7 miles east of Cougar (35 miles from Interstate 5). The trailhead is on the left just over 11 miles later. The entire route is paved.

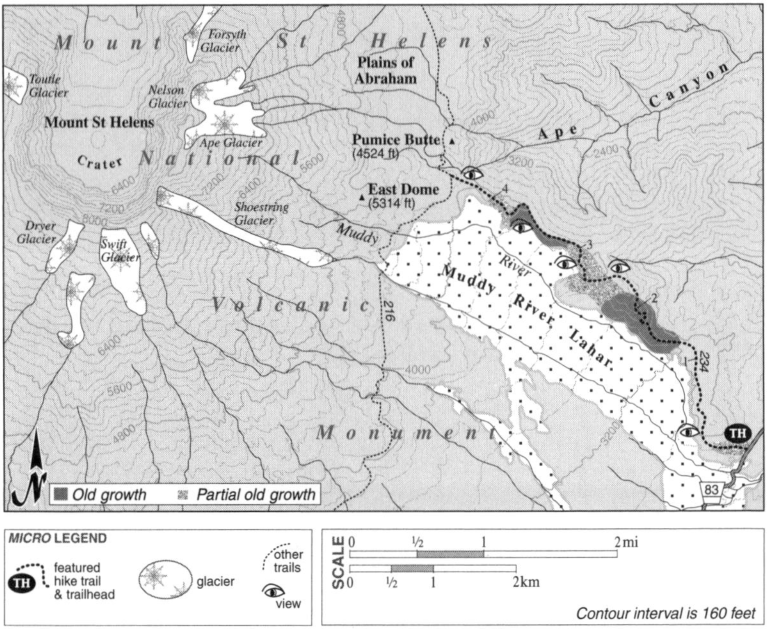

CEDAR FLATS

One of the most impressive old-growth forests in the Cascades sits on the deep alluvial soils of the Cedar Flats Research Natural Area (RNA). The 1-mile-long Cedar Flats Trail (32) loops through a small portion of the RNA past mammoth western redcedar and Douglas-fir. Five to eight-foot-thick monoliths are common, and occasional titans stretch to 9 or 10 feet through the base. Unfortunately, the largest Douglas-fir known in the Cascades, the Cedar Flats Sentinel, toppled to the forest floor in the summer of 2002. This giant was 264 feet tall and 11.8 feet in diameter. Important research on the vegetation and wildlife of old-growth forests, and on the effects of mudflows on soils and vegetation, has occurred in the RNA. Help protect this research, and the vegetation and soils in the area, by staying on the trail. Although accessible by wheelchair, be prepared for short steep pitches.

How to get there: Continue east on Forest Road 90 to the junction with FR 25, less than a quarter mile past the Pine Creek Work Center (approximately 48 miles east of Interstate 5). Stay to the left (heading north) onto FR 25 at the junction, and continue for 3.75 miles to the trailhead parking area on the right.

42 LEWIS RIVER

Length	**3 to 5 miles one way**
Difficulty	Moderate
Season	Early spring to autumn
Lowest point	1,130 feet
Highest point	1,300 feet
Human imprint	Moderate (hikers, mountain bikers, horseback riders)
Information	Gifford Pinchot National Forest; Mount St. Helens National Volcanic Monument

Primary Old-Growth Feature
Classic Douglas-fir and western hemlock old growth

Magnificent stands of Douglas-fir and western hemlock old growth are just part of the lure of the lower Lewis River Trail (31). Hikers, mountain bikers, and equestrians alike are attracted to the lovely river and gentle trail grade. The low-elevation trail can be enjoyably hiked for most any distance, although the finest old forest is found on riverside flats in the first 3 miles.

Start off heading through a stand with two cohorts of Douglas-fir. The younger and more numerous age class regenerated following a fire 350 to 400 years ago. Older fire-scorched survivors overtop this cohort. Less than a mile from the trailhead the trail enters a dynamite patch of luxuriant old growth featuring Douglas-fir and western redcedar 5 to 7 feet thick.

From here the trail briefly follows the edge of an older plantation, reenters old growth, and comes to restored Bolt Camp Shelter a little more than

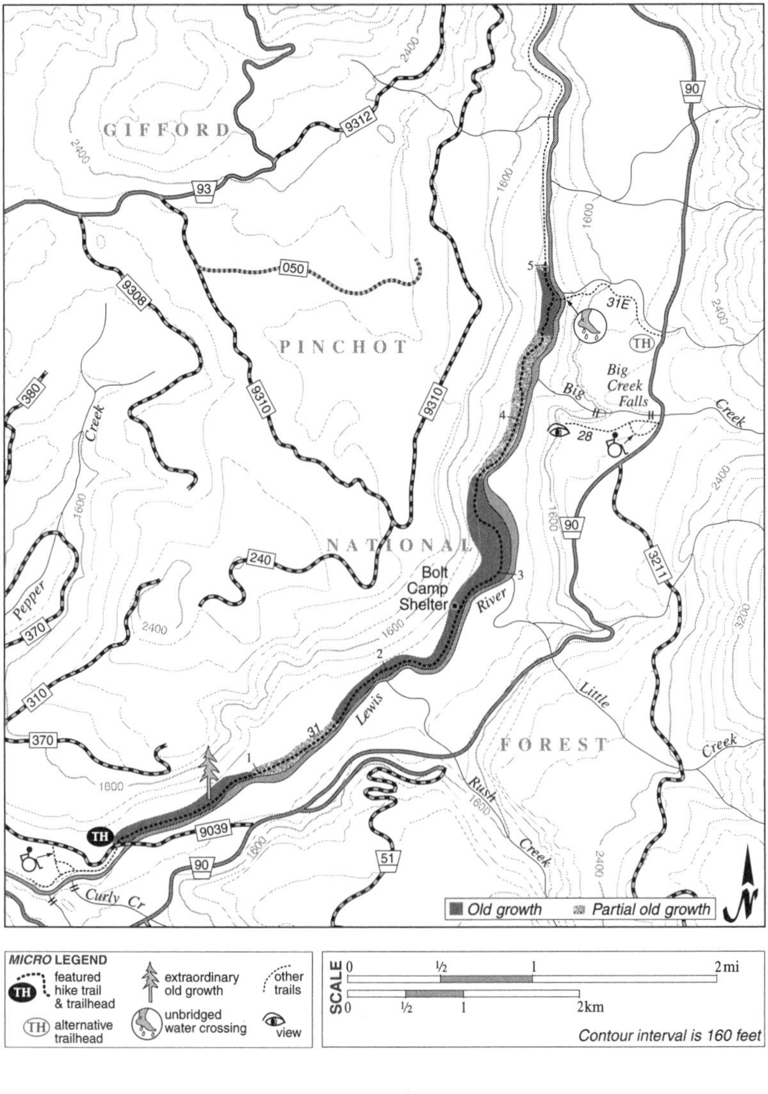

2.5 miles from the trailhead. Bolt Camp was once a redcedar bolt processing site for downriver settlements. Beyond the shelter the trail crosses another fine flat graced by stately western redcedar, grand fir, Douglas-fir, black cottonwood, and bigleaf maple swaying over dense swordfern.

Trillium

The trail continues near the river through mixed older and younger forest coming to another flat stocked with fat trees about 5 miles from the trailhead. This stand marks a logical turnaround spot for day hikers. A steep and seldom-maintained alternative route to the river known as the Speed Trail (31E) intersects the Lewis River Trail here. Used mainly by anglers, the trail requires fording the river, practical only during late summer or autumn. Huge Douglas-fir and western redcedar populate the bench above the canyon walls along this trail.

Heading north, the trail intersects Forest Road 90 about 9.5 miles from the lower trailhead. Scenic highlights along the 4.5 miles above the flat include a drippy, moss-softened columnar basalt outcrop, and vantage points overlooking a rocky gorge.

How to get there: From Interstate 5 at Woodland (exit 21), go east on State Route 503, which becomes 503-Spur at Yale, and then FR 90 about 3 miles east of Cougar. At the junction with FR 25 less than a quarter mile past the Pine Creek Work Center (48 miles east of Interstate 5), turn right, staying on FR 90. Turn sharply left onto Curly Creek Road (FR 9039) just over 5 miles from the junction. Trailhead parking is on the left by the bridge two-thirds of a mile later.

To reach the Speed Trail, continue on FR 90 another 4 miles or so past Curly Creek Road and park on the left just before the stream crossing.

BIG CREEK FALLS

A quarter-mile-long, wheelchair-accessible trail circles through an inviting patch of lowland old growth above Big Creek Falls. The trail hugs the gorge rim in places, offering striking views of the falls plunging 125 feet to a deep pool. A spur trail (28) branches off from the loop at the halfway point, continuing down the canyon brim for almost three-quarters of a mile past more big trees. A particularly massive Douglas-fir (9.5 feet in diameter) stands apart from the crowd near the trail junction.

How to get there: Continue on Forest Road 90 another 3.75 miles past the Curly Creek Road and park on the left in a well-signed lot.

43 GOTCHEN CREEK

Length ■ **11.2-mile loop**
Difficulty ■ Moderate to difficult
Season ■ Summer to early autumn
Lowest point ■ 3,590 feet
Highest point ■ 5,580 feet
Human imprint ■ High (cattle, timber harvest, fire suppression effects)
Information ■ Gifford Pinchot National Forest (Mount Adams Ranger District)

Primary Old-Growth Feature
Old-growth ponderosa pine and associated dry-site conifers

The forest on the south side of Mount Adams lies east of the Cascade crest, favoring tree species adapted to drier conditions. Ponderosa pine, grand fir, western larch, Engelmann spruce, and Douglas-fir were historically maintained in a relatively open condition by frequent, low-severity fires. Twentieth-century fire suppression has greatly altered this forest and set the stage for an ongoing outbreak of western spruce budworm. Yet despite widespread defoliation and mortality, many older trees still stand in the area. Two trails and a portion of a road can be linked to form an interesting 11-mile loop through this dynamic forest.

The western spruce budworm is currently at outbreak population levels in many eastside forests in south and central Washington, posing a difficult dilemma. Closely spaced understory trees, a lot of grand fir, and continuous foliage throughout the stand all result from fire suppression, and all favor the budworm. Ironically, these are also habitat characteristics that favor the northern spotted owl, leading to the presence of owls in places not likely used much by the owl prior to fire suppression. High levels of dead wood and the vertical ladderlike effect of the dense understory risk an extreme fire event that could cause widespread mortality and loss of older forest habitat.

Head northwest on the Gotchen Creek Trail (40) through highly variable old forest featuring platy-barked ponderosa pine, stout Douglas-fir, and statuesque grand fir. Past timber cutting is evident in the first mile or so, and cattle continue to graze in the area. A major

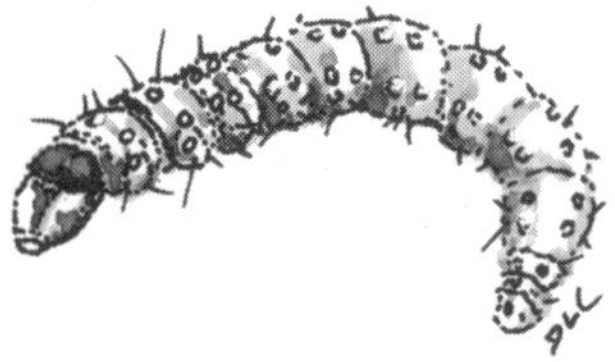
Western spruce budworm

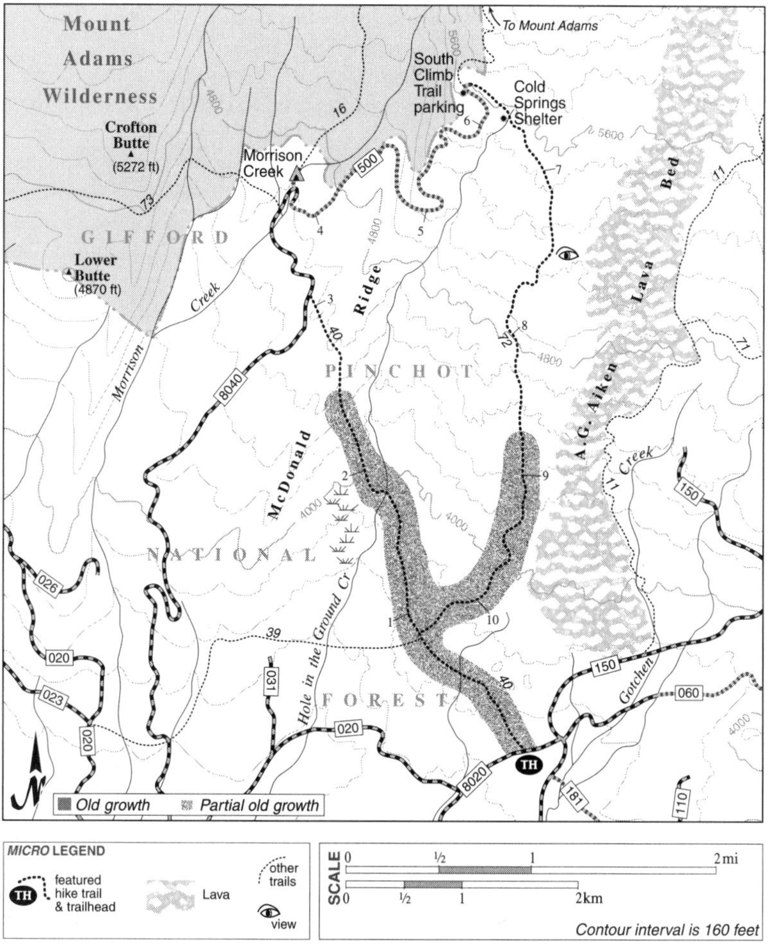

sheep and cattle driveway passed through the Gotchen Creek area from 1880 to 1940. Continue past the junction with the Morrison Creek Trail (39) and the Cold Springs Trail (72) leaving the old forest behind after a couple of miles.

Climb into a higher-elevation zone dominated by considerably smaller lodgepole pine and subalpine fir, coming to the upper trail terminus on Forest Road 8040 a little more than 3 miles from the trailhead. Turn right, and then turn right again onto rough FR 500 two-thirds of a mile later. Follow FR 500 uphill for 3 miles to the parking area for the South Climb Trail.

Take the Cold Springs Trail (72) heading south through more high-elevation forest and intermixed dry meadows. Stately ponderosa pine, Douglas-fir, and grand fir 3 to 4 feet thick hold sway over younger scions along lower portions of the trail. About 10.5 miles into the hike turn left onto the Gotchen Creek Trail to return to the trailhead.

For a shorter hike to the best of the old forest, start on the Gotchen Creek Trail, then turn right onto the Cold Springs Trail and follow it uphill for a mile or 2.

How to get there: Follow the Mount Adams Recreation Highway due north out of Trout Lake (22 miles north of White Salmon on State Route 141), and stay right where Forest Road 23 veers left 1.3 miles later. Veer left onto FR 80 in a half mile, then turn right onto FR 8020 in 2.75 miles. The trailhead is on the left 3.6 miles later.

BIG TREE TIP—TROUT LAKE BIG TREE

Pull over to the right to see the Trout Lake Big Tree just after turning onto Forest Road 8020. This giant ponderosa pine is 7 feet thick and reported as 213 feet tall, although the top appears to be broken off lower than that. This impressive tree is the second largest pine by volume in Washington.

44 SISTER ROCKS

Length ■ **2.8 miles to Observation Peak**
Difficulty ■ Moderate
Season ■ Summer to early autumn
Lowest point ■ 3,540 feet
Highest point ■ 4,207 feet
Human imprint ■ Minimal
Information ■ Gifford Pinchot National Forest (Mount Adams Ranger District)

Primary Old-Growth Feature
Climax Pacific silver fir forest

A nearly pure stand of Pacific silver fir old growth just to the north of Sister Rocks was recognized as a superlative example of a "climax" forest several decades ago, resulting in designation of the Sister Rocks Research Natural Area in 1967. The forest is considered to represent climax conditions because the distribution of young, middle-aged, and old trees indicate that Pacific silver fir is sustaining itself over time. The tree species expected to occur at this site in earlier successional stages (primarily Douglas-fir and noble fir) are limited to widely scattered old individuals, or snags or down logs. In the absence of fire or climatic shifts, Pacific silver fir may be able to regenerate itself on this site indefinitely.

Head south on the Observation Trail (132) splitting the Research Natural Area (RNA) in half along the ridgeline. The trail is in the RNA for the first mile, furnishing excellent views of this exemplary stand. Painted trees and other markings indicate the presence of long-term monitoring plots. Please stay on the trail in the RNA so that important long-term forest research can continue undisturbed.

The trail exits the old forest in a little under a mile and enters a younger forest that regenerated following a 1902 fire. The trail stays on the ridgeline, skirting the northern boundary of the Trapper Creek Wilderness, and comes to a trail junction at Berry Camp a little under 2 miles from the trailhead. The Big Hollow Trail (158) heads downhill to the east, and a little farther down the trail the Trapper Creek Trail (192) heads downhill to the west.

Continue southeast on the ridgeline for another mile, taking the Observation Peak Trail (132A) up to the summit. For obvious reasons the rocky knoll once hosted a fire lookout. Cascade peaks from Mount Rainier to Mount Jefferson dominate the skyline.

How to get there: Turn north onto the Wind River Road from State

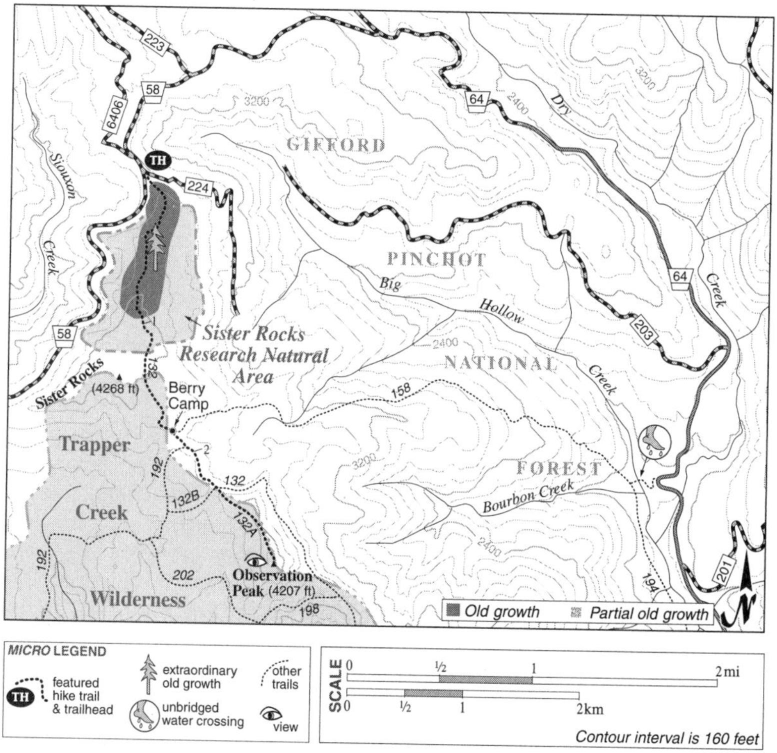

Route 14 approximately 3 miles east of Stevenson. Go north through Carson and come to a junction with Mineral Springs Road 14.5 miles from SR 14. Stay right on Wind River Road for 2 miles, then turn left onto Forest Road 64. Follow FR 64 for 6 miles then turn left onto FR 58. The trailhead is on the left just over 2 miles later.

Beadlily

45 Trapper Creek

Length	**4.8 miles one way**
Difficulty	Moderate
Season	Early spring to autumn
Lowest point	1,150 feet
Highest point	2,400 feet
Human imprint	Minimal
Information	Gifford Pinchot National Forest (Mount Adams Ranger District)

Primary Old-Growth Features
Lowland riparian old growth; huge Douglas-fir

The Trapper Creek Wilderness holds one of few remaining sizable blocks of intact low-elevation forest in southern Washington. Patches of old growth along lower slopes and riparian areas survived a mid-nineteenth-century fire that burned much of the wilderness. The Trapper Creek Trail bisects the heart of the wilderness, running along the creek up to a cliff-top perch overlooking Trapper Creek Falls.

Head west on the Trapper Creek Trail (192) in mature forest overtopped by a few older Douglas-fir and western redcedar. Pass a junction with the Observation Trail (132), a node for a possible loop hike, in about three-quarters of a mile. The best of the old growth begins near the first junction with the Deer Cutoff Trail (209) nearly 3 miles from the trailhead. Prime streamside old growth featuring the characteristic lowland trio (Douglas-fir, western hemlock, and western redcedar) continues for another mile past the second junction with the Deer Cutoff Trail. Larger trees reach 5 to 7 feet in diameter. The trail then crosses Trapper Creek and switchbacks up a steep headwall to a surprising viewpoint facing 100-foot-tall Trapper Creek Falls.

Hikers with additional energy can continue uphill past the falls to make a 14.5-mile loop through the north half of the wilderness. Most of the remainder of the loop is through younger forest, except for small, protected areas near streams where pockets of old growth survived the last fire. Follow the Trapper Creek Trail to the ridgeline and turn right on the Observation Trail (132) for the return leg. The truly energetic can take an additional side trip up to Observation Peak for expansive views over a wide swath of the Cascades (see Hike 44). Other, shorter, loop hikes are possible using one of the primitive connector trails (Big Slide, 195; Sunshine, 198; or Rim, 202) built by the Mazamas hiking club out of Portland.

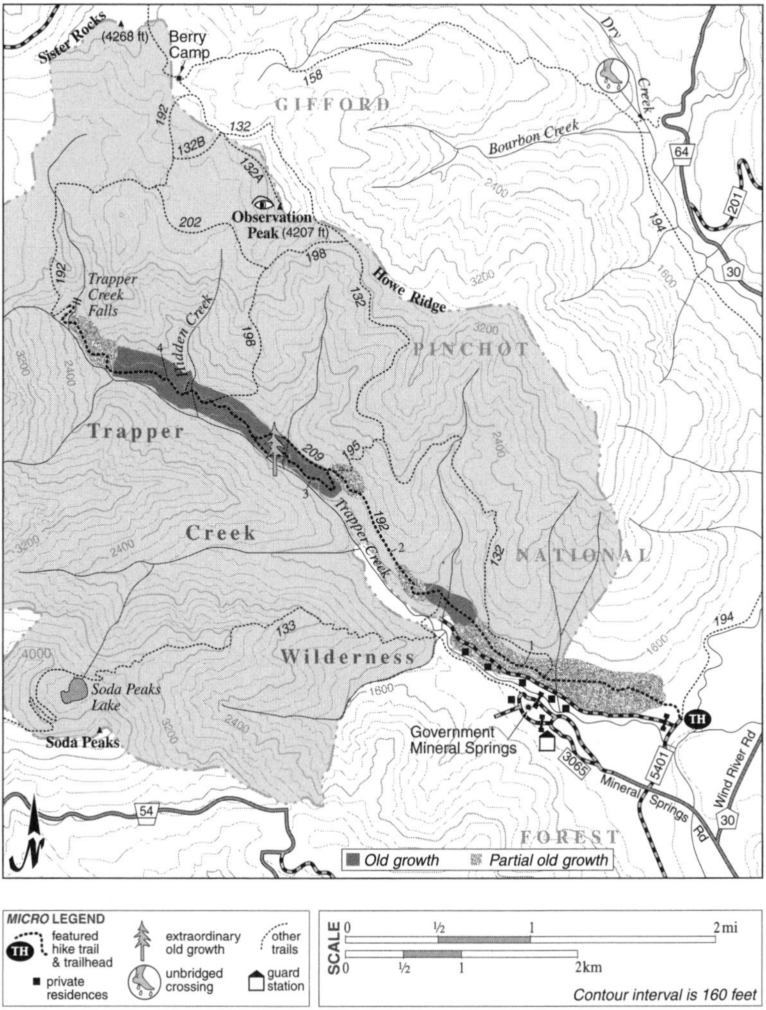

How to get there: Turn north onto Wind River Road from State Route 14 approximately 3 miles east of Stevenson. Go north through Carson and come to a junction with Mineral Springs Road 14.5 miles from SR 14. Continue straight onto Mineral Springs Road, then turn right onto Forest Road 5401 in four-tenths of a mile. Trailhead parking is straight ahead after another four-tenths of a mile.

Hooker's fairybells

GOVERNMENT MINERAL SPRINGS

Mammoth conifers still stand near Government Mineral Springs, site of a well-known resort that operated in a bygone era. An impressive Douglas-fir with a diameter of nearly 9 feet towers over a historic guard station by the entrance to the grove. Follow Forest Road 3065 past the guard station for an easy stroll through the area.

How to get there: Go straight onto Mineral Springs Road at the junction described above and park near the guard station at the head of the first loop, about 1.25 miles from the junction.

WIND RIVER CANOPY CRANE

A unique facility for studying old-growth forests was erected in 1995 on the nearby Thorton T. Munger Research Natural Area. A 250-foot-tall construction crane, operated jointly by the University of Washington and the U.S. Forest Service, allows access from above to nearly six acres of 500-year-old forest. Scientists are studying this forest in great detail in three dimensions, learning how the forest canopy exchanges gases with the atmosphere and how it provides unique habitats for plants and animals. The crane is closed to the public for safety reasons and access is strictly controlled. Visit *www.depts.washington.edu/wrccrf/* for more information.

NORTHERN OREGON CASCADES

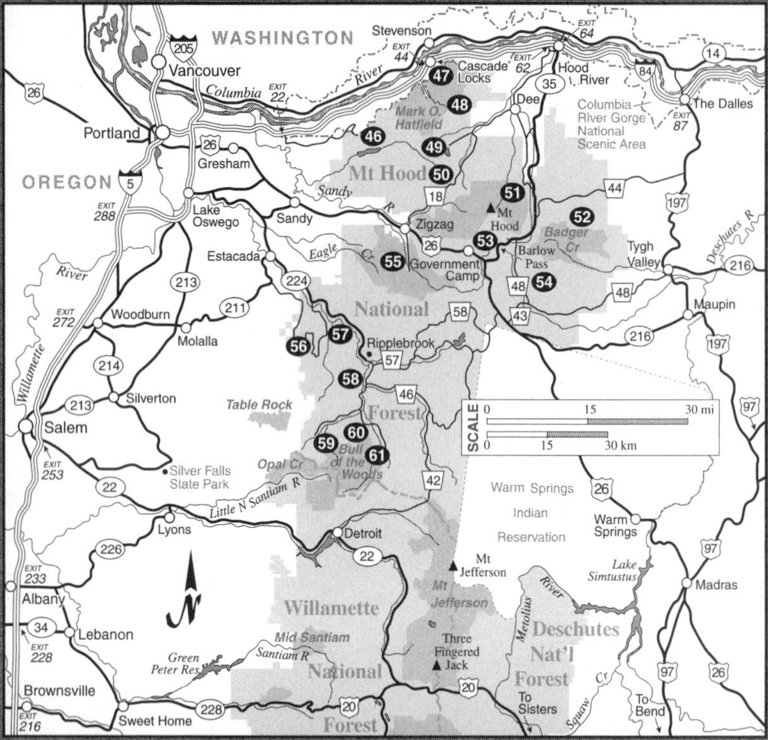

Hike locations

46 LARCH MOUNTAIN BASIN

Length ■ **6-mile loop**
Difficulty ■ Moderate
Season ■ Late spring to autumn
Lowest point ■ 2,820 feet
Highest point ■ 3,910 feet
Human imprint ■ Moderate (hikers, mountain bikers, old road, old clearcut)
Information ■ Columbia River Gorge National Scenic Area

Primary Old-Growth Feature
Extensive stand of Douglas-fir, western hemlock, and noble fir old growth

An extensive and well-trailed patch of old growth lies sheltered in the crater of Larch Mountain, a misnamed but popular destination less than 40 miles from Portland. Early lumbermen marketed the noble fir found near the mountaintop as larch because of the high quality of the noble fir wood, and it's been called Larch Mountain ever since. Although the mountain receives heavy use on weekends, most visitors drive to the top for the view and leave the trails to the more energetic. A 6-mile loop allows relatively easy exploration of the old forest in the heart of the basin, and links to other hiking options. The loop is also well-used by mountain bikers.

Head down the Larch Mountain Trail (441) from the main parking lot, coming to a small patch of large western hemlock and noble fir a mile or so down the trail. Cross over the ridge onto east-facing slopes and continue downhill across a gravel road until reaching the Multnomah Creek Way Trail (444). For a delightful detour to an impressive stand, continue downhill on the Larch Mountain Trail until reaching a particularly productive site about a half mile from the junction. Douglas-fir reach 5 to 6 feet in girth on this herb-rich spot. The Larch Mountain Trail eventually leads to Multnomah Falls passing through riparian old growth most of the way.

King bolete

Back at the junction head downhill to the southeast on the Multnomah Creek Way Trail (444). Stay right on

Trail 444 at the junction with the Multnomah Spur Trail (446) a quarter mile later. Start the climb back uphill on Trail 444 through a beautiful, open stand of Douglas-fir, western hemlock, and occasional noble fir. The largest of these giants approach 6 feet in diameter. The trail skirts the marshy remains of a post-glacial lake and continues uphill through old forest until crossing a secondary ridge and joining an old logging road in younger forest. Trail 444 ends at a junction with the Oneonta Trail (424) on the main ridgeline. Turn right and follow the Onenota Trail back to Larch Mountain Road. The parking lot is another half mile up the highway.

Another option is to take a slightly longer loop starting downhill on the Oneonta Trail. Continue past the Multnomah Creek Way Trail, cross an old road bed, and enter an ancient western hemlock and Douglas-fir forest.

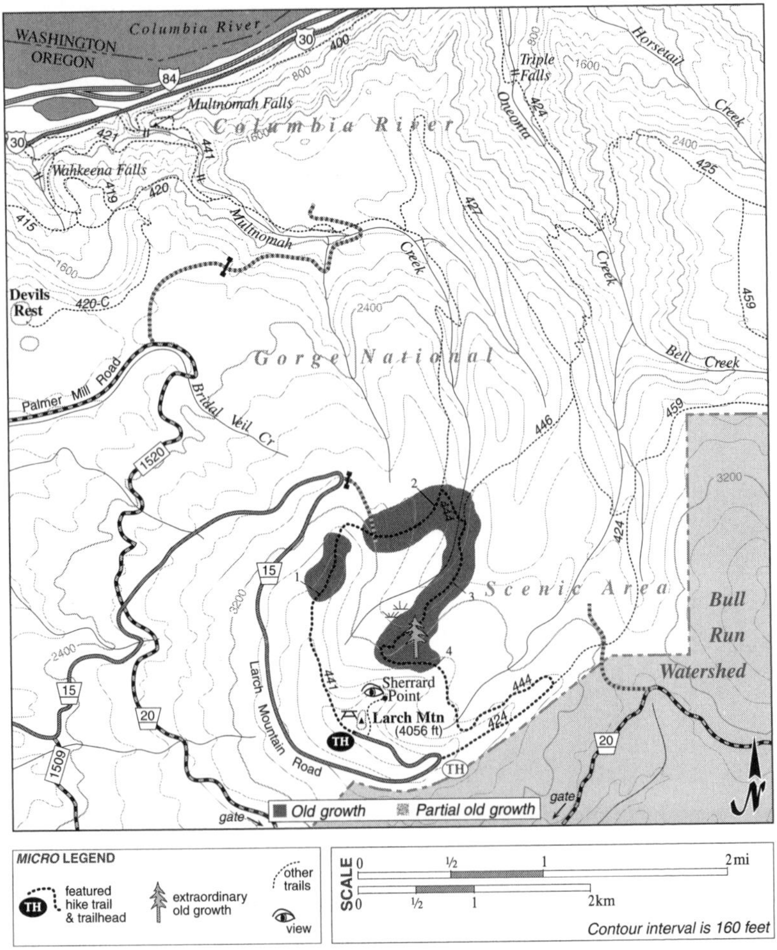

For another old-growth detour, turn right on the Bell Creek Trail (459) about 2 miles from the trailhead. Venerable Douglas-fir and western redcedar stand along the trail for the first mile or so. To continue the loop, resume hiking on the Oneonta Trail. Turn left onto the Multnomah Spur Trail about three-quarters of a mile from the junction with the Bell Creek Trail, and turn left again at the junction with the Multnomah Creek Way Trail in another mile, picking up the loop described above.

How to get there: Turn off Interstate 84 (Corbett exit 22) 13 miles east of the I-84/I-205 junction and head uphill toward Corbett. Turn left onto the Columbia Gorge Highway after 1.5 miles, and then turn right onto the paved Larch Mountain Road after another 1.75 miles. Park in the large lot at the top of Larch Mountain 14 miles later.

47 HERMAN CREEK

Length ■	**7.3 miles one way**
Difficulty ■	Difficult
Season ■	Spring to autumn
Lowest point ■	220 feet
Highest point ■	2,900 feet
Human imprint ■	Minimal
Information ■	Columbia River Gorge National Scenic Area; Mount Hood National Forest (Hood River Ranger District)

The Herman Creek Trail (406) heads up the middle of the East Fork Herman Creek valley to classic Douglas-fir old growth and majestic western redcedar. These topographically favored groves escaped major twentieth-century fires that consumed much of the forest in the Columbia Gorge. Although situated in the northeastern corner of the Mark O. Hatfield Wilderness, Herman Creek is easily accessible from Interstate 84.

Primary Old-Growth Features
Classic Douglas-fir old growth; old-growth western redcedar grove

From the trailhead, switchback uphill through an attractive, mature forest, then cross a powerline corridor. Stay left at the junction with the Herman Creek Bridge Trail (406E) a half mile from the trailhead, soon converging with an old road at a minor saddle. Follow the road until reaching a junction with the Wyeth Trail (400) and the Gorton Creek Trail (408) at Herman Camp. Continue straight, soon reaching another trail junction (Nick Eaton Trail, 447). Stay straight again continuing to track a parallel

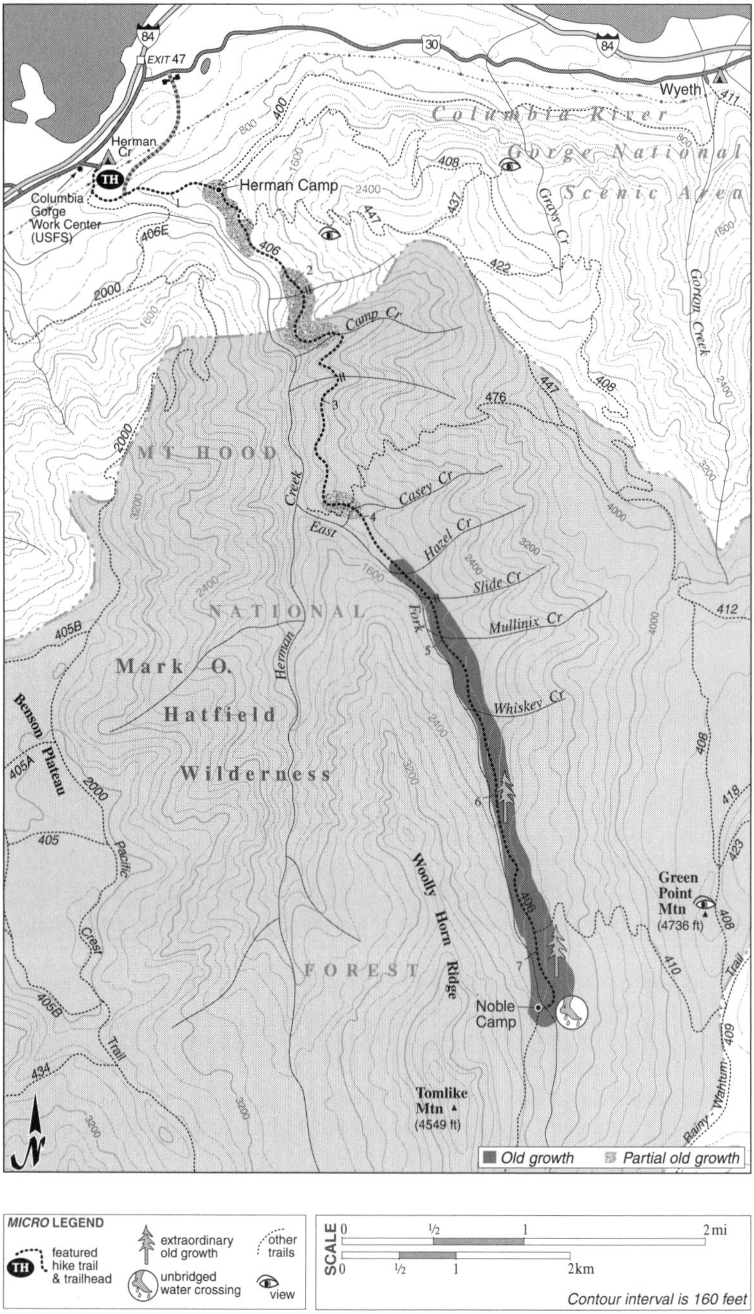
84
EXIT 47
30
84
Wyeth
411
Herman Cr
TH
Herman Camp
Columbia Gorge Work Center (USFS)
406E
406
400
800
1600
2000
2400
3200
4000
Columbia River Gorge National Scenic Area
408
437
447
422
Grays Cr
Gorton Creek
Camp Cr
476
MT HOOD
NATIONAL
FOREST
Casey Cr
East Fork
Herman Creek
Hazel Cr
Slide Cr
Mullinix Cr
Whiskey Cr
412
405B
405A
405
Benson Plateau
Mark O. Hatfield Wilderness
Pacific Crest Trail
Woolly Horn Ridge
Green Point Mtn (4736 ft)
418
423
410
409
Noble Camp
Tomlike Mtn (4549 ft)
434
Rainy - Wahtum Trail
Old growth
Partial old growth
MICRO LEGEND
featured hike trail & trailhead
extraordinary old growth
unbridged water crossing
other trails
view
SCALE
0 ½ 1 2 mi
0 ½ 1 2km
Contour interval is 160 feet

Starflower

course with Herman Creek. Shortly after passing the Nick Eaton Trail the road ends and real trail resumes, about 1.6 miles from the trailhead.

From here the hike takes on more of a wilderness character. The trail steadily ascends, tracing contours into draws where numerous waterfalls splash and sparkle, and then heading out around the interlaced ridges separating each tributary. The Casey Creek Trail (476) intersects the Herman Creek Trail from the left about 4 miles from the trailhead, where a short spur trail downhill to the right leads to a view of the forks of Herman Creek. Many hikers turn back at this point, missing the fine forest ahead.

Once past Hazel Creek the influence of historic fire fades as the trail penetrates farther into this remote patch. Douglas-fir up to 6 feet thick tower over understory western hemlock and Pacific silver fir, while infrequent noble fir diversifies the upper canopy. The Herman Creek Cutoff Trail (410) joins the trail on the left almost 7 miles from the trailhead. Dead ahead stands a glorious grove of shreddy barked western redcedar capable of tolerating the relatively high levels of soil moisture in this area. Soon thereafter the trail crosses the East Fork Herman Creek heading toward Wahtum Lake, leaving the elders behind shortly beyond Noble Camp.

A shorter hiking route to the heart of the old forest is available via the Rainy-Wahtum Trail (409) and the Herman Creek Cutoff Trail (410). This route is much steeper, though, and requires more driving, including almost 11 miles on gravel roads.

How to get there: Turn off Interstate 84 at Cascade Locks (exit 44) 34 miles east of the I-84/I-205 junction. Proceed east through town for 1.5 miles to a stop sign by the I-84 eastbound entrance ramp. Go straight, then left, toward the Oxbow Fish Hatchery, heading northeast parallel to I-84. Turn right onto the Herman Creek Campground access road, 1.7 miles from the stop sign. Trailhead parking is to the right.

Eastbound travelers will want to take exit 47 and head toward the hatchery. The campground access road is on the left a half mile from the freeway.

48 WAHTUM LAKE

Length	**3.6-mile loop**
Difficulty	Easy
Season	Summer to early autumn
Lowest point	3,720 feet
Highest point	4,240 feet
Human imprint	Moderate (campers, hikers, nearby road)
Information	Mount Hood National Forest (Hood River Ranger District)

Primary Old-Growth Feature
Mixed Douglas-fir and true fir old growth

Old-growth forests surround peaceful Wahtum Lake, a glistening gem tucked into the head of the Eagle Creek basin along the eastern margin of the Mark O. Hatfield Wilderness. Douglas-fir and western hemlock, species typically found at low elevations, intermingle with noble fir and Pacific silver fir on the hillslopes above the lake. Portions of three trails in the area can be linked together to form a 3.6-mile loop around the basin.

Prince's pine

Start by stepping down 254 stairs to the lake, then turn right onto the Pacific Crest Trail (PCT, 2000). Hike around the east side of Wahtum Lake through an exemplary stand of true fir and Douglas-fir old growth. Head up across the slope curving westward, first passing a junction with the Herman Creek Trail (406) on the right, then coming to a junction with the Chinidere Mountain Trail (445). Head steeply downhill to the left on the Chinidere Mountain Trail back to Wahtum Lake. Turn left onto the Eagle Creek Trail (440), then rejoin the Pacific Crest Trail for the final leg of the loop.

If the sky is clear, a detour to the top of Chinidere Mountain is well worth the time and energy. Continue straight on the PCT at the junction with the Chinidere Moun-

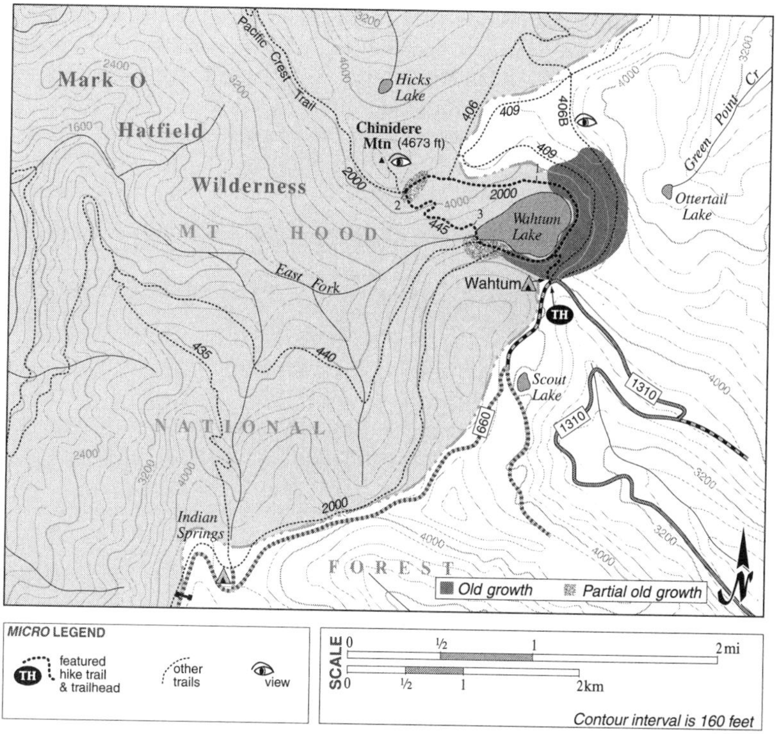

tain Trail and take a right about 100 yards later. Switchback up the slope for less than half a mile to reach the summit for wide-ranging views of Cascade peaks near and far.

Another option to extend the hike is to turn right on the Eagle Creek Trail at the southwest corner of the lake. The first mile or so traverses a fine stand of stately noble fir. The old forest ends at a tributary just over a mile from the lake, but if you continue another three-quarters mile a small streamside pocket of old Douglas-fir and western hemlock along Indian Springs Creek provides a pleasant picnic spot.

Two other trails that depart from the Wahtum Lake trailhead can be linked together to form a 4-mile loop through the same patch of old growth above the lake. From the Wahtum Campground, start off beyond the gate on the old roadbed now known as the Rainy-Wahtum Trail (409). After 2 miles turn right on the Anthill Trail (406B) and head south back toward the trailhead.

How to get there: Head south through the town of Hood River on 12th Street and follow signs toward Odell. Turn left on Tucker Road approximately 2 miles south of Hood River. Cross to the south side of Hood River 2 miles later and immediately bear right toward Tucker Park and Dee. At a junction in 5.7 miles turn right toward Lost Lake. Cross the East Fork Hood River in a third of a mile and bear left onto Lost Lake Road (which becomes Forest Road 13). After 4.8 miles, turn right onto a single-lane, paved road (also FR 13) toward Wahtum Lake. Turn right onto FR 1310 after another 4.3 miles, and 6 miles later park in the Wahtum Lake pullout at the end of the pavement.

49 LOST LAKE

Length ■	3.4-mile loop
Difficulty ■	Easy
Season ■	Spring to autumn
Lowest point ■	3,180 feet
Highest point ■	3,240 feet
Human imprint ■	High (hikers, boaters, large campground)
Information ■	Mount Hood National Forest (Hood River Ranger District)

Majestic old forests border scenic Lost Lake, a popular destination northwest of Mount Hood. A well-used trail circles the lake passing by some particularly impressive western redcedar on the northwest and southeast lakeshores. A large campground on the east shore of the lake and two day-use areas attract hordes of weekend outdoor enthusiasts. A visit during the week, though, is well worthwhile and relatively quiet. Although subject to change, the site is not currently part of the Northwest Forest Pass network and a special day-use fee (currently $5) is charged to enter the developed area. Ask at the entrance station.

Primary Old-Growth Feature
Patches of huge western redcedar

From the day-use trailhead on the north shore of the lake, head counterclockwise on the Lakeshore Trail (656) and immediately enter a stellar old forest. Large western hemlock and western redcedar dominate the first mile, accompanied by Douglas-fir and occasional noble fir. An opening in the forest frames a famous picture-postcard view of snow-draped Mount Hood rising spectacularly over the lake. Pockets of big western redcedar are rooted in seasonally soaked soils near a small marsh by Inlet Creek. Continue around the lake through an old western hemlock forest before entering a younger forest.

Approximately 1.5 miles from the trailhead, the Lakeshore Trail intersects the Huckleberry Mountain Trail (617) a couple hundred yards from

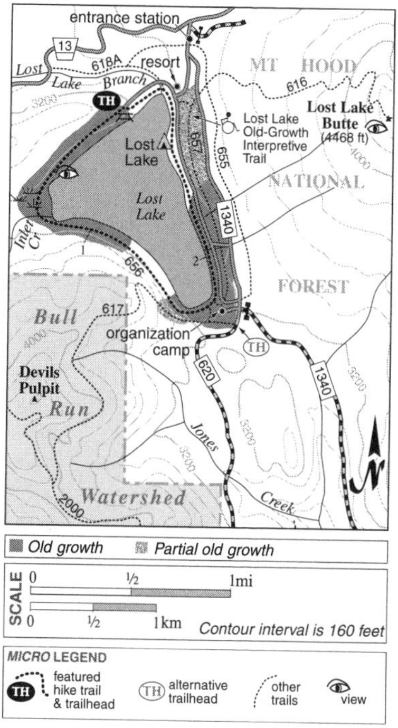

its trailhead near the southern tip of the lake, providing an alternative starting point for the loop. Hikers with an annual Northwest Forest Pass can park at this trailhead and avoid the additional day-use fee.

Another trail intersection lies to the east a couple hundred yards farther up the trail, offering two options for the closing leg of the loop. Stay left along the lakeshore, or turn right to head up toward the organization camp to pick up the southern end of the Lost Lake Old-Growth Interpretive Trail (see sidebar). Both routes are scenic and lead north through the campground back to the trailhead.

How to get there: Head south through the town of Hood River on 12th Street and follow signs toward Odell. Turn left on Tucker Road approximately 2 miles south of Hood River. Cross to the south side of Hood River 2 miles later and immediately bear right toward Tucker Park and Dee. At a junction in 5.7 miles turn right toward Lost Lake. Cross the East Fork Hood River in a third of a mile and bear left onto Lost Lake Road (which becomes Forest Road 13). Continue straight at a junction near Lost Lake 13.4 miles later coming to an entrance station in a couple hundred yards. Follow the signs downhill to the right to park in the picnic and day-use area on the north shore. Stay to the left and head south for a mile or so to reach the alternative trailhead on the south end of the lake.

Vine maple

LOST LAKE OLD-GROWTH INTERPRETIVE TRAIL

The Lost Lake Old-Growth Interpretive Trail runs parallel to the eastern shore of Lost Lake, sandwiched between the lake and Forest Road 1340. The barrier-free, mile-long trail is accessible to wheelchairs (trail grade does not exceed 5 percent). The southern portion of the trail is a single-lane boardwalk with pullouts and is particularly well endowed with colossal western redcedar (6 to 8 feet thick) and regal noble fir. A series of interpretive displays along this portion of the trail explain many features of old-growth forests.

How to get there: Pick up the north end of the trail from the day-use area on the northeastern lakeshore. Turn left at the stop sign by the lake and park by the kiosk on the left a couple hundred yards later.

Wheelchair users may want to start from the south end near the boardwalk. Inquire at the entrance station to verify that there is space in the organization camp parking lot, or, if the station is not staffed, head south on FR 1340 for a mile or so and turn right into the lot.

50 Lolo Pass

Length ■ **5 miles to Preachers Peak; 8 miles to Buck Peak**
Difficulty ■ Moderate to difficult
Season ■ Summer to early autumn
Lowest point ■ 3,420 feet
Highest point ■ 4,751 feet
Human imprint ■ Minimal
Information ■ Mount Hood National Forest (Hood River Ranger District)

Primary Old-Growth Feature
Pacific silver fir and noble fir old growth

Excellent examples of ridgeline old growth straddle the Pacific Crest Trail (PCT, 2000) for much of the 8 miles from Lolo Pass to Buck Peak. Pacific silver fir, noble fir, and mountain hemlock dominate the canopy, joined on warmer sites by Douglas-fir and western hemlock. This easily accessible hike can be enjoyed at any length, although deep forest blocks wide-angle vistas after the first quarter mile until reaching Buck Peak.

The trail rolls along the east side of a prominent ridgeline separating the Bull Run watershed to the west from the West Fork Hood River watershed to the east. Bull Run supplies the city of Portland with drinking water and has been the site of many controversies over the years. To

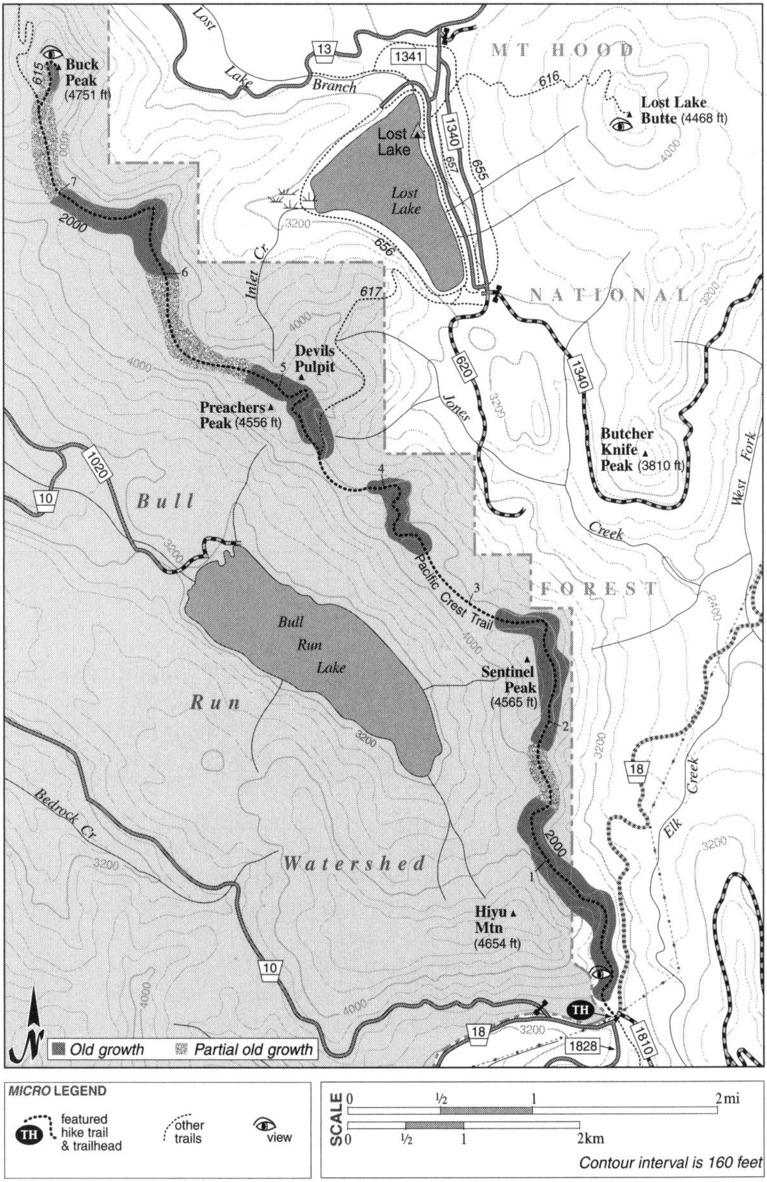

Beargrass

protect water quality public entry to the watershed is prohibited.

Start north on the PCT (2000) out of Lolo Pass immediately passing under crackling powerlines. The trail follows a repeating pattern of striking old forest interrupted by occasional patches of blowdown and young forest. Where the forest is protected from strong winds blowing through the Columbia Gorge by the ridge to the west, excellent examples of high-elevation forest have developed. Stately silver fir and noble fir are particularly memorable in the first stretch of old forest. Strong winds funnel through gaps between high points along the ridge, frequently toppling taller trees and resetting the successional process.

The saddle between Preachers Peak and Devils Pulpit (approximately 5 miles from the trailhead) makes a good turnaround spot for those not planning on going the distance to Buck Peak. Although not visible from the trail, a massive landslide off the southwestern shoulder of Preachers Peak is currently thought to be the origin of the natural dam that forms Bull Run Lake. The Huckleberry Mountain Trail (617) intersects the PCT from the right about a half mile prior to the saddle (4.5 miles from the trailhead). The Huckleberry Mountain Trail leaves the southern end of Lost Lake about 2 miles from this junction, offering an alternative and somewhat shorter route to Buck Peak via Lost Lake.

Old Pacific silver fir and mountain hemlock forests stand astride the PCT much of the way from Preachers Peak to Buck Peak. Take the Buck Peak Trail (615) to reach the summit for a lofty view of Mount Hood and sister peaks to the north.

How to get there: Turn north onto East Lolo Pass Road (Forest Road 18) from U.S. Highway 26 at Zigzag (29 miles southeast of Gresham). Follow FR 18 for 10.6 miles to Lolo Pass. Parking is in a small lot around the corner to the right; the trail is to the left.

LOLO PASS SOUTH

Head south out of Lolo Pass on the Pacific Crest Trail (PCT) for an alternative ridgeline ramble through high-elevation old growth and for dramatic views of Mount Hood. A small, north-facing basin about 1 mile up the PCT harbors a grove of towering Pacific silver fir and some impressive hemlock. Above this basin the trail continues on the ridge top through more old forest until reaching a four-way trail junction (2.75 miles from Lolo Pass). You could return from here, but continuing another half mile straight ahead on the PCT delivers a stunning view of Mount Hood from the open slopes of Bald Mountain. You will want to sit a spell for this one.

51 TILLY JANE

Length	**2.8-mile loop**
Difficulty	Easy
Season	Summer
Lowest point	5,720 feet
Highest point	6,620 feet
Human imprint	Moderate (hikers, climbers)
Information	Mount Hood National Forest (Hood River Ranger District)

Primary Old-Growth Feature
Mountain hemlock and Pacific silver fir old-growth grove

Hikers can experience a fine example of snow-zone old growth on a short loop near timberline on the north side of Mount Hood. Hearty old mountain hemlock and Pacific silver fir not only survive in the deep snows found at this elevation, but grow to impressive dimensions (3 to 4 feet thick) along the lower portions of the loop. Dramatic views of Eliot Glacier and Mount Hood rise in the foreground along upper portions of the loop.

From Tilly Jane Campground head northwest (to the right) toward Cloud Cap Saddle on the Tilly Jane Trail (600A). At Cloud Cap, a half mile from Tilly Jane Campground, turn left (south) and start uphill on the Timberline Trail (600). Climb above the old forest to breathtaking views of the retreating Eliot Glacier, the steep and active lateral moraines left behind, and the north face of Mount Hood. Look for rock cairns to mark the path through the cinders and rocks. Continue on through whitebark pine krummholz (stunted, shrublike trees of the subalpine zone) to a four-way trail junction. Turn left on the Tilly Jane Trail (600A) to head back down toward Tilly Jane Campground.

For those with time and energy to spare, take the Cooper Spur Trail (600B) to the right at the four-way junction. The trails climbs moderately for 2.7 miles before dead-ending. This route is often used by climbers and offers spectacular views of Mount Hood and the surrounding landscape to the east and north.

The return leg of the loop parallels gaping Polallie Canyon, the site of a highly destructive debris-flow in December of 1980. A major, warm rain-on-snow flood triggered a massive landslide and debris-flow that traveled for many miles downstream, ripping out 6 miles of State Route 35 and killing one person. Take a look across the canyon and imagine the immense mass of material unleashed in mere minutes during this event. The trail reenters old forest for the last three-quarters of a mile before returning to the trailhead. This loop can be hiked just as easily in the opposite direction, or from Cloud Cap Saddle.

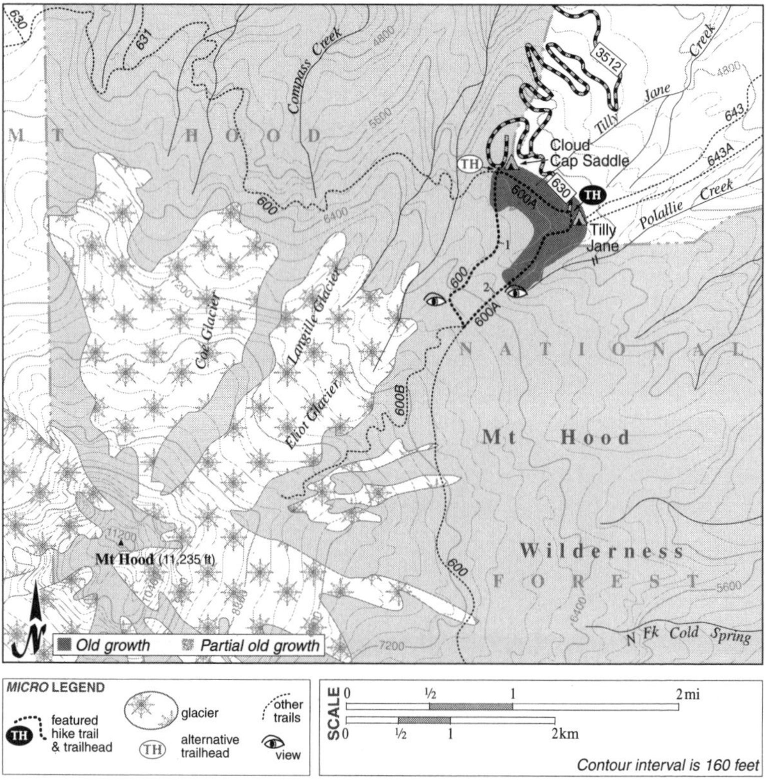

Douglas-fir, Brown Mountain, Rogue River National Forest

Western hemlock, Milk Creek, Mount Baker–Snoqualmie National Forest

Western redcedar, Baker River, Mount Baker-Snoqualmie National Forest

Pacific silver fir, Elbow Lake, Mount Baker-Snoqualmie National Forest

Alaska-cedar, Laughingwater Creek, Mount Rainier National Park

Mountain hemlock, Caldera Rim, Crater Lake National Park

Incense-cedar, Grasshopper Meadow, Umpqua National Forest

Western white pine, Brown Mountain, Rogue River National Forest

Shasta red fir, Red Blanket Creek, Rogue River National Forest

Ponderosa pine, Pine Bench, Umpqua National Forest

Western larch, Fret Creek, Mount Hood National Forest

Noble fir, Yocum Ridge, Mount Hood National Forest

Whitebark pine, Caldera Rim, Crater Lake National Park

Sugar pine, Larison Creek, Willamette National Forest

Pacific yew, Big Swamp, Willamette National Forest

Distinctive Douglas-fir crown, Druid Grove, Mount Baker-Snoqualmie National Forest

Understory western hemlock, Wind River, Gifford Pinchot National Forest

Large snag, Ipsut Creek, Mount Baker-Snoqualmie National Forest

Large down western hemlock, Heather Lake, Wenatchee National Forest

Fire-scorched Douglas-fir, Clear Lake, Willamette National Forest

Fire-scarred ponderosa pine, Metolius River, Deschutes National Forest

Trillium and oxalis, Fall Creek, Willamette National Forest

Oak fern, Cow Creek, Umpqua National Forest

Bunchberry, French Pete Creek, Willamette National Forest

Lobaria oregana lichen, Middle Santiam River, Willamette National Forest

Sulphur shelf fungus, North Fork Sauk River, Mount Baker-Snoqualmie National Forest

Old man's beard

How to get there: From State Route 35 turn west onto Cooper Spur Road approximately 22 miles south of the town of Hood River. Stay left onto Forest Road 3512, travel past Cooper Spur Resort, and stay left again on FR 3512 at a junction 3.3 miles from the highway. Switchback up the mountain until reaching Forest Road 630 to Tilly Jane Campground 12.75 miles from SR 35. Turn left onto FR 630 and park at the campground a half mile later. Staying right on FR 3512 will take you up to Cloud Cap Campground and an alternative trailhead.

52 FIFTEENMILE CREEK

Length ■ **10.2-mile loop**
Difficulty ■ Moderate
Season ■ Late spring to autumn
Lowest point ■ 2,750 feet
Highest point ■ 4,640 feet
Human imprint ■ Moderate (mountain bikes, roads, past timber harvest)
Information ■ Mount Hood National Forest (Barlow Ranger District)

Primary Old-Growth Feature
Ponderosa pine old growth

Impressive groves of old ponderosa pine still stand east of Mount Hood along the bluffs above Fifteenmile Creek. Douglas-fir, grand fir, and other conifers mingle with burnt-orange pines in the much drier conditions prevailing east of the Cascade crest. The Cedar Creek Trail joins the Fifteenmile Trail in two places forming a 10.2-mile loop through the finest

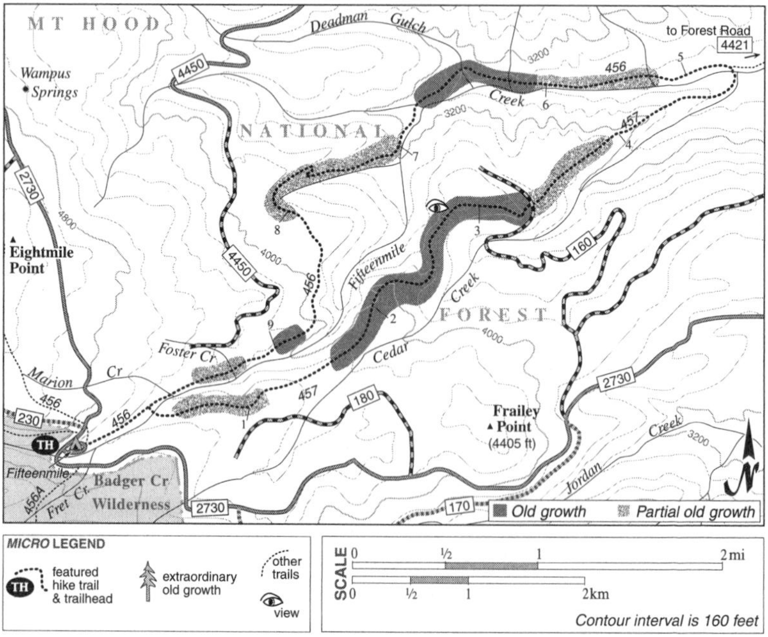

forest remaining in the area. This loop is also popular with mountain bikers, resulting in localized trail erosion.

Start downhill on the Fifteenmile Trail (456) from Fifteenmile Campground. Turn right onto the Cedar Creek Trail (457) in about half a mile to cross the creek and climb to the ridge separating Fifteenmile Creek from Cedar Creek. Follow the ridgeline trail northeast coming to an extensive stand of old ponderosa pine and Douglas-fir approximately 1.5 miles from the trailhead. For the next 2 miles, park-like pines reign over a sparse herb and shrub understory in some places, and overtop dense thickets of younger trees in other spots.

Continue steeply down the spine of the ridge until rejoining the Fifteenmile Trail just across the bridge over Fifteenmile Creek, about 4.75 miles from the trailhead. This point can also be reached from the lower trailhead for the Fifteenmile Trail on Forest Road 4421. The trail leads up the north bank of Fifteenmile Creek through a scenic canyon for 3.3 miles, in scrub white oak for the first mile or so, then in a mixed-age stand with scattered large ponderosa pine, Douglas-fir, and grand fir. A few big western redcedar hug the stream.

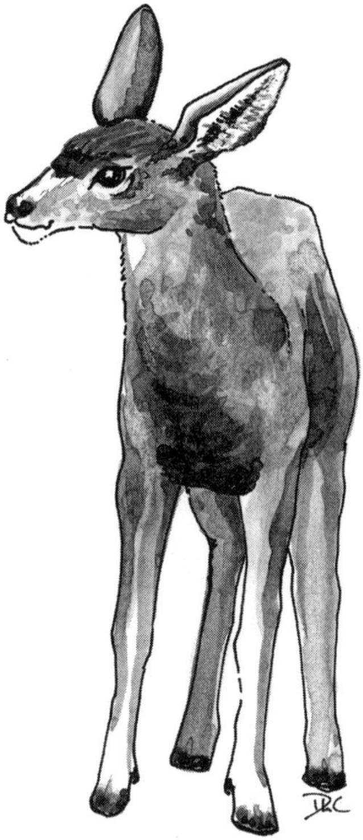

Mule deer

Follow the Fifteenmile Trail up the north bank of Fifteenmile Creek through patches of older trees for 2.5 miles, including some over 400 years old. Then, switchback up to a secondary ridgeline where scattered large ponderosa pine grace a relatively open, grassy site. The trail then curves southward and reenters the forest. Turn left onto an old logging road about 8 miles from the trailhead and enter a ponderosa pine plantation. The trail leaves the old roadbed and comes to some cliffs on the edge of a picturesque gorge a mile later. Follow the trail southwest to complete the loop.

How to get there: From State Route 35 turn northeast onto the Dufur Mill Road (Forest Road 44) about 25 miles south of the town of Hood River (13.3 miles north of U.S. Highway 26/SR 35 junction). Turn right onto FR 4420 in 8.5 miles, then veer left onto FR 2730 in another 2 miles. The trailhead is on the left in Fifteenmile Campground 1.9 miles later.

FRET CREEK

Pockets of veteran western larch, a unique deciduous conifer, dot the hillslopes above Fret Creek. The orange-barked larches are quite distinctive, especially when the soft green clusters of needles turn yellow in the fall. The thick, fire-resistant bark of old larches, and the ability of young larches to grow rapidly in open sunlight, earned western larch a niche of its own in the historic fire cycle. Larch seems to fare particularly well on higher elevation, north-facing slopes of the east side.

Head south up Fret Creek on a branch of the Fifteenmile Trail (456A) found just east of Fifteenmile Campground off FR 2730. After a steep beginning, the trail climbs on a moderate grade for 2 miles until it intersects the Divide Trail (458). Turn left on the Divide Trail and ascend to the ridge for great views of the Badger Creek Wilderness and major Cascade peaks. Watch your step around the cliffs.

53 Barlow Pass

Length	**4 miles one way**
Difficulty	Moderate
Season	Summer
Lowest point	4,160 feet
Highest point	5,280 feet
Human imprint	Minimal
Information	Mount Hood National Forest (Zigzag Ranger District)

Primary Old-Growth Feature
Excellent noble fir, Pacific silver fir, and mountain hemlock old growth

The portion of the Pacific Crest Trail (PCT, 2000) heading north from Barlow Pass features prime old growth on the south flank of Mount Hood. The fragmented noble fir forest found in the vicinity of Barlow Pass and nearby Bennett Pass was one of the finest in Oregon prior to clearcutting, and still boasts some noteworthy stands. The hike begins on the edge of the noble fir forest, and ascends from there into a Pacific silver fir and mountain hemlock forest, and finally emerges in a subalpine zone where whitebark pine and subalpine fir persevere. A stunning view of Mount Hood caps the hike.

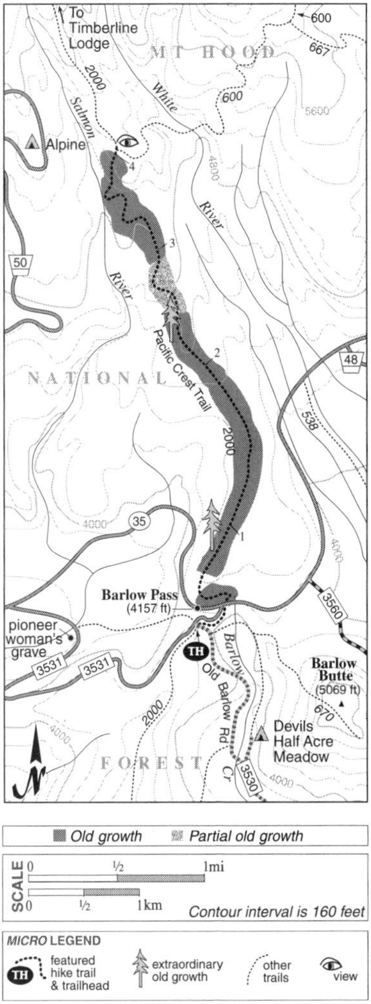

Pick up the PCT behind the signboard on the east side of the parking area and head left back toward the highway. After a quarter mile, cross State Route 35 on a right diagonal to pick up the trail by the end of the guardrail. The trail bisects a relatively small clearcut one-half mile later, and then enters a glorious stand of noble fir and Douglas-fir. The long, seemingly taper-free, noble fir trunks tower high overhead on this productive site.

Pacific silver fir and mountain hemlock gradually replace noble fir and Douglas-fir as the trail gains elevation, leaving the species behind approximately 2 miles from the trailhead. Continue up the PCT through excellent examples of high-elevation old growth to timberline where islands and peninsulas of subalpine fir and whitebark pine intersperse with mountain meadows. Consider the energy expended climbing up as the purchase price for a front-row seat to a first-rate mountain spectacle; dead ahead lie glaciers, deep valleys, moraines, and waterfalls dancing down the flanks of ice-capped Mount Hood.

Return as you came, or continue climbing north on the PCT another 2 miles or so to historic Timberline Lodge. With a little help from your friends and a shuttle, an alternative is to start at the lodge for a 6-mile, mostly downhill, one-way hike to Barlow Pass.

How to get there: From State Route 35 at Barlow Pass (2.5 miles east of the U.S. Highway 26/SR 35 junction), turn right onto Forest Road 3531. Barlow Pass trailhead parking is on the right a quarter mile down FR 3531.

To reach Timberline Lodge, head northeast on a well-signed, paved

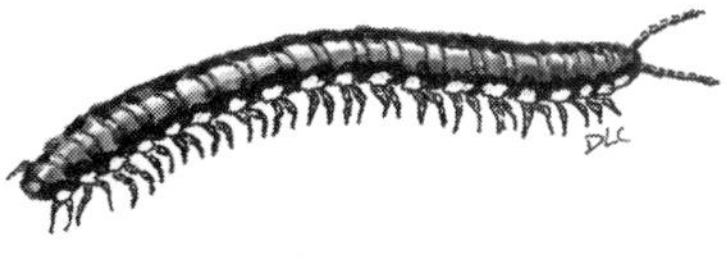

Yellow spotted millipede

road out of Government Camp approximately 2.4 miles west of the US 26/ SR 35 junction. The lodge is at the end of the road 6 miles later.

BARLOW BUTTE

Outstanding old-growth noble fir continues on the south side of State Route 35 draped across the northwest shoulder of Barlow Butte. From the Barlow Pass trailhead, proceed downhill to the east on the Barlow Butte Trail (670), initially on the Old Barlow Road (Forest Road 3530) before splitting off to the left. Continue on the Barlow Butte Trail all the way to the top of Barlow Butte. The second mile of the trail climbs on a very steep grade through enchanting noble fir, Douglas-fir, western hemlock, and Pacific silver fir old growth. The noble fir is especially impressive with its unique blue-hued crown and long, massive trunks. The surrounding landscape and high Cascade peaks reveal themselves at the top where you emerge into beautiful open country.

54 BOULDER CREEK

Length	**7.5-mile loop**
Difficulty	Moderate
Season	Summer
Lowest point	4,060 feet
Highest point	5,520 feet
Human imprint	Moderate (roads)
Information	Mount Hood National Forest (Barlow Ranger District)

Primary Old-Growth Features
Wide variety of old-growth types; impressive eastside Douglas-fir

Upper Boulder Creek basin holds some of the finest old growth left on the east side of Mount Hood National Forest. Segments of three trails and a road can be linked together forming a 7.5-mile loop through an ever-changing assemblage of forest types. Alternatively, hikers can take a half-mile jaunt up to Boulder Lake or down to Boulder Creek, in fine old forest in either direction.

Start uphill (west) on the Boulder Lake Trail (463) and immediately enter an old-growth stand dominated by noble fir and Douglas-fir 4 to 5 feet thick. Two trail junctions are reached just prior to arrival at pretty Boulder Lake less than a half mile from the trailhead. The first (463A) extends a half mile to Little Boulder Lake; the second (463B) loops around cliff-lined Boulder Lake, rejoining the Boulder Lake Trail by the northeast corner of the lake.

To continue the loop, head north past the lake over a minor ridge quickly coming to Kane Springs where hefty noble fir, Engelmann spruce, Pacific silver fir, and mountain hemlock cluster nearby. Switchback up the hill to

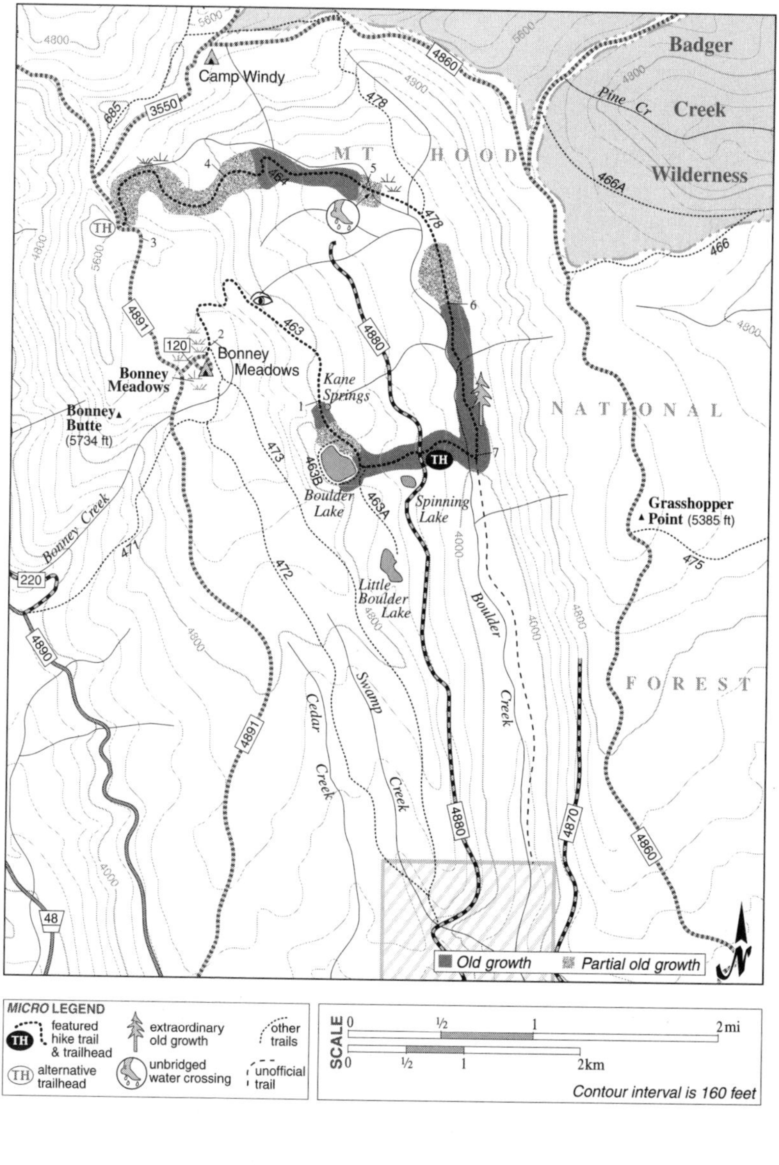

Bonney Meadows and campground. Find your way through the campground out to Forest Road 4891 and take a right. Follow the road for a mile, coming to the Crane Prairie Trail (464) on your right.

Head downhill passing through a 300-year-old mountain hemlock and Pacific silver fir forest. The trail steepens along the spine of a narrow ridge a mile later where hefty Douglas-fir 4 to 5 feet thick crown the ridgeline. The trail soon flattens out, first crossing the stream on the right side of the ridge, then crossing the larger stream on the left side of the ridge. Once across the stream the trail enters a small marshy area populated by stout Engelmann spruce. If the trail is underwater in places just look for the cut ends of logs and flagging to find your way to drier ground.

Turn right onto the Crane Creek Trail (478) a half mile past the stream crossing (5.5 miles from the trailhead) and soon enter an old Engelmann spruce, Pacific silver fir, and noble fir forest. Look for a fat, solitary black cottonwood a half mile past the trail junction. Douglas-fir, western white pine, and western larch replace the spruce and true firs as the trail loses elevation. Several immense, fire-scorched Douglas-fir 6 to 7 feet in diameter squeeze the trail near a talus slope where groves of quaking aspen tremble in the breeze. Turn right back onto the Boulder Lake Trail (463) shortly thereafter, crossing a trail bridge back over Boulder Creek and heading uphill through more old forest for the final half mile.

Another option for the hardy hiker is to continue downstream on the Crane Creek Trail (478). The trail is no longer maintained below the trail

Belted kingfisher

junction, is hard to follow in places, and is becoming littered with large down logs. Nevertheless, determined hikers will find a wonderful streamside forest dense with big Douglas-fir all the way down to the boundary with a section of private land (2.25 miles).

How to get there: Turn southeast onto FR 48 from State Route 35 approximately 4.5 miles northeast of the U.S. Highway 26/SR 35 junction (33.5 miles south of the town of Hood River). Follow FR 48 for 14 miles and turn left onto FR 4880. Stay on FR 4880, bearing right where the road becomes gravel-surfaced after 2.5 miles. Trailhead parking is on the left 4 miles later.

55 OLD SALMON RIVER TRAIL

Length	**2.4 miles one way**
Difficulty	Easy
Season	Year round
Lowest point	1,450 feet
Highest point	1,600 feet
Human imprint	High (hikers, campers, mountain bikers, paved road)
Information	Mount Hood National Forest (Zigzag Ranger District)

Primary Old-Growth Feature
Immense Douglas-fir and western redcedar

Easy access from Portland to giant trees and a beautiful river practically guarantees company on the Old Salmon River Trail (742A). This well-known and heavily used trail is an easy stroll through striking old forest, and suitable for walkers of all ages. Low elevations mean the trail is generally open year round. The trail follows the east bank of the Salmon River in a narrow roaded strip nearly surrounded by the Salmon-Huckleberry Wilderness. The nearby river provides rock-tossing and feet-dipping opportunities for kids large and small.

The trail travels through a lush riverside forest dominated by large Douglas-fir and western redcedar most of the way. The larger redcedar reach 8 feet or more in diameter. Portions of the forest show evidence of a mid-1800s era fire where mature Douglas-fir are common. Pockets of deciduous red alder and bigleaf maple intermix with towering conifers.

The trail briefly joins the road about 1.3 miles from the lower trailhead, and then comes to the Green Canyon Campground in another half mile. A half mile beyond the campground, the trail ends where it intersects the

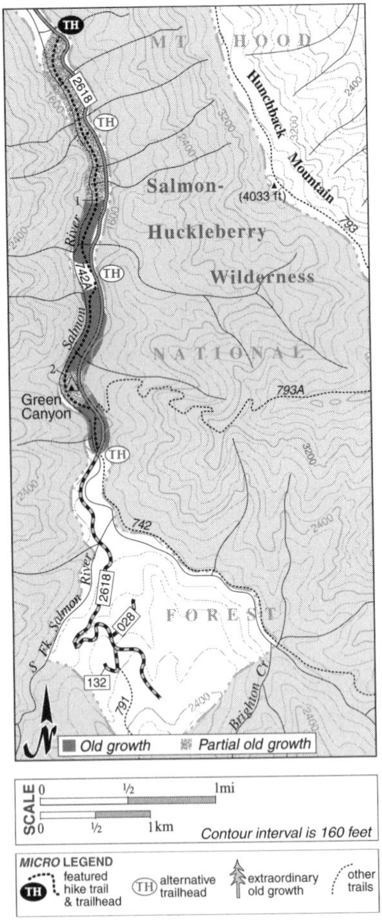

Salmon River Road. Each of these spots provides an option for a shorter hike, or a potential drop-off point for a one-way hike with a shuttle.

On the south side of the road, the Salmon River Trail (742) continues another dozen miles upriver into the Salmon-Huckleberry Wilderness. The trail follows a fairly level grade near the river for the first couple of miles, and then veers upslope away from the river through mostly younger forest. A nice patch of old growth stands on a riverside terrace below the trail less than a half mile from the road.

How to get there: Turn south onto the Salmon River Road (Forest Road 2618) from U.S. Highway 26 in Zigzag approximately 29 miles southeast of Gresham. Park on the right just after entering the national forest 2.7 miles from US 26. The trail can also be accessed in several places farther up FR 2618, including from Green Canyon Campground (approximately 4.6 miles from the highway) and by the Salmon River bridge (5 miles from the highway).

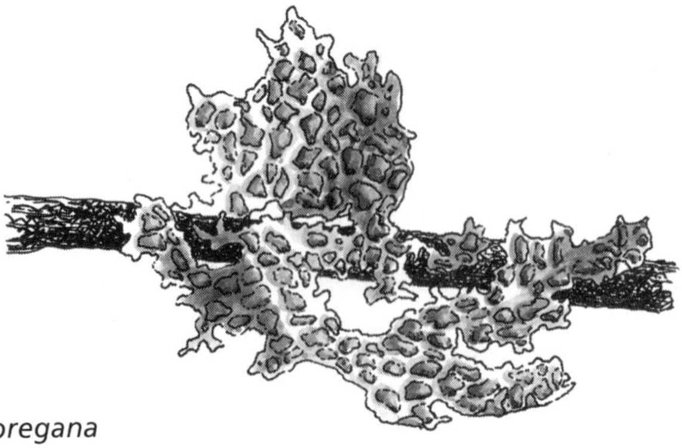

Loberia oregana

56 MEMALOOSE LAKE

Length	**1.3 miles one way**
Difficulty	Moderate
Season	Late spring to autumn
Lowest point	3,600 feet
Highest point	4,120 feet
Human imprint	Moderate (nearby clearcuts, hikers)
Information	Mount Hood National Forest (Clackamas River Ranger District)

Primary Old-Growth Feature
Rich noble fir forest

An isolated fragment of stunning old forest in the Clackamas River watershed shelters delightful Memaloose Lake. Surrounded by clearcuts, stately noble fir and Douglas-fir touch the heavens in this spectacular old-growth island. A trip to Memaloose Lake from Portland makes a perfect half-day outing.

While the lake is the destination of choice for most hikers, the journey to the lake is exceptional. Wind your way up toward the lake on the Memaloose Lake Trail (515) through a wall of wood stacked with 3 to 5-foot-thick noble fir and Douglas-fir. Relatively warm, well-drained soils near the lower elevational limit for noble fir support a lush herbaceous ground cover and a densely stocked forest of towering titans. Switchback up to old-growth rimmed Memaloose Lake for a relaxing break 1.3 miles from the trailhead.

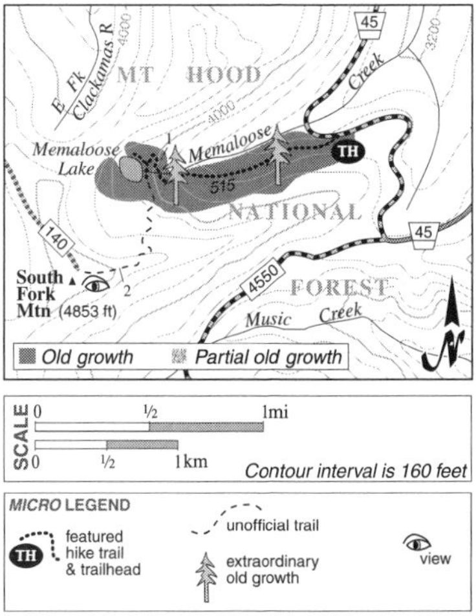

The trail continues another mile to the top of South Fork Mountain, but the trail is no longer maintained past the lake. Switchback up across the basin headwall through large Pacific silver fir and western hemlock, then swing right onto the ridgeline. Grand views encompassing all the major Cascade peaks from Mount Rainier to the Three Sisters can be had from the mountaintop, once the site of a fire lookout. This point can also be reached by vehicle via Forest Road 140 (take FR 4540 from FR 45), providing a shuttle option for a one-way, downhill hike.

How to get there: Turn right onto Memaloose Road (FR 45) from State Route 224 approximately 9 miles southeast of Estacada. Follow FR 45 for 11 miles where the road becomes gravel surfaced at a junction with FR 4550. Stay right on FR 45 and park at the trailhead in eight-tenths of a mile.

Oxalis

57 CLACKAMAS RIVER

Length ■ **8.1 miles one way**
Difficulty ■ Moderate
Season ■ Year round
Lowest point ■ 880 feet
Highest point ■ 1,360 feet
Human imprint ■ Moderate (near highway, powerlines)
Information ■ Mount Hood National Forest (Clackamas River Ranger District)

Primary Old-Growth Features
Beautiful western redcedar glades; huge Douglas-fir

The Clackamas River Trail (715) is a year-round wonder tracing the cliffs and riverbanks south of the river for just over 8 miles. Low-elevation old growth adorns the hiker-only trail over most of its length, attaining peak conditions in two particularly enjoyable groves. Rewarding as an out-and-back hike for most any length, the trail can also be hiked one way with a shuttle. Although not overly difficult at most times, unbridged stream crossings can be problematic during high stream flows in winter.

Head upriver from the Fish Creek trailhead, on an old road at first, but soon coming to an older forest abutting a true trail. The trail then climbs above riverside cliffs for a mile or so before returning to the shore. The Bowl Fire burned adjacent to portions of the first couple miles of trail in September 2002, consuming understory vegetation and killing scattered large trees.

Highlights of the first half of the trail include a particularly beautiful spot about 2.5 miles from the trailhead where massive western redcedar and Douglas-fir 4 to 6 feet thick shade a rich, riparian grotto. The trail reaches a short, side trail to Pup Creek Falls just under 4 miles from the trailhead, a logical stopping point for a moderate two-way hike. Take the path to the right just before the stream to view an impressive three-step falls, well over 100 feet tall.

The trail continues upriver through younger forest for another 1.3 miles to The Narrows, where the river churns through a constricting gorge. Just beyond The Narrows the trail gently rises onto a deep-soiled bench harboring a fine fleet of immense western redcedar and Douglas-fir 4 to 6 feet in girth. A lush swordfern and oxalis understory perfectly complements the fluted base and shreddy bark of the redcedars.

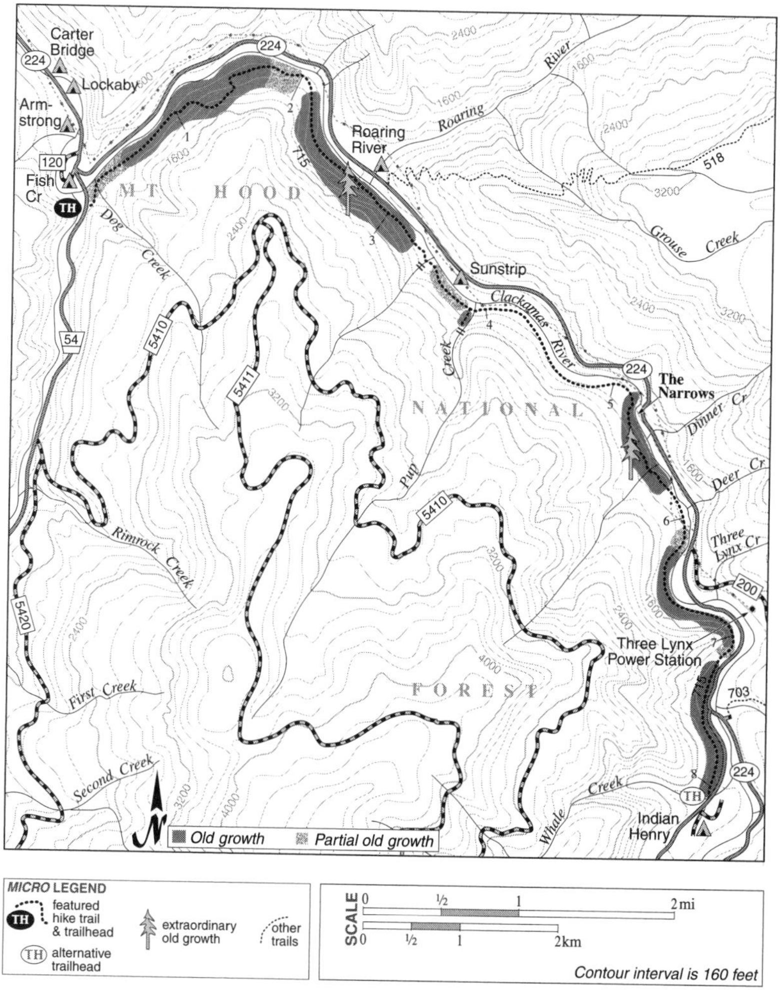

From here the trail passes under a long-distance powerline and then reenters patchy old forest for the last couple miles. Scorched bark on older trees from past fires helps explain the highly variable pattern of large trees over this portion of the trail. Minor waterfalls dash over riverside cliffs in places. Trailhead parking at Indian Henry Campground provides an alternative starting point for the hike, or a potential shuttle pick-up point. The southern trailhead is a few more miles up State Route 224 than the western trailhead; consequently, this end of the trail receives less use.

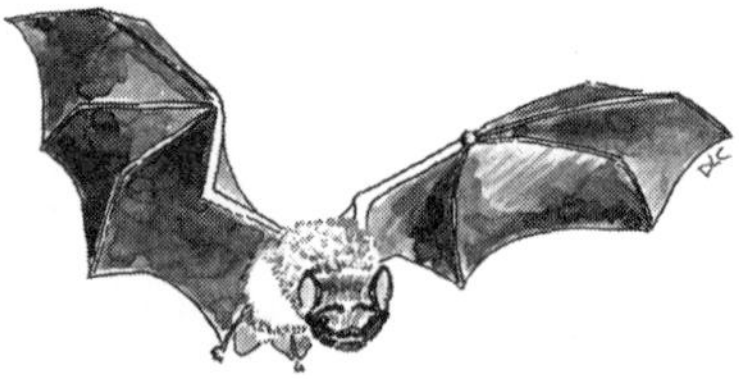

Hoary bat

How to get there: To reach the Fish Creek trailhead, turn right onto Fish Creek Road (Forest Road 54) from SR 224 approximately 14.9 miles southeast of Estacada. Park in the large lot on the right by the boat launch just after crossing the bridge; the trail is to the left across FR 54.

To reach the southern trailhead by Indian Henry Campground, continue another 6.6 miles up SR 224 and turn right onto FR 4620 (signed "Indian Henry Campground") just prior to a bridge. Park on the right in a half mile.

58 RIVERSIDE TRAIL

Length ■ **4 miles one way**
Difficulty ■ Easy to moderate
Season ■ Year round
Lowest point ■ 1,410 feet
Highest point ■ 1,480 feet
Human imprint ■ High (hikers, anglers, campers, nearby road)
Information ■ Mount Hood National Forest (Clackamas River Ranger District)

Primary Old-Growth Feature
Douglas-fir and western redcedar old-growth groves

The Riverside Trail (723) stays true to its name, remaining close to the east side of the Clackamas River for most of its length. Excellent examples of lowland old growth and impressive western redcedar are located at opposite ends of the trail. Though designated as a national recreation trail, the Forest Service no longer allows parking at the logical start-

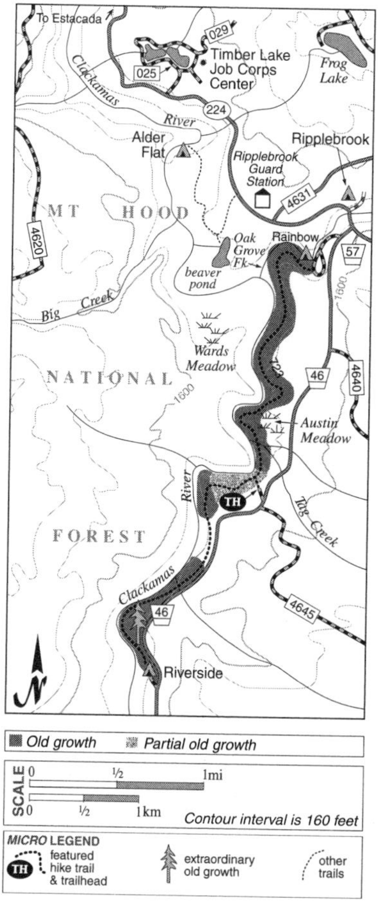

ing points for the hike in the two campgrounds at either end of the trail. The official trailhead is now located midway along the path.

A mossy old grove of Douglas-fir and western redcedar is tucked in the corner formed by the confluence of the Oak Grove Fork and the Clackamas River by the northern end of the trail. Heading south, the path soon climbs to the top of a shoreline cliff with a sweeping view up the Clackamas River. From here the path heads south along the Clackamas, alternately swinging away from the river through beautiful old forest, then veering back to the rims of the riverside bluffs. A short spur trail on the left about 2.5 miles south of Rainbow Campground leads to the official trailhead.

A little farther south the path curves away from the river, in places nearly abutting the main road. Then the trail swerves riverward tracing the inside line of a graceful bend in the river. Here, on a rich riparian terrace, stands the finest old-growth forest of the hike. Majestic Douglas-fir and western redcedar reach 5 feet in diameter, with occasional old-timers attaining even greater dimensions. Coming out of the curve the trail dead-ends in Riverside Campground.

The Clackamas River is a good place to witness a natural phenomenon common to many Northwest rivers. Adult steelhead trout return to

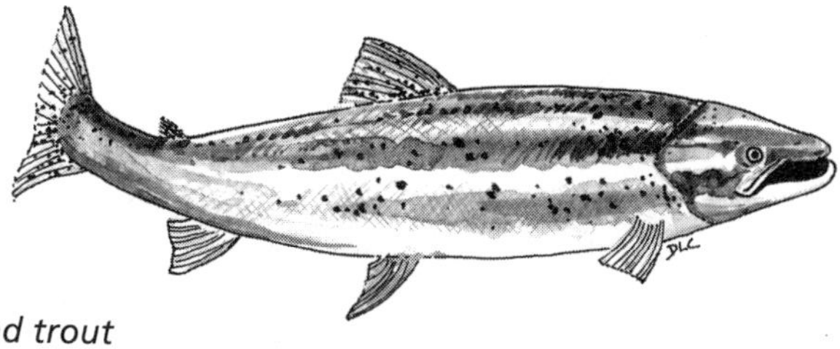

Steelhead trout

the upper river from the ocean in late summer to deposit and fertilize eggs in riverbed gravels, splashing and churning in an annual ritual of regeneration.

How to get there: Turn right into the official trailhead from Forest Road 46 about 2.3 miles south of the Ripplebrook Guard Station (approximately 26.8 miles southwest of Estacada, and 1.7 miles south of Rainbow Campground).

ALDER FLAT

Another option for an easy old-growth hike in the area is to amble along the 1-mile trail to Alder Flat through big Douglas-fir, western hemlock, and western redcedar. The trail skirts a beaver pond not far from the trailhead. The trail dead-ends in a stand of red alder by the river, where a walk-in campground provides an attractive option to the many car campgrounds along the Clackamas River.

How to get there: Park on the south side of State Route 224 about eight-tenths of a mile past the Timber Lake Job Corps Center (a quarter-mile west of the Ripplebrook Guard Station).

59 HOT SPRINGS FORK

Length ■ **1.5 miles one way to Bagby Hot Springs; 8 miles to Silver King Lake**
Difficulty ■ Easy to difficult
Season ■ Spring to autumn
Lowest point ■ 2,080 feet
Highest point ■ 4,160 feet
Human imprint ■ Very high to hot springs; minimal beyond hot springs
Information ■ Mount Hood National Forest (Clackamas River Ranger District)

Primary Old-Growth Features
Massive Douglas-fir and western redcedar on lower stretch; huge hemlock near Silver King Lake

The Bagby Trail (544) delivers attractive old growth in servings suitable for an easy streamside stroll, or for an all-day venture up to Silver King Lake and back. The trail parallels the course of the Hot Springs Fork, one of three major streams draining the north side of the Bull of the Woods Wilderness. The Bull of the Woods is the last large patch of unfragmented, low-elevation old growth left in the southern end of the Mount Hood National Forest, a condition that finally brought this primeval forest wilderness designation in 1984.

Although the old forest along the trail is fantastic, most users are here for another reason: the well-known Bagby Hot Springs. The hot springs lie about 1.5 miles up the trail, and from the parking lot to the springs the trail sometimes resembles a city sidewalk. Even so, the walk is quite pleasant and use of the hot springs has evolved over the years to a relatively clean and comfortable environment as these things go. If you are planning on a soak, expect a wait and remember these rules: no soap, no music, and no unleashed pets. Clothing is optional.

Most of the old growth in the area appears to have regenerated about 300 years ago following a large forest fire. Douglas-fir and western hemlock 3 to 4 feet thick and of that age dominate the forest. However, the segment of trail stretching from the bridge (a little over a mile from the trailhead) for another mile upstream passes by a more open forest with scattered Douglas-fir reaching 6 feet in diameter. Still larger veterans reach 8 feet thick in places, including in the vicinity of the hot springs.

Visitor use drops off rapidly above the springs, although some soakers wander up the trail another third of a mile to Shower Creek. Aptly named, this tiny tributary drops over trailside rocks giving well-positioned travelers another refreshing, though much cooler, soaking. The trail enters the wilderness shortly after Shower Creek.

A mile or so above the hot springs the forest becomes more varied. Small patches of old growth, areas that blew down during a 1990 windstorm, and younger forest alternate for about 2 miles before settling back in to a long unbroken stretch of old forest above Betty Creek. As you near Silver King Lake, the trail enters a particularly striking stand of enormous trees 4 to 6 feet thick, including some outstanding western hemlock. Take a right at a junction about 7.5 miles from the trailhead onto a short spur trail uphill to quaint little Silver King Lake. With a shuttle, hikers can start on the Whetstone Trail (546) and connect with the upper end of the Bagby Trail for an excellent 13-mile, one-way hike down the Hot Springs Fork.

How to get there: From Forest Road 46, approximately 4.2 miles south of the Ripplebrook Guard Station (29 miles southeast of Estacada), turn right onto FR 63. Approximately 3.5 miles later turn right onto FR 70. Park on the left at the Bagby Hot Springs parking lot in 6 miles.

To reach the Whetstone trailhead, continue on FR 70 past the hot springs parking lot, staying right on FR 7030 at a junction with FR 7020 in

Oregon slender salamander

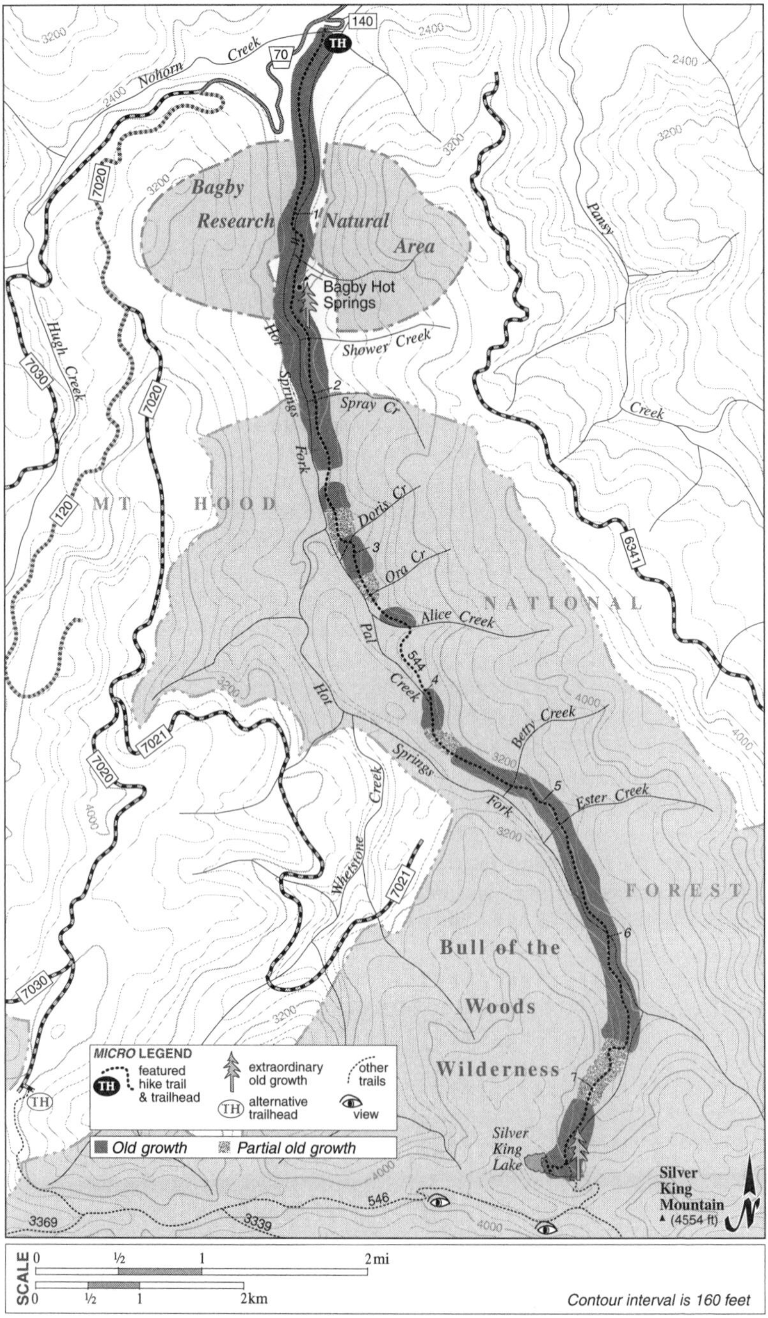

140
70
TH
Nohorn Creek
7020
Bagby Research Natural Area
Bagby Hot Springs
Shower Creek
Hot Springs Fork
Spray Cr
Pansy Creek
Hugh Creek
7030
120
MT HOOD NATIONAL FOREST
Doris Cr
Ora Cr
Alice Creek
Pal Creek
544
6341
Betty Creek
Ester Creek
Whetstone Creek
7021
Bull of the Woods Wilderness
Silver King Lake
Silver King Mountain
(4554 ft)
546
3369
3339
MICRO LEGEND
featured hike trail & trailhead
extraordinary old growth
other trails
alternative trailhead
view
Old growth
Partial old growth
SCALE
0 ½ 1 2 mi
0 ½ 1 2 km
Contour interval is 160 feet

1.4 miles. Then stay left on FR 7030 at the junction with FR 7040 about 1.6 miles later. Follow FR 7030 for 5.5 miles until it ends at FR 7020. Turn right and follow FR 7020 for three-quarters of a mile, then turn left on FR 028. The trailhead is one-tenth of a mile down this short spur.

60 DICKEY CREEK

Length ■ **3 miles one way**
Difficulty ■ Moderate, with occasional very steep pitches
Season ■ Spring to autumn
Lowest point ■ 2,540 feet
Highest point ■ 2,960 feet
Human imprint ■ Minimal
Information ■ Mount Hood National Forest (Clackamas River Ranger District)

Primary Old-Growth Feature
Douglas-fir and western hemlock old growth

The Dickey Creek Trail (553) accesses the northeastern corner of the Bull of the Woods Wilderness, a unique, low-elevation, old-growth stronghold. This is a quiet, little-noticed nook of the wilderness, perfect for a few hours of solitude and contemplation. Trailside wonders include beautiful lowland old growth and a strangely distorted forest.

The trail starts off fairly gently through an older plantation, and then the tread steepens, precipitously in places, as it enters a large earthflow. Many standing trees are tipped in a variety of directions in response to this slow-motion phenomenon. Deep-seated earthflows typically move at nearly imperceptible rates, ranging from fractions of an inch to a few inches per year, enough to tilt trees but not topple them immediately. The jumbled and hummocky surface of the ground provides an additional indicator of earthflow activity and causes the trail to follow an uneven course. Upon close inspection, some of the apparently dry stream drainages turn out to be tension cracks between portions of the ground moving at different rates.

Red alder

The top of the earthflow can be

viewed at a distance from the road to the lower Elk Lake Creek trailhead. The brown line visible to the west is a rock scarp face along a geologic discontinuity between hard rock along the ridgeline and the landslide. A look at the map reveals that the landslide has gradually pushed Dickey Creek to the east, feeding the stream with gravel, sediment, and trees as the toe of the slide erodes during high streamflows.

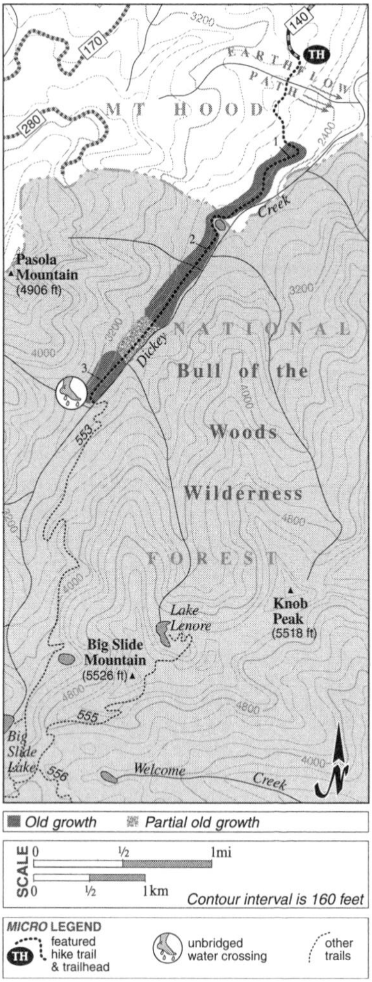

Old growth begins in earnest after leaving the landslide and continues for approximately 2 miles. Dazzling Douglas-fir 5 feet and larger in thickness mingle with smaller western hemlock and western redcedar. Individual trees are larger near streams where soils are deeper and well watered.

A few big red alders thrive in a wet meadowy area by a small pond, adding diversity to the otherwise coniferous forest. Red alder is a relatively short-lived species (usually dead by age 100) typically found near streams and on lower slopes in the Oregon Cascades. These 2 to 3 feet thick specimens are near the upper limit of diameter growth for forest-grown red alder.

The trail briefly climbs around a rock outcrop about 3 miles from the trailhead, and then drops down to a final patch of old growth before reaching a bridgeless crossing of Dickey Creek. The stream crossing marks an excellent lunch spot and a sensible turnaround point for most day hikers. The trail does continue though, turning steeply uphill through mostly younger forest on a tack toward Big Slide Lake and multiple trail junctions on the distant ridgeline.

How to get there: From Forest Road 46, approximately 4.2 miles south of the Ripplebrook Guard Station (29 miles southeast of Estacada), turn right onto FR 63. Turn right 5.6 miles later onto FR 6340. Turn left onto FR 140 after 2.8 miles, then stay right on FR 164 at an unsigned junction 1 mile later. Park at the end of the road in a half mile.

61 ELK LAKE CREEK

Length ■ **5.1 miles one way**
Difficulty ■ Moderate to difficult
Season ■ Spring to autumn
Lowest point ■ 2,480 feet
Highest point ■ 2,800 feet
Human imprint ■ Minimal
Information ■ Mount Hood National Forest (Clackamas River Ranger District)

Primary Old-Growth Feature
Large Douglas-fir and western redcedar

Old-growth-lined Elk Lake Creek drains the southern portion of the Bull of the Woods Wilderness into the north-flowing Collawash River. The trail parallels the creek from Elk Lake nearly to its confluence with the river, in and out of pockets of large Douglas-fir and western redcedar the entire distance. Three bridgeless creek crossings can be boulder-hopped in the summer or early fall, but will likely require a wade when flows are higher. Hikers starting from either end are likely headed for the destination old growth near the confluence of Battle Creek and Elk Lake Creek, site of the old Battle Creek Shelter.

The lower trailhead is easier to access and provides a more interesting route. From here the Elk Lake Creek Trail (559) heads upstream on the northern shore, entering old forest shortly after leaving the trailhead plantation. The trail continues along the creek all the way to the old shelter, crossing and then recrossing Elk Lake Creek, and then crossing Battle Creek just before reaching the shelter site. Streamside vistas of crystalline Elk Lake Creek become more frequent above the first stream crossing. Bigger trees flourish along slope bottoms near the stream where the soil is thicker; diameters diminish where the trail swings upslope. High and mighty Douglas-fir and western redcedar, some reaching 5 to 6 feet in diameter, tower over visitors on the flats where Battle Creek, Mother Lode Creek, and Elk Lake Creek join near the former shelter 5 miles from the trailhead. Although now demolished, the shelter site is still popular as a wilderness camping spot.

American dipper

An alternative route to the shelter site, or a one-way hike downhill over the entire length of the trail, entails starting at the upper trailhead by Elk Lake. Enormous Douglas-fir 4 to 6 feet thick provide a wilderness welcome as soon as you hit the trail. Continue downhill parallel to Elk Lake Creek for about 4 miles to reach the grove of elegant elders near the old shelter. Without a high-clearance vehicle add 1.5 miles each way to this route.

How to get there: To reach the lower trailhead, turn right onto Forest Road 63 from FR 46, approximately 4.2 miles south of the Ripplebrook Guard Station (29 miles southeast of Estacada). Continue on FR 63 for 12.6 miles, then stay right onto FR 6380. Cross the Collawash River in 2.4 miles, and turn left at a junction. Park at the trailhead a half mile later.

To reach the upper trailhead, turn north onto FR 4696 from FR 46 approximately 4.2 miles northeast of the State Route 22/FR 46 junction in Detroit (approximately 50 miles east of Salem). Turn left onto FR 4697 in a little over three-quarters of a mile. Travel uphill for 4.5 miles until intersecting a rough, boulder-laden road suitable for high-clearance vehicles only. Either turn left and park at the trailhead 1.5 miles later, or park at this junction and hike west on the road to the trailhead by the northeast corner of Elk Lake.

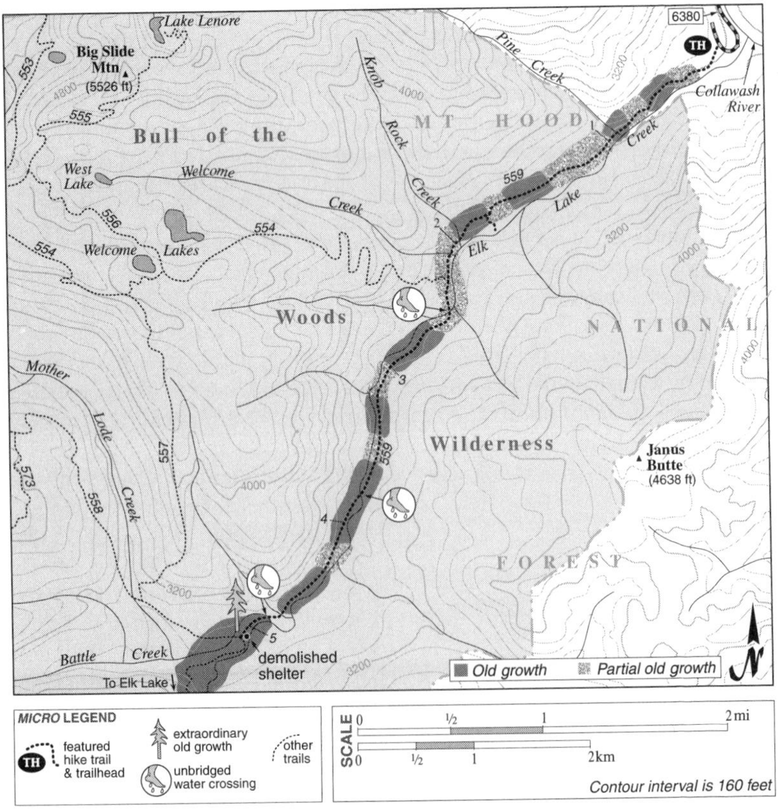

CENTRAL OREGON CASCADES

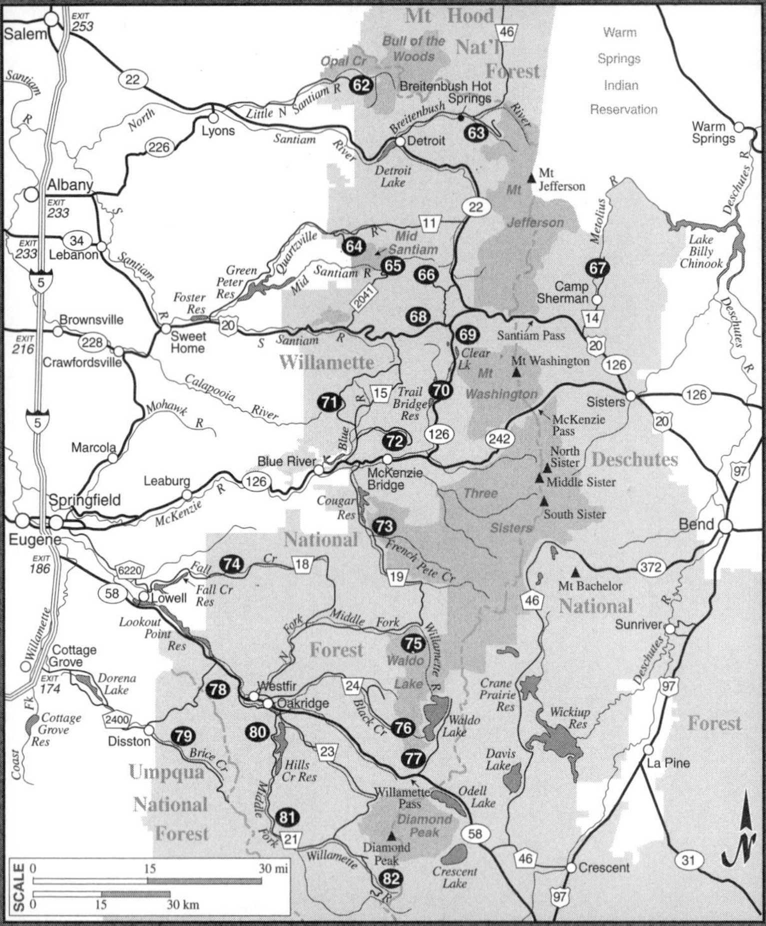

Hike locations

62 OPAL CREEK

Length ■ **5.1 miles to Beachie Creek**
Difficulty ■ Moderate
Season ■ Spring to autumn
Lowest point ■ 1,860 feet
Highest point ■ 2,400 feet
Human imprint ■ High (road, mining, tree plantation, hikers)
Information ■ Willamette National Forest (Detroit Ranger District)

Primary Old-Growth Feature
Extensive stand of diverse, low-elevation old forest

Opal Creek became a national rallying ground for the old-growth preservation movement in the late 1980s, ultimately leading to designation of the Opal Creek Wilderness in 1996. Renowned as one of few remaining extensive tracts of low-elevation old forest in western Oregon, Opal Creek attracts thousands of visitors each year. A complex fire history and broad range of growing conditions have produced a very diverse and patchy forest. Enormous Douglas-fir and western redcedar populate the more productive sites, while smaller trees occupy sites with shallow or recently disturbed soils. Opal Creek itself is justly prized for its crystal-clear pools and dazzling waterfalls.

The first 2 miles of the path are on an old road closed to public four-wheeled vehicles. Head up the road past the gate through a predominantly young forest overtopped by giant Douglas-fir (7 to 8 feet diameter) that survived a nineteenth-century fire. Cross Gold Creek in less than a half mile, soon traversing the unique half bridges built to get the old mining road around steep rock walls. Shortly thereafter the road bisects the most attractive old growth of the hike, traveling through a beautiful forest stacked with Douglas-fir 4 to 6 feet thick.

A junction is reached a little over 2 miles up the road, just a few hundred yards past the old Merten Mill site. The main road continues to privately owned Jawbone Flats, site of the Opal Creek Environmental Education Center. Turn right instead, soon crossing a trail bridge over the Little North Santiam River. The Opal Creek Trail (3372) heads upriver from here toward the mostly untouched Opal Creek basin.

The trail starts off in patchy old growth for the first mile, briefly passes through an older plantation across the river from Jawbone Flats, and then reenters older forest. Opal Pool, a worthy destination itself, lies just off the trail to the left near the beginning of the Opal Creek watershed proper.

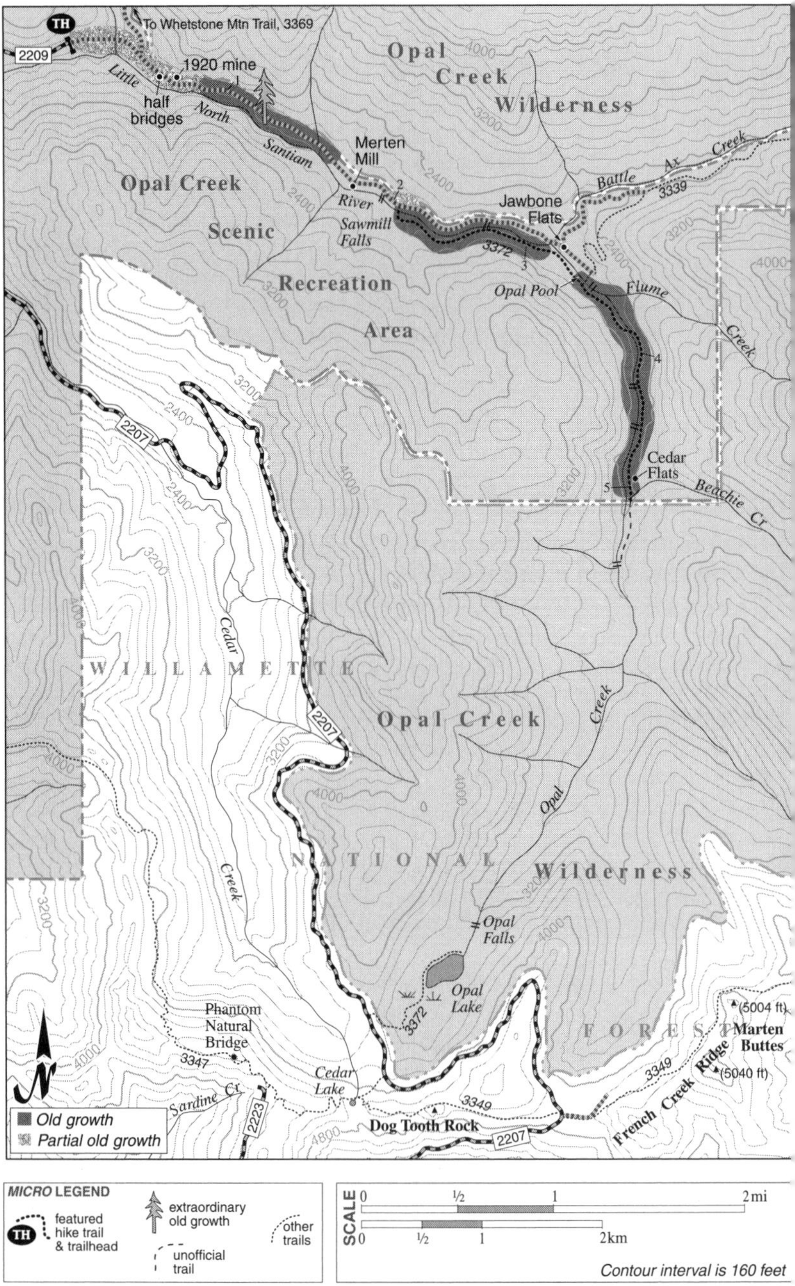
TH
2209
To Whetstone Mtn Trail, 3369
Opal Creek Wilderness
1920 mine
half bridges
Little North Santiam River
Merten Mill
Opal Creek Scenic Recreation Area
Sawmill Falls
Jawbone Flats
Battle Ax Creek
3339
3372
Opal Pool
Flume Creek
Cedar Flats
Beachie Cr
2207
WILLAMETTE NATIONAL FOREST
Cedar Creek
Opal Creek
Opal Creek Wilderness
Opal Falls
Opal Lake
Phantom Natural Bridge
3347
Sardine Cr
2223
Cedar Lake
3349
Dog Tooth Rock
French Creek Ridge
Marten Buttes
(5004 ft)
(5040 ft)
Old growth
Partial old growth
MICRO LEGEND
featured hike trail & trailhead
extraordinary old growth
unofficial trail
other trails
SCALE
0 ½ 1 2mi
0 ½ 1 2km
Contour interval is 160 feet

The Battle Ax Trail (3339) intersects the Opal Creek Trail just above Opal Pool. From this junction the Opal Creek Trail continues up the valley for another 1.2 miles, crossing over to the east bank of Opal Creek for the last mile. Several waterfalls and more old forest fill out the scenery. Large western redcedars at Cedar Flats mark a convenient turnaround spot for day hikers. The trail currently ends near Beachie Creek, although long-range plans call for extending the trail through some rugged country up to Opal Lake.

How to get there: From State Route 22 at milepost 23 near Mehama, turn northeast onto Little North Fork Road. The road is paved for 16 miles, where it becomes gravel-surfaced Forest Road 2209 at the national forest boundary. Follow FR 2209 for another 5 miles and park by the gate.

Sulphur shelf fungus

OPAL LAKE

Opal Lake sits at the head of the drainage surrounded by some of the most impressive forest in the area. Descend steeply on a washed-out trail grade (the southern end of the Opal Creek Trail 3372) through a plantation, then negotiate a path through a wet, boggy area near the south end of Opal Lake. The trail then tracks around the west and north shores of Opal Lake through a splendid stand of colossal Douglas-fir, western hemlock, noble fir, and Alaska-cedar.

How to get there: The trailhead lies off Forest Road 2207, about 6 miles north of the junction with FR 2223 and 10 miles from Detroit if coming from the south, or about 9 miles from FR 2209 if approaching from the north. FR 2207 is steep and rocky in places, but generally passable to careful drivers.

63 South Fork Breitenbush River

Length ■	**4.5 miles one way**
Difficulty ■	Easy to moderate
Season ■	Spring to autumn
Lowest point ■	2,380 feet
Highest point ■	3,050 feet
Human imprint ■	Moderate (hikers, nearby road, some timber harvest)
Information ■	Willamette National Forest (Detroit Ranger District)

Primary Old-Growth Feature
Easily accessed riparian old growth

The South Breitenbush Gorge Trail (3366) bisects winsome old growth along the northeast flank of the South Fork Breitenbush River. The low-elevation old forest in this area is a little younger (approximately 300 years old) and smaller than most old growth in the Willamette National Forest, but impressive nonetheless. Four trailheads on Forest Road 4685 provide access to this national recreation trail, creating options for hikes of varying length and difficulty.

The best old growth and most interesting portion of the trail can be enjoyed in an easy hike from the lower trailhead up to the second trailhead 2 miles later. This trail segment cuts through several patches of trees blown down during a January 1990 windstorm. The trail was cleared through the middle of the jack-strawed old growth, lending a glimpse of Mother's power. Stand back when she wants to play pick-up sticks! Beyond the largest patch of blowdown the trail nears Breitenbush Gorge, a narrow chute now partially covered by trees toppled by the same storm. Continue

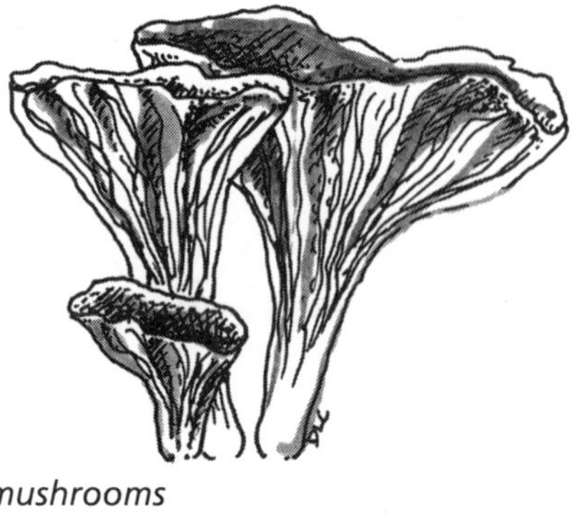

Chanterelle mushrooms

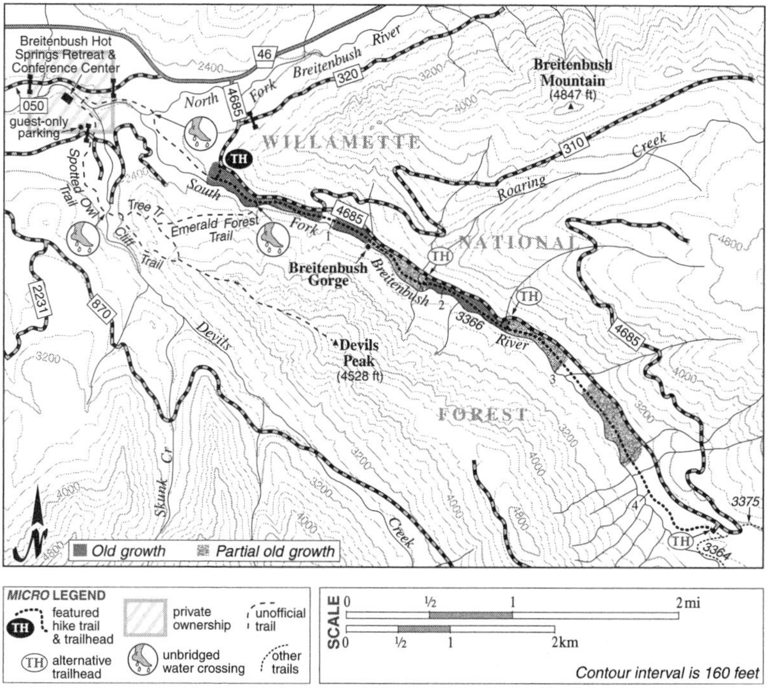

upriver and cross aptly named Roaring Creek, a suitable spot for a trailside break. Shortly after crossing the Creek, a short spur trail heads uphill to the second trailhead.

The trail continues for another 2.5 miles through a mix of forest types to the final trailhead. This portion of the trail is lightly used and infrequently maintained, and may be hard to follow in places.

Several unofficial trails connect the South Breitenbush Gorge Trail to the nearby Breitenbush Hot Springs Retreat and Conference Center. Trail junctions are usually signed, although the trails are rough and steep in some places. In particular, trail crossings over the north and south forks of the Breitenbush River may be unbridged and hazardous. The retreat center and Forest Service intend to work together to improve these trails as funds become available. These trails are intended for retreat center guests, although portions of the trails on public lands are open for all to enjoy. The Breitenbush Hot Springs Retreat and Conference Center only permits retreat center guests on its property to maintain a quiet, healing environment.

How to get there: Head northeast on Forest Road 46 out of Detroit (or travel south on FR 46 from the Clackamas area). Turn right (south) onto FR 4685 approximately 11.5 miles east of Detroit. Trailheads are located on the right side of FR 4685 about half a mile, 2.2 miles, 2.7 miles, and 4.7 miles up the road.

SPOTTED OWL LOOP

Hikers can also link together three unofficial trails to form a 3-mile loop around the northwest flank of Devils Ridge. These trails are maintained by the Breitenbush Hot Springs Retreat and Conference Center for resort guests. The trails are on public land though, and are available for all to hike.

The Spotted Owl Trail begins by winding through plantations and mature forest. After crossing Devils Creek, stay left at the trail junction on the Tree Trail and head uphill through the finest old forest on the loop. Classic Douglas-fir and western hemlock old growth cloak the hillside. Continue to the ridgeline veering right up the ridge towards two trail junctions. Stay right at both junctions and head very steeply downhill on the Cliff Trail to complete the loop.

How to get there: Turn right onto Forest Road 2231 about 9 miles east of Detroit, and stay left after crossing the bridge. Veer left onto FR 890 two-thirds of a mile later. The parking lot for the retreat center is on the left in another two-thirds of a mile, just before reaching a locked gate across the main road. Guests of the retreat center can pick up the trail from the retreat center parking lot. Other hikers need to park in a public parking area on the left about a quarter mile prior to the gate, or in wide spots along the road. The trail is on the right about 150 feet past the gate.

64 CHIMNEY PEAK

Length	**6 miles one way**
Difficulty	Difficult
Season	Summer to autumn
Lowest point	2,640 feet
Highest point	4,965 feet
Human imprint	Minimal
Information	Willamette National Forest (Sweet Home Ranger District)

Primary Old-Growth Feature
Large patch of old-growth Douglas-fir

Chimney Peak sits atop a ridge defining the northern boundary of the Middle Santiam Wilderness, providing visitors with a raven's-eye view of unbroken old growth in the wilderness and adjacent lands to the north. A dramatic vista to the south from Chimney Peak highlights the opposing choices modern society has made concerning human use of forest landscapes. The unharvested wilderness to the southeast contrasts starkly with the industrial-strength clearcut stretching to the west as far as the eye can see.

The first half mile of the infrequently traveled McQuade Creek Trail (3397) requires bridgeless crossings of the two forks of McQuade Creek, although neither is likely to wet your feet during the summer and fall low-flow

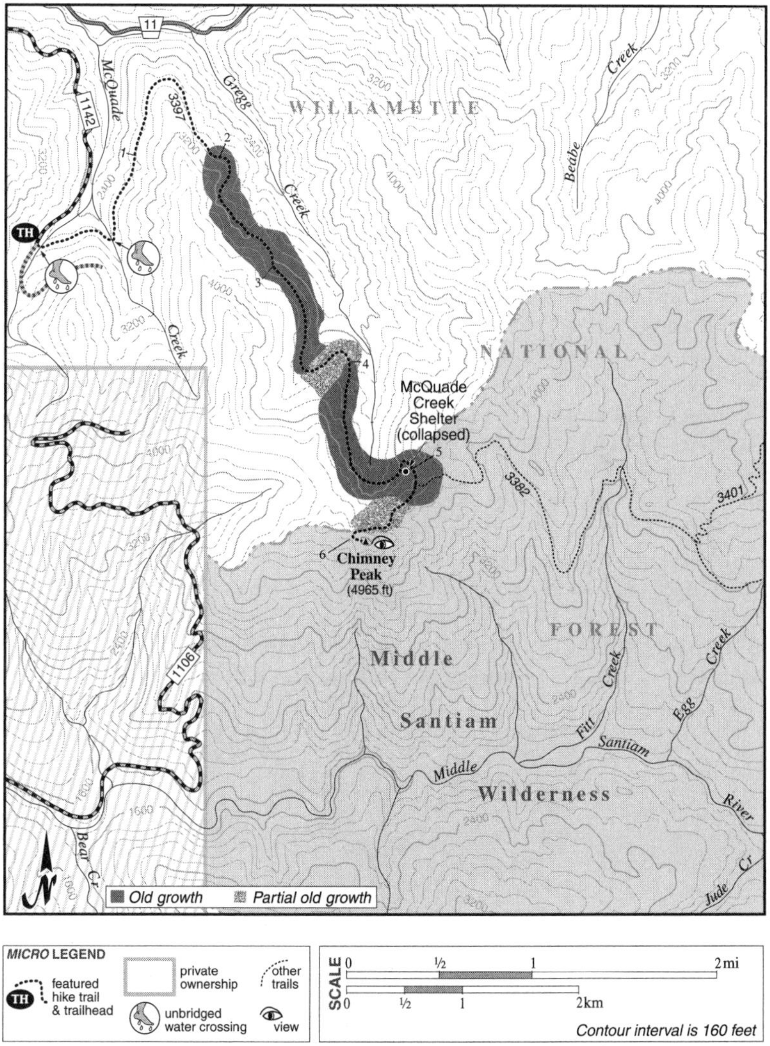

seasons. The trail climbs a steady, moderate grade through plantations and a younger, fire-initiated stand for the first 2 miles. Old conifers begin to dominate the forest shortly after the trail rounds the ridge and crosses into the Gregg Creek drainage. The forest varies from lush and large in the moist, protected draws to sparse and shrubby on the drier, less productive ridges. Windthrow has significantly altered forest structure in places.

The finest old forest is located in the upper reaches of the basin. Large western hemlock grace north-facing slopes in a scene more typical of forests farther north. The McQuade Creek Shelter, a third of a mile from the ridgeline, has collapsed, but provides a pleasant camping or break spot surrounded by titanic hemlocks. Continue on to the ridgeline trail junction and take a right on the Chimney Peak Trail (3382), reaching Chimney Peak two-thirds of a mile later.

An alternate, longer route (8 miles) to Chimney Peak travels for mile after mile through one of the largest stands of old growth in Oregon. Head southwest on the Swamp Peak Trail (3401), drop over the ridge into the Middle Santiam Wilderness, and take the Chimney Peak Trail (3382) west for the last 4 miles. Classic old growth commanded by Douglas-fir and western hemlock characterize most of the hike; noble fir and Pacific silver fir intermingle on cooler, north-facing slopes. An interesting, slow-moving earthflow is evident in the area around Fitt Creek. Tipsy trees, a jumbled and hummocky surface, and tension cracks in the ground provide the telltale clues.

How to get there: From U.S. Highway 20 by the upper end of Foster Reservoir (4 miles east of Sweet Home), turn north onto the Quartzville Road and head toward Green Peter Reservoir. Drive well past the reservoir, staying right on Forest Road 11 at a fork in the road 24.7 miles from the highway, then turn right onto FR 1142 about 2.6 miles later. The trailhead is on the left, 4 miles from FR 11.

To reach the Swamp Peak trailhead (see Hike 65 map), travel past Green Peter Reservoir as above, and turn right onto FR 1152 approximately 9.3 miles past the fork in the road. Turn right onto FR 640 about 3.25 miles later. The trailhead is on the right a half mile up FR 640.

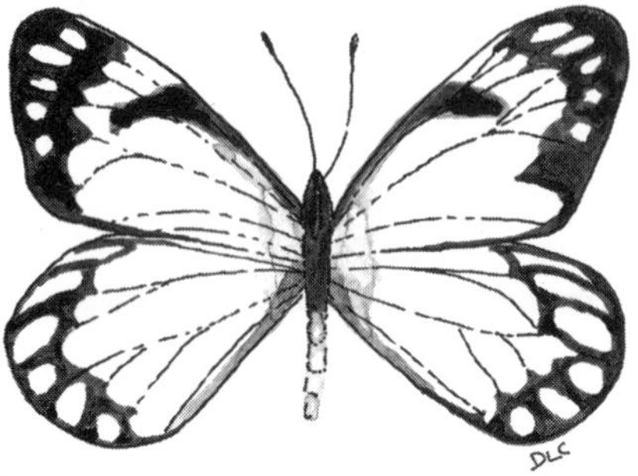

Pine white moth

65 DONACA LAKE

Length ■ **7 miles one way**
Difficulty ■ Difficult
Season ■ Spring to autumn
Lowest point ■ 2,000 feet
Highest point ■ 2,720 feet
Human imprint ■ Minimal
Information ■ Willamette National Forest (Sweet Home Ranger District)

Primary Old-Growth Features
Excellent examples of low-elevation old growth; patches of very old forest

The Middle Santiam Wilderness and adjacent lands are well known for outstanding old growth and contain one of the largest stands of old forest in western Oregon. Environmental groups fought long and hard to protect this area, and though the battle was eventually won, scarred hillsides nearby attest to the incomplete nature of the victory. A long hike through several stunning stands of old growth on the southeast end of the Chimney Peak Trail leads hikers to Donaca Lake, the most popular destination in the wilderness.

After leaving the trailhead plantation, the Chimney Peak Trail (3382) enters the first of several great groves. Large trees, snags, and down logs are abundant on this wondrous hillslope. The trail soon reaches a short waterfall on the Middle Santiam River by the Shedd Camp Shelter, where a delightful pool beckons summer swimmers.

Crossing the unbridged river can be problematic during high streamflows, and wet feet are likely in every season. A junction with the South Pyramid Creek Trail (3403) lies just beyond the river, providing alternative access to this point via the Forest Road 747 trailhead. Taking the South Pyramid Creek Trail to this junction avoids the river crossing and is also a gorgeous walk through exceptional old forest, but it adds 1.5 miles each way to the trip.

Beyond the trail junction, the Chimney Peak Trail contours around the hillside through a superb 700-year-old forest. Another fine example of old growth occurs near the bridgeless crossing of Pyramid Creek at about 3 miles, marking another potential turnaround spot for those intending to keep their feet dry.

Find your way across the creek and continue up and over FR 2041 (blocked farther back by several major landslides) to reenter diverse old forest. Younger forest prevails in the vicinity of the junction with the Gordan Peak Trail (3387), but from Swamp Creek to Donaca Lake the forest is superlative. Craggy Douglas-fir 5 to 7 feet thick and scattered old sugar pine impress all wilderness visitors. Pocket-sized Donaca Lake is a peaceful destination.

Another option is to visit Donaca Lake along a long loop (approximately 15

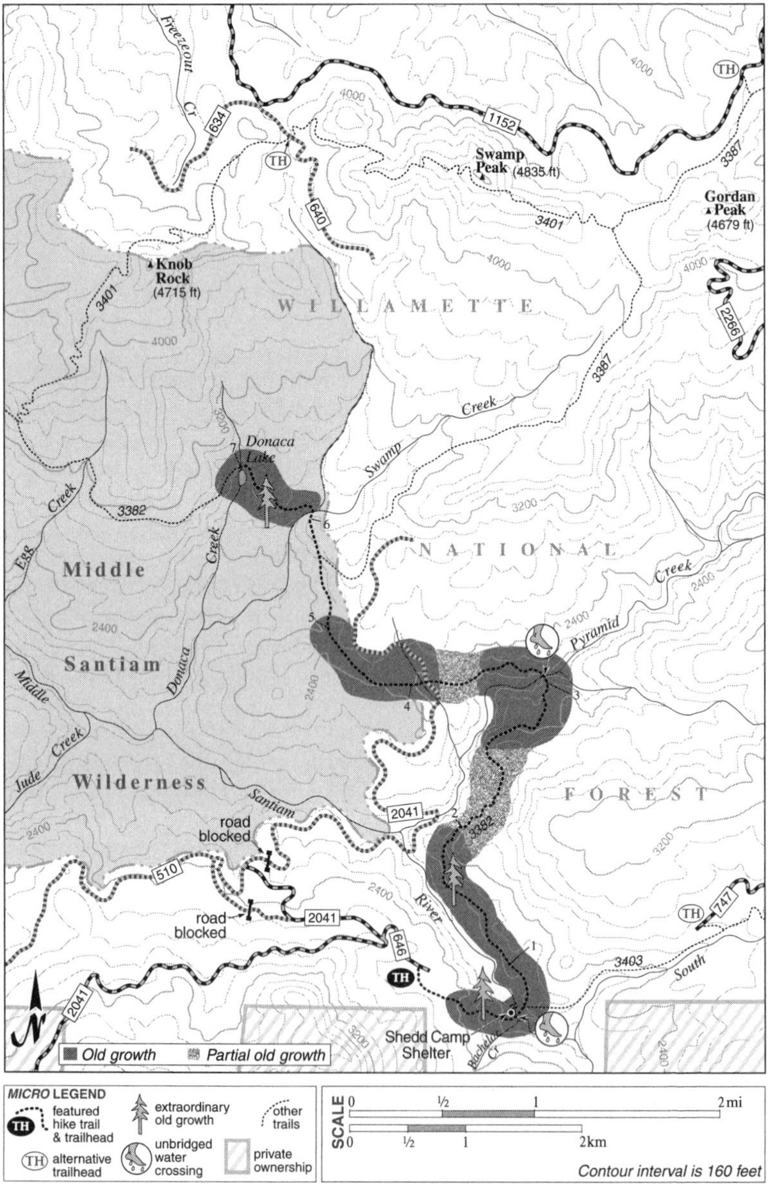

Rocky Mountain elk

miles) through abundant old forest. Head west on the Swamp Peak Trail (3401; see alternative trailhead description for Hike 64) from FR 640, then turn left on the Chimney Peak Trail (3382) to Donaca Lake. Continue past the lake and turn left onto the Gordan Peak Trail (3387), hiking up the trail to the eastern terminus of the Swamp Peak Trail. Turn left and return to the trailhead.

How to get there: Turn northeast onto Soda Fork Road (FR 2041) from U.S. Highway 20 at Upper Soda (24 miles east of Sweet Home). Stay on FR 2041 through an abused, mixed-ownership landscape until reaching Forest Road 646, approximately 12.25 miles from the highway. Turn right and the trailhead is on the right a half mile later.

To reach the South Pyramid Creek Trail via the FR 747 trailhead, turn left (north) onto Sheep Creek Road (FR 2047) from US 20, approximately 28 miles east of Sweet Home. Turn left onto FR 747, about 13.25 miles from the highway, and go a mile or so to the trailhead at the end.

BIG TREE TIP—SODA FORK GIANT

On your way to the trailhead stop off to see the Soda Fork Giant, an enormous (10.5-foot diameter), solitary Douglas-fir standing by the stream on private land. Even though a large portion of the treetop is broken off, this is the second largest Douglas-fir by volume known in Oregon due to the slow taper of the massive trunk. **How to get there:** Pull off to the right by the stream just over 2 miles from U.S. Highway 20 on Soda Fork Road. Although the tree is not marked or signed, you'll know it when you see it.

HOUSE ROCK

A short loop trail near the southern route to the Middle Santiam Wilderness circles through a lush and productive old forest by the banks of the South Santiam River. Some of the old Douglas-fir reach 7 to 8 feet in diameter, and at least one stretches 9 feet across. Cross the trail bridge over the river by the House Rock Campground and turn left heading upriver. The three-quarter-mile long trail passes House Rock—a giant overhanging boulder large enough to shelter small groups—and an impressive waterfall, then comes to a junction with the historic Santiam Wagon Road. Constructed in the late 1860s, the wagon road was a primary travel and trade route across the Oregon Cascades until the 1930s. Turn right, then turn right again a quarter mile later to close the loop. Hikers can also continue northwest on the wagon road in fantastic old forest for another mile.

How to get there: Turn right (south) onto Forest Road 2044 toward House Rock Campground from U.S. Highway 20 approximately 26 miles east of Sweet Home. Parking is on the right by the campground a quarter mile later.

66 THREE PYRAMIDS

Length ■ **2.2 miles one way**
Difficulty ■ Moderate to difficult
Season ■ Summer to autumn
Lowest point ■ 3,940 feet
Highest point ■ 5,618 feet
Human imprint ■ Minimal
Information ■ Willamette National Forest (Sweet Home Ranger District)

Primary Old-Growth Feature
Noteworthy noble fir forest

This diverse hike switchbacks up through a fine stand of noble fir old growth on the way to the scenic summit of Middle Pyramid. Together with sister pyramids on both flanks, the Three Pyramids dominate the eastern boundary of the Pyramid Creek watershed. The Pyramids Trail links with several other trails to form a 27-mile loop around the upper Middle Santiam watershed, known as the Old Cascade Crest Loop.

Start off on the Pyramids Trail (3380), bearing right at a junction with the

South Pyramid Creek Trail (3403) just after crossing a log bridge. The Pyramids Trail immediately enters a stately grove of mixed noble fir and Douglas-fir old growth, trending towards cold-hardy true firs as the trail quickly gains elevation. The long, seemingly taper-free noble fir trunks stretch skyward to impressive heights lending a strong vertical feel to the stand. The trail briefly nears a couple of small waterfalls before crossing the stream and entering a brushy meadow dotted with small patches of large noble fir (up to 5 feet thick) and a few big Engelmann spruce.

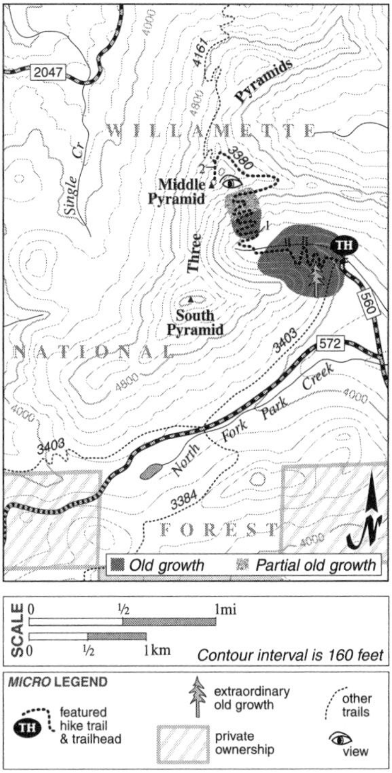

Resume a switchbacking ascent, now up a steep basin sidewall through scattered patches of noble fir and several other conifers. The slopes become increasingly rocky as the trail reaches the crest of a secondary ridge about 1.5 miles from the trailhead. Head west along the north face of this ridge reaching a trail junction with the North Pyramid Trail (4161) a third of a mile or so later. Turn left heading towards Middle Pyramid on the west slope of the main ridge, and climb the final switchbacks up to the site of an old lookout. Old Cascade peaks born during an ancient period of volcanism 18 to 40 million years ago stretch across the skyline to the north, south and west, while younger and higher New Cascade peaks (3 to 8 million years old) poke out of the plateau to the east.

Vaux's swift

To extend your hike and sample more of the enchanting forest on the lower slopes of the Middle and South Pyramids, turn left (southwest) at the trail junction by the trailhead. The eastern end of the South Pyramid Creek Trail (3403) traverses the same superb stand of mixed noble fir and Douglas-fir old growth described above, and merits a short stroll on that basis alone.

How to get there: Turn north onto the Lava Lake Road (Forest Road 2067) from U.S. Highway 20 approximately 42 miles east of Sweet Home (just over a half mile west of the junction with State Route 126.) Stay on the main road for 5.7 miles and turn left onto FR 560. The road ends at the trailhead 3.6 miles later. This spot can also be reached from SR 22 approximately 26 miles southeast of Detroit by turning west onto the Lava Lake Road, then turning right onto FR 560 approximately 2 miles later.

67 METOLIUS RIVER

Length ■ **1 to 9 miles one way, loop options**
Difficulty ■ Easy to moderate
Season ■ Spring to autumn
Lowest point ■ 2,680 feet
Highest point ■ 3,050 feet
Human imprint ■ Moderate to high (hikers, anglers, roads, hatchery)
Information ■ Deschutes National Forest (Sisters Ranger District)

Primary Old-Growth Feature
Extensive groves of ponderosa pine old growth

The fabulous Metolius River area harbors one of the most extensive stands of ponderosa pine old growth remaining in the Oregon Cascades. Mile after mile of flaming-orange pine spreads across trails on both flanks of a river famed for its trout fishery and several major springs. The West Metolius River Trail (4018) runs north from Canyon Creek Campground to Candle Creek Campground, while the East Metolius River Trail (4020) stretches from the Gorge Campground to Lower Bridge.

The most popular trail segment is on the west shore between Canyon Creek Campground and the Wizard Falls State Fish Hatchery. Spectacular springs come pouring out of the hillslope a few feet above the river's surface about a third of a mile downstream from Canyon Creek Campground. Old ponderosa pine, some with multiple fire scars evident, are scattered along the entire segment; large Douglas-fir intermingle with the pine inside a picturesque gorge near the springs.

The East Metolius River Trail also runs through the gorge, generally hugging the river's edge after the first mile. Start out from the Gorge Campground heading north through a nearly pure stand of pretty pines on a flat above the

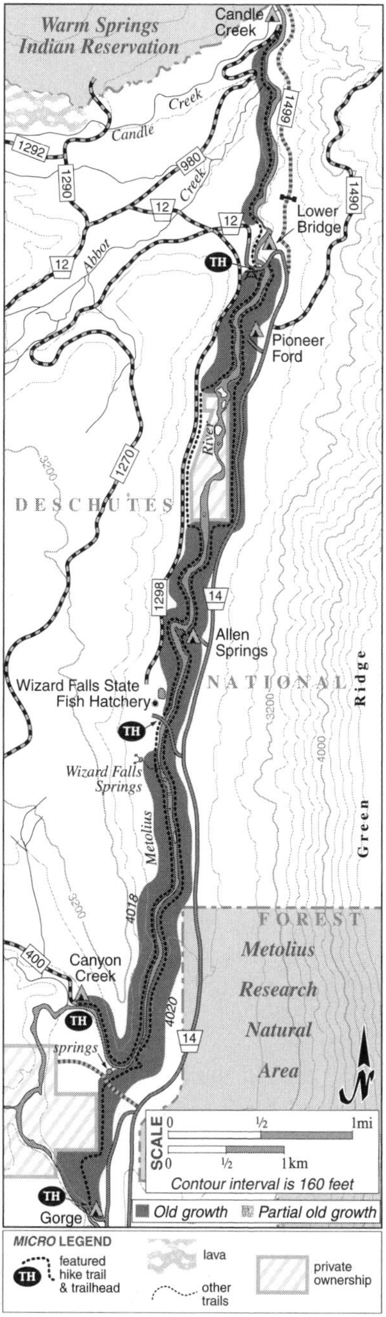

gorge. The trail then switchbacks down the gorge sidewall to the river and follows the shoreline downriver through large old pine and Douglas-fir. Several pullouts along Forest Road 14 also provide easy access to the trail.

The bridges by the hatchery and Lower Bridge to the north link these two trails together to form a 6.5-mile loop downstream from the hatchery. Accessible at either end, and from two campgrounds and several pullouts on the east side of the river, the loop traverses attractive old forest of ponderosa pine, incense-cedar, grand fir, and Douglas-fir. Ospreys and mergansers are frequently visible along this segment.

The final segment of the West Metolius River Trail downstream from Lower Bridge offers the best opportunity for a little solitude along the river. This quiet, 1.3-mile shoreline stroll rolls through still more old ponderosa pine, incense-cedar, and Douglas-fir. If your timing is right you may glimpse the annual autumnal return of bright orange kokanee salmon. Kokanee salmon, a landlocked variety of sockeye salmon, migrate upstream from Lake Billy Chinook to spawn in the Metolius, turning from silver to orange during the journey.

How to get there: Turn north onto Forest Road 14 from U.S. Highway 20 approximately 10 miles west of Sisters (10 miles east of Santiam Pass). To reach Canyon Creek Campground, continue straight onto FR 1419 at a junction 2.5 miles from the highway. Continue straight onto FR 1420 at a stop sign, then turn right onto FR

400 approximately 5.4 miles from the junction with FR 14. The campground and trailhead are at the end of the road 1 mile later.

Kokanee salmon

To reach Gorge Campground, stay to the right on FR 14 at the junction 2.5 miles from the highway. Turn left toward Camp Sherman in about 3.5 miles, and then turn right in a couple hundred yards. The Gorge Campground is about 1.75 miles from the junction, the last of a series of Forest Service campgrounds.

Wizard Falls Fish Hatchery lies off FR 14 on the left about 10.25 miles from the highway, and Lower Bridge is another 2.5 miles down FR 14. Parking is on the left just across the bridge in both cases.

BIG TREE TIP

An excellent patch of eastside old growth, including a couple of exceptional Douglas-fir, stands along the first half mile of the Jefferson Lake Trail. The largest one measures almost 8 feet in diameter, one of the largest known Douglas-fir on the east side of the Cascades.

How to get there: Follow Forest Road 12 over Lower Bridge heading west and turn right onto FR 1290 after 1.3 miles. Turn left onto FR 1292 after one third of a mile, reaching the trailhead 2.4 miles later.

68 ECHO BASIN

Length ■	**2.5-mile loop**
Difficulty ■	Easy
Season ■	Summer to autumn
Lowest point ■	4,160 feet
Highest point ■	4,800 feet
Human imprint ■	Moderate (plantation)
Information ■	Willamette National Forest (Sweet Home Ranger District)

Echo Basin holds a unique stand of old Alaska-cedar and Pacific silver fir, including the largest known Alaska-cedar in Oregon. The forest sits in the palm of the basin where

Primary Old-Growth Feature
Very old and large Alaska-cedar

cold air pools, fostering a forest similar to those found around Mount Rainier and farther north. An easy, 2.5-mile loop leads hikers through this forest where impressive Alaska-cedar and occasional noble fir stand by the trail.

Head up the Echo Basin Trail (3410) through a rapidly growing noble fir plantation, coming to the loop junction a half mile from the trailhead. From here the loop circles through the old forest and interspersed meadows. Very large Alaska-cedar are scattered throughout the loop. The largest, about 8 feet in diameter, is the first of the big Alaska-cedar encountered along the trail, and is recorded as the largest in Oregon. Diverse meadow, shrub, and forest communities draped over the basin sidewalls are visible from the more open areas.

Echo Basin is well along the pathway toward a self-perpetuating forest of shade-tolerant trees. The young forest that regenerated following the last major fire in the basin four or more centuries ago was likely dominated by blue-hued noble fir, an early-successional species capable of out-competing other trees at this elevation in a high-light, post-fire environment. Shade-tolerant Alaska-cedar and Pacific silver fir established in the understory and grew into the upper canopy as older trees died. Only a few scattered large noble fir trees and snags now remain, protruding markedly above the general canopy layer. Forests dominated by shade-tolerant trees are uncommon in the Oregon Cascade Range below 4,000 to 5,000 feet elevation, due to the long life spans of the primary, early successional conifers (Douglas-fir and

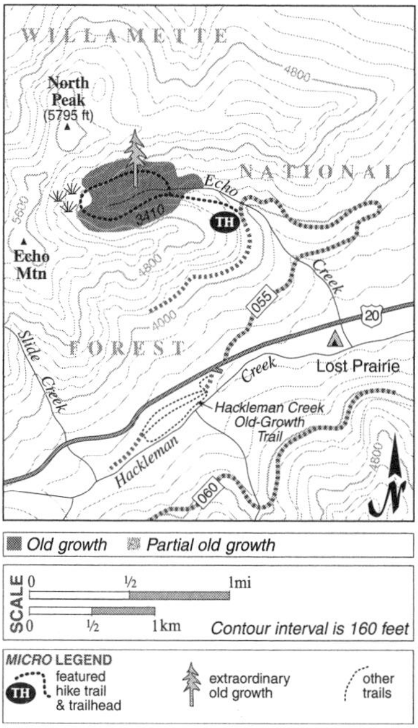

Alaska-cedar

noble fir) and the multiple fires that occurred within those life spans on most sites. Shade-tolerant conifers are typically thin-barked and more susceptible to fire-induced mortality.

How to get there: Turn northeast onto Forest Road 055 from U.S. Highway 20, approximately 38 miles east of Sweet Home. The trailhead is on the right, 2 miles from US 20.

HACKLEMAN CREEK

The Hackleman Creek Old-Growth Trail provides a perfect companion hike to Echo Basin. This short trail (1.25 miles) loops past interpretive stations in a small stand of classic old growth surrounded by plantations. A secondary trail swings down by the creek and back, adding another half mile to the trip. The primary loop is wheelchair accessible; the second segment is not.

How to get there: The trailhead lies across U.S. Highway 20 slightly west of the road to Echo Basin (Forest Road 055, described above).

69 CLEAR LAKE

Length	**7-mile loop; 2 miles one way to viewpoint turnaround**
Difficulty	Easy to moderate
Season	Spring to autumn
Lowest point	3,015 feet
Highest point	3,120 feet
Human imprint	High (hikers, boaters, highway noise)
Information	Willamette National Forest (McKenzie River Ranger District)

Primary Old-Growth Features
Mid-elevation Douglas-fir old growth; lava-flow old growth

Immense conifers north of Clear Lake easily justify adding a couple of gentle miles onto the north end of a popular 5-mile loop around the lake. Aquamarine Clear Lake was formed approximately 3,000 years ago when a lava flow dammed the McKenzie River. It is well known for its clarity, attracting scuba divers interested in exploring the few pockets of a 3,000-year-old snag forest still standing underwater. A beautiful setting, easy access, and recreational developments along the lakeshore bring heavy use on summer weekends.

From the upper McKenzie River Trail parking area, head south on the McKenzie River Trail (3507) across a footbridge and immediately enter a luxuriant old forest. Enormous Douglas-fir (5 to 7 feet in girth) and hardy Pacific yew garnish the trailside. The Clear Lake Trail (4341) intersects the McKenzie River Trail 1 mile from the

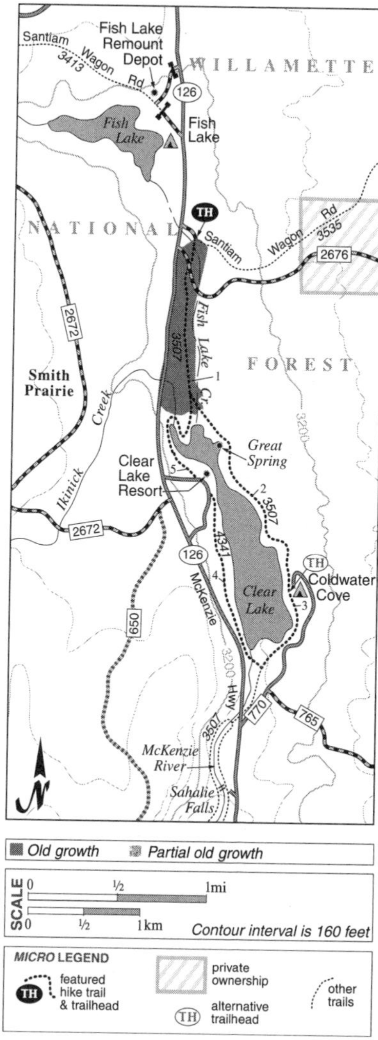

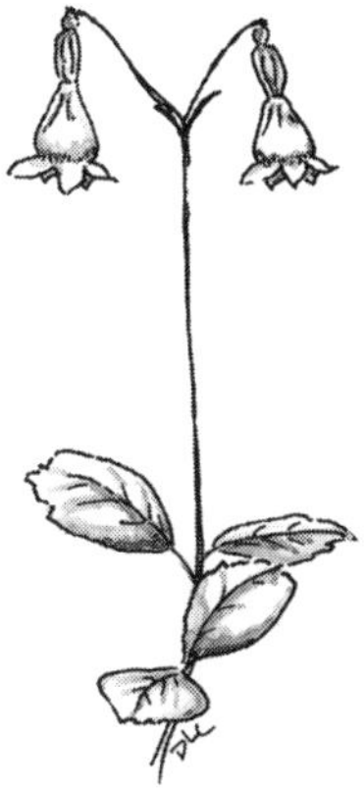

Twinflower

trailhead, forming the northern apex of the Clear Lake loop. Stay left on the McKenzie River Trail across a footbridge, continuing in old forest until reaching gurgling Great Spring a quarter mile later. Then the trail enters a unique form of old growth: lava-flow old growth! These amazing sentinels appear to sprout out of sheer lava. One giant Douglas-fir over 7 feet thick grows out of lava adjacent to the trail.

The trail continues in and out of old growth and lava before leaving the old trees altogether near Coldwater Cove Campground. The trail then intersects the southern end of the Clear Lake Trail approximately 2.25 miles from the northern intersection. Turn right to return north to the trailhead. Note that the southwestern end of the Clear Lake loop may be closed from January 1 to July 15 due to the presence of nesting bald eagles, a threatened species. Check with the McKenzie River Ranger District (see Appendix E) for the latest information. A lakeside viewpoint on the lava flow approximately 2 miles south of the northern trailhead provides a convenient turnaround point when the Clear Lake loop is closed, or for those looking for a shorter hike.

How to get there: Travel the McKenzie Highway (State Route 126) approximately 76 miles northeast of Eugene (1 mile north of Clear Lake, and 2 miles south of the U.S. Highway 20/SR 126 junction) and turn east into the upper McKenzie River Trail parking area. The trail is also accessible from the Clear Lake Resort on the west shore of the lake, and from Coldwater Cove Campground on the east shore.

SANTIAM WAGON ROAD–FISH LAKE

A leg of the historic Santiam Wagon Road also departs from the upper McKenzie River Trail parking area. Head east on the wagon road (Trail 3535) through huge Douglas-fir scattered across a lava flow, then through 3 miles of an open forest comprised of 200 to 300-year-old Douglas-fir, grand fir, and occasional ponderosa pine. The wagon road (Trail 3413) also stretches to the west on the other side of SR 126, from the Fish Lake Campground, heading past the lake and then through nearly 3 miles of colossal Douglas-fir and western hemlock. Historic Fish Lake Remount Depot was used as the summer headquarters for the old Santiam National Forest from 1921–1933, when the Willamette National Forest was first formed. The main cabin is now available as a ski-in winter rental.

70 TAMOLITCH FALLS

Length ■ **2.1 miles to Tamolitch Falls; 5.5 miles to Carmen Reservoir**
Difficulty ■ Easy to moderate
Season ■ Spring to autumn
Lowest point ■ 2,225 feet
Highest point ■ 2,800 feet
Human imprint ■ Moderate (hikers, mountain bikers)
Information ■ Willamette National Forest (McKenzie River Ranger District)

Primary Old-Growth Features
Riparian old growth; grove of huge incense-cedar

Riverside old growth and impressive incense-cedar border the dual phases of the McKenzie River along this segment of the McKenzie River Trail. The river tumbles rapidly in a

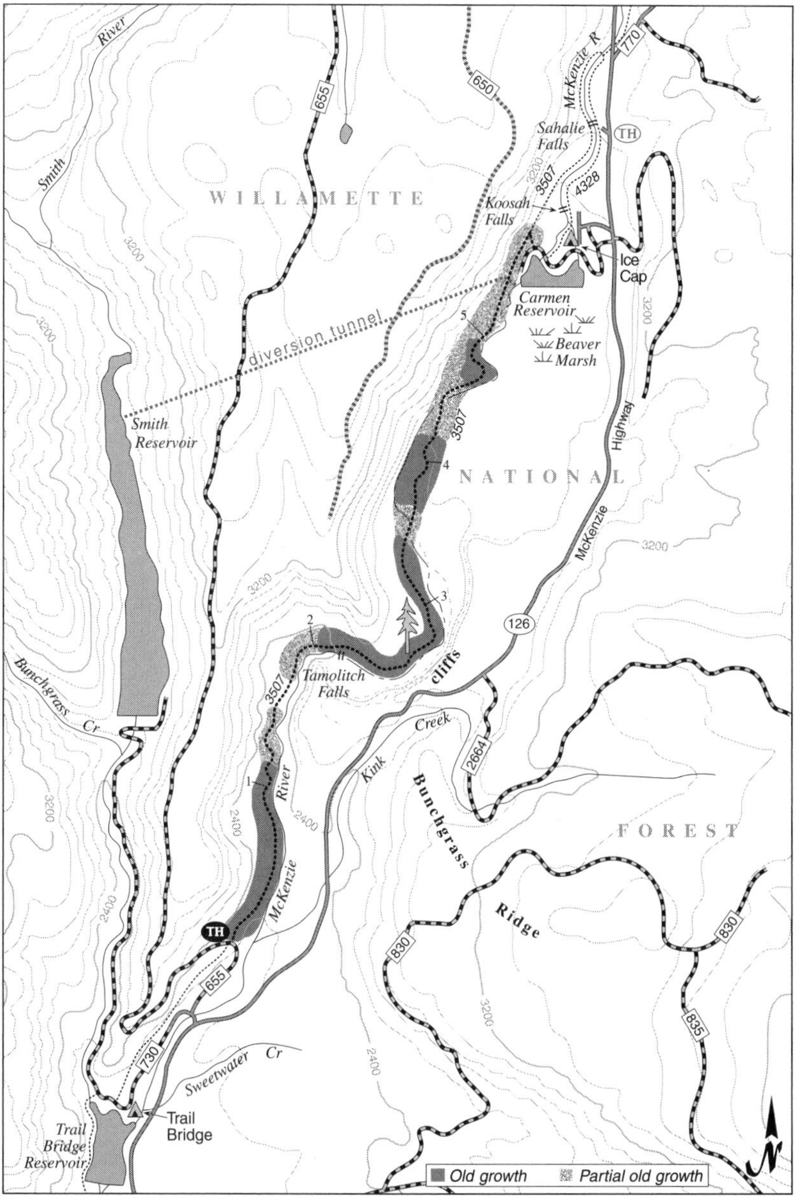

MICRO LEGEND

TH featured hike trail & trailhead

extraordinary old growth

TH alternative trailhead

other trails

SCALE 0 ½ 1 2 mi

0 ½ 1 2 km

Contour interval is 160 feet

Harlequin duck

whitewater frenzy downstream from eerily dry Tamolitch Falls, but disappears below ground from the falls up to Carmen Reservoir. The trail is easy to get to and free of snow most of the year; spring and autumn are particularly pleasant times to visit.

From the trailhead off Forest Road 655 above Trail Bridge Reservoir, head north on the McKenzie River Trail (3507) and soon descend to the banks of the river. Large western redcedar and Douglas-fir 3 to 6 feet wide occupy the streambank, floodplain, and riparian terraces along this stretch of trail. After a mile or so the trail climbs slightly onto an old lava flow where smaller old trees grow scattered across the lava surface.

Viewpoints of Tamolitch Falls are reached 2.1 miles from the trailhead, near lava casts of toasted trees. It will take good timing to see the river actually falling over Tamolitch Falls, however. The falls are dry most of the year and during these times the river emerges from a lava flow in a picturesque pool at the base of the falls. This phenomenon is due in part to the natural tendency of the river to vanish below ground in the lava flow filling the valley above the falls, and due in part to an incredible dewatering of the river engineered by the Eugene Water and Electric Board. A 2-mile long tunnel diverts McKenzie River water from Carmen Reservoir through a ridge over to Smith Reservoir for hydropower generation. Spring snowmelt sometimes overwhelms the capacities of both water diversion processes, and the river briefly runs freely from Carmen Reservoir downstream over Tamolitch Falls.

The next mile above Tamolitch Falls passes through an unusual stand of old-growth incense-cedar, Douglas-fir, and grand fir. A crescent-shaped patch of old trees has been protected from fire by a lava flow to the west and the river channel to the east. Incense-cedar growing along the margin of the lava flow are unusually large for this area (5 to 7 feet diameter), perhaps the largest incense-cedar in the Willamette National Forest. The next couple of miles follow the river in and out of patches of older forest until reaching Carmen Reservoir, a potential drop-off point for a one-way, shuttle hike.

How to get there: Travel the McKenzie Highway (State Route 126) to just north of the Trail Bridge Reservoir (approximately 68 miles northeast of Eugene), and turn left (west) onto Forest Road 730. Cross the McKenzie River and turn right on FR 655, intersecting the trail a half mile later.

WATERFALLS LOOP

A segment of the McKenzie River Trail joins both ends of the Waterfalls Trail to form a scenic 2.3-mile loop along both sides of the river. Although bordered by large Douglas-fir, the frothing river and foreground vistas of thundering Koosah Falls and Sahalie Falls take center stage on this hike. From Sahalie Falls, take the Waterfalls Trail (4328) upriver to the junction with the McKenzie River Trail (3507). Cross the river via the footbridge and descend along the west bank until reaching Carmen Reservoir, where a trail junction is marked by a 6-foot-thick Douglas-fir. Take a short spur trail down to the road by the reservoir, cross the river on the road, and turn left on the Waterfalls Trail back to Sahalie Falls.

How to get there: Turn west into the Sahalie Falls parking area from the McKenzie Highway (State Route 126), approximately 74 miles northeast of Eugene.

71 TIDBITS MOUNTAIN

Length ■ **2.25 miles one way**
Difficulty ■ Moderate
Season ■ Summer to autumn
Lowest point ■ 4,080 feet
Highest point ■ 5,185 feet
Human imprint ■ Moderate (nearby roads and clearcuts)
Information ■ Willamette National Forest (McKenzie River Ranger District)

Primary Old-Growth Feature
Mid-elevation transition forest of large western hemlock, Douglas-fir, and noble fir

Magnificent old forests on the upper slopes of Tidbits basin are readily accessible along a little-used trail to the top of Tidbits Mountain. The Tidbits Mountain Trail (3328) crosses several ecological zones, demonstrating the influence of elevation and aspect (the direction the slope faces) on the plant species able to dominate a site. Sensational views of the Oregon Cascades richly reward hikers reaching the summit.

Hammond's flycatcher

The trail quickly enters an impressive old-growth forest on a warm, southwest-facing slope. Huge Douglas-fir up to 6 feet thick and massive western hemlock up to 5 feet in diameter dominate this splendid stand. As the trail ascends toward the ridgeline, cold-hardy noble fir and Pacific silver fir become more abundant. The coarse, bluish crowns of noble fir and the smooth, silver bark of Pacific silver fir are the diagnostic clues.

Continue heading west on the left fork at a trail junction in the saddle 1.5 miles from the trailhead, crossing over to the colder, north side of Tidbits Mountain. Here Douglas-fir and western hemlock drop out of the stand altogether and are replaced by mountain hemlock and Pacific silver fir, species better adapted to cooler temperatures and a persistent snowpack. Continue through talus slopes beneath a multipinnacled peak and small patches of trees until reaching another trail junction on the west side of the mountain. Turn sharply left and scramble up to the mountaintop, site of a former lookout and current target of dive-bombing cliff swallows.

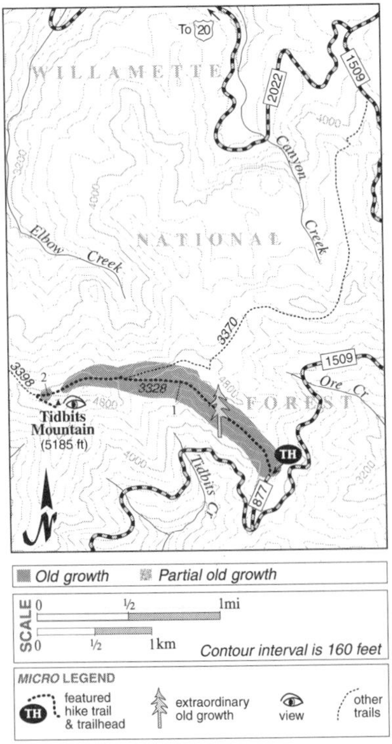

Tidbits Mountain sits astride the divide between predominately federally managed land to the east and predominately private land to the west, highlighting the lasting imprint contrasting land use patterns impose on the landscape. Three distinct zones are evident: unharvested wilderness along the crest of the Cascades; federal lands harvested extensively from the end of World War II through 1990 with dispersed clearcuts; and the industrial, private lands clearcut nearly entirely in large blocks. Views to the east range from Mount Hood to Diamond Peak. Marys Peak, the highest point in the Oregon Coast Range, is visible to the west.

After returning to the trail junction in the saddle, hikers can extend the hike by continuing northeast on the Gold Hill Trail (3370), following the ridgeline through attractive old growth for another couple miles.

How to get there: From the McKenzie Highway (State Route 126) approximately 48 miles east of Eugene, turn left (north) onto Forest Road 15 toward Blue River Reservoir. Stay left onto gravel-surfaced FR 1509 shortly after crossing the bridge over Blue River at 4.8 miles. Wind your way up the basin on FR 1509 for 8.4 miles, then turn left onto FR 877. Trailhead parking is on a short spur to the left less than a quarter mile later.

72 Lookout Creek

Length	**3.6 miles one way**
Difficulty	Moderate
Season	Spring to autumn
Lowest point	2,430 feet
Highest point	3,440 feet
Human imprint	Minimal
Information	Willamette National Forest (McKenzie River Ranger District)

Primary Old-Growth Features
Long, unbroken expanse of Douglas-fir old growth; patches of large western redcedar; large down and standing dead wood

Step into the forest primeval on the Lookout Creek Old-Growth Trail (4105), a 3.6-mile journey through unbroken old growth in the H.J. Andrews Experimental Forest (see sidebar). Massive Douglas-fir up to 7 feet thick, a well-developed understory of western hemlock and western redcedar, and large snags and down logs are all abundant in this classic example of an old-growth, Douglas-fir forest. The trail has two trailheads 3 miles apart on Forest Road 1506, providing an option for a bike or car shuttle, or for a loop hike partially on the road. Particularly impressive pockets of old growth are located near both trailheads.

Head downhill from the lower trailhead, soon encountering an interesting example of forest dynamics. A canopy gap created by a windstorm in January of 1990 was enlarged in subsequent years as Douglas-fir bark beetles moved from the downed trees into adjacent, standing live trees in search of nutrition. The gap is now ringed by standing dead trees courtesy of this natural mortality agent.

Another interesting example of ecosystem dynamics and the interactions of forest and stream can be seen by the lower crossing of Lookout Creek. A large wedge of gravel, cobble, and boulders was deposited in this area during the floods of 1964, burying the base and ultimately killing several western redcedar standing in the riparian zone. Another major flood in February of 1996 cut down through the earlier deposit reexposing the discolored trunks of several of these redcedars. Perhaps the next flood will undercut the roots of the redcedar snags and finally topple them into the creek.

Head upslope from the log-bridge crossing and contour around the base of Lookout Mountain through ideal spotted owl habitat. Large western redcedars cluster near the midpoint of the hike where tributaries to Lookout Creek come crashing down debris torrent chutes. The trail recrosses Lookout Creek and heads uphill through a magnificent forest toward FR 1506 and the end of the hike. "Reference Stand #12," a permanent study plot located near the upper trailhead, contains one of the highest biomasses ever measured in the Cascades.

Note: Various painted trees, flagging, marking pins, and other signs indicate the proximity of long-term research plots. Please stay on the trail to avoid damaging these areas.

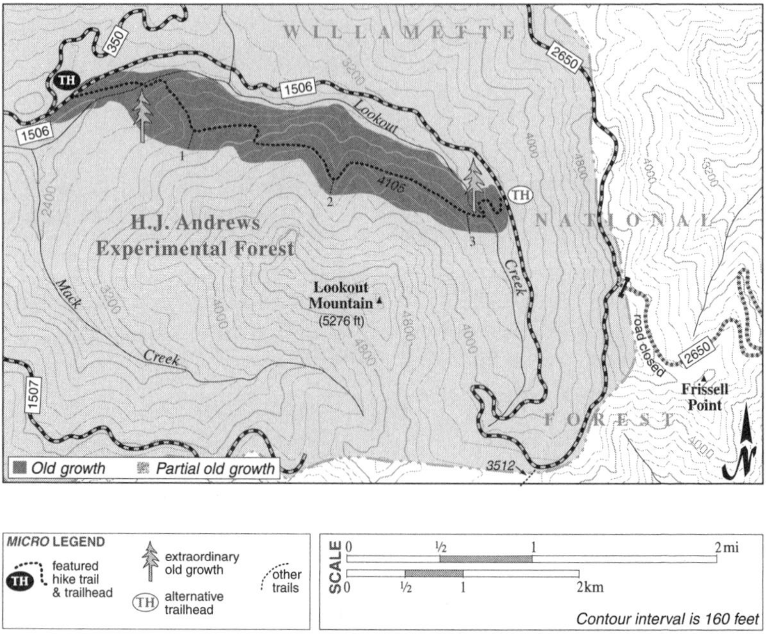

Northern spotted owl

How to get there: Travel State Route 126 approximately 48 miles east of Eugene and turn left (north) onto FR 15 heading toward Blue River Reservoir. Turn right onto FR 1506 after 3.4 miles. The lower trailhead is on the right 7 miles later, just past the junction with Carpenter Mountain Road (FR 350). The upper trailhead is another 3 miles up FR 1506, also on the right.

H.J. ANDREWS EXPERIMENTAL FOREST

Established in 1948, the H.J. Andrews Experimental Forest has been a major site of forest and stream ecosystem research since the late 1960s, including pioneering work describing old-growth Douglas-fir forests and the habitat needs of the northern spotted owl. The Andrews forest is one of two dozen Long-Term Ecological Research (LTER) sites in the United States designated and sponsored by the National Science Foundation. The LTER program is a national and international network of research sites intended to better understand the potential ecological consequences of climate change, natural disturbance, and human activities. Studies are conducted on the Andrews to better understand vegetation development and mortality, carbon dynamics, fire history, climatic patterns, stream ecology, insect ecology, and many other topics (visit *www.fsl.orst.edu/lter* for more information).

73 FRENCH PETE CREEK

Length ■ **4.5 miles one way**
Difficulty ■ Difficult (unbridged water crossings)
Season ■ Summer to autumn
Lowest point ■ 1,840 feet
Highest point ■ 2,800 feet
Human imprint ■ Minimal
Information ■ Willamette National Forest (McKenzie River Ranger District)

Primary Old-Growth Feature
Riparian Douglas-fir old growth

The French Pete Creek area was an early front in the protracted political warfare surrounding the fate of Northwest old-growth forests and was eventually added to the Three Sisters Wilderness in 1978. This historic event marked the first time a large block of highly prized, low-elevation forest was reserved from logging in the Willamette National Forest, the national forest with the highest timber harvest in the nation at that time. While most of the basin is occupied by a mature forest that originated following fires in the mid-1800s, isolated pockets of old growth dot the valley floor. The French Pete Creek Trail (3311) bisects the lower watershed and two of these old-growth groves while paralleling turbulent French Pete Creek.

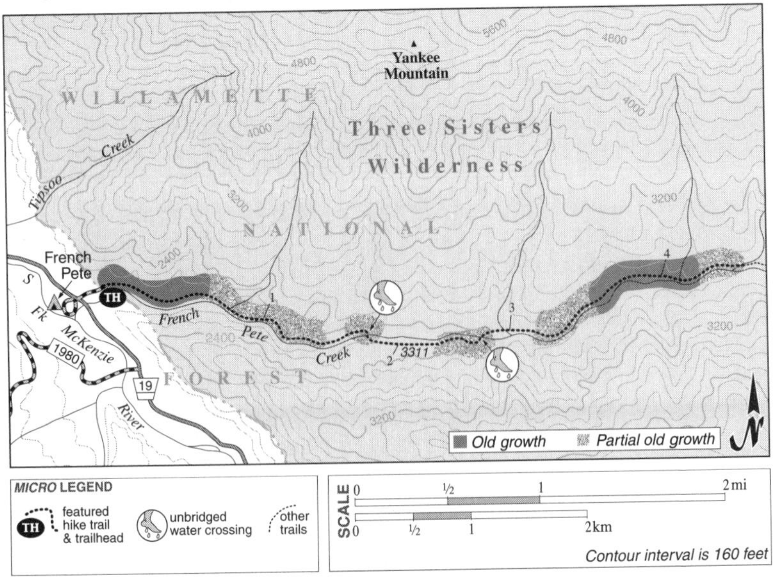

Red tree vole

Veteran hikers may fondly remember several notable wooden trail bridges, all of which have now been removed due to their deteriorating condition and wilderness considerations. Two crossings of French Pete Creek will require fording the stream, a feasible proposition during low streamflows, but a hazardous proposition at other times. Large, channel-spanning logs are available near the trail crossings, but are not ideal for the task and may also be hazardous. Trail use has declined accordingly and formerly battered streamside camping sites are now recovering.

The trail starts out in an old-growth grove featuring chunky Douglas-fir on a streamside terrace. After leaving the old forest, the path cuts through a several acre patch of windthrown trees leveled by a storm in early 1998. The resulting canopy gap allows increased sunlight to reach the forest floor, fostering understory development and adding diversity to the forest. The trail first crosses French Pete Creek 1.7 miles from the trailhead, and re-crosses to the north side of the stream a mile later. Turn back at the first crossing if unsure of your footing.

The trail resumes in younger forest on the north bank of the stream. Old trees increase in abundance shortly after crossing a rocky slope sparsely stocked with scrubby Oregon white oak and a few large incense-cedar. The second grove of old-growth giants is soon reached, featuring more large Douglas-fir (5 to 7 feet thick). Pick a spot for a break, then return the way you came. The trail does continue past this stand, swerving upslope through mostly younger forest farther into the wilderness.

How to get there: Turn south onto Aufderheide Drive (Forest Road 19) from the McKenzie Highway (State Route 126), approximately 49 miles east of Eugene. Follow FR 19 past Cougar Reservoir and Terwilliger Hot Springs until spotting the French Pete trailhead on the left side of the road 11 miles south of the highway. The heavily used hot springs reside in a grove of big trees and require a separate fee for soaking.

DELTA NATURE TRAIL

This well-used trail loops through a showcase old-growth stand on the delta formed at the confluence of the mainstem McKenzie River and the South Fork of the McKenzie River. Enormous Douglas-fir (5 to 7 feet) and moss-enshrouded maples highlight the hike. An interpretive brochure explains how indigenous people used native flora found along the trail. The half-mile loop is wheelchair friendly and open year round.

How to get there: Turn right toward Delta Campground from Forest Road 19 a quarter mile from the McKenzie Highway. The trailhead is at the far end of the campground, 1.25 miles from FR 19.

74 FALL CREEK

Length ■ **13.6 miles one way, five access points**
Difficulty ■ Easy to difficult
Season ■ Year round
Lowest point ■ 960 feet
Highest point ■ 1,450 feet
Human imprint ■ Moderate to high (hikers, roads, campgrounds)
Information ■ Willamette National Forest (Middle Fork Ranger District)

Primary Old-Growth Features
Classic, low-elevation Douglas-fir old growth; riparian old growth

Year-round excursions into the excellent old-growth forests of Fall Creek are available via the Fall Creek Trail (3455). This national recreation trail is scenic in all seasons and heavily used during summer weekends. Big Douglas-fir hug the riverbanks above beckoning pools and boulder perches. Please stay on the trail to avoid damaging the understory, and use existing side trails to reach the stream. Five trailheads provide several hike-length and difficulty options, especially for those who can arrange vehicle shuttles.

The trail segment from the western trail terminus to Forest Road 1821 is an easy and popular hike that maximizes woods-time while minimizing drive-time. Just 45 minutes from Eugene-Springfield, this trail segment closely parallels Fall Creek for about 3 miles. The trail starts out in predominantly younger forest with occasional old-growth trees, then enters and remains in attractive riparian old growth most of the way until reaching FR 1821.

The middle segment (between FR 1821 and FR 1828) stays on the sunny side of the stream, highlighting striking colors in the autumn, and providing a little more warmth in the winter. Beefy Douglas-fir beautifully frame the pools and riffles of the stream from FR 1821 to Bedrock Campground. East of the campground the trail switchbacks above a section of private land to the south, then returns riverside and enters a burned area. An escaped slash fire moved into the crowns of adjacent trees in the spring of 1999, eventually covering almost 200 acres. Interestingly, the east-wind driven fire spread from tree crown to tree crown by igniting dried lichens in the canopy without burning the still-moist forest floor. The trail soon

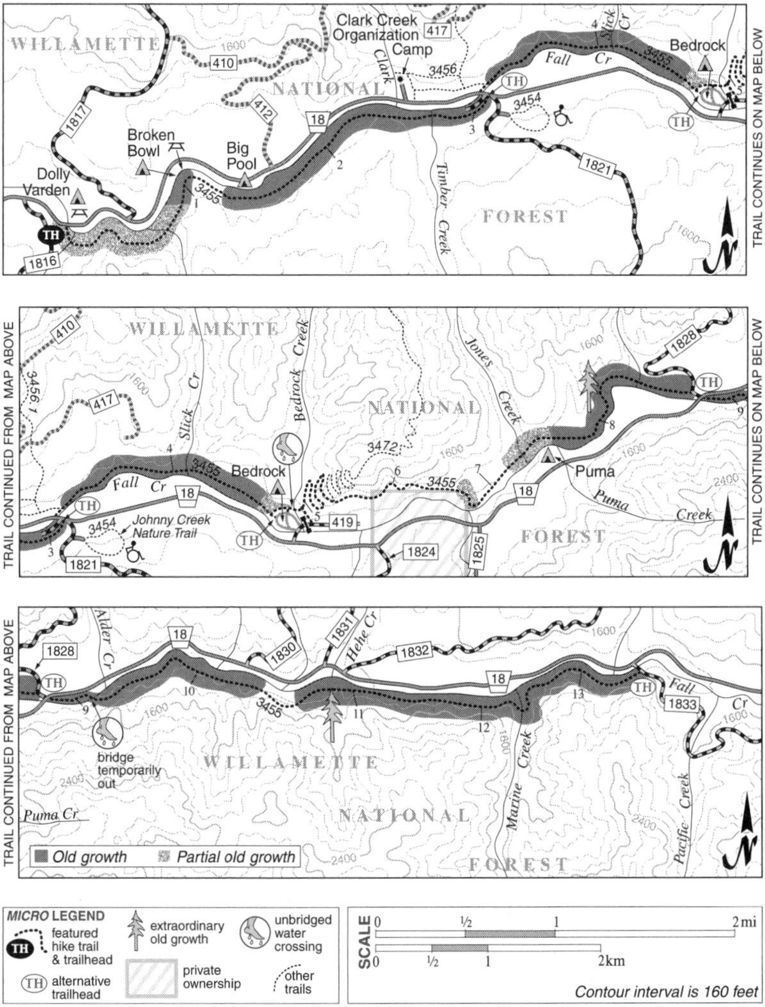

reenters sumptuous old growth, featuring massive Douglas-fir (5 to 8 feet in diameter) and licorice fern–adorned bigleaf maple.

Douglas-fir

The upper section of the trail (above FR 1828) returns to the shady south shore passing through miles of resplendent old growth. This section is much less heavily traveled, yet provides easy access to extraordinary old forest and eye-catching river views. An exceptional stand on the floodplain approximately 2 miles east of the FR 1828 trailhead contains particularly prodigious Douglas-fir (6 to 8 feet thick).

Note: Several bridges along the trail are scheduled for replacement, and in the interim period stream crossings may be unbridged, including the main bridge crossing over Fall Creek about 9 miles from the western trailhead.

How to get there: At the covered bridge on State Route 58, 20 miles southeast of Eugene, turn left (north) to head toward Lowell. Turn left, then right through Lowell, and come to a four-way stop by another covered bridge 2.5 miles later. Turn right on County Road 6204 (which becomes FR 18 at the national forest boundary) and follow it for about 10.25 miles to the westernmost trailhead on the right just before crossing a bridge over Fall Creek. Additional trailheads are located to the right just off FR 18 on FR 1821; in the Bedrock Campground; on the left just off FR 18 on FR 1828; and on the left side of FR 1833 after crossing the bridge.

NEARBY NATURE TRAILS

The mile-long Clark Creek Trail (3456) loops through a predominately mature (120 to 140-year-old) forest sprinkled with varying densities of fire-scorched, 400 to 500-year-old Douglas-fir. Interpretive signs describe features of the forest. The paved Johnny Creek Nature Trail (3454) circles through a lush riparian forest in a three-quarters-mile loop accessible to wheelchairs. A few big Douglas-fir are scattered amidst a mature forest. An impressive fern- and herb-covered 270-foot-long log lies adjacent to the trail.

How to get there: To reach the Clark Creek trailhead, turn left from Forest Road 18 into the trailhead parking lot 2.25 miles past the westernmost Fall Creek trailhead. To reach the Johnny Creek trailhead, turn right onto FR 1821 a half mile later. Trailhead parking is on the left in a quarter mile.

TALL TREES TRAIL

The quarter-mile-long Tall Trees Trail (4269) winds around a warm, sunny ridge into the cool shade of a rich streamside forest. Amidst this classic old growth tower Douglas-fir reportedly more than 300 feet tall. These lofty spires are some of the tallest trees known in Oregon. An interpretive station at the end of the trail explains unique features of the old forest.

How to get there: Turn left onto Forest Road 1817 a half mile past the westernmost Fall Creek trailhead. Follow FR 1817 for approximately 10 miles, then turn left onto FR 1806. Follow FR 1806 downhill for 2.75 miles and turn left onto FR 427. Parking is on the right a half mile later.

75 SHALE RIDGE TRAIL

Length ■ **2.7 miles one way to the North Fork crossing**
Difficulty ■ Easy
Season ■ Spring to autumn
Lowest point ■ 2,940 feet
Highest point ■ 3,040 feet
Human imprint ■ Minimal
Information ■ Willamette National Forest (Middle Fork Ranger District)

Primary Old-Growth Features
Very large Douglas-fir; nice western redcedar grove

Massive Douglas-fir and western redcedar embellish the nearly level Shale Ridge Trail (3567), a northern port of entry to the Waldo Lake Wilderness. This easy path parallels the North Fork of the Middle Fork Willamette River as it descends from Waldo Lake, a major headwater of the Willamette River. Although much of the area is covered by a younger, post-fire forest, some of the surviving Douglas-fir are quite impressive.

At the Shale Ridge trailhead take the trail to the left and head south. The first 2 miles pass in and out of three distinct patches containing scattered, fire-scorched old conifers. Gargantuan Douglas-fir in the second patch about 1 mile from the trailhead reach 9 feet in diameter. A brushy swamp nearby to the west sometimes shelters Roosevelt elk. The trail crosses Skookum Creek and into the Three Sisters Wilderness as it enters the third patch of large trees 1.7 miles from the trailhead.

The trail then enters a charming western redcedar grove about 2.5 miles from the trailhead just prior to reaching the North Fork. Gigantic redcedar, some over 7 feet thick, mix with moss-shrouded maple and ancient Douglas-fir in an idyllic glen perfect for picnics. The trail then crosses the North Fork leaving the old forest behind, and heads deeper into the wilderness. The unbridged river crossing can be treacherous in the spring and makes a natural stopping point for day hikers.

Another old-growth touring option is segment #5 of the North Fork Trail (3666.5) to the right from the trailhead. The upper 3 miles of the North Fork Trail pass through some outstanding old forest between the Shale Ridge Trail and Constitution Grove (see sidebar). A moist and mossy streamside environment supports hefty western redcedar, Douglas-fir, and western hemlock. A particularly impressive site approximately 1 mile east of Constitution Grove shelters unusually large Pacific yew (2 to 3 feet in diameter).

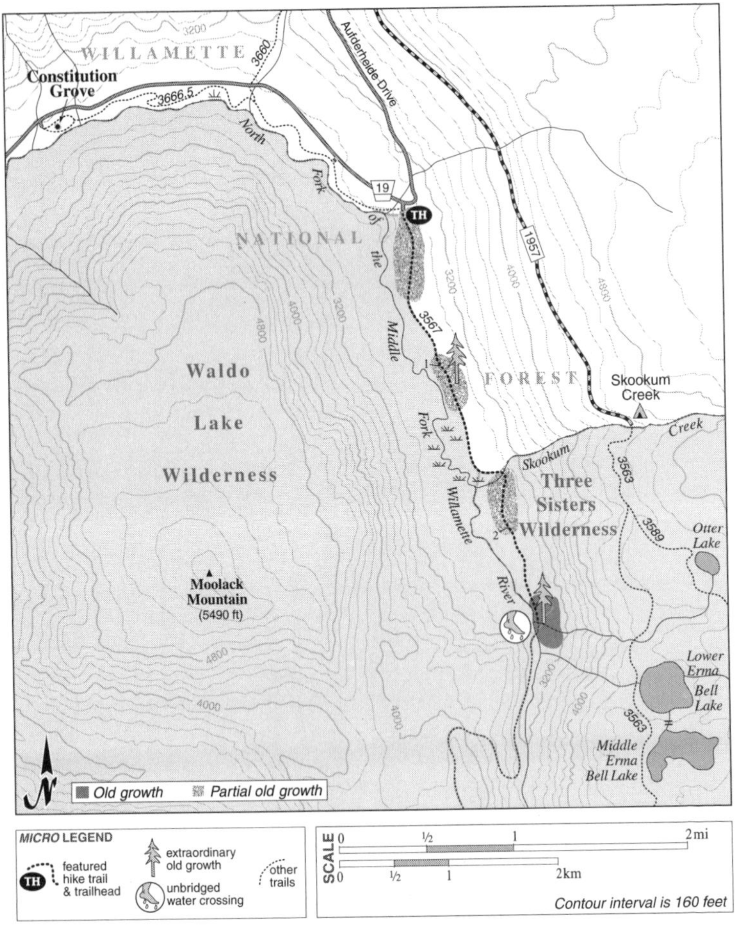

How to get there: Turn left onto the Westfir Highway from State Route 58 approximately 37 miles southeast of Eugene. Turn left onto Westfir-Oakridge Road a half mile later, and continue straight through the Westfir junction. This road becomes Forest Road 19 (Aufderheide Drive) where it enters the Willamette National Forest. The trailhead is on the south side of a large switchback in FR 19, about 33 miles from Westfir.

Oregon megomphix

CONSTITUTION GROVE

An easy jaunt through Constitution Grove provides a cultural perspective on the meaning of old growth. The quarter-mile loop trail through the grove was established on the 200-year anniversary of the U.S. Constitution in 1988. This area was selected because the trees were close to 200 years in age at that time (slightly older actually), hence trees in the grove have not yet attained the great size characteristic of older forests in the area. In another federal twist, commemorative wooden plaques, each recognizing a signer of the Constitution, are attached to these old trees.

How to get there: The trailhead is on the right side of Forest Road 19, about 3 miles prior to reaching the Shale Ridge trailhead.

76 Black Creek

Length	**3.8 miles one way**
Difficulty	Moderate to difficult
Season	Summer to early autumn
Lowest point	3,360 feet
Highest point	5,550 feet
Human imprint	Minimal
Information	Willamette National Forest (Middle Fork Ranger District)

Primary Old-Growth Features
Beautiful riparian old growth; valley bottom to high plateau old growth

The Black Creek Trail (3551) travels through a variety of old-growth types and glaciated landforms before terminating at Waldo Lake, a world-class wonder. After leaving the initial plantation, the trail ascends steadily on a moderate grade through a marvelous stand of old growth. Immense Douglas-fir (5 to 6 feet in diameter) and patches of Pacific yew screen Black Creek rumbling below. The bark of Pacific yew was briefly in high demand in the early 1990s as a source of the cancer-fighting chemical taxol. Harvest of yew for taxol became one of the battlegrounds in the old-growth wars since slow-growing, long-lived yews are more abundant in older stands. A combination of increased nursery-grown yews and synthetic taxol production quelled the roar.

Graceful Lillian Falls marks the head of the glacial valley and provides a perfect place to rest and refuel, 1.2 miles from the trailhead. From here the trail switchbacks up the steep valley sidewall for approximately a half mile onto a relatively level and cooler surface where true firs dominate. After another mile resume climbing on a moderate grade to reach Waldo Lake, one of Oregon's crown jewels. Mountain hemlock replaces Douglas-fir and western hemlock at higher elevations.

Waldo Lake is known far and wide for spectacular beauty and crystal clear waters, and is thought by many to be among the world's purest lakes. As is the case with many such treasures, human use and abuse threatens the very qualities that attract us in the first place. Long-term monitoring has shown decreases in water clarity. A number of changes are underway at Waldo Lake in an attempt to reverse this trend, including removal of some lakeside campsites, replacement of flush toilets in the campgrounds with composting toilets, elimination of fish stocking, and potential prohibition of non-emergency motorized boat use.

For a historical lesson, turn right at the eastern end of the Black Creek Trail onto the Waldo Lake Trail (3590) to reach Klovdahl Bay, where a seriously misguided engineer once tried to tap Waldo Lake for irrigation and hydropower. Fortunately Simon Klovdahl's scheme fell through, but the

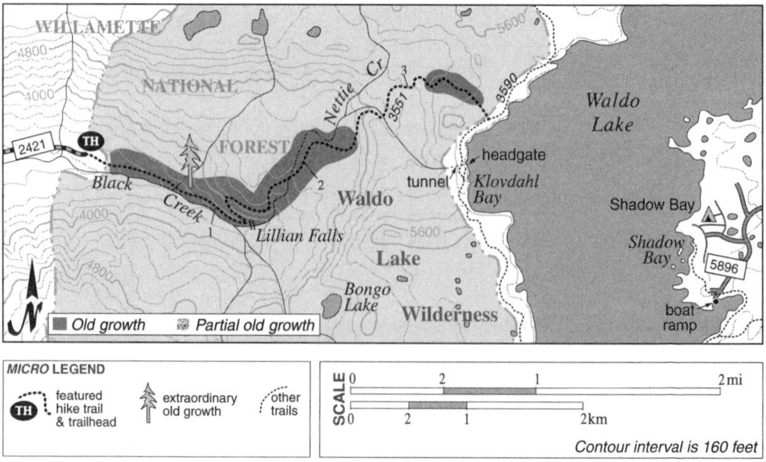

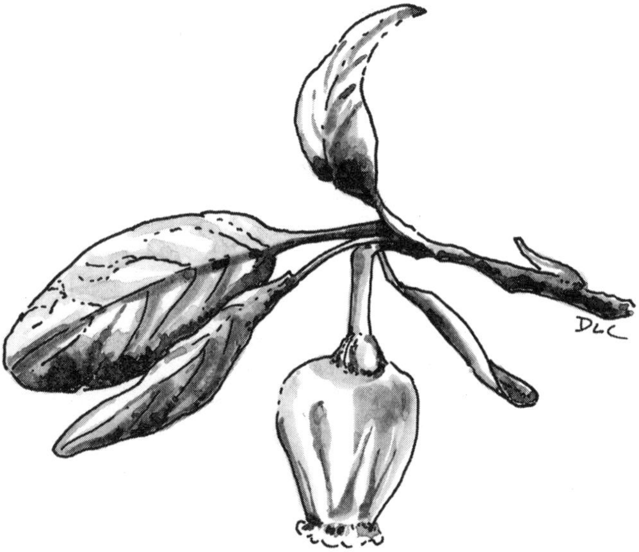

Oval-leaf huckleberry

tunnel headgate his crew built still stands on the lakeshore bearing mute testimony to the senseless extremes some will pursue for profit.

How to get there: Turn north off of State Route 58 at the traffic light in Oakridge, cross the bridge, and turn right onto Main Street. Travel east through town onto Forest Road 24. Follow FR 24 until the pavement ends, staying right on FR 24 at the intersection with FR 2417. Then stay right onto FR 2421 where the gravel begins, continuing up the valley bottom until FR 2421 ends at the trailhead, 23.5 miles from Oakridge.

JOE GODDARD NATURE TRAIL

Take a few minutes while in the area to visit a small grove of enormous trees known as the Goddard Grove. A half-mile loop trail circles this small fragment of old growth containing some of the largest and oldest (600 plus) trees in the Willamette National Forest. Three Douglas-fir more than 100 inches in diameter stand in close proximity to one another, and impressive western redcedar and Pacific yew stand nearby. The longevity of the grove may be due in part to a swamp just to the east that has likely prevented east-wind driven fires from reaching the grove. Many major fires in the western Cascades are pushed by warm, dry east winds.

How to get there: Turn south and park off Forest Road 2421 approximately 1.5 miles before the Black Creek trailhead.

77 ISLAND LAKES LOOP

Length ■ **10-mile loop**
Difficulty ■ Moderate
Season ■ Summer to early autumn
Lowest point ■ 4,850 feet
Highest point ■ 6,200 feet
Human imprint ■ Minimal
Information ■ Willamette National Forest (Middle Fork Ranger District)

Primary Old-Growth Feature
Extensive stand of impressive old-growth mountain hemlock

The eastern slopes of Fuji Mountain harbor an extensive stand of remarkable mountain hemlock old growth, perhaps the finest in central Oregon. Several hundred acres of huge hemlock populate the area. A loop hike past the two Island Lakes provides an ideal way to sample this noteworthy stand.

Cross Waldo Lake Road and switchback up the Fuji Mountain Trail (3674) to a relatively flat plateau. The trail soon enters an extensive stand of western white pine, many still healthy. Most white pine throughout the Northwest have succumbed to white pine blister rust, a pathogenic fungus inadvertently introduced from France in 1906 on nursery seedlings. The fungus is present in this stand as well, but higher genetic resistance to the fungus, or environmental conditions unfavorable to spread of the fungus, boost survival rates in this stand.

The old mountain hemlock forest greets hikers just prior to reaching Birthday Lake and increases in stature and girth soon thereafter. Turn right onto the South Waldo Trail (3586) at a trail junction 3.3 miles from the trailhead. Continuing straight at this junction leads through more old hemlock on the way to Fuji Mountain (see sidebar). Plan to stop at Lower Island Lake, the most appealing lake in the cluster, for a lengthy rest break. When ready to resume, continue north in splendid mountain hemlock and Pacific silver fir old growth more than 400 years old.

Mountain hemlock

Another four-way trail junction marks the halfway point of the

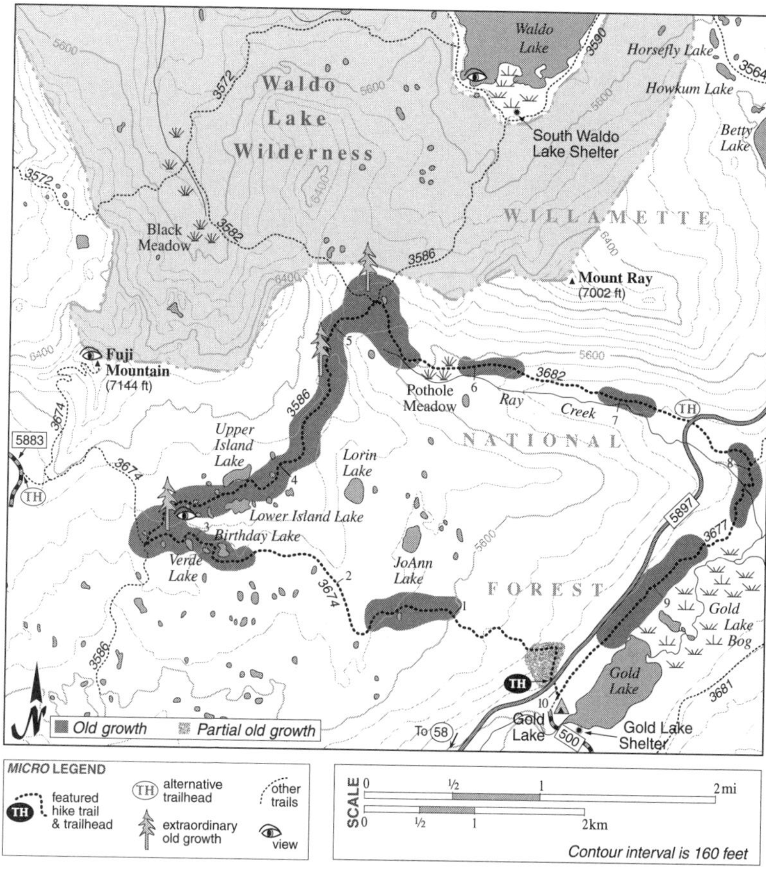

loop. Continuing straight on the South Waldo Trail leads to Waldo Lake through 2 more miles of old mountain hemlock. To continue the loop though, turn right at the junction onto the Mount Ray Trail (3682) and head toward Pothole Meadow where Mount Ray and Fuji Mountain dominate the skyline. Continue east past the meadow back toward Waldo Lake Road.

To complete the loop, turn right once again onto the Gold Lake Trail (3677) approximately a third of a mile after crossing the road. This final segment bisects a unique stand of large, shallow-rooted Engelmann spruce near Gold Lake Bog, an area reserved long ago for its botanical diversity and well-known as a mosquito breeding ground. Please stay on the trail through here to protect the bog vegetation. Near the southern end of Gold Lake, take a short spur trail to the right toward your vehicle.

How to get there: Turn left (north) onto Waldo Lake Road (Forest Road 5897) from State Route 58, approximately 22 miles southeast of Oakridge. Trailhead parking is on the right side of the road about 2 miles from the highway.

FUJI MOUNTAIN

Fuji Mountain is a popular destination, and the 1.5-mile path to the top from Eagle Creek Road is an easy way to reach the scenic summit. Start off in a plantation on a short spur trail, then turn left onto the Fuji Mountain Trail (3674). The path winds through a basin of nearly pure old-growth mountain hemlock, then switchbacks out of the old growth toward the rocky crest. The peak (elevation 7,144 feet) offers spectacular views of Waldo Lake and the Three Sisters. **How to get there:** Turn left (north) onto Eagle Creek Road (Forest Road 5883) from State Route 58 just east of the railroad trestle, 14 miles southeast of Oakridge. The trailhead is on the left, 11.5 miles up the road.

78 Patterson Mountain

Length ■ **2.5 miles one way**
Difficulty ■ Easy
Season ■ Late spring to autumn
Lowest point ■ 3,820 feet
Highest point ■ 4,350 feet
Human imprint ■ Moderate (old clearcuts nearby)
Information ■ Willamette National Forest (Middle Fork Ranger District)

Primary Old-Growth Feature
Upper slope Douglas-fir old growth

The infrequently traveled Lone Wolf/Patterson Mountain Trail (3470) offers easy access through older forest to the gentle summit of Patterson Mountain. The north-facing slope on the second half of the hike holds a choice stand of colossal Douglas-fir. Easily completed as a half-day venture, hikers may be able to time the lifting of the clouds on a misty day to reach the mountaintop in time for a rewarding view.

Start off along the edge of a plantation and an older forest, entering an intact stand a little over a third of a mile from the trailhead. At first the forest is fairly open beneath a closed canopy of mature Douglas-fir approximately 150 to 200 years old. Soon, elements of a much older Douglas-fir stand (400 to 500 years old) intermingle with the mature forest. The trail intersects the Lawler Trail (3473) three-quarters of a mile from the trailhead and winds around an interesting small meadow before

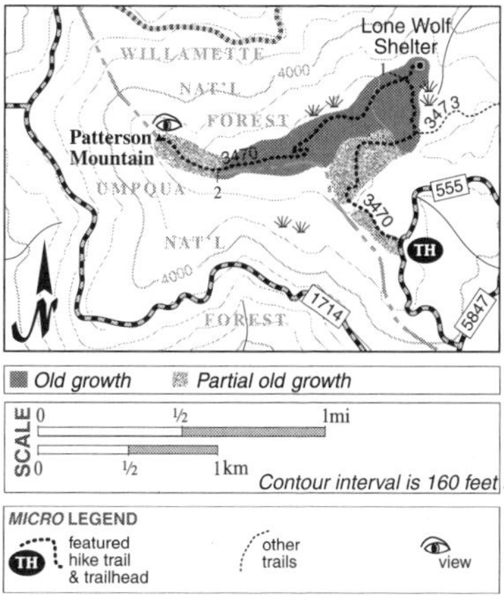

reaching a short spur trail on the right approximately a third of a mile later. The Lone Wolf Shelter sits a hundred yards or so down this trail.

Once past the shelter, the trail gently climbs the north slope of Patterson Mountain, staying in the forest above a series of small shrub fields. Big Douglas-fir 4 to 5 feet thick grace the hillside until the trail reaches the ridge top. Ice and snowstorm battered, broken-topped Pacific silver fir add character to the trailside forest. Scattered vine maple, rhododendron, and hemlock overtop an extensive carpet of oxalis and starry Solomon's seal.

Grand fir mixes with Douglas-fir in a mature ridgetop forest along the last half mile of the trail. The trail dead-ends at a rock outcrop where the regrowing patchwork of clearcuts and mature forest on the Willamette National Forest is visible to the north. Lookout Point Reservoir and private forestlands to the west are also apparent.

How to get there: Turn right (west) onto Krueger Rock Road (Forest Road 5847) from State Route 58, approximately 35 miles southeast of Eugene. Follow FR 5847 approximately 8 miles to the junction with FR 555 near the ridgeline. Turn right on FR 555; the trailhead is on the left a little less than a half mile later. You can also get there via Patterson Mountain Road (FR 5840) and FR 1714; but it is a longer, more circuitous route.

Rhododendron

79 BRICE CREEK

Length ■ **5.5 miles one way, multiple trailheads**
Difficulty ■ Easy to moderate (one section is wheelchair accessible)
Season ■ Year round
Lowest point ■ 1,380 feet
Highest point ■ 2,800 feet
Human imprint ■ High (hikers, mountain bikers, road nearby)
Information ■ Umpqua National Forest (Cottage Grove Ranger District)

Primary Old-Growth Feature
Low-elevation riparian old growth

An attractive old forest, a cascading mountain stream, and close proximity to Cottage Grove and the Eugene-Springfield area all serve to lure a steady stream of visitors to Brice Creek. Generally snow-free year round, the Brice Creek Trail is particularly alluring during winter and early spring when snow still covers most mountain trails. The trail is also open to mountain bikes and is popular with bikers.

By strict definition very little pure old growth lies along the Brice Creek Trail (1403), but strict definitions have their limits and big trees punctuate the incipient old-growth near Brice Creek. The dominant forest canopy consists of Douglas-fir 200 to 250 years old. That's enough time to grow big trees but not enough time to develop the craggy crowns and abundant large dead trees and logs characteristic of an old-growth forest on these sites. A few older and larger Douglas-fir are also scattered throughout the forest, survivors of the fire responsible for regenerating most of this stand.

Fairyslipper

Four trailheads provide hikers and bikers with options for trips of varying length. The western trailhead is the first encountered, and a favorite entry point for mountain bikers. The Cedar Creek Campground is the next trailhead in line and a popular summertime spot. The trail tread has been widened and hardened for wheelchair access from the camp-

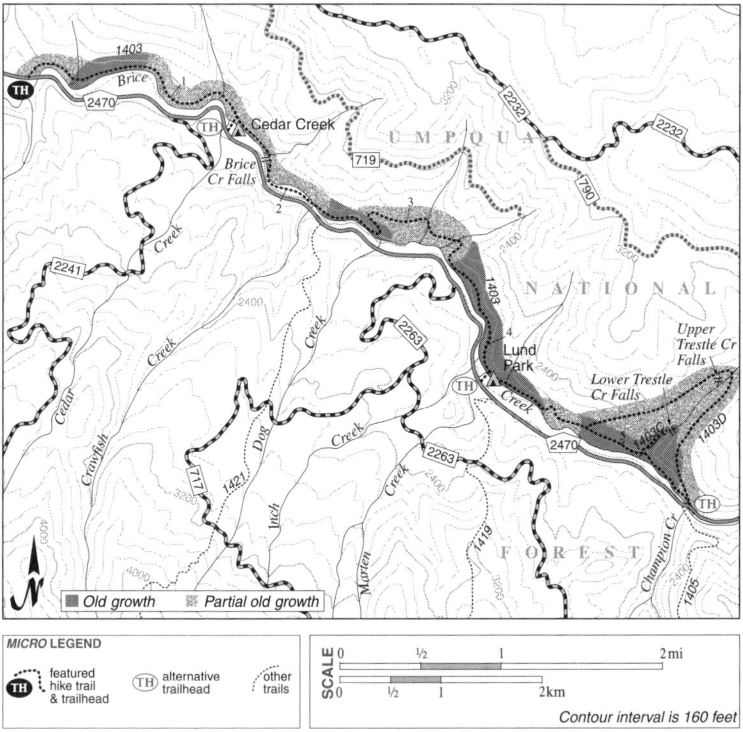

ground upriver for about a third of a mile to a viewpoint of Brice Creek Falls. Ideal sunning rocks and dipping pools upstream from the falls entice water lovers to cool off in the creek. Lund Park Campground (approximately 4 miles from the western trailhead), and the eastern trailhead at Champion Creek (5.5 miles from the western trailhead) provide access to the less-frequently traveled upper half of the trail.

Two hiker-only trails join the main trail near the eastern trailhead, offering additional options to extend the hike. Lower Trestle Creek Falls Trail (1403C) leaves the main trail just under a half mile from the eastern trailhead, and heads up a beautiful, old-growth filled, valley bottom to the falls. Trestle Creek drops gracefully into a ferny, moss-lined grotto about a third of a mile from the Brice Creek Trail. Upper Trestle Creek Trail (1403D) joins the Brice Creek Trail at the eastern trailhead and intersects it again just under a mile west of the eastern trailhead. In between these two points the trail veers upslope and passes behind Upper Trestle Creek Falls before returning to the Brice Creek Trail 2 miles from its origin.

How to get there: Take the northern Cottage Grove exit (174) from Interstate 5 and head east toward Dorena Lake. Follow Shore View Drive around the south shore of the lake, continuing east on Row River Road once around the lake (approximately 11 miles from Cottage Grove). The main road turns into Brice Creek Road (County Road 2470) by the junction with Layng Creek Road 7.5 miles later, and enters the Umpqua National Forest in another 2.5 miles. The western trailhead is on the right about two-thirds of a mile past the national forest entrance sign; Camp Creek Campground is on the left 1.4 miles later; Lund Park trailhead is also on the left another 2.3 miles up the road; and the eastern trailhead is just over the Champion Creek bridge 1.2 miles later. All roads are paved.

80 LARISON CREEK

Length ■ **6.5 miles one way**
Difficulty ■ Easy to moderate
Season ■ Early spring to late autumn
Lowest point ■ 1,580 feet
Highest point ■ 2,960 feet
Human imprint ■ Moderate (mountain bikers, nearby clearcuts)
Information ■ Willamette National Forest (Middle Fork Ranger District)

Primary Old-Growth Features
Low elevation old growth; some large sugar pine

The Larison Creek Trail (3646) offers an easy and attractive way to sample one of the larger blocks of old forest remaining in the southern end of the Willamette National Forest. Usually snow-free most of the year, Larison Creek can be a stellar winter or early spring hike into an outstanding old-growth grove. The Larison Creek Trail is also popular with mountain bikers, so expect to share the trail.

The trail starts off skirting the northern edge of Larison Cove, a canoe-only arm of Hills Creek Reservoir. Occasional trailside poison oak threatens unwary hikers on these warm, south-facing slopes. The lower 3 miles of trail pass through patches of old forest, young forest, and a mixed-age forest containing trees from both cohorts.

Poison oak

Then the trail enters one of those magical places. Magnificent sugar pine, western redcedar, grand fir, and bigleaf maple intermingle with massive Douglas-fir. Pacific yew is abundant in places, adding character to the forest. All too soon the trail exits the old forest and enters an old clearcut.

Before long though, the trail returns to lush, riparian old growth sporting enormous Douglas-fir (6 to 8 feet diameter).

A log bridge at the forks of Larison Creek a little over 5 miles from the trailhead provides a logical turnaround point for hikers returning to the lower trailhead. Otherwise, switchback up the slope, initially passing through diverse old growth. Finally, the trail passes through another clearcut leading to the upper trailhead, a potential drop-off point for a one-way hike.

How to get there: From State Route 58, less than 1 mile southeast of Oakridge, turn right (south) onto Forest Road 23 heading toward Hills Creek Reservoir. Turn right onto FR 21 in about a half mile. The trailhead

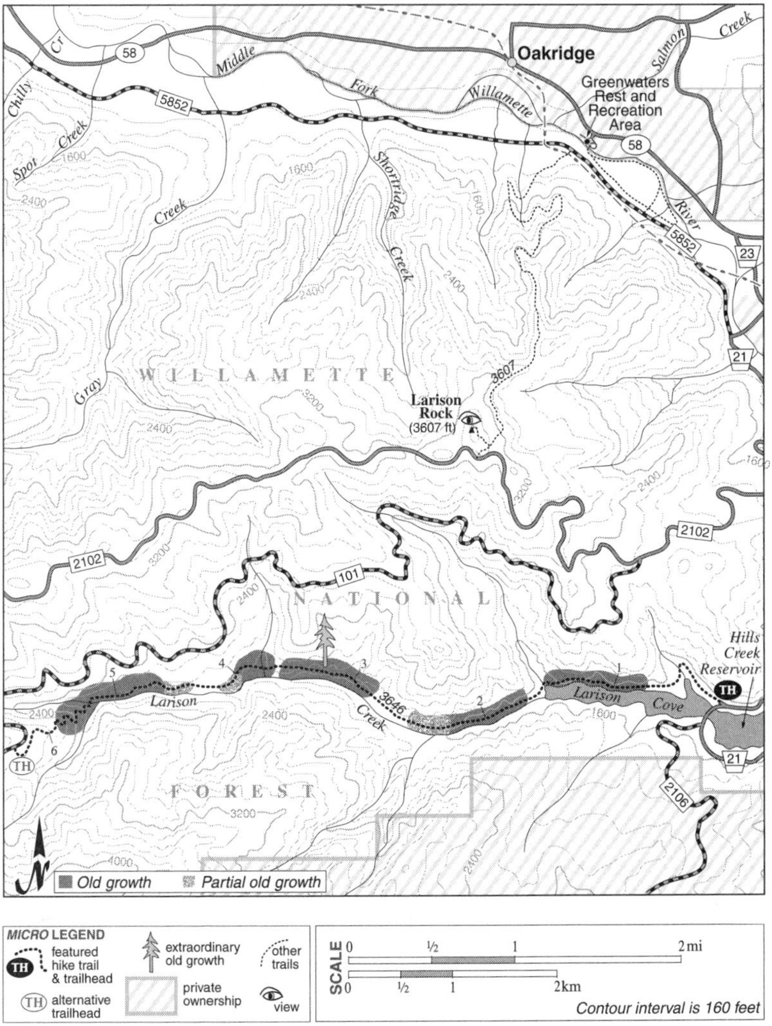

is on the right in 3.25 miles on the north side of Larison Cove.

The upper trailhead is on FR 101, reachable from the east via FR 2102 or from the west via FR 5850 and FR 2106. Note that FR 101 is maintained infrequently and may be very brushy.

LARISON ROCK

Another delightful patch of low-elevation old growth stands along the lower end of the Larison Rock Trail (3607), just a few miles north of Larison Creek. From the lower trailhead, the 4-mile-long trail curls up a north-facing slope through old Douglas-fir, western hemlock, and western redcedar on a steep course toward Larison Rock. The effects of the last major fire in this stand become more visible as you progress uphill and cross over to drier south- and west-facing slopes. Old growth first gives way to a younger forest overtopped by scattered old fire survivors, before the old trees fade away completely over the last mile. A half-mile side trail near the upper trailhead leads to the top of Larison Rock. Views from the rock are partially obstructed by growing conifers.

How to get there: Turn onto the west end of Forest Road 5852 from State Route 58, approximately 2.5 miles west of Oakridge. The trailhead is on the right side of FR 5852 in 2.5 miles. The trailhead can also be reached from the east end of FR 5852 via FR 21.

81 ┆ YOUNGS ROCK

Length ■	6.5 miles one way
Difficulty ■	Moderate to difficult
Season ■	Summer to autumn
Lowest point ■	2,080 feet
Highest point ■	5,180 feet
Human imprint ■	Moderate (mountain bikers)
Information ■	Willamette National Forest (Middle Fork Ranger District)

The northernmost stand of ponderosa pine in the western Cascades covers the slopes below Youngs Rock, one of two impressive rock monoliths framing the headwaters of Youngs Creek. Stands like this on the northern margin of a species

Primary Old-Growth Feature
Ponderosa pine old growth near the northern limit of its range in the western Cascades

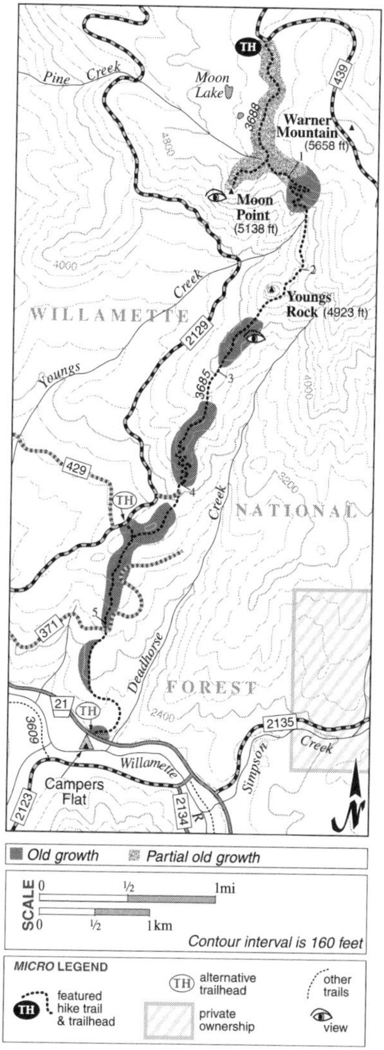

range may provide seed for northward expansion if the climate warms appreciably. The scenery along the trail is also popular with mountain bikers; expect to encounter bikers on summer weekends.

From the upper (northern) trailhead, head south on the Moon Point Trail (3688) through scattered old grand fir, noble fir, and Douglas-fir interspersed with flower-filled meadows and shrub fields. Stay right at the junction eight-tenths of a mile from the trailhead to reach the top of Moon Point, a rocky spire with a grand view of the Middle Fork Willamette valley. Return to the trail junction and turn right onto the Youngs Rock Trail (3685). Switchback downhill through a headwall bowl of attractive Douglas-fir and grand fir old growth, and head across the slope to Youngs Rock.

The forest changes rather abruptly below Youngs Rock. Orange-bellied ponderosa pine more typical of southern or eastern Oregon suddenly appear in the midst of a westside Douglas-fir forest. Scattered old-growth pine, Douglas-fir, and incense-cedar protrude above a younger understory along most of the lower (southern) 3 miles of the trail.

Historically, frequent low-severity fires kept stands like this in a relatively open condition while doing little damage to the thick-barked, old-growth pine and Douglas-fir. However, a dense understory has now developed following several decades of fire suppression, creating new competitive pressures for water and nutrients, and more potential fuel for future forest fires. Many of the old pines in this stand are now snags. In August 1996, a lightning storm spawned several dozen fires in this area, including one that burned over about a mile of the trail above Forest Road 371. Fortunately, burning conditions were such that few large overstory trees were killed.

Continuous forest cover is interrupted in several places below Youngs Rock where the trail traverses flowery dry meadows, roads, or older timber harvest units. Sugar pine, grand fir, and poison oak are notable minor components of the vegetative community. The lower trailhead along FR 21 provides an alternative, generally snow-free starting point, and a potential drop-off or pick-up point for a one-way hike.

Hermit thrush

How to get there: From State Route 58, less than 1 mile southeast of Oakridge, turn right (south) onto Forest Road 23 toward Hills Creek Reservoir. Turn right onto FR 21 a half mile later, and follow it around the west side of the reservoir. Turn left onto FR 2129 approximately 18 miles from SR 58, and turn right onto FR 439 about 8 miles later. The trailhead is on the right side of FR 439 about 1.5 miles from the FR 2129 junction. The lower end of the trail intersects FR 21 about 20 miles from SR 58.

82 Big Swamp

Length	**5.8 miles one way**
Difficulty	Easy to difficult
Season	Summer to autumn
Lowest point	3,600 feet
Highest point	4,920 feet
Human imprint	Minimal
Information	Willamette National Forest (Middle Fork Ranger District)

Primary Old-Growth Feature
Large patch of remote ancient forest

The Middle Fork Trail (3609) ascends the Middle Fork Willamette River above Hills Creek Reservoir for more than 33 miles to the headwaters of the Willamette River near Timpanogas Lake. Although most of the trail passes through territory previously disturbed by the hand of man, a large patch of seldom-visited old growth sits at the head of the Middle Fork valley near Big Swamp. The upper end of the Middle Fork Trail links the glacially carved valley floor and headwall—where the old-growth grove resides—with the Timpanogas basin.

From the trail's start, head off to the right through a plantation, coming

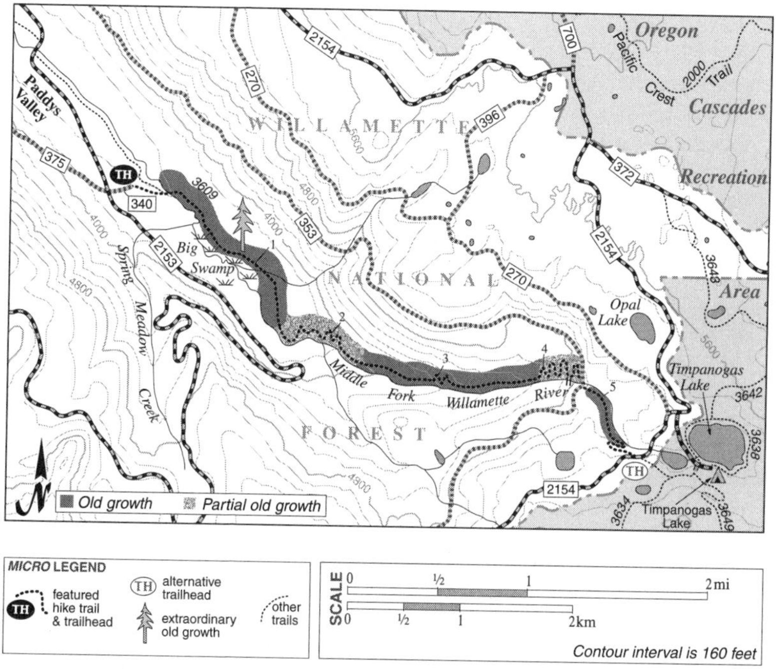

quickly to a new trail bridge over the Middle Fork. Remains of the old bridge are visible just downstream where it was smashed against the bank by a 1996 flood. Once across the river the trail soon enters a spectacular old forest. Hefty Douglas-fir (4 to 7 feet thick), some well over 700 years old, and chunky western hemlock (3 to 5 feet thick) fill the valley floor. Scattered western white pine and Engelmann spruce add diversity to the forest.

The trail starts up the valley headwall after 1.5 miles, climbing moderately with occasional switchbacks. Small patches of beautiful Douglas-fir and western hemlock old growth populate the more productive sites. The trail steepens and starts a series of switchbacks about 4 miles from the trailhead, periodically nearing several waterfalls and cascades. Mountain hemlock and Pacific silver fir become more common as the trail gains elevation and take over entirely above Forest Road 353 in the more gently sloped upper basin. Forest Road 2154 marks a logical stopping point a little under 6 miles from the trailhead.

Rosy gomphidius

How to get there: From State Route 58 less than 1 mile southeast of Oakridge, turn right (south) onto FR

23 heading toward Hills Creek Reservoir. Turn right onto FR 21 a half mile later. Follow FR 21 around the west side of the reservoir and continue south, taking the right fork onto FR 2153 approximately 31.5 miles from the highway. After 3.5 miles, turn left onto FR 340. The trailhead is a short way down this rough road by a large waste pile.

CHUCKLE SPRINGS

The old-growth-clad hillslopes near Chuckle Springs appear to have sprung a few leaks. Numerous gurgling springs and surging streams deliver copious quantities of water from a natural underground pipeline. Head downhill on the Chuckle Springs Trail (3614), arriving at charming Chuckle Springs in about 300 yards. Please stay on the trail around this delicate old-growth alcove.

For a 1.6-mile old-growth loop, head downhill and turn left on the "Horse Trail" bypass. Turn right on the Middle Fork Trail (3609) a quarter mile later heading downhill toward the river. The Chuckle Springs Trail comes in on the right a little farther downriver for the return leg. Continuing downriver on the Middle Fork Trail extends the hike through sterling, riverside old growth. Impressive Douglas-fir and western redcedar 5 to 7 feet thick stand streamside for most of the next 2.5 miles.

How to get there: From Forest Road 21 south of Hills Creek Reservoir, turn right onto FR 404 less than a mile past Indigo Springs (about 30 miles from State Route 58). The trailhead is on the right a little more than a half mile down the road.

SOUTHERN OREGON CASCADES

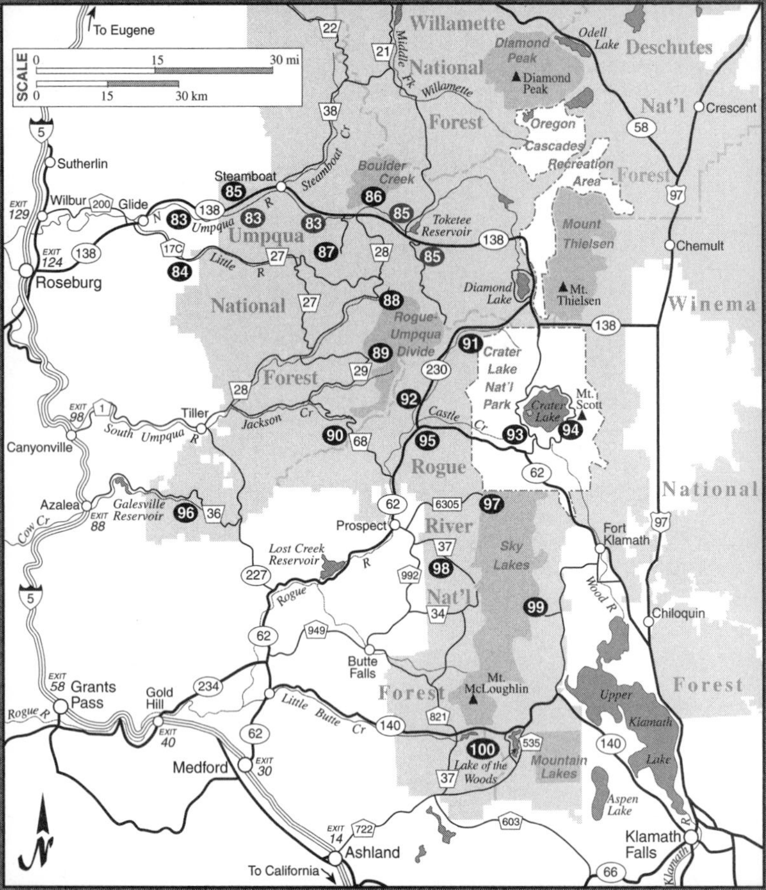

Hike locations

83 North Umpqua River

Length	■	**Tioga segment: 4.6 miles to viewpoint. Mott segment: 5.5 miles one way. Marsters segment: 3.6 miles one way**
Difficulty	■	Easy to moderate
Season	■	Year round
Lowest point	■	800 feet
Highest point	■	1,560 feet
Human imprint	■	High (nearby highway, hikers, anglers)
Information	■	Roseburg Bureau of Land Management; Umpqua National Forest (North Umpqua Ranger District)

Primary Old-Growth Features
Low elevation riverside old growth; scattered large sugar pine

The North Umpqua River Trail (1414) parallels the famous river for 79 miles, linking the low-elevation forests on the western margins of the Cascades to the Pacific Crest Trail. The trail profiles the breathtaking beauty of this frolicking Cascade river while traversing a wide range of ecological conditions, including stands of attractive old forest and scattered ancient giants. Although many trail segments include small patches of old growth, the most impressive stands are found in three segments along the western half of the trail. All three segments are easily reached on paved roads, are generally open year round, and can be hiked one-way with a vehicle shuttle. Although not abundant, poison oak is scattered along the trail.

The westernmost portion of the trail, the Tioga segment, starts out in a mature forest with scattered older trees, including a few impressive sugar pine. A short, graveled path leads off to a viewpoint of Deadline Falls just a couple hundred yards from the trailhead. Salmon and steelhead can be seen launching themselves over the falls in season. The best old forest begins shortly after passing modest Fern Creek Falls, 1.7 miles from the trailhead. The trail drops down onto a rich riparian surface where an older forest of Douglas-fir, sugar pine, and grand fir flourish for the next 2 miles. The trail climbs away from the river to avoid a section of private land, and then turns a corner as it starts back toward the river. An oak-fringed rock outcrop near this point overlooks the broad valley below—a good turnaround spot for day hikers, 4.6 miles from the trailhead.

Farther upriver, large, fire-scorched Douglas-fir adorn the Mott segment nearly the entire 5.5 miles from the Wright Creek trailhead to the Mott trailhead. A flat, fertile surface just across the river and downstream from the well-known Steamboat Inn supports the greatest density of impressive old trees. The trail hugs the riverbank most of the way, showcasing the emerald pools, rapids, and cascades of one of the great rivers of Oregon. Unfortunately, the North Umpqua Highway is also nearby the entire trip, generating regular traffic noise.

The third trail segment profiled here, the Marsters segment, lies a little farther upriver and receives less use than the other two segments. Short

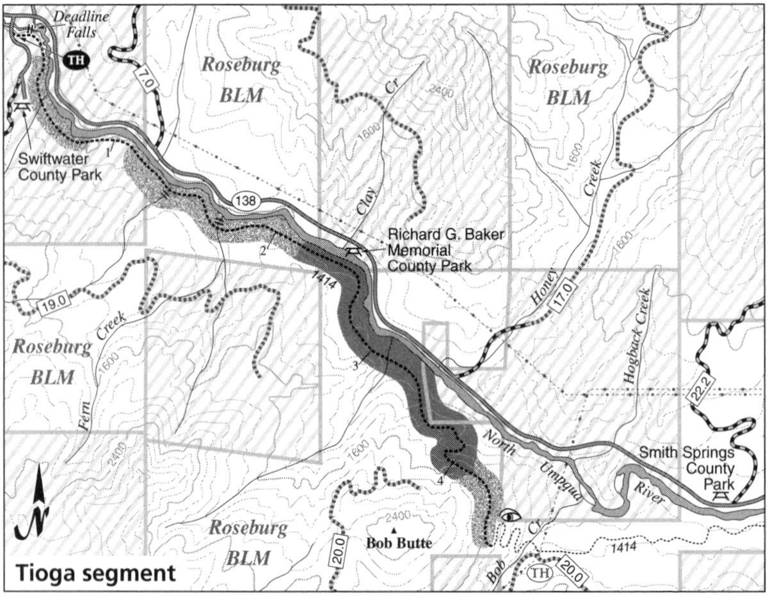

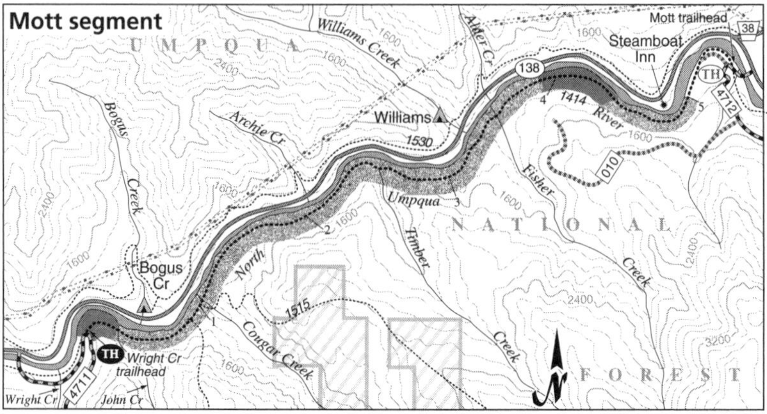

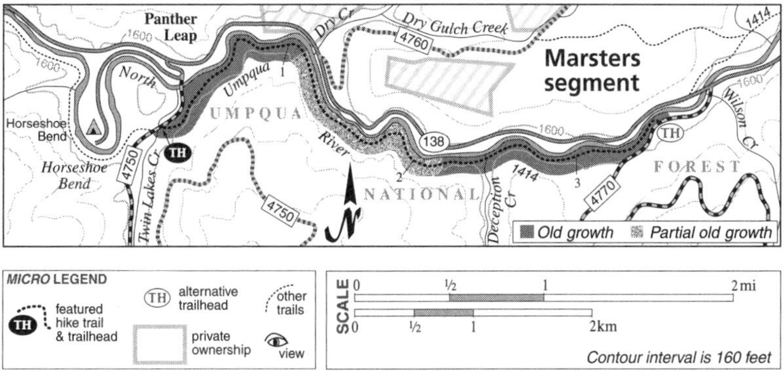

pitches of this 3.6-mile trail segment climb up and over rock outcrops; elsewhere the trail skirts below a line of cliffs. Douglas-fir, sugar pine, and western redcedar old growth lie along both ends of this segment. The largest trees cluster on a bench below the trail about a mile or so from the western trailhead, where Douglas-fir commonly reach 5 to 6 feet in diameter.

How to get there: From Interstate 5, take exit 124 at Roseburg and head east toward Diamond Lake on the North Umpqua Highway (State Route 138). The western trailhead for the Tioga segment is approximately 5 miles east of Glide (22 miles from Roseburg) by Swiftwater County Park. Turn right (south) across the bridge, then turn left into the paved parking area.

The western trailhead for the Mott segment is farther upriver, approximately 17 miles east of Glide. Turn right (south) onto Wright Creek Road (4711), cross the bridge, and park on the left in about a quarter mile.

To reach the western trailhead of the Marsters segment, turn right (south) onto Forest Road 4750 by the Horseshoe Bend Campground approximately 29 miles east of Glide. Continue straight over the bridge. Trailhead parking is on the right in four-tenths mile; the trail is on the left.

Sugar pine

84 WOLF CREEK FALLS

Length	**1.25 miles one way**
Difficulty	Easy
Season	Year round
Lowest point	1,050 feet
Highest point	1,200 feet
Human imprint	Moderate (hikers)
Information	Roseburg Bureau of Land Management

Primary Old-Growth Feature
Classic lowland old growth

Follow the gentle path along Wolf Creek through a marvelous old-growth forest to reach the base of sweeping Wolf Creek Falls. The trail is open throughout the year, except for those infrequent occasions in the Cascades when substantial snowfall reaches down to 1,000 feet elevation. Old Douglas-fir dominates the wayside, although western hemlock and western redcedar are also abundant.

From the parking lot, immediately cross a long, arching trail bridge over

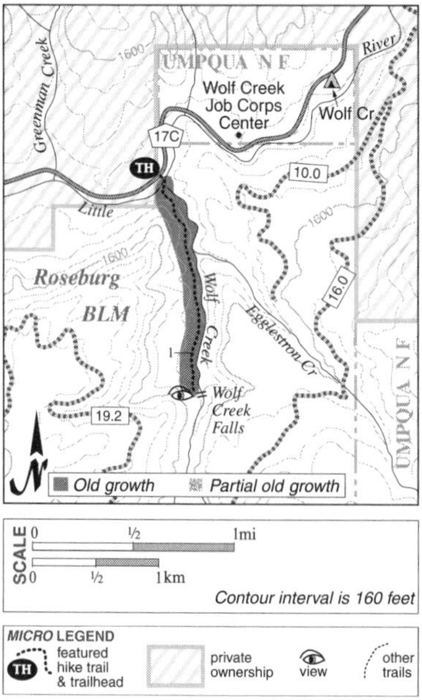

Licorice fern

the bedrock flats of Little River, and then cross a second arched trail bridge over to the west bank of Wolf Creek. The trail then heads due south, hugging the gurgling creek all the way to the falls. Easy access to the stream is sure to attract the rock-tossers in your entourage. Grand fir and occasional bigleaf maple by the streamside add diversity to the forest. Scorched bark along the base of old Douglas-firs clearly indicates the passage of a ground fire since the stand established.

The trail dead-ends after 1.25 miles at the base of curvaceous Wolf Creek Falls. The setting is dramatic; at the head of a bowl, huge basalt cliffs box visitors in on two sides. Wolf Creek Falls slides over a cliff face curving gracefully as it falls 75 feet toward the pool at the base of the falls. A second falls drains the pool dropping another 50 feet as Wolf Creek accelerates toward Little River. Enjoy the view and return as you came.

How to get there: Turn south onto Little River Road (County Road 17C) from State Route 138 (North Umpqua Highway) approximately 18 miles east of Roseburg (just west of Glide). Follow the paved road 10.8 miles and pull into a signed parking area on the right.

BIG TREE TIP—EMILE SHELTER BIG TREE, BILL TAFT TREE

Two enormous Douglas-fir stand in the upper reaches of Emile Creek, a tributary to Little River. The largest of the two trees is known as the Emile Shelter Big Tree. A short path leads through a very old forest to the base of this ancient giant (11.75 feet in diameter). The roots of this massive tree extend into a wet, shrubby area nearby, likely contributing to the tree's great age and size. Scattered, gnarly old Douglas-fir, abundant big snags and logs, and a lot of large western hemlock characterize this very impressive forest.

The Bill Taft Tree stands nearby, dominating a small patch known as the Emile Big Tree Botanical Area. Measuring almost 10 feet thick and 235 feet tall, this monster Douglas-fir emerges above its peers in an awesome yet tiny grove surrounded by clearcuts.

How to get there: To reach the Emile Shelter Big Tree, continue on Little River Road another 5.4 miles (16.2 miles from the North Umpqua Highway) to Lookout Mountain Road (Forest Road 2703), across from Coolwater Campground. Turn left onto FR 2703 and follow it for 9 miles into the Umpqua National Forest and on to a junction with FR 450, just past Emile Shelter. Turn right and follow FR 450 for a quarter mile, then turn left onto FR 500. The trailhead is on the left three-quarters of a mile later.

To reach the Bill Taft Tree, turn left onto Wright Creek Road (FR 4711) from Lookout Mountain Road, 7.5 miles from Little River Road. Park on the left by the sign a quarter mile later.

85 Falls of the North Umpqua River

FALL CREEK FALLS

Length ■ **0.9 mile one way**
Difficulty ■ Easy
Season ■ Year round
Lowest point ■ 1,300 feet
Highest point ■ 1,400 feet
Human imprint ■ High (hikers, nearby highway)
Information ■ Umpqua National Forest (North Umpqua Ranger District)

TOKETEE FALLS

Length ■ **0.4 mile one way**
Difficulty ■ Easy
Season ■ Early spring to autumn
Lowest point ■ 2,320 feet
Highest point ■ 2,400 feet
Human imprint ■ High (hikers)
Information ■ Umpqua National Forest (Diamond Lake Ranger District)

WATSON FALLS

Length ■ **0.5-mile loop**
Difficulty ■ Easy
Season ■ Early spring to autumn
Lowest point ■ 2,700 feet
Highest point ■ 3,280 feet
Human imprint ■ High (hikers)
Information ■ Umpqua National Forest (Diamond Lake Ranger District)

Primary Old-Growth Feature
Lush lowland old growth

Showy waterfalls plunging over massive basalt bluffs are among the many charms of the North Umpqua River watershed. These three are among the finest, and the path to each passes through splendid old forest. Sample these three easy ambles in the order encountered heading upriver finishing with Watson Falls, the most impressive of the lot.

Fall Creek Falls

Fall Creek Falls is particularly well suited to an early springtime visit when streamflows are high and the snowpack in the higher mountains is still deep. Head up the path parallel to Fall Creek through a mossy, ferny forest stacked with 3 to 4-feet-thick Douglas-fir and western redcedar. Numerous boulders lie strewn along the trail, at one point constricting the path to a narrow slot between two cottage-sized rocks. A short spur trail one-half mile from the trailhead leads to a big pile of weathered and tilted basalt columns known as Jobs Garden. The main trail reaches the lower half of a two-tiered falls three-quarters of a mile from the trailhead, and then switchbacks up to a view of the upper half.

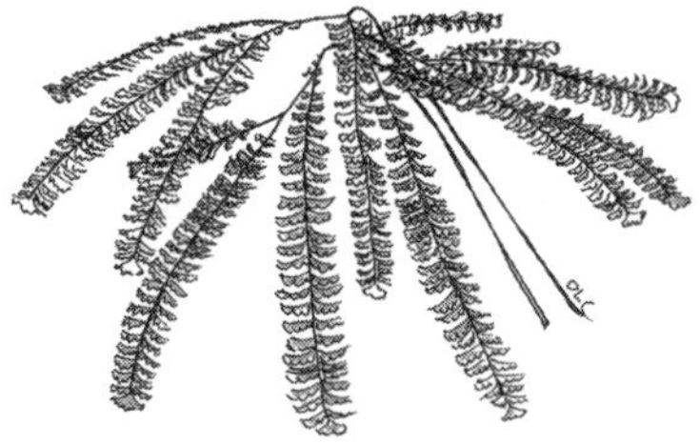

Maidenhair fern

Toketee Falls

Large Douglas-fir and sugar pine line the well-worn path to Toketee Falls, one of the more unique and picturesque falls in the Oregon Cascades. The largest trees reach almost 5 feet in diameter and half a millennium in age. The trail first ascends and then descends a total of 231 steps to a wood-decked platform overlooking the spectacular falls. The upper falls sits back in a grotto where it empties into a small pool before plunging 80 feet over columnar basalt cliffs into a large pool at the base of the falls.

Watson Falls

Capping the trio of waterfall hikes is Watson Falls, dropping 272 feet in a huge bowl along the margin of a massive lava flow. Ancient Douglas-fir and western hemlock tower above the trail, some reaching 5 feet in girth. Cross the road and head uphill for a third of a mile or so to reach the apex of the loop on a sturdy wooden bridge and viewing platform. The falls appear as long, wispy veils trailing in the breeze. A short side trail switchbacks uphill to another viewpoint above the base of the falls. Return on the opposite side of the cascading stream back to the parking lot below.

HOW TO GET THERE

Fall Creek Falls

Turn north off the North Umpqua Highway (State Route 138) approximately 32 miles east of Roseburg (16 miles east of Glide) into a paved parking lot.

Toketee Falls

Turn north onto Forest Road 34 off the North Umpqua Highway (SR 138) toward Toketee Lake, approximately 59 miles east of Roseburg (42 miles east of Glide). Stay left over the bridge, and take an immediate left onto a gravel road. Park at the end of the road a few hundred yards later by a leaky river diversion pipe.

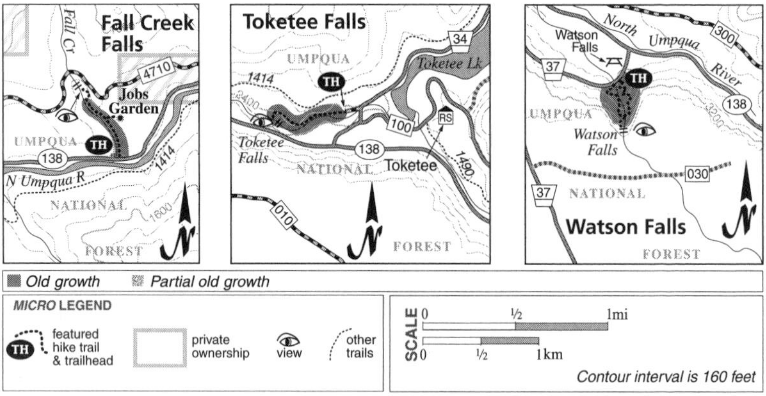

Watson Falls

Continue upriver on the North Umpqua Highway (SR 138) past FR 34 for another 2 miles to Fish Creek Road (FR 37; 44 miles east of Glide). Turn right (south) onto FR 37 and park in a large lot on the right.

86 PINE BENCH

Length ■	**2.2 miles to Pine Bench; 4 miles to Boulder Creek**
Difficulty ■	Moderate
Season ■	Year round
Lowest point ■	2,000 feet
Highest point ■	2,610 feet
Human imprint ■	Minimal
Information ■	Umpqua National Forest (Diamond Lake Ranger District)

Primary Old-Growth Features
Ponderosa pine grove; recent fire

Old ponderosa pine mingles with other ancient conifers more typical of western Oregon on Pine Bench, a prime low-elevation destination in the Boulder Creek Wilderness. The Spring Fire burned through much of the wilderness and surrounding lands following a lightning burst in August of 1996, adding greatly to the variability and appeal of the hike. The Bradley Trail is the most interesting approach, although an alternative route chains together segments of three trails and a road to form a loop through Pine Bench.

Head west on the Bradley Trail (1491), intersecting the Soda Springs Trail

(1493) about three-quarters of a mile from the trailhead. Soda Springs themselves trickle out of the ground just before the trail junction, lightly scenting the air and leaving a yellowish residue. The fire burned throughout this area, mostly as an underburn leaving older, more fire-resistant sugar pine, incense-cedar, Douglas-fir, and occasional ponderosa pine. The fire flared up into the overstory in places though, creating small patches of mortality.

From the trail junction, the trail begins sloping upward, continuing through the underburned forest. A larger patch of mortality is encountered where the trail crosses onto a southeast-facing slope just before cresting onto the flat surface of Pine Bench. Pine Bench is the eroded remnant of an ancient lava flow that once filled the valley bottom and is now topped by a relatively open forest of large ponderosa pine and Douglas-fir. This stand is one of the more northerly extensions of ponderosa pine on the west side of the Cascades. The fire burned through the bench in a very patchy pattern, killing few overstory trees except along the margins of the bench where flames roared up the steep slopes.

Turn right on the Boulder Creek Trail (1552) 2.2 miles from the trailhead, near the grassy edge of the flats, to continue strolling through Pine Bench. For more views of Boulder Creek canyon, turn left on a short spur trail to a cliff-top overlook just under a half mile from the Bradley Trail. Return to the main trail and continue north through underburned forest for another 1.4 miles to Boulder Creek, 4 miles from the trailhead. The Boulder Creek cross-

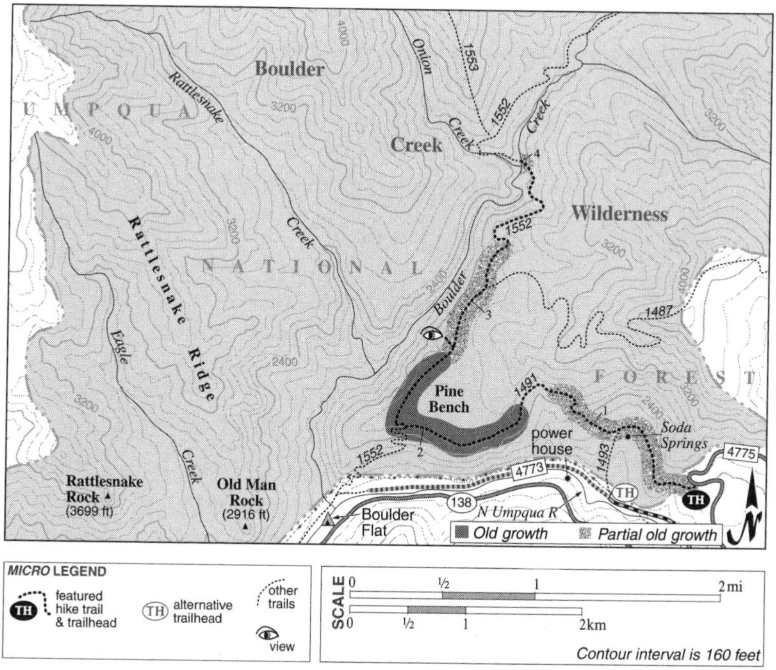

ing makes a fine destination for a day hike, offering a large Douglas-fir bridge log for a rest stop. When body and mind are rejuvenated, return the way you came.

Ponderosa pine

Another option is to make a loop starting on the Soda Springs Trail (1493). Head uphill until joining the Bradley Trail (1491) in less than half a mile. Turn left and continue on to Pine Bench. To return from Pine Bench, head south on the Boulder Creek Trail (1552) from the junction with the Bradley Trail. Switchback downhill and turn left on an old jeep road, soon coming to a gate at the end of the Soda Springs Road. Poison oak is abundant on this south-facing hillslope. Follow the road back to the trailhead.

How to get there: For the Bradley Trail, turn left onto Medicine Creek Road (Forest Road 4775) from the North Umpqua Highway (State Route 138) approximately 55 miles east of Roseburg. Follow Medicine Creek Road for approximately 1 mile and park on the right.

For the Soda Springs Trail, turn left onto Medicine Creek Road and take an immediate left onto Soda Springs Road and park on the left in 1.3 miles.

87 TWIN LAKES

Length ■ **4.2-mile loop; 7.2 miles including side trip to viewpoint**
Difficulty ■ Easy to moderate
Season ■ Summer to autumn
Lowest point ■ 4,880 feet
Highest point ■ 5,040 feet; 5,600 feet at viewpoint
Human imprint ■ Moderate (hikers, campers)
Information ■ Umpqua National Forest (North Umpqua Ranger District)

Primary Old-Growth Features
Remarkable old Douglas-fir; nearly pure Shasta red fir stand

Although most visitors come to twinkling Twin Lakes for the forested lake setting, it is a worthy destination for old-forest enthusiasts as well. The Twin Lakes Trail (1500) immediately enters an ancient forest inhabited by craggy Douglas-fir, some reaching 6 to 7 feet in diameter. The original tops of most of these giants broke off long ago, rerouting chemicals within the tree in a sort of midlife crisis causing former branches to start growing straight up in a bid to become the new leader.

The path soon leaves this stand and enters a mature forest of Douglas-fir and grand fir interspersed with a few older trees. A fine view of the Boulder Creek Wilderness and several Cascade peaks at the half mile point serves as an appetizer for the spectacular view to be had from the cliffs above Twin Lakes. Turn right onto the Twin Lakes Loop (1521) at a trail junction about 1 mile from the trailhead, then stay left at the next junction with the Deception Trail (1510) a couple hundred yards later. Wind your way toward Twin Lakes passing through attractive meadows studded with camas, paintbrush, and other wildflowers.

Both lakes are quite nice and quite chilly judging from the shrieks of bold bathers. The lower lake (Big Lake) is more heavily used, while the upper lake (Small Lake) offers a little more privacy. A mature forest of Douglas-fir, grand fir, and white pine surrounds both lakes. Small groups of Alaska-cedar, a common species farther north but confined to scattered high-elevation sites in Oregon, grow along both lakeshores.

To extend your hike on the way out, stay right at the first junction encountered on the way in and head upslope. The trail passes through small meadows embedded in a forested matrix, including Shasta red fir, grand fir, and some huge Douglas-fir. A nearly pure patch of old Shasta red fir stands astride the trail just before crossing over to the south side of the ridge.

Turn right on an unsigned spur trail a half mile later and ascend about 50 yards to the top of a massive, windswept cliff overlooking cerulean blue Twin Lakes. This raven's-eye viewpoint provides a grand and unobstructed view of Three Sisters, Diamond Peak, Boulder Creek Wilderness, and Mounts Thielsen and Bailey. The Apple Fire burned the slopes directly below Twin Lakes in August 2002, portions of which are also visible from the cliff top. These cliffs are not for small children, and stringent caution needs to be exerted by all.

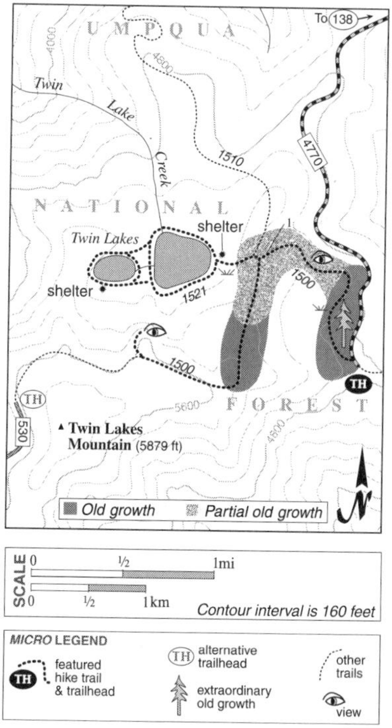

How to get there: From Interstate 5 take exit 124 at Roseburg and head east toward Diamond Lake on the North Umpqua Highway (State Route 138). Follow the highway up the river and turn right (south) onto Forest Road 4770 approximately 34 miles east of Glide. Trailhead parking is at the end of the graveled road, 9 miles from the highway.

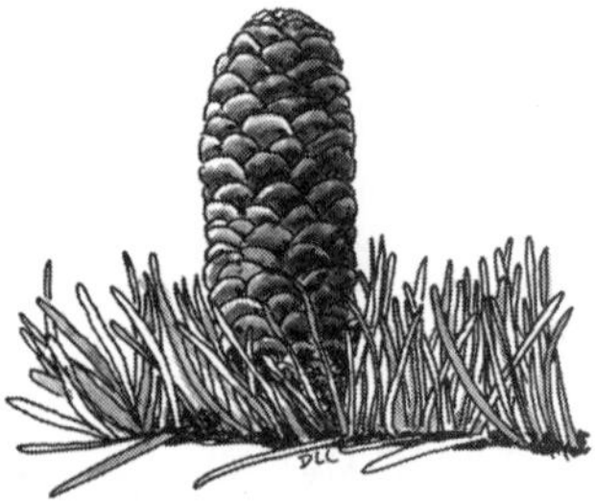

Grand fir

88 CASTLE CREEK

Length	**6 miles one way**
Difficulty	Moderate to difficult
Season	Spring to autumn
Lowest point	3,040 feet
Highest point	3,920 feet
Human imprint	Minimal
Information	Umpqua National Forest (Tiller Ranger District)

Primary Old-Growth Features
Long, unfragmented expanse of Douglas-fir forest in remote valley; recent forest fire

The Castle Creek Trail is a trail for tree lovers. No misty mountains, alpine lakes, winsome waterfalls, or flower-filled meadows, just mile after mile of 220 to 300-year-old Douglas-fir. Other tree species and a few older Douglas-fir add variety and character to this vast, unbroken forest in a seldom-visited corner of the Rogue-Umpqua Divide Wilderness. Although the trees are not exceptionally large by Northwest standards (2 to 4 feet diameter), the Castle Creek Trail (1576) offers an unusual level of deep-forest solitude.

The summer of 2002 saw a spate of large fires strike southern Oregon, including a group of lightning-ignited fires in this area known as the Tiller Complex. One of these fires, the Big Bend Fire, burned over the first two miles of the Castle Creek Trail creating an opportunity to observe first-hand the effects of a low-severity ground fire on an old forest. In this case, the fire burned understory vegetation in most areas, skipped some areas altogether, and killed few overstory trees. The fire may actually accelerate development of complex forest habitats by increasing the variability of the forest.

The trails soon enters an attractive forest of stately, fire-scorched Douglas-fir sprinkled with singed grand fir, incense-cedar, sugar pine, and ponderosa pine. The trail stays above the stream on this relatively dry, southeast-facing slope for 3 miles or so, then heads down towards the stream. A rocktop perch provides the first views of the Castle Rock Fork.

The trail then stays close to the stream for about a mile, passing beneath an interesting streamlet dribbling over the mossy edge of a house-sized boulder. A large, down log offers an alternative to fording Castle Rock Fork, about 4 miles from the trailhead. This section of stream shows obvious effects from large floods that occurred in the fall of 1996. Flood flows created new deposits of gravel and cobble in some places, downcut through pre-flood deposits in other areas, and left the flood zone littered with logs.

The trail soon heads upslope to a broad bench, staying mostly on the level for a half mile or so. Here the trail is on a northeast-facing slope hosting conifers that require more soil moisture to prosper. Western hemlock, Pacific silver fir, and occasional Shasta red fir mingle with still dominant Douglas-fir. The trail contours along a steep sideslope for another half mile before heading back down to the Castle Rock Fork, a likely stopping point for day hikers. The trail crosses Castle Rock Fork here and continues steeply up a ridge another 4 miles to Fish Creek Valley Road.

How to get there: From Canyonville (exit 98 off Interstate 5), head east

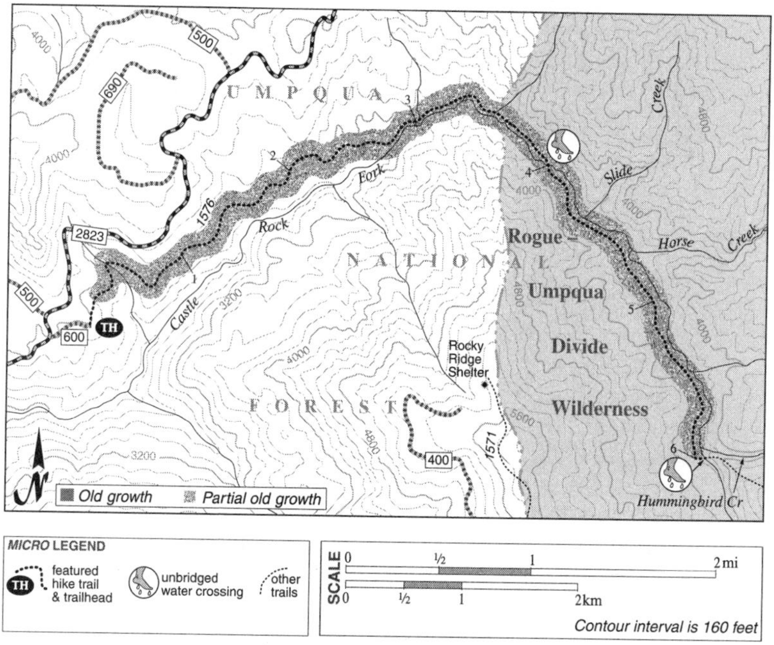

towards Days Creek and Tiller on County Road 1. Turn left onto South Umpqua Road (County Road 46) just before crossing the bridge over the South Umpqua River in Tiller, approximately 23 miles from Canyonville. This road turns into Forest Road 28 about 6.5 miles later where it enters the Umpqua National Forest. Continue on FR 28 until reaching FR 2823, approximately 24 miles from Tiller, and turn right onto FR 2823. Stay left on FR 2823 at a junction 2.4 miles later where the pavement ends, then turn right after 3.7 miles onto a poorly marked and brushy spur road (FR 600). The trail begins at the end of the road in a third of a mile.

Note: The Forest Service plans to move the trailhead when funding is available so that the trail comes directly off of FR 2823 a little farther up FR 2823.

CAMP COMFORT TRAIL

An easy jaunt on the nearby Camp Comfort Trail may be a perfect way to cap your day. The wheelchair-accessible trail heads gently downhill through a beautiful riverside forest towards a scenic pool and potential swimming hole. Large Douglas-fir near the path tower over western redcedar, western hemlock, and incense-cedar. An immense sugar pine snag stands just below the trail. The trail dead-ends in just over a quarter mile where the Black Rock and Castle Rock Forks join to form the South Umpqua River.

How to get there: Follow the directions for the Castle Creek Trail, but continue on FR 28 an additional 2 miles until reaching Camp Comfort. Turn right into the campground and continue straight ahead to a small trailhead parking area.

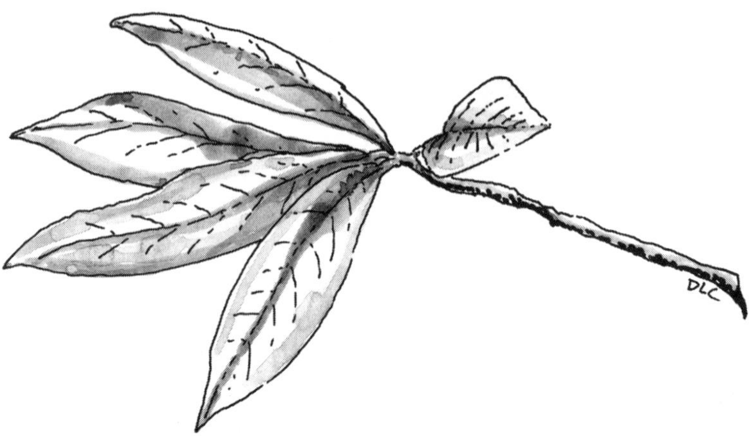

Golden chinquapin

89 HIGHROCK MOUNTAIN

Length ■ **15-mile loop**
Difficulty ■ Difficult
Season ■ Summer to early autumn
Lowest point ■ 3,540 feet
Highest point ■ 5,880 feet
Human imprint ■ Minimal
Information ■ Umpqua National Forest (Tiller Ranger District)

Primary Old-Growth Feature
Enormous Douglas-fir and incense-cedar

Spectacular and varied old growth is abundant along this loop through the heart of the Rogue-Umpqua Divide Wilderness. Huge Douglas-fir dominate the forest in several locations; immense incense-cedar rim mountain meadows; and splendid Shasta red fir tower over the trail at higher elevations. Several remarkable trees of exceptional girth in an ancient forest just below Highrock Meadow are themselves a worthy destination.

Turn right onto the Acker Divide Trail (1437) within a couple hundred yards of the trailhead and soon enter an open, attractive forest of large Douglas-fir, incense-cedar, grand fir, and sugar pine. Turn left onto the Grasshopper Trail (1574) a little over a mile from the trailhead, and circle the western and northern perimeter of Grasshopper Meadow. Incense-cedar line the meadow margin, including a particularly large and gnarly specimen near the northwest corner of the meadow. Angle uphill through a forest underburned by the Grasshopper Fire in 2002 to a saddle where the Grasshopper Mountain Trail (1580) heads off to the west.

If you have the time and energy to spare, take this side trip (three-quarters of a mile each way) to the peak for outstanding and educational views. The trail follows the ridge through a mixed-age forest and small scattered meadows until reaching a mortality patch created by the Grasshopper Fire near the end of the ridge. Vistas from the top of Grasshopper Mountain include a foreground view of Highrock Mountain and portions of the Grasshopper Fire, Buckeye and Cliff Lakes directly below the mountain, and distant views of vegetation patterns shaped in part by several fires in the Tiller Complex (2002).

Continue to the north on the Grasshopper Trail, now heading downhill through Shasta red fir and mountain hemlock. Douglas-fir and incense-cedar gain prominence as the trail loses elevation. Join the Lakes Trail (1578) approximately 3.75 miles from the trailhead, and turn right to continue the loop (left leads to Cliff and Buckeye Lakes). Follow the Lakes Trail downslope approximately 2.6 miles, glimpsing Fish Lake from above before intersecting the Fish Lake Trail (1570) at the lowest elevation of the loop.

Turn right here and begin a second uphill stretch, through mostly younger forest for the first 1.5 miles, then abruptly enter a magnificent old forest about 8 miles from the trailhead. Massive Douglas-fir, incense-cedar, western hemlock, grand fir, and Shasta red fir intermingle with numerous small meadows. Several remnant Douglas-fir approach 10 feet or more in diameter in a forest well on the way towards dominance by more shade-tolerant species. One Douglas-fir has a lateral branch well over 3 feet thick.

Continue on through Highrock Meadow, then curve south through more Shasta red fir old growth. Join the Rogue-Umpqua Divide Trail (1470) on the way to the saddle south of Jackass Mountain. Briefly leave the wilderness by the Hershberger Mountain Road (Forest Road 530), an alternative starting point for the hike. Reenter the wilderness on the eastern end of the Acker Divide Trail (1437) heading southwest. The trail passes more meadows and big trees, reaching a particularly impressive forest of mammoth Douglas-fir about a mile from the road. This spectacular forest continues for almost 2 miles, capped by a massive, open-grown Douglas-fir shading the recently-restored Cripple Camp Shelter. Most of the last mile before reaching Grasshopper Meadow passes through an area under-

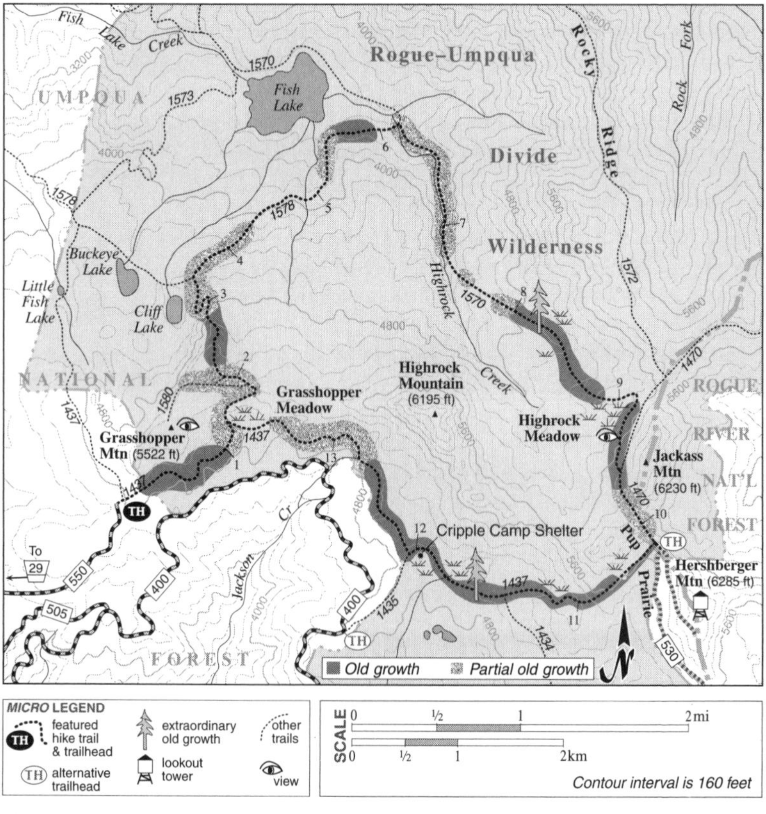

burned by the Grasshopper Fire, killing only a few scattered overstory trees. Pick up the return leg of the loop from the southwest corner of the meadow.

How to get there: From Canyonville (exit 98 off Interstate 5), head east towards Days Creek and Tiller on County Road 1. Turn left onto South Umpqua Road (County Road 46) just before crossing the bridge over the South Umpqua River in Tiller, approximately 23 miles from Canyonville. This road becomes FR 28 about 6.5 miles later where it enters the Umpqua National Forest. Continue on FR 28 for 18.6 miles, then turn right onto FR 29 heading up Buckeye Creek. Note that this is the second junction with FR 29, approximately 4.8 miles past Boulder Creek Campground. Follow FR 29 for 12.2 twisty miles, then turn left onto FR 550. The trail begins at the end of the road 1 mile later.

Vanilla leaf

90 DONEGAN PRAIRIE

Length ■ **3.7 miles one way; 5.4-mile loop with road segment**
Difficulty ■ Moderate
Season ■ Summer to early autumn
Lowest point ■ 5,150 feet
Highest point ■ 5,750 feet
Human imprint ■ Minimal
Information ■ Umpqua National Forest (Tiller Ranger District)

Primary Old-Growth Features
Nice stand of Shasta red fir and mountain hemlock; unique stand of incense-cedar and Douglas-fir

Impressive Shasta red fir and mountain hemlock drape across the ridge separating the Umpqua and Rogue River watersheds near Donegan Prairie. The lightly used Donegan Prairie Trail (1431) and a connecting dirt road segment showcase this forest, along with a unique stand of old incense-cedar and a variety of meadow communities. The trail itself is 3.7 miles long and intersects Forest Road 800 at two junctures about 2 miles

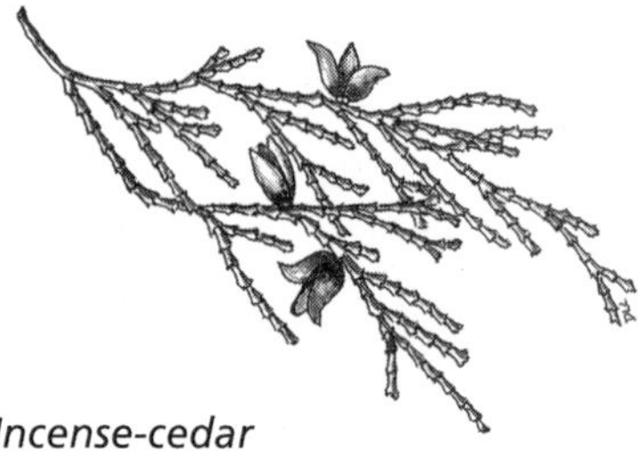

Incense-cedar

apart. An easy loop can be readily formed by connecting the two trailheads with the intervening road segment.

Starting from the eastern trailhead, the first mile of trail passes through relatively open forest and several attractive, moist meadows. Scattered large Shasta red fir, mountain hemlock, and grand fir mix with abundant snags, younger trees, and brushy patches. A larger meadow is encountered a little more than a mile from the trailhead. Keep going straight where the trail becomes difficult to follow near the middle of the meadow, heading for a tree at the meadow's edge marked with trail blazes. Several large, gnarly incense-cedar stand guard along the northern fringe of the meadow.

A younger forest predominates for the next mile or so until the trail reaches a dry meadow undergoing rapid colonization by waves of young lodgepole pine and incense-cedar. Dry meadow communities in the Cascades, and elsewhere in the West, are shrinking in extent due to changes in fire frequency, grazing, and climate over the last century or so.

Once past this meadow, the trail enters a stand of large incense-cedar and Douglas-fir on a south-facing slope. A crossing of Dead Horse Creek leads back to a cooler and wetter, north-facing slope stocked with Shasta red fir and mountain hemlock 3 to 4 feet thick and 300 to 350 years old. The trail continues upslope to the western trailhead on FR 800. Close the loop by returning on the narrow road flanked by an open forest of regal Shasta red fir and mountain hemlock. With a vehicle shuttle the trail can be hiked 3.7 miles one way, although FR 800 is a little rough in places and may not be suitable for low-clearance vehicles.

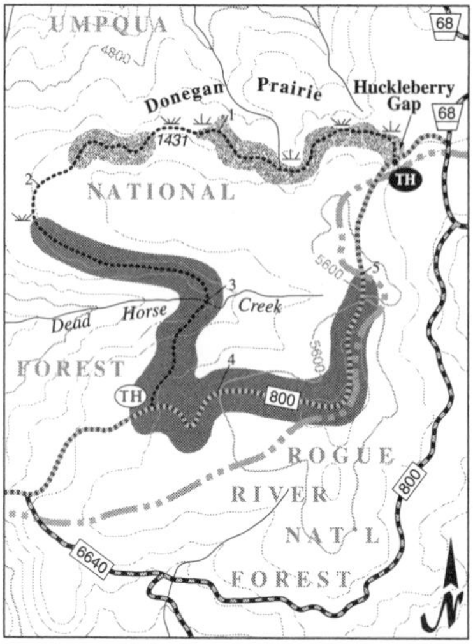

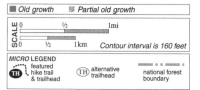

How to get there: To reach the primary trailhead from the Rogue River side of the divide, turn northwest onto FR 68 from the Crater Lake Highway (State Route 62), approximately 50 miles northeast of Medford (7 miles past Prospect). FR 68 reaches the ridgetop junction with FR 800 in 12.6 miles.

To reach this point from the South

Umpqua side, turn right (southeast) onto Jackson Creek Road (FR 29) off South Umpqua Road 5.3 miles past Tiller. Turn right onto FR 68 approximately 12.4 miles later, reaching the ridgetop junction in another 15.6 miles.

The primary trailhead is just a third of a mile from FR 68; the western trailhead is another 2 miles up FR 800.

BIG TREE TIP—JACKSON CREEK PINE

A noteworthy sugar pine, formerly the world's tallest, stands nearby less than a mile from Jackson Creek Road. The sugar pine is a truly impressive specimen, 7.5 feet in diameter and 265 feet tall, but has been in questionable health since a despicable and senseless act of vandalism in late 2000. The tree was girdled by a deranged individual who inserted a chainsaw around the entire circumference of the tree, thus greatly reducing the flow of water, nutrients and photosynthetic products among the tree crown and the tree roots. Time will tell if this venerable giant can withstand such an indignity.

How to get there: Turn right onto Jackson Creek Road (Forest Road 29) from South Umpqua Road 5.3 miles past Tiller. Then head right onto FR 2925 approximately 9.7 miles later, and veer left onto FR 2950 after another third of a mile. The tree is signed on the left just over a half mile later.

91 ROUGH RIDER FALLS

Length	**4.2 miles one way**
Difficulty	Moderate
Season	Late spring to autumn
Lowest point	4,080 feet
Highest point	4,700 feet
Human imprint	Minimal
Information	Rogue River National Forest (Prospect Ranger District)

Primary Old-Growth Feature
Large Douglas-fir and pine above the Rogue River

Big-tree lovers and waterfall seekers alike will enjoy this lightly used segment of the Upper Rogue River Trail (1034). Starting from Forest Road 6530, the first 1.25 miles of trail stays up on a plateau above the Rogue River, where a cast of conifers adapted to relatively dry conditions (Douglas-fir, sugar pine, ponderosa pine, and incense-cedar) dominate the site. The trail then veers off the plateau surface angling downhill through hefty Douglas-fir. The open, exposed slope affords striking views of the Rogue River meandering through the adjacent valley bottom. The trail then comes to the river by a peaceful, unnamed falls 1.7 miles from the trailhead.

The trail continues past the falls, sometimes near the river and sometimes a couple hundred yards or more from the shore. Tree species adapted to more mesic conditions (western hemlock, Pacific silver fir, and Shasta red fir) become more common as the trail heads farther upstream into a canyon. About 3.5 miles from the trailhead, the trail bends uphill to the left at the elbow of a sharp switchback. Straight ahead lies Rough Rider Falls where the river drops precipitously approximately 40 feet, then cascades over the bedrock another 20 feet or so. A short bushwack across the slope leads to the base of the falls and good views.

To continue the hike, take the switchback to the top of the falls. The trail then continues along the river for another third of a mile or so, through a particularly impressive stand of stout Douglas-fir, some more than 600 years old. From here, the trail angles up the canyon sidewall through more big trees, topping out in a younger forest on the plateau surface 4.2 miles from the trailhead.

The canyon rim provides several suitable spots for a break prior to the return trip. Alternatively, continue another 4 miles on the plateau to Crater Rim viewpoint, a potential drop-off point for an 8.3-mile, one-way, downhill hike. These 4 miles are usually within earshot of the highway. Views into and across the canyon are common along this stretch, although big trees are not.

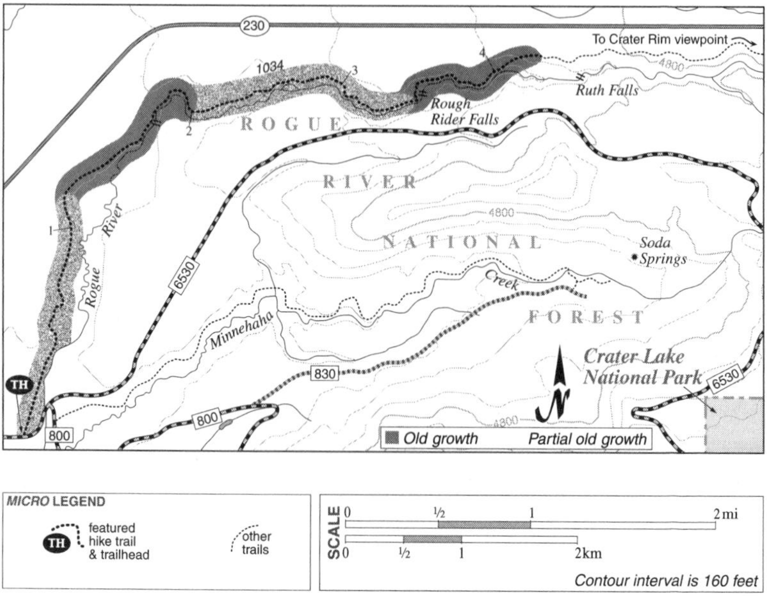

How to get there: Approximately 11.6 miles southwest of the junction of State Route 230 with SR 138 (approximately 70 miles northeast of Medford), turn east from SR 230 onto the upper end of Forest Road 6530, heading toward Hamaker Campground. Note that FR 6530 also intersects SR 230 approximately 6 miles to the southwest of this junction. Following FR 6530 from this lower junction is the long way around. From the upper junction, stay left on FR 6530 a half mile from SR 230 and start looking for a trail sign on the left in another quarter mile. Ample room for parking is provided on the right just past the trail sign.

To reach the Crater Rim viewpoint, continue east on SR 230 for another 6.3 miles and park in the designated area on the south side of the road.

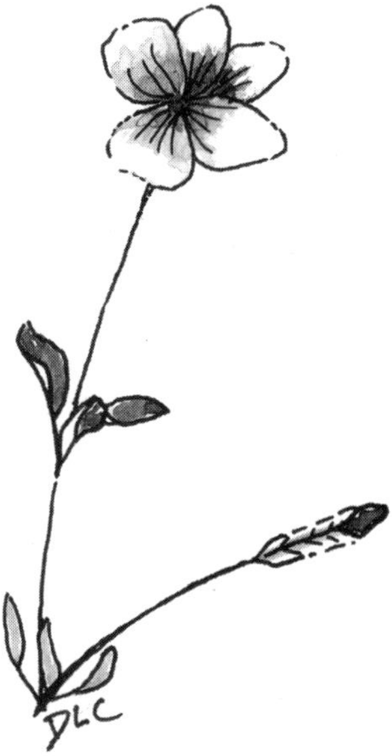

Wood violet

92 UPPER ROGUE RIVER

Length ■	**6.5 miles one way**
Difficulty ■	Moderate
Season ■	Spring to autumn
Lowest point ■	3,520 feet
Highest point ■	3,640 feet
Human imprint ■	Moderate (nearby road, some partial cutting)
Information ■	Rogue River National Forest (Prospect Ranger District)

Primary Old-Growth Feature
Classic Douglas-fir old growth on the banks and bluffs of the Rogue River

Outstanding old forest straddles the trail along this relatively gentle and quiet stretch of the remarkable Rogue River. This segment of the Upper Rogue River Trail (1034) follows the river as it bounces from

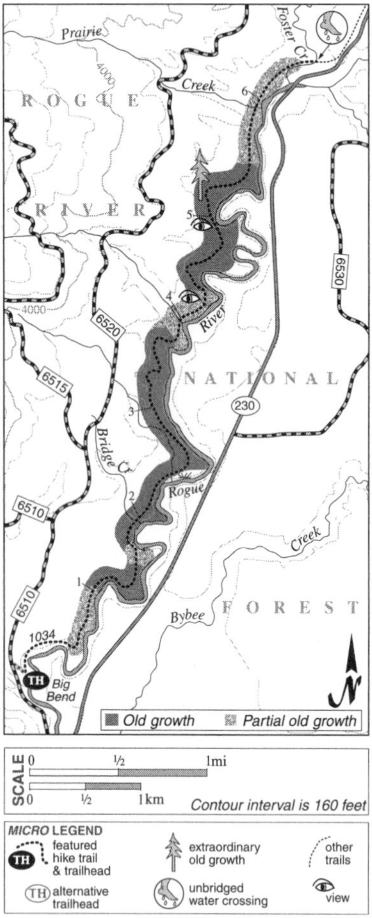

bluff to bluff above the Rogue River Gorge. The trail alternates from tracing the river shoreline to brief ascents up and over bluff-top vantage points, passing through classic Douglas-fir old growth much of the way. Lucky visitors may happen upon a family of river otters that live and play along this stretch of the river.

Head upriver from the Big Bend trailhead, passing through disturbed portions of the forest and visiting two smaller bluffs in the first 1.7 miles. A nearly 2-mile-long section of handsome riverside Douglas-fir–western hemlock old growth follows, mostly on an old river terrace. Occasional western white pines add diversity and character. At one point the trail crosses a marsh and beaver pond, where telltale tooth marks indicate busy beavers.

The trail then briefly enters a more open and patchy area about 4 miles from the trailhead before quickly climbing to the top of the first of two dramatic bluffs. Views both upriver and downriver reveal 60 to 100-foot-tall bluffs carved out of deep deposits of ash and pumice emitted from the explosive collapse of Mount Mazama approximately 7,700 years ago. Be very careful near the top of these bluffs as they may be undercut and unstable.

Over the next mile or so, the trail leaves the immediate riverside environment, crossing the contours repeatedly in a series of ravines holding small tributary streams. Impressive and long-undisturbed Douglas-fir, western hemlock, and western white pine are tucked away in this remote section.

The trail emerges onto the riverbank and passes through a more open and patchy environment for almost a mile before coming to the banks of unbridged Foster Creek, 6.5 miles from the trailhead. The stream is easily forded most of the time, although the crossing marks a good turnaround point for those headed back to the Big Bend trailhead. For those on a one-way hike, the trail continues past Foster Creek, passing next to the highway by the highway bridge over the Rogue River just above where Foster Creek joins the Rogue River.

How to get there: Turn west onto Forest Road 6510 off State Route 230 about 58 miles northeast of Medford (just under a mile north of the junction with the Crater Lake Highway, and approximately 23 miles southwest of the junction with SR 138). The Big Bend trailhead is down a short road on the right, eight-tenths of a mile from SR 230. To reach the roadside pulloff above Foster Creek, continue north on SR 230 approximately 4.2 miles and look for a safe place to park after crossing the highway bridge over the Rogue River.

River otter

93 CRATER LAKE CALDERA RIM

Length ■	**2.5 miles one way along rim; or 13.7-mile loop**
Difficulty ■	Easy; difficult
Season ■	Summer to early autumn
Lowest point ■	5,950 feet
Highest point ■	7,260 feet
Human imprint ■	High along rim (hikers, sightseers, paved road); moderate otherwise
Information ■	Crater Lake National Park

Primary Old-Growth Feature
Large mountain hemlock and Shasta red fir

Stroll beside big trees growing at the upper fringes of the forest while gazing at one of the world's scenic wonders on this hike along the rim of Crater Lake. The forest is sparse and interlaced with subalpine meadows at this elevation, but sprinkled with chunky old, mountain hemlock and occasional whitebark pine. Those looking for a short and easy hike can stay along the rim trail and return along the same route. Those seeking greater exertions and a more varied hike can link together portions of several trails to form a 13.7-mile loop starting and ending at Rim Village.

Start out among the throngs of sightseers at Rim Village and head northwest along the rim on a hiker-only, alternate route for the Pacific Crest Trail (PCT). This rim trail was completed in 1995 to add 6 miles of scenic rim hiking for PCT hikers. Many day hikers now enjoy this trail.

The pavement soon ends and the crowds rapidly thin out as you leave the village behind. Rim Drive comes back to the rim three more times in the first 2.5 miles of the hike after leaving the Rim Village area. In between these intersections the trail treads up and over small inclines, each populated with craggy conifers. The larger mountain hemlocks are well over 400 years old. Sensational views of Crater Lake, Wizard Island, Mount Scott, and Llao Rock abound. This section of trail is also accessible in the winter for a spectacular snowshoe or ski trip.

If you're up for the longer, loop hike, meet Rim Drive at the fourth pullout from the village and head diagonally across the road toward the

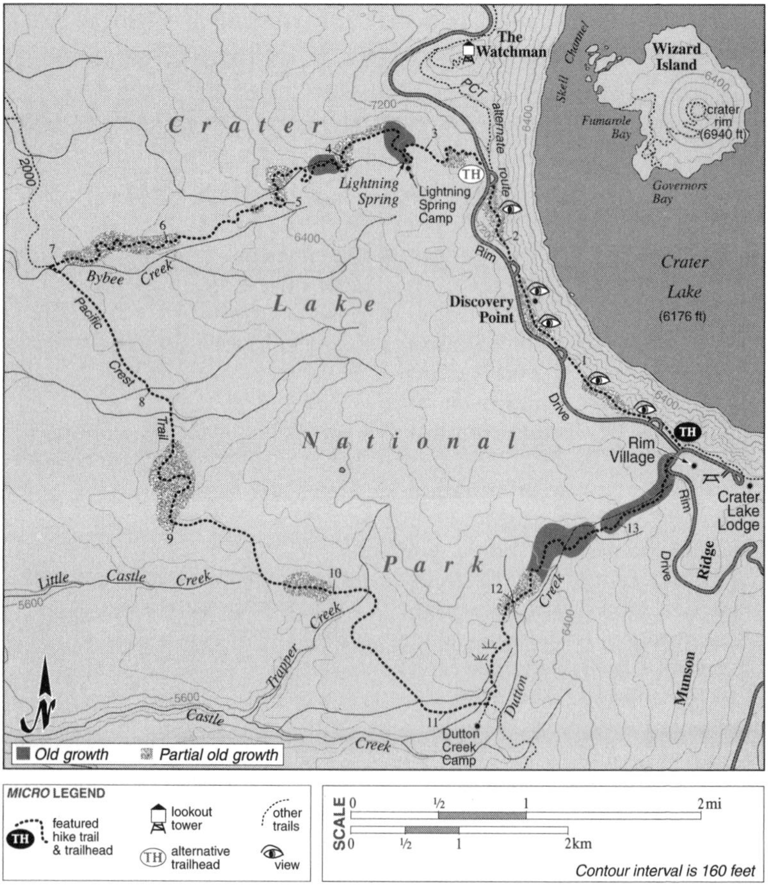

Lightning Spring trailhead. Head downhill on the Lightning Spring Trail, passing Lightning Spring and Lightning Camp about eight-tenths of a mile from Rim Drive. The upper 2 miles of this trail pass in, out, and around large pumice plains and dry meadows rimmed by impressive mountain hemlock. The lower portion of the Lightning Spring Trail passes through younger forest, overtopped in places by scattered, large, Shasta red fir.

Steller's jay

At 4.6 miles from Rim Drive turn left onto the PCT and head southeast on a relatively even contour for another 4.2 miles until intersecting the Dutton Creek Trail. Most of this segment is in young lodgepole pine and other high-elevation conifers intermixed with grassy meadows. Older Shasta red fir, mountain hemlock, and western white pine shade the younger forest in places. Turn left on the Dutton Creek Trail and head back uphill to complete the loop. The final 1.5 miles of the Dutton Creek Trail reenters a venerable old forest of fat mountain hemlocks, a few approaching 5 feet in diameter.

How to get there: The north entrance to the park is usually open from July through mid-October. Just south of the junction of State Routes 230 and 138, turn south off State Route 138 heading toward the national park, reaching the entrance station (fee required) eight-tenths of a mile later, and the junction with Rim Drive in another 8.4 miles. Turn right and follow Rim Drive approximately 6 miles to Rim Village.

The south entrance is open year round. Turn north toward the park off SR 62, reaching the south entrance station in a quarter mile (fee required). Rim Village lies approximately 7 miles ahead.

GODFREY GLEN NATURE TRAIL

The Godfrey Glen Nature Trail loops through a pleasant, relatively open stand of large Shasta red fir, mountain hemlock, and western white pine on the edge of Godfrey Glen. Striking palisades formed from eroded ash and tephra deposited during the eruption and collapse of Mount Mazama highlight the glen. The mile-long trail is accessible to wheelchairs.

How to get there: Turn right into the nature trail parking area approximately 1.6 miles north of the south park entrance station, reached from the Crater Lake Highway (State Route 62).

94 MOUNT SCOTT

Length ■ **2.5 miles one way**
Difficulty ■ Moderate
Season ■ Summer to early autumn
Lowest point ■ 7,600 feet
Highest point ■ 8,929 feet
Human imprint ■ Moderate (hikers)
Information ■ Crater Lake National Park

Primary Old-Growth Feature
Old whitebark pine

A hike that starts at 7,600 feet and goes up from there may seem like an unlikely spot to find an old-growth forest, but the climb to the summit of Mount Scott passes through a very interesting and ancient forest of whitebark pine. Whitebark pine is common on many high-elevation inland sites, assuming a variety of growth forms in the subalpine and alpine zones. Crater Lake lies along the western margin of its range and the trail to Mount Scott offers a chance to simultaneously view this distinctive species and obtain a bird's-eye view of Crater Lake. The trail is well used and like other trails in the national park is closed to pets.

The trail starts out level and soon begins a steady ascent on a moderately graded path. Whitebark pine is the dominant species all along the trail, although mountain hemlock is interspersed throughout the stand. Here, at 8,000 feet, old forests are necessarily smaller and more open than old-growth forests of lower elevations. The oldest and largest whitebark pines are found after the

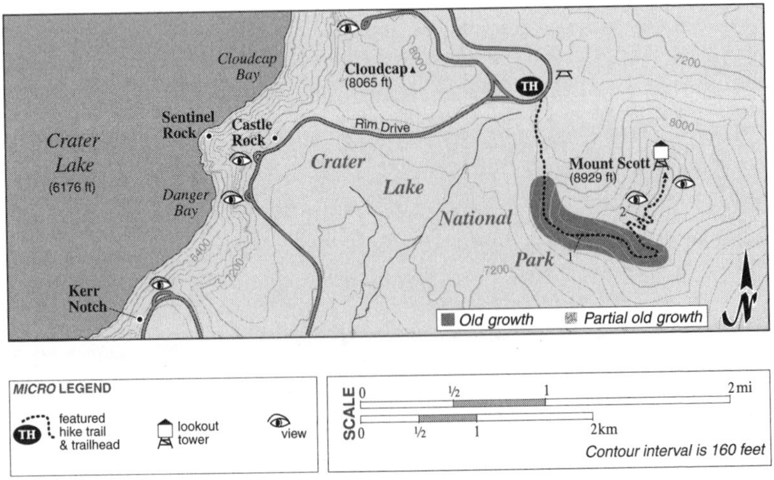

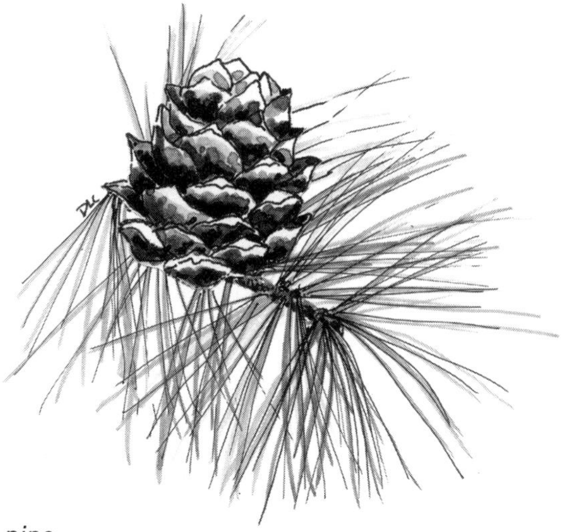

Whitebark pine

trail winds around onto the southwest-facing flank of Mount Scott. Short, stout, wind-whipped veterans are scattered across this hillslope. The largest pines are approximately 30 inches in diameter, 40 to 50 feet tall, and 400 or more years old. Large snags and down logs complete the picture of an old whitebark pine forest.

Many stands of whitebark pine have been decimated by an exotic fungus, white pine blister rust, and maintenance of whitebark pine is an important conservation issue. The stand on Mount Scott is unusually healthy with a low mortality rate. Park ecologists believe that the microclimate on this southwest-facing slope is too warm and dry in September when rust spores are dispersed for the rust to have a significant effect. Hopefully this stand maintains its vigor in the coming decades and centuries.

After 1.5 miles the trail begins switchbacking up the slope. From here the pines take on an increasingly shrubby growth form known as krummholz due to severe winds and icy storms. The final third of a mile straddles the ridge heading north to a lookout on the summit. Although not regularly staffed, the Mount Scott lookout is the highest remaining fire lookout in Oregon. Mount Scott is also the highest point (8,929 feet) in the park and provides a spectacular view of Crater Lake and Cascade peaks from the Three Sisters to Mount McLoughlin.

How to get there: From the Crater Lake Highway (State Route 62) on the south side of the park, turn north into the park and follow the road for approximately 4 miles, then turn right onto Rim Drive. Follow Rim Drive for approximately 11 miles and park on the right at the signed trailhead. From the north park entrance, turn left onto Rim Drive and park on the left 13 miles later.

95 UNION CREEK

Length ■ **4.4 miles one way**
Difficulty ■ Easy
Season ■ Spring to autumn
Lowest point ■ 3,330 feet
Highest point ■ 3,760 feet
Human imprint ■ Moderate (hikers)
Information ■ Rogue River National Forest (Prospect Ranger District)

Primary Old-Growth Features
Immense riparian Douglas-fir; abundant Pacific yew

Union Creek provides a peaceful backdrop for a streamside stroll among gigantic Douglas-fir, some reaching 6 to 7 feet in girth. Huge trees, vast amounts of dead wood, and a gappy overstory canopy all indicate a very old forest, likely in the 550 to 600-year-old range. Fire scorches on many of the thick-barked Douglas-fir show that low-severity fire has visited the stand within that same time period, leaving many of the bigger trees unharmed.

Head upstream along the south side of Union Creek, crossing over to the north bank on a large log bridge just past the cabins of Union Creek Resort. The trail is practically level the entire way, ideal for an after-dinner stroll for the entire family. The trail stays near the shore for almost 4 miles before taking a hard turn to the left at Union Creek Falls, reaching the upper trailhead

Pacific dogwood

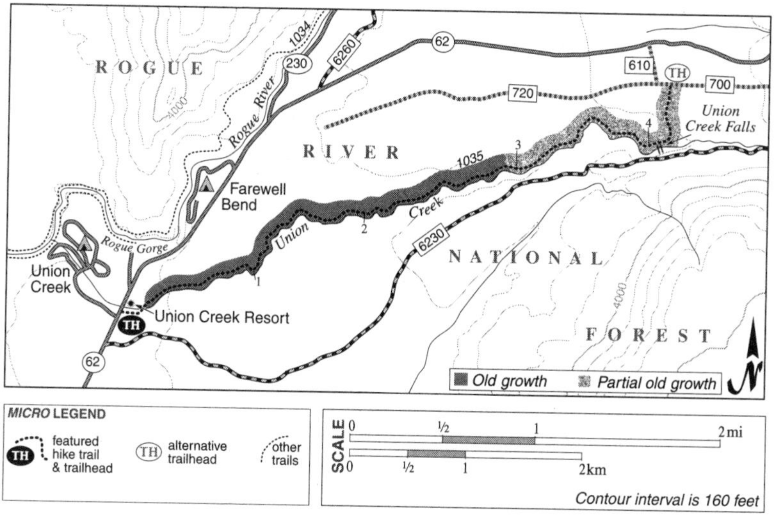

less than a half mile later. The 10-foot falls cap a long stretch of the creek featuring numerous mini-falls and cascades where the stream is constrained by a lava flow to a narrow channel. The upper trailhead provides an alternative starting point or a potential shuttle drop-off for a one-way hike.

While immense Douglas-fir attract most of the attention along this hike, other conifers add diversity and interest. Some impressive old western white pine, noteworthy for their general good health, are sprinkled along the trail. Many western white pine throughout the west have succumbed to an introduced fungal pathogen, white pine blister rust, increasing the value of the healthy old pines remaining in the forest as a seed source for future generations of rust-resistant white pine.

The forest along the trail also supports an unusually large number of Pacific yew. Pacific yew is a thin-barked conifer capable of surviving for long periods in the deep shade of the understory. A slow growth habit and long life leads to a very dense, hard wood historically preferred by many Northwest Indian tribes for uses requiring wood strength and durability. Yew wood was used for ceremonial purposes, weapons, digging sticks, and many forms of vessels and utensils. Look for the papery bark, flat needles, and red berries of this diminutive tree.

How to get there: The western trailhead starts by the Union Creek Resort on the east side of the Crater Lake Highway (State Route 62), about 56 miles northeast of Medford (1.2 miles south of the junction with SR 230). Park in the pullout by the trail sign. To reach the eastern trailhead, continue northeast on the Crater Lake Highway 2 miles east of the junction with SR 230 and turn right (south) onto Forest Road 610. Turn left in a quarter mile onto FR 700 and park at the trailhead a few hundred yards later.

96 COW CREEK

Length	**4 miles one way**
Difficulty	Moderate to difficult
Season	Early spring to late autumn
Lowest point	2,450 feet
Highest point	4,120 feet
Human imprint	Minimal
Information	Umpqua National Forest (Tiller Ranger District)

Primary Old-Growth Feature
Beautiful riparian old growth

Tucked into a little-visited corner of the Umpqua National Forest, the Cow Creek Trail (1424) rambles through a herb-rich floodplain stocked with mature and old Douglas-fir, some of impressive dimensions. The Cow Creek Trail was designated as a national recreation trail in recognition of its scenic qualities and can be hiked enjoyably for any distance up to 6.5 miles each way. Unbridged stream crossings may be a limiting factor for some hikers, although large channel-spanning logs nearby and a normally shallow stream make for relatively easy crossings.

The trail starts off winding through a mature Douglas-fir forest, then heads downslope to the first of three unbridged stream crossings in the first 1.5 miles. Once across the creek the trail continues south on the luxuriant Cow Creek floodplain, where giant Douglas-fir take advantage of productive, well-watered soils. These craggy veterans, some reaching 6 feet or more in diameter and well over 500 years in age, have survived multiple fires that burned in this drainage during the last 500 years. Many of these trees have now fallen to the

Oak fern

ground and across Cow Creek, trapping sediment and gravel and increasing the complexity of stream habitats. Western hemlock and grand fir join the Douglas-fir throughout the valley bottom, while occasional sugar pine and incense-cedar add diversity on drier sites.

The trail then veers slightly upslope out of the floodplain, briefly entering a young forest before returning to older forest about 2 miles from the trailhead. The trail then heads back downslope toward Cow Creek, reaching another unbridged crossing of the stream approximately 4 miles from the trailhead. The stream junction is a pleasant place for a rest break, and a suitable turnaround point.

For those with extra energy, the trail crosses to the eastern banks of Cow Creek, briefly in streamside old growth, and comes to the edge of the Angel Fire a quarter mile from the stream crossing. A burst of more than 110 lightning strikes during a 2-hour period in 1987 quickly overwhelmed fire suppression efforts. Several fires grew together eventually burning approximately 3,500 acres. Afterwards much of the fire was salvaged logged and replanted, primarily to Douglas-fir. The trail forms the southern boundary of the fire offering close-up views of the recovering forest. The trail continues upslope through a younger forest sprinkled with fire-scorched remnant trees, and recrosses Cow Creek one more time before ending at Railroad Gap, 6.5 miles from the trailhead.

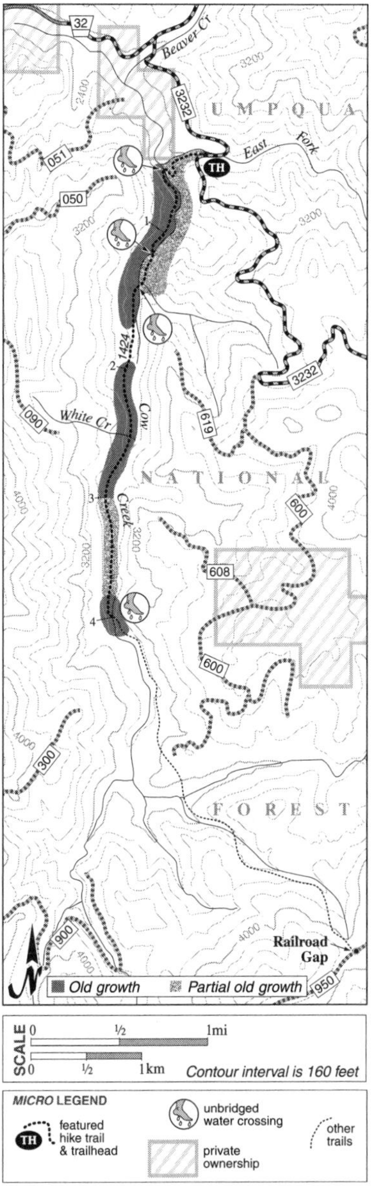

How to get there: From Interstate 5 take exit 88 at Azalea (approximately 34 miles south of Roseburg) and head east on County Road 36, which turns into Forest Road 32 at the end of county maintenance inside the Umpqua National Forest. Turn right onto FR 3232 approximately 19

miles from I-5. The trailhead is on the right just after crossing the East Fork of Cow Creek about 1 mile later.

97 RED BLANKET CREEK

Length ■ **2.9 miles one way to Red Blanket Falls; 10-mile loop**
Difficulty ■ Moderate
Season ■ Summer to autumn
Lowest point ■ 3,940 feet
Highest point ■ 5,430 feet
Human imprint ■ Minimal
Information ■ Rogue River National Forest (Prospect Ranger District)

Primary Old-Growth Features
Extensive stand of "young" old growth; excellent Shasta red fir

An extensive patch of older forest covers the slopes of upper Red Blanket Creek valley, where numerous waterfalls mark the transition from high-elevation plateau to a formerly glaciated valley. The Red Blanket Creek Trail (1090) leads hikers through the heart of this stand to Red Blanket Falls, passing several lesser falls along the way. Energetic hikers can double their pleasure by continuing up the trail to Stuart Falls and returning to Red Blanket Falls via a loop formed by the Stuart Falls Trail and the Lucky Camp Trail.

The trail enters the northwest corner of the Sky Lakes Wilderness immediately after leaving the trailhead, passing near the southern boundary of Crater Lake National Park. The first 2 miles of the trail bisect an attractive stand with a relatively open low-shrub and herb understory. Douglas-fir and grand fir approximately 250 years old and 2 to 4 feet thick form the dominant overstory canopy; scattered old sugar pine and incense-cedar add diversity to the forest. While the overstory contains sufficient large trees to meet most old-growth definitions, the stand has not yet developed a complex, continuous tree canopy or abundant large dead wood.

Shasta red fir

The trail comes abruptly to the edge of a canyon about 2 miles from the trailhead, where a princely pic-

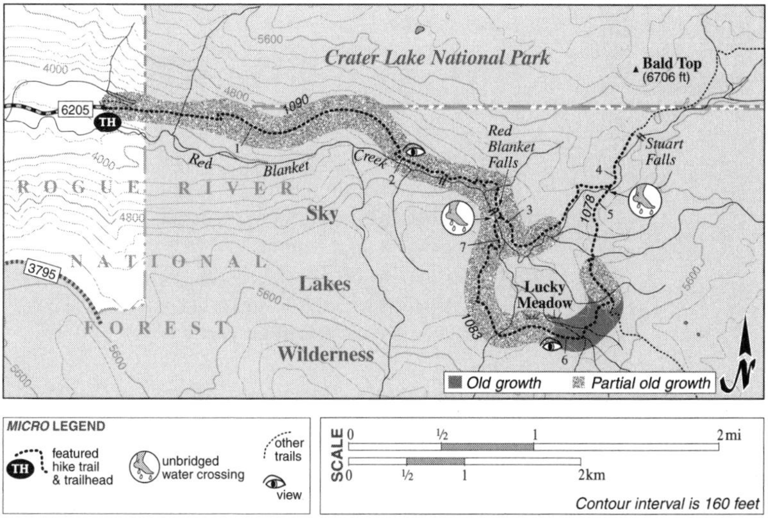

nic site looks directly upon a small waterfall stepping down the opposing canyon wall. From here the trail heads up the canyon rim past a series of waterfalls and bedrock chutes, culminating in dramatic Red Blanket Falls a mile later. Shasta red fir, Engelmann spruce, western white pine, and mountain hemlock all make an appearance in this section, foreshadowing the higher-elevation forest to come.

While Red Blanket Falls makes a perfectly suitable objective for a day hike, additional waterfalls and a stellar stand of Shasta red fir reward those who venture forward. Stay left at two trail junctions, continuing on the north side of the stream past a couple of small falls, reaching Stuart Falls 1.4 miles later. Stuart Falls spreads fan-like across the face of an old lava flow dropping 40 to 50 feet to another fine spot for a rest break.

To visit new country for the return leg, turn left onto the Stuart Falls Trail (1078) at the first trail junction below Stuart Falls, and cross the creek. Then turn right onto the Lucky Camp Trail (1083) eight-tenths of a mile later where striking Shasta red fir stretch skyward to impressive heights. Continue down the trail for another mile or so, closing the loop at the junction with the Red Blanket Creek Trail. Be careful crossing the stream just before the junction; the stream can be forded and large channel-spanning logs are nearby, but Red Blanket Falls lies just below the crossing.

How to get there: Turn toward Prospect off Crater Lake Highway (State Route 62) approximately 45 miles northeast of Medford, and then turn east onto Butte Falls–Prospect Road by the Prospect Hotel. Turn left onto Red Blanket Creek Road in about 1 mile, and turn left again onto gravel-surfaced Forest Road 6205 in four-tenths of a mile. Stay on the main road for 11.4 miles to the trailhead parking lot.

98 SOUTH FORK ROGUE RIVER

Length ■ **11.6 miles one way**
Difficulty ■ Moderate to difficult
Season ■ Summer to early autumn
Lowest point ■ 3,400 feet
Highest point ■ 4,420 feet
Human imprint ■ Moderate (roads, nearby plantations)
Information ■ Rogue River National Forest (Butte Falls Ranger District)

Primary Old-Growth Features
Picturesque pine and Douglas-fir; some amazingly large Pacific yew

Diverse, large conifers typical of mid-elevation forests in the southern Oregon Cascades congregate along the scenic lower slopes of the South Fork Rogue River. Conveniently enough the South Fork Rogue River Trail (988) traverses these shady hillsides where old Douglas-fir, sugar pine, and ponderosa pine highlight the woody assemblage. Forest Road 34 slices the trail into two, easily hiked segments, both containing fine old forest. The lower half is open to mountain bikers as well as hikers and receives more use; the upper portion is closed to bikes and feels a little more remote.

From the lower trailhead, round the corner and head upriver, passing the South Fork Dam a couple hundred yards west of the trailhead. The dam diverts a significant portion of the South Fork into a canal for downstream power generation. The first 2.5 miles offer a bit of a contrast as the trail frequently lies at the edge between tree plantations above the trail and large Douglas-fir and sugar pine below the trail. The trail then angles downhill to the river entering an excellent old-growth grove populated by Douglas-fir, western hemlock, western white pine, and white fir. The trail detours uphill through another patch of veterans before heading back to the river. Shortly before crossing Green Creek, a spur trail heads uphill to Forest Road 3775, and continues on to the giant sugar pines (see sidebar). Ponderosa pine dominates the flats before intersecting FR 34 approximately 6.3 miles from the lower trailhead.

Pacific yew

The upper half of the trail (5.3 miles long) continues through highly varied forest and crosses four good-sized tributaries, all with solid log crossings. The best old

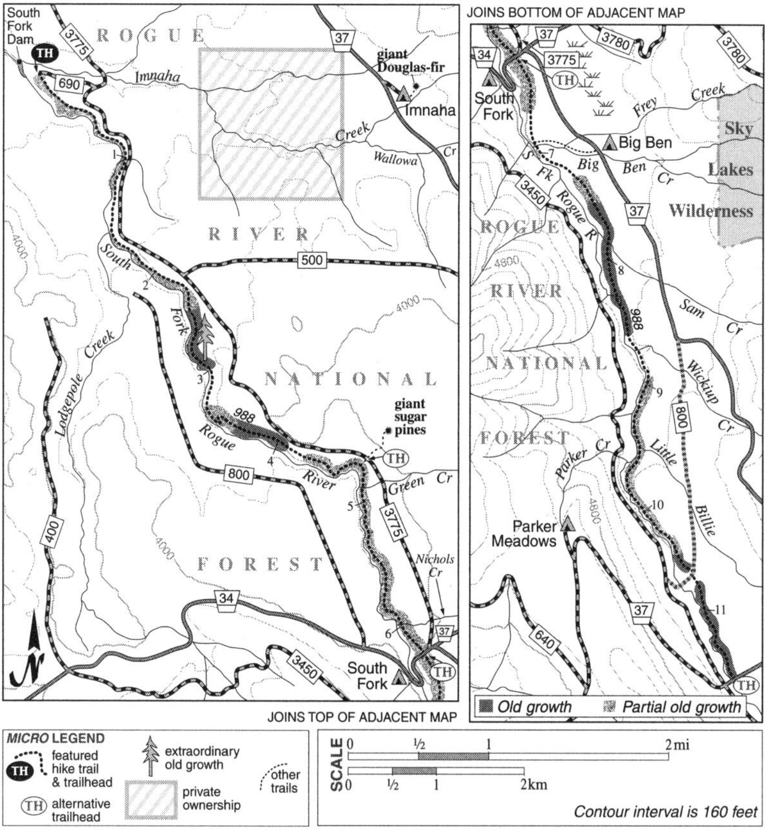

growth lies in the vicinity of Sam Creek about 2 miles from FR 34, and again over the last mile of the trail. Engelmann spruce and mountain hemlock join the cast of conifers as the trail gains elevation. Both stands also feature a profusion of Pacific yew, including some very large and gnarly specimens (2 to 2.5 feet thick). The largest trees of the hike stand along the last half mile or so of the trail where Douglas-firs reach 7 feet in girth.

How to get there: To reach the lower trailhead from Prospect (about 43 miles northeast of Medford on the Crater Lake Highway), turn east onto the Butte Falls–Prospect Road by the hotel in Prospect. Stay left on Bessie Creek Road (FR 37) about 3 miles later, and turn right onto gravel-surfaced FR 3775 after another 7 miles. Turn right again onto FR 690 a little over 3 miles from FR 37; the trailhead is at the end of the road in a third of a mile.

To reach the middle trailhead, continue past the junction with FR 3775 on FR 37 for another 5.8 miles until intersecting FR 34. The trailhead is on the left just past the junction. This point can also be reached from Butte Falls via the Butte Falls–Prospect Road and FR 34 (17.5 miles).

To reach the upper trailhead, continue south another 5.4 miles on FR 37; the trailhead is on the right.

BIG TREE TIP—GIANT SUGAR PINES

Take a few minutes to visit a trio of giant sugar pine while you are in the area. The largest is 7.5 feet in diameter, 160 feet tall, and is estimated to be 535 years old. A short trail (less than one-quarter mile) passes through a patch of old growth and ends by an interpretative sign at the base of the stout pines.

How to get there: Follow the directions given above for the lower trailhead, only continue another 3.9 miles on Forest Road 3775 past the junction with FR 690. Trailhead parking is on the right. From the middle trailhead, the trailhead is on the left 1.3 miles from the junction with FR 37.

BIG TREE TIP—GIANT DOUGLAS-FIR

Stop off at the Imnaha Campground on your way to the middle or upper trailheads for a quick look at the largest Douglas-fir in the area. This 9-foot-thick giant stands at the end of a compacted-gravel trail, a couple hundred yards from the campground.

How to get there: Follow the directions given above for the lower trailhead, only continue another 1.2 miles on Forest Road 37 past the junction with FR 3775 and turn left into the campground. Park by the old guard station.

99 Cherry Creek

Length ■ **5.3 miles one way**
Difficulty ■ Difficult
Season ■ Summer to autumn
Lowest point ■ 4,700 feet
Highest point ■ 5,960 feet
Human imprint ■ Minimal
Information ■ Fremont-Winema National Forests (Klamath Ranger District)

Primary Old-Growth Feature
Impressive Engelmann spruce

The Cherry Creek portal to the Sky Lakes Wilderness passes through a delightful and diverse mixed-conifer forest featuring several impressive patches of Engelmann spruce. The

Sky Lakes Wilderness straddles the Cascade Range crest and true to its name is populated with dozens of picturesque lakes typical of the high Cascades. The Cherry Creek Trail (3708) follows Cherry Creek on a gentle grade before switchbacking upslope to dead-end by Trapper Lake.

The first 3.5 miles of trail pass through stellar groves of old Engelmann spruce interspersed among patches of young Engelmann spruce in a mixed-age forest. Relatively dense young forest with an overstory component dominated by scattered large ponderosa pine, Douglas-fir, and grand fir is common along this stretch of trail, and typical of the fire suppression era in eastside forests. Nice little pockets of large Engelmann spruce 3 to 4 feet in diameter lie adjacent to Cherry Creek on the north shore by the crossing (at 2 miles) and recrossing (at 3.2 miles) of Cherry Creek. Both crossings are unbridged, but easy to cross during low stream flows. Remnants of an old log bridge slammed against the south bank of the second crossing vividly demonstrate how crossing in high flows during spring and early summer may be more problematic.

Soon after regaining the south shore of Cherry Creek the trail crosses a tributary and starts switchbacking up the hill. Shasta red fir make an occasional appearance lower on the slope and increase in number as the trail gains elevation. An unexpected and marvelous stand of Engelmann spruce and Shasta red fir ring the trail near the end of the switchbacks a little more than 4 miles from the trailhead. Here at almost 6,000 feet above sea level, 3 to 4-foot-thick Shasta red fir, Engelmann spruce, and Douglas-fir extend skywards. The trail then crosses over onto the summit plateau and joins the Sky Lakes Trail (3762) at Trapper Lake.

Luther Mountain rises behind Trapper Lake providing a rugged counter-

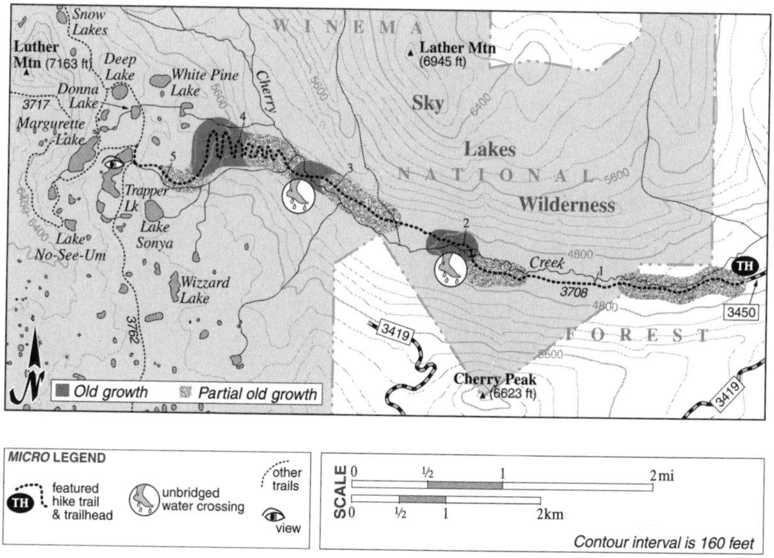

point to the placid lake. If you have the energy and appetite for further adventure, a short loop (1.5 miles) can be taken from Trapper Lake to three more scenic lakes (Margurette Lake, Deep Lake, and Donna Lake) and two other small tarns.

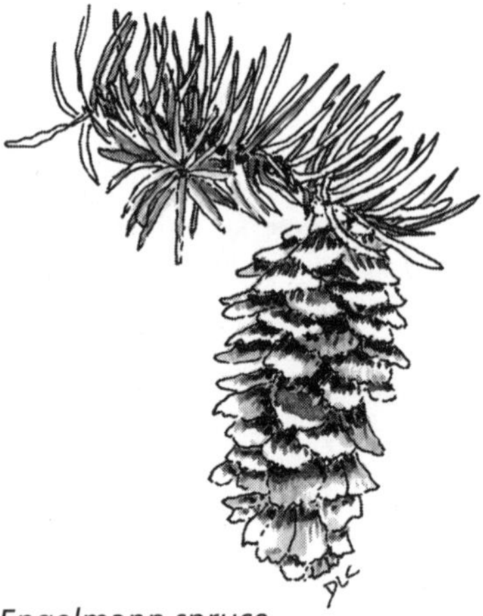

Engelmann spruce

How to get there: From Klamath Falls take State Route 140 northwest approximately 25 miles to the junction with Westside Road (County Road 531); from Medford take SR 62 and then SR 140 east approximately 44 miles to reach this junction. Take Westside Road north toward Crater Lake and Fort Klamath for 10.8 miles to reach Forest Road 3450. Turn left and park at the end of the graveled road 1.8 miles later.

100 Brown Mountain

Length	**7.75 miles one way**
Difficulty	Moderate
Season	Summer to autumn
Lowest point	4,870 feet
Highest point	5,620 feet
Human imprint	Moderate (roads, plantations)
Information	Rogue River National Forest (Ashland Ranger District), Fremont-Winema National Forests (Klamath Ranger District)

Primary Old-Growth Features
Giant Douglas-fir; stately Shasta red fir and western white pine

The Brown Mountain Trail (1005 and 3724) samples one of the finest stands of old growth left in the southern Cascade Range of Oregon. A diverse mixture of old conifers surrounds the trail nearly the entire way, with the first 5 miles passing some particularly noteworthy stands. Oddly enough this trail is signed with two trail numbers, one for the Rogue River National Forest side of the trail (1005), and another for the Winema National Forest side (3724). The entire length of the trail can be easily hiked one-way with a vehicle shuttle.

Head east on a gentle grade paralleling a willow- and alder-shrouded tributary of Little Butte Creek. The primary canopy layer is dominated by Douglas-fir approximately 250 years old, overtopped by scattered veterans of older vintage (650 to 700 years old). A cluster of impressive Douglas-fir towers over a dense patch of Pacific yew about a half mile from the trailhead.

Where the trail intersects a road approximately 1.5 miles from the trailhead, turn right on the road and cross the stream, then look for the trail on the left. Resume an eastward bearing, hiking now on the south side of the stream. Douglas-fir continues to dominate the stand, although a few Engelmann spruce are rooted by the stream. Cross a second road a mile past the first intersection, continuing through old forest. Shasta red fir mixes with Douglas-fir through this stretch, increasing in number as the trail slowly gains elevation. Cross the Pacific Crest Trail (PCT, 2000) about 3 miles from the trailhead and enter a lovely stand of Shasta red fir.

Brown Mountain comes into view a half mile or so after crossing the PCT,

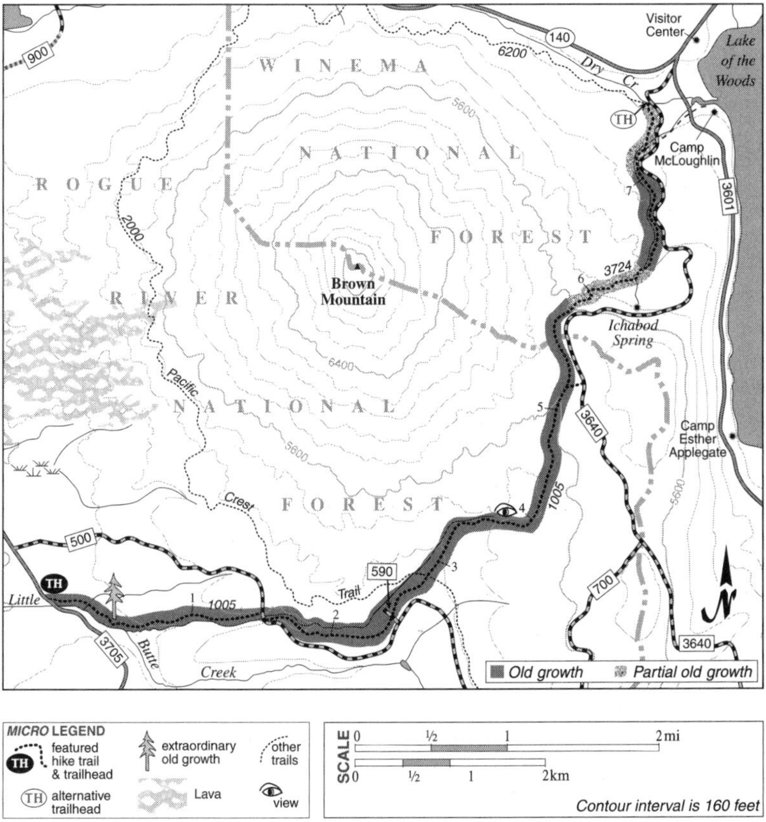

rising above the blocky lava flows that envelop the peak. Mountain hemlock, western white pine, lodgepole pine, and quaking aspen add diversity to the forest by the jumble of lava. This opening provides a nice lunch stop or a potential turnaround point. From here the trail continues around the eastern flank of the mountain, in excellent old forest for another couple of miles. The final 2 miles of the trail travel through a mix of old and young forest, swerving close to the road in places.

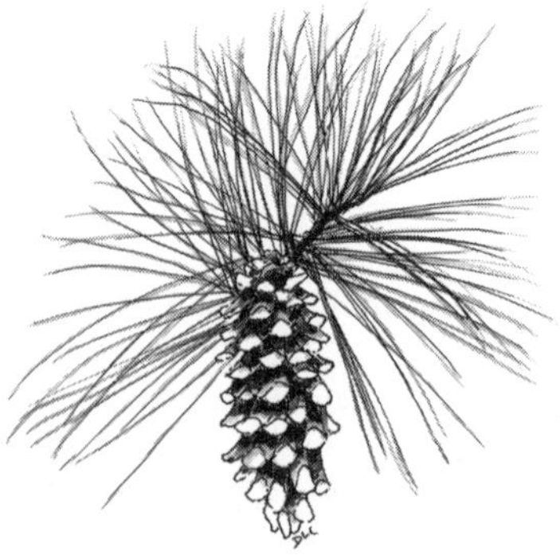

Western white pine

How to get there: Turn south onto Forest Road 37 from State Route 140 a little more than 28 miles east of the Crater Lake Highway (SR 62). Turn left onto FR 3705 a little over 2 miles later; trailhead parking is on the right in another 3.2 miles.

To reach the eastern trailhead for a possible shuttle, continue east on SR 140 for another 7.1 miles, then turn south onto FR 3601. Turn right onto FR 3640 a few hundred yards later. Brown Mountain trailhead parking is on the right in another four-tenths of a mile.

BIG TREE TIP—FISH LAKE PINE

An immense western white pine, the former national champion and still largest in Oregon, stands approximately 100 yards from the trailhead at the end of a short path. This gnarly veteran once stood 242 feet tall, has a 6.7-foot diameter, and is estimated to be approximately 400 years old. While still impressive, national champion status was lost when the treetop was broken off in a storm. **How to get there:** Turn north onto County Road 821 from State Route 140 approximately 28.5 miles east of the Crater Lake Highway (SR 62). Turn left onto Forest Road 3735 in a half mile, then turn right into a tree plantation on FR 795 a little over a half mile later. Trailhead parking is on the right in another third of a mile.

APPENDIX A. BIBLIOGRAPHY

References in this appendix identify publications that provided useful background information for this book.

Agee, James K. "Fire history of Douglas-fir forests in the Pacific Northwest." In *Wildlife and vegetation of unmanaged Douglas-fir forests.* edited by L. F. Ruggiero, K. B. Aubry, A. B. Carey, and M. H. Huff. USDA Forest Service, Pacific Northwest Research Station, General Technical Report PNW-285, 1991. pp. 25–33.

Agee, James K. and M. Vaughn. "The headwaters old growth of Canyon Lake Creek." Unpublished report submitted to Trillium Corporation and Whatcom County Land Trust, 1993. 52 p.

Arno, Stephen F., and R. P. Hammerly. *Northwest Trees: Identifying and Understanding the Region's Native Trees*. Seattle: The Mountaineers Books, 1999.

Cissel, John H., and D. L. Cissel. *50 Old-Growth Day Hikes in the Mt. Hood National Forest.* Eugene, OR: Old-Growth Day Hikes, 1993. Double-sided, large-format annotated map.

———. *50 Old-Growth Hikes in the Southern Washington Cascades.* Eugene, OR: Old-Growth Day Hikes, 1996. Double-sided, large-format annotated map.

———. *50 Old-Growth Hikes in the Willamette National Forest,* 2nd edition. Eugene, OR: Old-Growth Day Hikes, 1998. Double-sided, large-format annotated map.

Dittmar, Ann, D. Dittmar, J. Dittmar, T. Dittmar, J. Dittmar, and S. Dittmar. *Visitor's Guide to Ancient Forests of Western Washington.* Washington, DC: The Wilderness Society, 1989.

Durbin, Kathie. *Tree Huggers—Victory, Defeat and Renewal in the Northwest Ancient Forest Campaign.* Seattle: The Mountaineers Books, 1996.

Eifert, Larry. *Field Guide to Old-Growth Forests: Exploring Ancient Forest Ecosystems from California to the Pacific Northwest.* Seattle: Sasquatch Books, 2000.

Franklin, Jerry F., K. Cromack, Jr., W. Denison, A. McKee, C. Maser, J. Sedell, F. Swanson, and G. Juday. "Ecological characteristics of old-growth Douglas-fir forests." USDA Forest Service, Pacific Northwest Research Station, General Technical Report PNW-118, 1981. 48 p.

Franklin, Jerry F., and T. A. Spies. "Ecological definitions of old-growth Douglas-fir forests." In *Wildlife and vegetation of unmanaged Douglas-fir forests,* edited by L. F. Ruggiero, K. B. Aubry, A. B. Carey, and M. H. Huff. USDA Forest Service, Pacific Northwest Research Station, General Technical Report PNW-285, 1991. pp. 61–69.

Gaines, William L., P. Singleton, and A. L. Gold. "Conservation of rare carnivores in the North Cascades Ecosystem, western North America." *Natural Areas Journal* 20 (2000):366-375.

Halverson, Nancy M., compiler. *Major indicator shrubs and herbs on national forests of western Oregon and southwestern Washington.* USDA Forest Service Pacific Northwest Region, Portland, OR, R6-TM-229, 1986.

Henrie, Cheris, editor. *Old Growth Forests: A Casual Hikers' Guide.* Portland, OR: USDA-Forest Service/USDI-BLM/World Forestry Center, 1990. 64 p.

Hosie, R. C. *Native Trees of Canada,* 7th edition. Ottawa, Canada: Canadian Forestry Service, 1975. 380 p.

Jensen, Edward C., and C. R. Ross. *Trees to Know in Oregon.* Oregon State University Extension Service and Oregon Department of Forestry. Publication EC 1450. 1994. 128 p.

Johnson, Charles G., Jr. *Common Plants of the Inland Pacific Northwest.* USDA Forest Service Pacific Northwest Region, Portland, OR, R6-TP051-93, 1993. 389 p.

Kelly, David, and G. Braasch. *Secrets of the Old Growth Forest.* Layton, UT: Gibbs Smith, 1988. 99 p.

Leonard, William P., H. A. Brown, L. L. C. Jones, K. R. McAllister, and R. M. Storm. *Amphibians of Washington and Oregon.* Seattle: Seattle Audubon Society, 1993. 168 p.

Mathews, Daniel. *Cascade-Olympic Natural History.* Portland, OR: Raven Editions, Portland Audubon Society, 1990. 625 p.

Miller, Jeffrey C. *Caterpillars of Pacific Northwest Forests and Woodlands.* USDA Forest Service Pacific Northwest Region, Portland, OR, FHM-NC-06-95, 1995. 80 p.

Moir, William H. *Forests of Mount Rainier.* Seattle: The Pacific Northwest National Parks and Forests Association, 1989. 111 p.

Norse, Elliot. *Ancient Forests of the Pacific Northwest.* Washington DC: The Wilderness Society and Island Press, 1990. 344 p.

Peterson, Roger T. *A Field Guide to Western Birds,* 3rd edition. Boston: Houghton Mifflin Company, 1990. 432 p.

Plumb, Gregory A. *Waterfalls of the Pacific Northwest.* Seattle: The Writing Works, 1983. 182 p.

Pojar, Jim, and A. MacKinnon, editor *Plants of the Pacific Northwest Coast—Washington, Oregon, British Columbia and Alaska.* Vancouver, BC: Lone Pine Publishing, 1994. 527 p.

Ross, Robert A., and H. Chambers. *Wildflowers of the Western Cascades.* Portland, OR: Timber Press, 1988. 140 p.

Spring, Ira, and H. Manning. *50 Hikes in Mount Rainier National Park*, 3rd edition. Seattle: The Mountaineers Books, 1988. 138 p.

———. *100 Hikes in Washington's South Cascades and Olympics*, 2nd edition. Seattle: The Mountaineers Books, 1992. 240 p.

———. *100 Hikes in Washington's North Cascades National Park Region,* 2nd edition. Seattle: The Mountaineers Books, 1994. 256 p.

———. *100 Hikes in Washington's Glacier Peak Region: The North Cascades,* 3rd edition. Seattle: The Mountaineers Books, 1996. 240 p.

Spring, Vicky, I. Spring, and H. Manning. *100 Hikes in Washington's Alpine Lakes,* 2nd edition. Seattle: The Mountaineers Books, 1993. 240 p.

Stoltmann, Randy. *Hiking the Ancient Forests of British Columbia and Washington.* Vancouver, BC: Lone Pine Publishing, 1996. 191 p.

Sullivan, William L. *100 Hikes in Northwest Oregon.* Eugene, OR: Navillus Press, 1993. 240 p.

———. *100 Hikes in Southern Oregon.* Eugene, OR: Navillus Press, 1997. 240 p.

———. *100 Hikes in the Central Oregon Cascades,* 2nd edition. Eugene, OR: Navillus Press, 1998. 240 p.

Tekiela, Stan. *Birds of Oregon Field Guide.* Cambridge, MA: Adventure Publications, Inc., 2001. 307 p.

Van Pelt, Robert. *Champion Trees of Washington State.* Seattle: University of Washington Press, 1996. 120 p.

Van Pelt, Robert. *Forest Giants of the Pacific Coast.* Seattle: Global Forest Society and University of Washington Press, 2001. 200 p.

Vitt, Dale H., J. E. Marsh, and R. B. Bovey. *Mosses, Lichens and Ferns of Northwest North America.* Edmonton, Alberta: Lone Pine Publishing; Seattle: University of Washington Press, 1988. 296 p.

Wassink, Jan L. *Birds of the Pacific Northwest Mountains.* Missoula, MT: Mountain Press Publishing Company, 1995. 196 p.

Wood, Wendell. *A Walking Guide to Oregon's Ancient Forests.* Portland, OR: Oregon Natural Resources Council, 1991. 315 p.

APPENDIX B. QUICK GUIDE TO TREE IDENTIFICATION

Readers unfamiliar with Northwest tree species may benefit from the brief summary listed below. The ability to recognize tree species along trails will enhance readers' appreciation of the environment, and add to the pleasures of the hikes described in this book. A number of books are available that do a comprehensive job of identifying and describing tree species found in the Northwest (see Appendix A). Readers should consult Appendix C, Big Tree Data, to note the maximum dimensions attained by these tree species.

Species are organized into groups known singularly as genus, or in plural form as genera. For example, pines are a genus, and ponderosa pine is a species. The scientific name of a species includes the genus then the species, and is given in Latin; e.g., *Pinus ponderosa.* Ecologists, foresters, botanists, and other scientists frequently use scientific names when communicating with peers because scientific names are universally known, precise, and consistent. Common names can vary from region to region, and sometimes a single common name is used for multiple species. We use common names in this book since they are well understood for most species, and are easier for most people to recognize and remember.

Western white pine—*Pinus monticola* (illustration, p. 260; color insert, p. ii)

Distinguishing features: large cones (5 to 10 inches long); scaly ("alligator-skin"), dark gray bark; needles 2 to 4 inches long, in clusters of five

Habitat/ecology: tolerates wide range of conditions; sea level to 5,000 to 6,000 feet; typically a minor component of mixed-species stands; regenerates and competes well in a post-fire environment; much reduced in distribution and abundance due to mortality from white pine blister rust (an introduced fungus)

Cascades distribution: throughout the Cascades in Washington and Oregon

Sugar pine—*Pinus lambertiana* (illustration, p. 223; color insert, p. iv)

Distinguishing features: one of the giant conifers and the largest pine species; very large, heavy cones (10 to 18 inches long); reddish-brown, fissured bark; needles 2 to 4 inches long, in clusters of five

Habitat/ecology: mid-elevations (1,000 to 4,000 feet); dry sites; typically a minor component of mixed-species stands; much reduced in distribution and abundance due to white pine blister rust

Cascades distribution: Central Oregon Cascades south into California

Whitebark pine—*Pinus albicaulis* (illustration, p. 247; color insert, p. iv)

Distinguishing features: form varies including stout single-stemmed tree, multiple-stemmed windblown tree, or nearly prostrate shrub; scaly-grayish bark; small cones (approximately 2 inches long) that disintegrate at maturity; needles are stiff, approximately 2 inches long, in clusters of five

Habitat/ecology: subalpine forests along Cascade crest, above 5,000 feet; reduced in abundance on moist sites due to white pine blister rust

Cascades distribution: throughout the Cascades in Washington and Oregon

Ponderosa pine—*Pinus ponderosa* (illustration, p. 230; color insert, p. iii)

Distinguishing features: stately tree symbolic of the pioneer west; 5 to 8-inch-long needles in groups of two to three; bark becoming orange and flaky with age; 3 to 5-inch stocky cones armed with sharp prickles

Habitat/ecology: widespread, dominant conifer on many arid sites; extends from sea level to 5,000 feet on south-facing slopes; older trees tolerate fire well; historically grew in open, park-like stands, but now, due to fire suppression, frequently surrounded by dense stands of young conifers

Cascades distribution: throughout the Cascades east of the Cascade crest; reaches its northern limit on the west side of the Cascades east of Eugene, and is common in southern Oregon

Western larch—*Larix occidentalis* (illustration, p. 91; color insert, p. iii)

Distinguishing features: one of only two deciduous conifers in the Northwest; soft, lime-green needles turn golden in October then fall off; 1 to 2-inch needles in clusters on knobby, woody spurs off main branches; bark turns orange with age and is very thick at the base of the tree; cones are short (1 to 1.5 inches) and papery with small bracts

Habitat/ecology: a species that has adapted to and is capable of surviving fire, dispersing lightweight seed considerable distances, and growing rapidly in height at early ages; typically found at mid-elevations on moist sites east of the Cascade crest; repeated defoliation from an introduced insect, the larch casebearer, has caused increased mortality in recent decades

Cascades distribution: occurs in discontinuous patches throughout the Cascades east of the Cascade crest

Alpine larch—*Larix lyallii* (illustration, p. 41)

Distinguishing features: one of only two deciduous conifers in the Northwest; a relatively short (50 to 80-foot) tree of the subalpine zone; young branches are covered with woolly hairs; thin bark; erect, 1.5 to 2-inch cones with exserted bracts; light-green needles turn golden in September prior to dropping off

Habitat/ecology: a stout and hardy tree growing at the head of watersheds near timberline, frequently on sites uninhabitable by other trees, such as rock piles; shade intolerant and able to colonize newly exposed sites

Cascades distribution: very limited, only on the east side of the Cascades, from Wenatchee north to southern British Columbia

Sitka spruce—*Picea sitchensis* (illustration, p. 78)

Distinguishing features: attains prodigious dimensions, one of few tree species that reach 300 feet in height; needles are flat, stiff, and prickly, up to 1 inch long; bark is thin, reddish-brown, and scaly; cones are tan and papery with a wavy edge, 2 to 4 inches long, and hang down from branches

Habitat/ecology: thrives in wet, cool environments; can regenerate under itself, commonly on nurse logs; capable of extended rapid growth

Cascades distribution: a coastal species occurring inland along major river drainages, reaching the Cascades near Mount Rainier and farther north

Engelmann spruce—*Picea engelmannii* (illustration, p. 258)

Distinguishing features: needles are flat, stiff, and prickly, up to 1-inch long, with an unpleasant odor when crushed; bark is thin, reddish-brown, and scaly; cones are tan and papery with a wavy edge, about 2 inches long, and hang down; tall, narrow crown

Habitat/ecology: tolerates a wide range of conditions, but competes well on cool, moist sites at mid-elevations in the Cascades, especially on the east side; trees are considered shade-tolerant, retain branches low on trunk, and are shallow-rooted; susceptible to blowdown during windstorms

Cascades distribution: common on the east side of the Cascades in Washington and Oregon; western range limit is just west of the Cascade crest

Douglas-fir—*Psuedotsuga menziesii* var. glauca (illustration, p. 200; color insert, p. i)

Distinguishing features: the Oregon state tree; bark on young trees has resin blisters, becomes deeply furrowed up to a foot thick on older trees; 3 to 4-inch cones have three-pronged bracts that extend between the scales; buds are pointed and reddish-brown with overlapping scales; needles about 1 inch long with blunt tips

Habitat/ecology: most common tree in western Oregon; capable of rapid growth and great size; tolerates fire (thick bark), and regenerates and competes well in high-light, post-fire environment; usually the dominant post-fire tree in western Oregon and much of western Washington at low- to mid-elevations; tolerates wide range of environmental conditions, including partial shade, but does not establish without mineral soil seedbed; capable of surviving to great age (>1,000 years)

Cascades distribution: the coastal variety grows on both sides of the Cascades from mid–British Columbia to central California; the Rocky Mountain variety grows throughout the Rocky Mountains

Western hemlock—*Tsuga heterophylla* (illustration, p. 45; color insert, p. i)

Distinguishing features: the Washington state tree; tree tops droop; needles are short (0.25 to 0.75 inch long) rising predominantly from the sides of the twigs, but are also on the top of the twigs; egg-shaped cones are small (1 inch long), but abundant; bark is gray and thin (<1 inch thick), slightly furrowed with flattened ridges

Habitat/ecology: widespread at low- to mid-elevations; abundant lightweight seeds are widely dispersed; tolerates deep shade and retains branches low on the trunk; capable of surviving for centuries as a small, stunted tree in the understory, then growing rapidly into the upper canopy when nearby overstory trees die; casts dense shade limiting development of understory herbs and shrubs; competes best on moist, moderate sites; more abundant in northern Washington; susceptible to fire

Cascades distribution: found on both sides of the Cascades in Washington and Oregon

Mountain hemlock—*Tsuga mertensiana* (illustration, p. 206; color insert, p. ii)

Distinguishing features: cones are longer than western hemlock, 1.5 to 2 inches long; short (<1 inch long) needles appear in star-like pattern growing out of secondary branch shoots; bark somewhat thicker than western hemlock (1 inch thick) with narrow ridges

Habitat/ecology: grows in the snow-zone forests 3,500 to 6,000-foot elevations; tolerates dense shade; variety of growth forms from dense, closed-canopy stands to scattered gnarly shrubs in the subalpine zone; can regenerate by branch rooting ("layering") in the subalpine zone

Cascades distribution: found on both sides of the Cascades in Washington and Oregon

Noble fir—*Abies procera* (illustration, p. 115; color insert, p. iii)

Distinguishing features: largest and longest-lived true fir; long, clear, straight tree trunks; small distinctive crown composed of sturdy rigid branches; needles are stiff, blue-hued, and upturned with a bottle-brush appearance; bark contains resin blisters on young trees, becoming purplish-gray and forming flattened ridges with age; large (4 to 6 inches long), barrel-shaped cones disintegrate while on the tree

Habitat/ecology: shade intolerant; self-prunes lower branches; competes well in post-fire environment from 3,000 to 5,500 feet; prefers cool, moist sites

Cascades distribution: Stevens Pass in Washington is the northern limit, McKenzie River regarded as the southern limit; hybridizes with California red fir in southern Oregon to form Shasta red fir (see next entry)

Shasta red fir—*Abies magnifica* var. shastensis (illustration, p. 252; color insert, p. iii)

Distinguishing features: beautiful open, bluish crown; reddish-brown bark becoming furrowed with age; very similar to noble fir (see above)

Habitat/ecology: a natural hybrid among noble fir and California red fir, and considered a variety of California red fir; these three firs are similar ecologically and in appearance, though Shasta red fir better tolerates dry, warm sites, and can tolerate more shade than noble fir

Cascades distribution: southern Oregon Cascades south of the McKenzie River

Grand fir—*Abies grandis* (illustration, p. 232)

Distinguishing features: needles are "two-ranked," meaning they are flattened on the twig pointing in two opposite directions; needles are dark, shiny green about 2 inches long; mature trees have gray, moderately furrowed bark up to 2 to 3 inches thick; large (3 to 4 inches long), barrel-shaped cones disintegrate while on the tree

Habitat/ecology: a common shade-tolerant species, able to dominate sites too moist for ponderosa pine and too dry for western hemlock; capable of rapid growth and large size; susceptible to many fungi decomposers and insects; trees with these characteristics in the southern Cascades of Oregon are generally natural hybrids with white fir *(Abies concolor)*

Cascades distribution: on both sides of the Cascades in Oregon and Washington; predominately along rivers on the west side, although patches occur on dry upper slopes; on moist sites on the east side

Pacific silver fir—*Abies amabilis* (illustration, p. 56; color insert, p. i)

Distinguishing features: dark green needles on top, silvery underneath; needles on top are pointed forward like ski jumpers; large (3 to 6 inches long), barrel-shaped cones disintegrate while on the tree; thin, silvery bark becoming scaly when older

Habitat/ecology: ubiquitous on cool, moist sites in the Cascades above 3,000 feet; shallow rooted; very susceptible to fire; highly tolerant of shade; can persist in the understory for decades then emerge in canopy openings; becomes the dominant tree barring disturbance on many sites west of the Cascade crest

Cascades distribution: both sides of the Cascades in Washington, and in Oregon south to Mount Thielsen; only occurs close to the Cascade crest on the east side

Western redcedar—*Thuja plicata* (illustration, p. 51; color insert, p. i)

Distinguishing features: tree crowns composed of spreading droopy branches; old trees often have multiple dead tops (a "candelabra" appearance); gray, stringy, fibrous bark; base of trunk often strongly fluted; flat sprays of small, scale-like leaves pressed tightly to twigs; leaves are green on the top with a white "bow-tie" beneath; cones are small (0.5 inch), grow upright on the tops of twigs, and appear like tiny rosebuds

Habitat/ecology: grows up to 3,500 feet elevation; prefers moist sites, and restricted to moist sites east of the Cascade crest; can tolerate high-levels of soil moisture; shade tolerant; capable of attaining great mass and living more than 1,000 years; a durable species that resists pathogens in life and decomposers in death

Cascades distribution: on both sides of the Cascades in Washington and Oregon, but limited in distribution east of the Cascade crest in southern Oregon

Incense-cedar—*Calocedrus decurrens* (illustration , p. 238; color insert, p. ii)

Distinguishing features: bark flaky when young, becoming furrowed, orangish brown, and thick (<6 inches) with age; base of trunk often strongly fluted; tree trunk tapers rapidly; scale-like leaves press tightly to twigs, very little white on underside; scales are much longer than wide, forming a "wine-glass"; flat sprays of leaves often held in a vertical plane; distinctive cones are about 1 inch long; unopened cones have a "duck bill" appearance

Habitat/ecology: adapted to droughty soils and high temperatures; fire resistant; more shade tolerant than most dry-site associates, less shade-tolerant than moist-site associates; can regenerate in litter or duff

Cascades distribution: in Oregon Cascades, primarily from Santiam Pass south

Alaska-cedar—*Chamaecyparis nootkatensis* (illustration, p. 185; color insert, p. ii)

Distinguishing features: tree crown appears drooping, or weepy; trees appear yellowish from the distance; thin bark is shaggy, often peeling away from the trunk; small, scale-like leaves with pointy, flared tips pressed to twigs; no white on underside of leaves; leaves feel prickly to touch; small (0.5 inch diameter) round cones

Habitat/ecology: thrives in cold, wet environments; found above 3,000 feet, or higher in Oregon; forms shrub-like thickets on harsh sites, and closed-canopy forest with other species on better sites; moderately tolerant of shade; competes best on tough sites; limber branches tolerate deep snow-pack; can live well over 1,000 years

Cascades distribution: mainly on the west side of the Cascades in Washington through Oregon south to Three Sisters; found on a few north-facing, high-elevation sites farther south, and on the east side close to the Cascade crest

APPENDIX C. BIG TREE DATA

Champion trees of the Pacific Coast have been sought after, named, measured, publicized, and glorified for well over a century. Fascination with the biggest of most anything runs deep in our culture, but knowing the dimensions and location of our most massive, old trees lends important context both ecologically and culturally. The maximum size of a tree species conveys the growth potential of a species, and the characteristics of the site where a champion grows may indicate the optimum growing conditions for that species. Great size does not always imply great age as trees can rapidly attain high mass under optimum conditions, and in poor growing conditions trees may survive for many centuries and grow very little. Yet close encounters with these giants reinforces a feeling of human insignificance and recognition of the power of natural forces.

The size of trees is judged on a number of dimensions, such as tree height, diameter, volume, and even the width and length of the tree crown. American Forests, a national association of foresters, started a Big Tree Program in 1941 and standardized a measurement system to determine champion trees in the 1950s. The American Forests system defines the biggest tree according to a formula that awards points based on tree diameter, tree height, and crown spread. Specific rules govern how these measurements are taken.

The American Forests system works but has left many wondering if it really ranks the biggest trees accurately. Some foresters and ecologists have long felt that wood volume is a better measure of total tree size, but they have lacked the technology to readily estimate tree volume in a practical way. New technology, namely survey lasers, now enables relatively accurate measurements of tree volume in remote and rough terrain.

The listing below identifies the dimensions and general location of the largest known specimens of most tree species discussed in this book. Largest diameter is given in feet at breast height (standardized at 4.5 feet above the ground), tallest height is also given in feet, and greatest volume is reported in cubic feet as measured by a survey laser. Some of these trees are well known and access is easy. Others are remote and accessible to experienced off-trail travelers only.

These data are taken from *Forest Giants of the Pacific Coast* by Robert Van Pelt (University of Washington Press, 2001), *Champion Trees of Washington State* also by Robert Van Pelt (University of Washington Press, 1996), and from the extensive big-tree database he maintains. *Forest Giants of the Pacific Coast* is an excellent reference and beautiful book, highly recommended for all lovers of big trees.

	Measurement	Name	Location
Western white pine			
Largest diameter:	10.45 ft	Unnamed	El Dorado National Forest, CA
Tallest height:	232 ft	Unnamed	Floodwood State Forest, ID
Greatest volume:	3,210 cf	Fish Lake Pine	Rogue River National Forest, OR
Sugar pine			
Largest diameter:	11.54 ft	Pickering Pine	Dorrington, CA
Tallest height:	268 ft	Yosemite Giant	Yosemite National Park, CA
Greatest volume:	8,990 cf	Whelan Tree	Dorrington, CA
Whitebark pine			
Largest diameter:	8.78 ft	Unnamed	Sawtooth National Recreation Area, ID
Tallest height:	87 ft	Unnamed	Wenatchee National Forest, WA
Ponderosa pine			
Largest diameter:	9.07 ft	La Pine Giant	La Pine State Recreation Area, OR
Tallest height:	258 ft	Unnamed	Siskiyou National Forest, OR
Greatest volume:	4,460 cf	Grizzly Meadow Monarch	Sierra National Forest, CA
Douglas-fir			
Largest diameter:	15.92 ft	Queets Fir	Olympic National Park, WA
Tallest height:	329 ft	Doerner Fir	Coos Bay BLM, OR
Greatest volume:	12,320 cf	Red Creek Tree	Vancouver Island, BC
Western hemlock			
Largest diameter:	9.52 ft	Norvan's Castle	Lynn Headwaters Regional Park, BC
Tallest height:	241 ft	Unnamed	Olympic National Park, WA
Greatest volume:	4,270 cf	Enchanted Valley Hemlock	Olympic National Park, WA

	Measurement	Name	Location
Mountain hemlock			
Largest diameter:	7.35 ft	Unnamed	Stanislaus National Forest, CA
Tallest height:	194 ft	Unnamed	Olympic National Park, WA
Noble fir			
Largest diameter:	9.52 ft	Yellowjacket Creek Champion	Gifford Pinchot National Forest, WA
Tallest height:	295 ft	Unnamed	Mount St. Helens National Volcanic Monument, WA
Greatest volume:	5,700 cf	Yellowjacket Creek Champion	Gifford Pinchot National Forest, WA
Grand fir			
Largest diameter:	7.08 ft	Chilliwack Giant	Ecological Reserve 98, BC
Tallest height:	267 ft	Unnamed	Mount Baker–Snoqualmie National Forest, WA
Greatest volume:	2,770 cf	Chilliwack Giant	Ecological Reserve 98, BC
Pacific silver fir			
Largest diameter:	7.64 ft	Cabin Lake Tree	Cypress Provincial Park, BC
Tallest height:	236 ft	Unnamed	Olympic National Forest, WA
Greatest volume:	2,230 cf	Cabin Lake Tree	Cypress Provincial Park, BC
Engelmann spruce			
Largest diameter:	7.22 ft	North Joffre Spruce	Squamish Forest District, BC
Tallest height:	223 ft	Easy Pass Tower	Mount Baker–Snoqualmie National Forest, WA
Greatest volume:	1,910 cf	Easy Pass Tower	Mount Baker–Snoqualmie National Forest, WA

Sitka spruce			
Largest diameter:	17.68 ft	Quinault Lake Spruce	Olympic National Forest, WA
Tallest height:	317 ft	Unnamed	Prairie Creek Redwoods State Park, CA
Greatest volume:	11,290 cf	Queets Spruce	Olympic National Park, WA
Western larch			
Largest diameter:	7.24 ft	Seely Lake Giant	Lolo National Forest, MT
Tallest height:	192 ft	Unnamed	Umatilla National Forest, OR
Greatest volume:	2,940 cf	Seely Lake Giant	Lolo National Forest, MT
Alpine larch			
Largest diameter:	6.26 ft	Unnamed	Wenatchee National Forest, WA
Tallest height:	130 ft	Unnamed	Bitterroot National Forest, MT
Western redcedar			
Largest diameter:	19.65 ft	Kalaloch Cedar	Olympic National Park, WA
Tallest height:	234 ft	Unnamed	Mount Rainier National Park, WA
Greatest volume:	17,650 cf	Quinault Lake Cedar	Olympic National Park, WA
Incense-cedar			
Largest diameter:	12.92 ft	Tannen Lakes Titan	Siskiyou National Forest, OR
Tallest height:	229 ft	Unnamed	Umpqua National Forest, OR
Greatest volume:	7,860 cf	Devil's Canyon Colossus	Shasta-Trinity National Forest, CA
Alaska-cedar			
Largest diameter:	13.66 ft	Sergeant RandAlly	Kelsey Bay, BC
Tallest height:	200 ft	Sergeant RandAlly	Kelsey Bay, BC
Greatest volume:	6,650 cf	Admiral Broeren	Kelsey Bay, BC

APPENDIX D. ADDITIONAL MAPS

Maps in this book are accurate and current, but limited by a book format. The following list identifies U.S. Geological Survey 7.5-minute quadrangle topographic maps (1:24,000 scale), and Green Trails topographic maps (1:69,500 scale) for each hike. "NA" means "not available."

Hike Name	USGS maps	Green Trails maps
Northern Washington Cascades		
1. Canyon Lake Creek Community Forest	Canyon Lake	NA
2. Elbow Lake	Twin Sisters Mtn	Hamilton
3. Baker River	Mt Shuksan	Mt Shuksan
4. Baker Lake	Mt Shuksan, Bacon Peak	Mt Shuksan, Lake Shannon
5. Big Beaver Creek	Pumpkin Mtn, Mt Prophet	Ross Lake
6. Thunder Creek	Ross Dam, Forbidden Peak	Diablo Dam
7. South Creek	Gilbert, McAlester Mtn	Stehekin
8. Boulder River	Mt Higgins, Meadow Mtn	Oso, Granite Falls
9. Milk Creek	Lime Mtn	Glacier Peak
10. White Chuck River	Pugh Mtn, Lime Mtn, Glacier Peak West	Sloan Peak, Glacier Peak
11. Lake Twentytwo	Mallardy Ridge, Verlot	Silverton, Granite Falls
12. North Fork Sauk River	Sloan Peak, Glacier Peak West	Sloan Peak, Glacier Peak
13. Blanca Lake	Blanca Lake	Monte Cristo
14. West Cady Ridge	Blanca Lake, Bench Mark Mtn	Monte Cristo, Benchmark Mtn
15. Deception Creek	Scenic	Stevens Pass

16. Heather Lake	Labyrinth Mtn, Captain Point	Benchmark Mtn
17. Indian Creek	Mount David	Wenatchee Lake, Benchmark Mtn
18. Chiwaukum Creek	Winton, Big Jim Mountain	Leavenworth, Chiwaukum Mts
19. Icicle Creek	Jack Ridge, Chiwaukum Mts, Stevens Pass	Chiwaukum Mts, Stevens Pass
20. Denny Creek	Snoqualmie Pass	Snoqualmie Pass
21. Pete Lake	Polallie Ridge	Kachess Lake
22. Silver Creek	Kachess Lake	Kachess Lake
Southern Washington Cascades		
23. Federation Forest	Greenwater	Greenwater
24. Skookum Flats	Sun Top	Greenwater
25. Upper Clearwater Valley	Bearhead Mtn	Enumclaw
26. Green Lake	Mowich Lake	Mt Rainier West
27. Ipsut Creek	Mowich Lake	Mt Rainier West
28. Huckleberry Creek	Sun Top, White River Park, Sunrise	Greenwater, Mt Rainier East
29. Pleasant Valley	Goose Prairie	Bumping Lake
30. Paradise River	Mt Rainier West, Mt Rainier East	Mt Rainier West, Mt Rainier East
31. Olallie Creek	Chinook Pass	Mt Rainier East
32. Ohanapecosh River	Chinook Pass	Mt Rainier East
33. Laughingwater Creek	Chinook Pass, Ohanapecosh Hot Springs, Cougar Lake	Mt Rainier East, Bumping Lake
34. Packwood Lake	Packwood, Packwood Lake	Packwood
35. Clear Fork Cowlitz River	White Pass, Old Snowy Mtn	White Pass
36. Lewis and Clark State Park	Jackson Prairie	NA
37. Green River	Spirit Lake E, Spirit Lake W, Vanson Peak	Spirit Lake

38. Craggy Peak	McCoy Peak	McCoy Peak
39. Quartz Creek	Quartz Creek Butte	Lone Butte
40. Sheep Canyon	Goat Mtn, Mount St Helens	Mount St Helens (not fully covered)
41. Ape Canyon	Smith Creek Butte, Mount St Helens	Mount St Helens
42. Lewis River	Burnt Peak	Lone Butte
43. Gotchen Creek	King Mtn, Trout Lake, Mt Adams W, Mt Adams E	Mount Adams
44. Sister Rocks	Bare Mountain	Lookout Mtn
45. Trapper Creek	Termination Point, Bare Mountain	Wind River, Lookout Mtn
Northern Oregon Cascades		
46. Larch Mountain Basin	Multnomah Falls	Bridal Veil
47. Herman Creek	Carson, Wahtum Lake	Bonneville Dam
48. Wahtum Lake	Wahtum Lake	Bonneville Dam
49. Lost Lake	Bull Run Lake	Government Camp
50. Lolo Pass	Bull Run Lake	Government Camp
51. Tilly Jane	Mt Hood North	Mt Hood
52. Fifteenmile Creek	Flag Point, Fivemile Butte	Flag Point
53. Barlow Pass	Mt Hood South	Mt Hood
54. Boulder Creek	Badger Lake	Mt Hood
55. Old Salmon River Trail	Rhododendron	Government Camp
56. Memaloose Lake	Wanderers Peak	Fish Creek Mtn
57. Clackamas River	Bedford Point, Three Lynx, Fish Creek Mtn	Fish Creek Mtn
58. Riverside Trail	Fish Creek Mtn	Fish Creek Mtn

59. Hot Springs Fork	Bagby Hot Springs, Battle Ax	Battle Ax
60. Dickey Creek	Bull of the Woods	Battle Ax
61. Elk Lake Creek	Mother Lode Mtn, Bull of the Woods	Battle Ax
Central Oregon Cascades		
62. Opal Creek	Elkhorn, Battle Ax	Battle Ax
63. South Fork Breitenbush River	Breitenbush Hot Springs, Mount Bruno	Breitenbush
64. Chimney Peak	Quartzville, Chimney Peak	Detroit
65. Donaca Lake	Harter Mtn, Chimney Peak	Detroit
66. Three Pyramids	Echo Mtn, Coffin Mtn	NA
67. Metolius River	Black Butte, Candle Creek, Prairie Farm Spring	Whitewater River
68. Echo Basin	Echo Mtn	NA
69. Clear Lake	Echo Mtn, Santiam Junction, Clear Lake	NA
70. Tamolitch Falls	Tamolitch Falls, Clear Lake	NA
71. Tidbits Mountain	Tidbits Mtn	NA
72. Lookout Creek	McKenzie Bridge, Belknap Springs	NA
73. French Pete Creek	Cougar Reservoir	NA
74. Fall Creek	Saddleblanket Mtn, Sinker Mtn	NA
75. Shale Ridge Trail	Chucksney Mtn, Waldo Mtn	NA
76. Black Creek	Waldo Lake	NA
77. Island Lakes Loop	Waldo Lake	NA
78. Patterson Mountain	Westfir West	NA
79. Brice Creek	Rose Hill	NA
80. Larison Creek	Oakridge, Holland Point	NA

81. Youngs Rock	Warner Mtn	NA
82. Big Swamp	Emigrant Butte, Cowhorn Mtn	NA
Southern Oregon Cascades		
83. North Umpqua River	Glide, Old Fairview, Mace Mtn, Steamboat, Illahee Rock	NA
84. Wolf Creek Falls	Red Butte	NA
85. Falls of the North Umpqua River	Mace Mtn, Toketee Falls, Fish Creek Desert	NA
86. Pine Bench	Toketee Falls, Illahee Rock	NA
87. Twin Lakes	Twin Lakes Mtn	NA
88. Castle Creek	Buckeye Lake, Twin Lake Mtn, Fish Creek Desert, Fish Mtn	NA
89. Highrock Mountain	Buckeye Lake, Fish Mtn	NA
90. Donegan Prairie	Abbott Butte	NA
91. Rough Rider Falls	Hamaker Butte	NA
92. Upper Rogue River	Union Creek	NA
93. Crater Lake Caldera Rim	Crater Lake West	NA
94. Mount Scott	Crater Lake East	NA
95. Union Creek	Union Creek	NA
96. Cow Creek	Richter Mtn, Cleveland Ridge	NA
97. Red Blanket Creek	Red Blanket Mtn, Union Peak	NA
98. South Fork Rogue River	Prospect South, Imnaha Creek, Rustler Peak	NA
99. Cherry Creek	Crystal Spring, Pelican Butte	NA
100. Brown Mountain	Brown Mtn, Lake of the Woods South, Lake of the Woods North	NA

APPENDIX E. CONTACT INFORMATION

Please note that the following information is accurate as of the printing date, but is subject to change.

Northern Washington Cascades

1. Mount Baker–Snoqualmie National Forest

Mount Baker–Snoqualmie National Forest Headquarters
21905 64th Avenue West
Mountlake Terrace, WA 98043
425.775.9702
800.627.0062
www.fs.fed.us/r6/mbs

Darrington Ranger District
1405 Emmens Street
Darrington, WA 98241
360.436.1155

Glacier Public Service Center
Glacier, WA 98244
360.599.2714

Mount Baker Ranger District
810 State Route 20
Sedro-Woolley, WA 98284
360.856.5700

Skykomish Ranger District
74920 NE Stevens Pass Highway
P.O. Box 305
Skykomish, WA 98288
360.677.2414

Snoqualmie Ranger District
Enumclaw Office
450 Roosevelt Avenue East
Enumclaw, WA 98022
360.825.6585

Snoqualmie Ranger District
North Bend Office
42404 SE North Bend Way
North Bend, WA 98045
425.888.1421

Snoqualmie Pass Visitor Center
P.O. Box 17
Snoqualmie Pass, WA 98068
425.434.6111

Verlot Public Service Center
33515 Mountain Loop Highway
Granite Falls, WA 98241
360.691.7791

2. North Cascades National Park

North Cascades National Park
810 State Route 20
Sedro-Woolley, WA 98284
360.856.5700
www.nps.gov/noca/home

North Cascades Visitor Center
State Route 20
Newhalem, WA
206.386.4495

3. Wenatchee National Forest

Wenatchee National Forest
215 Melody Lane
Wenatchee, WA 98801
509.662.4335
www.fs.fed.us/r6/wenatchee

Cle Elum Ranger District
803 West 2nd Street
Cle Elum, WA 98922
509.674.4411

Lake Wenatchee Ranger District
22976 State Route 207
Leavenworth, WA 98826
509.763.3103

Leavenworth Ranger District
600 Sherbourne
Leavenworth, WA 98826
509.548.6977

Naches Ranger District
10061 U.S. Highway 12
Naches, WA 98937
509.653.2205

4. Okanogan National Forest
Okanogan National Forest Headquarters
1240 South 2nd Avenue
Okanogan, WA 98840
509.826.3275
www.fs.fed.us/r6/oka

Methow Valley Ranger District
502 Glover Street
P.O. Box 188
Twisp, WA 98856
509.997.2131

Visitor Information Center
Building 49, State Route 20
24 West Chewuch Road
Winthrop, WA 98862
509.996.4000

5. Whatcom County Parks and Recreation Department
Whatcom County Parks and Recreation Department
3373 Mount Baker Highway
Bellingham, WA 98226
360.733.2900

6. Outdoor Recreation Information Center
Outdoor Recreation Information Center
Trip Planning Section—REI
222 Yale Avenue North
Seattle, WA 98109
206.470.4060

SOUTHERN WASHINGTON CASCADES

1. Gifford Pinchot National Forest
Gifford Pinchot National Forest Headquarters
10600 NE 51st Circle
Vancouver, WA 98682
360.891.5000
www.fs.fed.us/gpnf

Cowlitz Valley Ranger District
024 U.S. Highway 12
P.O. Box 670
Randle, WA 98377
360.497.1100

Mount Adams Ranger District
2455 Highway 141
Trout Lake, WA 98650
509.395.3400

Packwood Information Center
13068 U.S. Highway 12
Packwood, WA 98361
360.494.0600

Wind River Information Center
1262 Hemlock Road
Carson, WA 98610
509.427.3200

Mount St. Helens National Volcanic Monument
42218 NE Yale Bridge Road
Amboy, WA 98601
360.247.3900

Mount St. Helens Visitor Center
3029 Spirit Lake Highway
Castle Rock, WA 98611
360.274.2100

2. Mount Rainier National Park
Mount Rainier National Park
Tahoma Woods Star Route
Ashford, WA 98304
360.569.2211
www.nps.gov/mora/home

3. Washington State Parks
Federation Forest State Park
49201 Highway 410 East
Enumclaw, WA 98022
360.663.2207

Lewis and Clark State Park
4583 Jackson Highway
Winlock, WA 98596
360.864.2643

Northern Oregon Cascades

1. Mount Hood National Forest
Mount Hood National Forest
16400 Champion Way
Sandy, OR 97055
503.668.1700
www.fs.fed.us/r6/mthood

Barlow Ranger District
Dufur Ranger Station
780 NE Court Street
P.O. Box 67
Dufur, OR 97021
541.467.2291

Clackamas River Ranger District
Estacada Ranger Station
595 NW Industrial Way
Estacada, OR 97023
503.630.8700
503.630.6861

Hood River Ranger District
6780 State Route 35
Mt. Hood–Parkdale, OR 97041
541.352.6002

Mount Hood Information Center
65000 East U.S. Highway 26
Welches, OR 97067
503.622.7674
503.622.4822
888.622.4822

Zigzag Ranger District
70220 East U.S. Highway 26
Zigzag, OR 97049
503.622.3191
503.668.1704

2. Columbia River Gorge National Scenic Area
Columbia River Gorge National Scenic Area
902 Wasco Avenue, Suite 200
Hood River, OR 97031
541.386.2333
www.fs.fed.us/r6/columbia

Skamania Lodge Visitor Center
1131 Skamania Lodge Drive
Stevenson, WA 98648
509.427.2528

Central Oregon Cascades

1. Willamette National Forest
Willamette National Forest
P.O. Box 10607
Eugene, OR 97440
541.225.6300
www.fs.fed.us/r6/willamette

Detroit Ranger District
HC73, Box 320
Mill City, OR 97360
503.854.3366

Lowell Service Center
60 South Pioneer Street
Lowell, OR 97452
541.937.2129

McKenzie River Ranger District
57600 McKenzie Highway
McKenzie Bridge, OR 97413
541.822.3381

Middle Fork Ranger District
46375 State Route 58
Westfir, OR 97492
541.782.2283

Sweet Home Ranger District
4431 U.S. Highway 20
Sweet Home, OR 97386
541.367.5168

2. Deschutes National Forest
Deschutes National Forest
1645 U.S. Highway 20 East
Bend, OR 97701
541.383.5300
www.fs.fed.us/r6/centraloregon

Sisters Ranger District
P.O. Box 249
Sisters, OR 97759
503.549.7700

Southern Oregon Cascades

1. **Umpqua National Forest**
   Umpqua National Forest
   P.O. Box 1008
   2900 NW Stewart Parkway
   Roseburg, OR 97470
   541.672.6601
   www.fs.fed.us/r6/umpqua

   Cottage Grove Ranger District
   78405 Cedar Park Road
   Cottage Grove, OR 97424
   541.767.5000

   Diamond Lake Ranger District
   2020 Toketee Ranger Station Road
   Idleyld Park, OR 97447
   541.498.2531

   North Umpqua Ranger District
   18782 North Umpqua Highway
   Glide, OR 97443
   541.496.3532

   Tiller Ranger District
   27812 Tiller Trail Highway
   Tiller, OR 97484
   541.825.3201

2. **Rogue River National Forest**
   Rogue River National Forest
   P.O. Box 520
   333 West 8th Street
   Medford, OR 97501
   541.858.2200
   www.fs.fed.us/r6/rogue

   Ashland Ranger District
   645 Washington Street
   Ashland, OR 97520
   541.482.3333

   Butte Falls Ranger District
   800 Laurel
   Butte Falls, OR 97522
   541.865.2700

   Prospect Ranger District
   47201 State Route 62
   Prospect, OR 97536
   541.560.3400

3. **Fremont-Winema National Forests**
   Fremont-Winema National Forests
   2819 Dahlia Street
   Klamath Falls, OR 97601
   541.883.6714
   www.fs.fed.us/r6/winema

   Klamath Ranger District
   1936 California Avenue
   Klamath Falls, OR 97601
   541.885.3400

4. **Roseburg Bureau of Land Management**
   Roseburg BLM
   777 NW Garden Valley Boulevard
   Roseburg, OR 97470
   541.440.4930
   www.or.blm.gov/roseburg

5. **Crater Lake National Park**
   Crater Lake National Park
   P.O. Box 7
   Crater Lake, OR 97604-0007
   541.594.2211
   www.nps.gov/crla/home

INDEX

ABOUT THE AUTHOR AND ILLUSTRATOR

John Cissel is the science liaison for the Bureau of Land Management in Western Oregon, and former director and science liaison for the H. J. Andrews Experimental Forest, a 16,000-acre ecological research site located in western Oregon. He holds a B.S. in forestry from Michigan State University, an M.S. in forestry and operations research from Pennsylvania State University, and has completed additional post-graduate work in forest ecology at Oregon State University. He hiked more than 2,000 miles through the old forests of the Northwest while researching this book.

Diane Cissel, also a veteran hiker, currently works as a graphic designer in Eugene, Oregon. She previously spent ten years as an illustrator and cartographer for a map-making company. She holds a B.F.A. from the University of Michigan and is an accomplished painter.

John and Diane Cissel are co-authors of *50 Old-Growth Day Hikes*, a series of annotated and illustrated maps covering the Willamette National Forest, Mount Hood National Forest, and the southern Washington Cascades. John is also the author of numerous publications on forest ecology and management.

THE MOUNTAINEERS, founded in 1906, is a nonprofit outdoor activity and conservation club, whose mission is "to explore, study, preserve, and enjoy the natural beauty of the outdoors. . . ." Based in Seattle, Washington, the club is now the third-largest such organization in the United States, with 15,000 members and five branches throughout Washington State.

The Mountaineers sponsors both classes and year-round outdoor activities in the Pacific Northwest, which include hiking, mountain climbing, ski-touring, snowshoeing, bicycling, camping, kayaking and canoeing, nature study, sailing, and adventure travel. The club's conservation division supports environmental causes through educational activities, sponsoring legislation, and presenting informational programs. All club activities are led by skilled, experienced volunteers, who are dedicated to promoting safe and responsible enjoyment and preservation of the outdoors.

If you would like to participate in these organized outdoor activities or the club's programs, consider a membership in The Mountaineers. For information and an application, write or call The Mountaineers, Club Headquarters, 300 Third Avenue West, Seattle, Washington 98119; 206-284-6310.

The Mountaineers Books, an active, nonprofit publishing program of the club, produces guidebooks, instructional texts, historical works, natural history guides, and works on environmental conservation. All books produced by The Mountaineers fulfill the club's mission.

Send or call for our catalog of more than 500 outdoor titles:

The Mountaineers Books
1001 SW Klickitat Way, Suite 201
Seattle, WA 98134
800-553-4453
mbooks@mountaineers.org
www.mountaineersbooks.org

The Mountaineers Books is proud to be a corporate sponsor of Leave No Trace, whose mission is to promote and inspire responsible outdoor recreation through education, research, and partnerships. The Leave No Trace program is focused specifically on human-powered (nonmotorized) recreation.

Leave No Trace strives to educate visitors about the nature of their recreational impacts, as well as offer techniques to prevent and minimize such impacts. Leave No Trace is best understood as an educational and ethical program, not as a set of rules and regulations.

For more information, visit *www.lnt.org*, or call 800-332-4100.